The Wise Wound

BANTAM NEW AGE BOOKS

This important imprint includes books in a variety of fields and disciplines and deals with the search for meaning, growth and change.

Ask your bookseller for the books you have missed.

The Wise Wound

The Myths, Realities, and Meanings of Menstruation

Penelope Shuttle and Peter Redgrove

R E V I S E D   E D I T I O N

Foreword by Margaret Drabble

BANTAM BOOKS
NEW YORK • TORONTO • LONDON • SYDNEY • AUCKLAND

AUTHOR'S NOTE: Due to custom it is inevitable that one or the other author's name takes apparent precedence on the title page. We would like to state that in this book we write as equal and complementary partners.

*This edition contains the complete text
of the original hardcover edition.*
NOT ONE WORD HAS BEEN OMITTED.

THE WISE WOUND: THE MYTHS, REALITIES, AND MEANINGS OF MENSTRUATION
A Bantam Book / published by arrangement with Grove Press

PRINTING HISTORY
*Grove Press edition published October 1988
First published in Great Britain by Victor Gollancz Ltd., 1978
Revised edition published in Great Britain by Grafton Books, a division of Collins
Publishing Group, 1986
First American publication by Richard Marek, Macmillan Books, 1978*

Bantam New Age and the accompanying figure design as well as "the search for meaning, growth and change" are trademarks of Bantam Books, a division of Bantam Doubleday Dell Publishing Group, Inc.

Bantam edition / July 1990

Book design by Ann Gold

Library of Congress Catalog Card Number: 88-11144.

Library of Congress Cataloging-in-Publication Data

Shuttle, Penelope, 1947–
    The wise wound : the myths, realities, and meanings of menstruation /
Penelope Shuttle and Peter Redgrove : foreword by Margaret Drabble.
    —Rev. ed.
        p.   cm.
    Includes bibliographical references.
    ISBN 0-553-34906-6
    1. Menstrual cycle.   2. Menstrual cycle—Psychological aspects.
3. Menstruation—Folklore.   I. Redgrove, Peter.   II. Title.
QP263.S58   1990
612.6′62—dc20   89-18369
                                                                                  CIP

ISBN 0-553-34906-6

Published simultaneously in the United States and Canada

Bantam Books are published by Bantam Books, a division of Bantam Doubleday Dell Publishing Group, Inc. Its trademark, consisting of the words "Bantam Books" and the portrayal of a rooster, is Registered in U.S. Patent and Trademark Office and in other countries. Marca Registrada. Bantam Books, 666 Fifth Avenue, New York, New York 10103.

PRINTED IN THE UNITED STATES OF AMERICA

O   0 9 8 7 6 5 4 3 2 1

Depression is one of the commonest experiences
known to mankind. . . . In all studies of depression
it has been shown conclusively that, although both sexes
suffer from this illness, women are far more likely to succumb
to emotional disturbance, particularly depression.

Jack Dominian

Depression is withheld knowledge.

John Layard

Contents

Acknowledgments

Grateful acknowledgments are due for endless help and advice given by all those with whom we have discussed and corresponded about this book. We should especially like to register our thanks to the following, though none of these generous correspondents and friends must be held responsible for opinions which we have subsequently arrived at that they may not share. Derek Toyne, B.A., F.L.A., Librarian at the Falmouth School of Art, has first place in our thanks for making the libraries of the world available to us through his bibliographical skill. The skill and energy of his transatlantic counterparts at the Colgate University Library, N.Y., and the Syracuse University Medical Center Library are also gratefully acknowledged, particularly those of Peter Haskell and Betty Rembert of the former. Peter Redgrove's colleagues and students at the Falmouth School of Art are thanked and praised for their patience and sensitivity in responding to the ideas of this book and providing much apposite information from their experience as creative artists: in particular we are grateful to Lionel Miskin for giving us so much of his time and attention and the benefit of his deep knowledge of analytical psychology. Deep thanks are also due to the staff of the Departments of Anthropology, Psychology, Physiology, and Astro-Archaeology at Colgate University, N.Y., who were also so patient and informative. We would also like to mention in thanks for particular help Mr. and Mrs. J.F. Almond and Angela Heape for research; Dorle Dymond and Karen Judd for translation; Sylvia Bruce for much useful commentary; Milton H. Erickson, M.D., for generous letters on hypnotism; Eileen Lamsmaa, Alison and Andrew Mac-Arthur, Kate Raby, Tony Thatcher, and Carole Tanner whose interpretive feminist work has been so stimulating; Cecil Williamson for his Witchcraft collections and informative conversation; Paddy Kitchen for her encouragement; Liz Calder for this and all her practical help too; Giles Gordon for his painstaking and vigorous championing of our book; and to the many women in Falmouth, London, and Hamilton, N.Y., who have endured and responded to our highly personal inquiries. Lastly, to the memory of John Layard, anthropologist, analytical psychologist, study with whom was a watershed in Peter Redgrove's life and indirectly in Penelope Shuttle's. Without the inspiration of his powerful and original mind the command "work on what has been spoiled" could not have been carried out.

Foreword

When *The Wise Wound* was first published in 1978, it was acclaimed as an important and pioneering work. It challenged prejudices, it explored the meaning of ancient taboos. It was the first comprehensive survey of the age-old, universal, natural, and distinctively human process of menstruation, a process which, as Penelope Shuttle and Peter Redgrove point out, has been largely ignored by the predominantly male traditions of doctors and psychoanalysts, priests and lawyers, natural scientists and anthropologists. It has tended to surface indirectly, in myth, in ritual, in the Grail legend, in poetry, in popular film. The authors have performed an invaluable service in collecting many scattered references from a wide variety of sources, and this edition has a new Afterword which includes discussion of recent publications and experiments, as well as practical advice on how to achieve relaxation and positive harmony with the menstrual cycle.

It is this unusual combination of scholarship and firsthand observation that gives the book much of its special quality. It attempts a rare synthesis of mind and body, of knowledge and instinct, and considers nothing above, beneath, or irrelevant to its quest. It is written by poets, and its interest in language, its delicate evocation of bodily sensation, its bold plain speaking, and its faith in the messages of the subcon-

1

scious and the imagination are an essential part of its own message. Where jargon enters, as the authors point out, it is because language itself, long restrained by taboo, has failed. The authors have curious, wide-ranging, eclectic minds: they quote from learned journals, from health manuals, from horror films, from fiction and folksong. They also draw images from the body, the landscape, the inner landscape of the body itself, and the interior world of dream. At the very least, this book is a fascinating compendium of extraordinary facts, figures, anecdotes, and speculations.

It has also been an influential work which has helped to form a changing climate of opinion. Menstruation is no longer an unmentionable topic: it provides jokes for television comedies, plots for films of the supernatural, and slogans for feminists, and PMT (premenstrual tension) has been, albeit controversially, admitted as a defense in law. It may be that this new openness will prepare the way to accepting menstruation as the woman's friend rather than the woman's curse. But we have a long way to go, and meanwhile millions of women all over the world continue to suffer from the depressing catalogue of bodily and mental pains, aches, and aberrations that Redgrove and Shuttle describe so vividly, and many of which they believe are culturally induced through repression of woman's creative energy. We fear the curse, and therefore it curses us. And yet, as most women agree, the menstrual period has a deeper meaning than pain and inconvenience. It colors our dreams and patterns our waking lives. It is both the familiar and the unmentionable, the known and the unknown. This book offers a possibility of greater understanding of one of the most neglected and most important of human experiences. It is also extremely informative, on a purely factual level, and answers many of the questions that one had never thought or dared to ask, and which I, for one, would never have been able to answer without its help.

Margaret Drabble

Prologue

I

This is a book of many questions and some answers. What is this menstruation that half the world undergoes? Has it any use, or any purpose? Is it like a vestigial organ, left over from an outworn evolutionary stage, or could it be the accompaniment of some hitherto unused ability in women? If it is an illness, why is it the lot of women to suffer in this way? To some women it can be like change and return, with depths and enhancements, even enchantments. To others its return is a torment. Which is it, blessing or curse? And, if curse, why does it fall on women alone?

This book of ours *The Wise Wound* cannot hope to give complete answers to these big questions. But it can do two things. It can, by asking these questions, contribute to a refusal to acquiesce in what appears to be a conspiracy of silence. It will, we hope, encourage women to ask these questions themselves, and to begin building up a body of information which is about what women actually experience and not what they are told they should experience by doctrinaire authority. In addition, we hope that some of the information we have gathered from very diverse fields will

3

provide signposts toward fresh ways in which women in today's world can think about their situation.

This implies a change of attitude toward and a reassessment of one's femininity. Is the menstrual cycle woman's curse, or is it an unexplored resource? We believe the latter. We also think that while to take up this challenge rather than to run from it will be a true liberation, it will also be for many a difficult challenge. Habits of thought will have to be broken—and, perhaps most difficult of all in our unnatural age, trust will have to be offered to feminine nature itself, before that nature will respond. This is what we mean by our title *The Wise Wound*. If menstruation is Eve's Curse, and the curse is a Wound, it is difficult and paradoxical to think of it as "wise." It is not our habit nowadays to assume (not even as a hypothesis) that life has a meaning, particularly human feminine life, and that menstruation, its invariable accompaniment, has a meaning also. This may be because it has a meaning that we are afraid of, or involves some development that we do not wish to acknowledge. Perhaps the inner life is concerned, and techniques for approaching that, and not just the outer life of science and medicine. Perhaps art and imagination and vision are involved as well as science. And if you can see it from this side of things, then perhaps the wound is no longer a wound, and the Curse of Eve what it is called in many languages: "Woman's Friend."

If this is true, as we believe it is, then the prize for women is so great as to be worth giving these ideas a try at least.

II

This is how the book came about. During early 1971 Penelope Shuttle was suffering bad premenstrual depressions, and menstrual pain when the period came. Peter Redgrove had studied analytical psychology and dream analysis for many years, and in particular had spent 1968–69 as a pupil of the famous analyst Dr. John Layard, who himself had studied with Homer Lane, C. G. Jung, and others and had published many distinguished contributions to psychology and anthropology. With the help of Layard's methods, Redgrove enabled Shuttle to draw pictures of the depressions, and then to dream vividly as a consequence. She dreamed every night for five months, and the dreams were analyzed every day, in sessions often lasting many hours.

It seemed the natural thing to relate each dream to its day of Penelope Shuttle's menstrual cycle, since it was the menstrual distress that had prompted the dream-analysis. However, we determined that we should not consult any book on the psychology of menstruation until the initial phases of the analysis were over, in case it prejudiced our observations.

In a few months, it was clear that the analysis was having a good effect, as the depressions were no longer severe, and the pains had eased. Instead, Penelope Shuttle had found a fresh attitude to her period, which enabled her to enjoy that time for its particular qualities, and no longer reject it. There were subsidiary effects, such as a radical improvement of eyesight, and an enhancement of her creative abilities.

At this stage, we thought it advisable to consult the literature. We went to our College Librarian, to ask him for some books on the psychology of menstruation, confident that such books existed and would help us. Greatly to the Librarian's surprise also THERE WERE NO SUCH BOOKS! *

---

* Astonishingly, this remained the situation until 1975, when Paula Weideger's *Menstruation and Menopause* broke new ground in the U.S. by bringing together a good deal of menstrual information, and pleading that women themselves should provide data so that the subject should not any longer be kept under a blanket of ignorance. Though it provides little guide to the inward experience and significance of the menstrual cycle, Weideger's is an extremely helpful book, and we were glad it appeared in time for us to draw upon it for some corroboration in the later stages of this study. By 1976 a second book had appeared (*The Curse*, by Janice Delaney, Mary Jane Lupton, and Emily Toth) which, though a fascinating digest of menstrual fact and lore, in our opinion lacks an overall sense of direction or

So we had to write our own, and this is it. The story of Penelope Shuttle's own quest in exploration of the menstrual cycle will be told in another book, as we thought it best to publish first a more general and objective study before offering the personal testimony: better to look at the situation at large rather than to put a single individual's experience at the center, however striking that might be.

We have tried to give you the facts as we have found them. We are not doctors, and we wish that the doctors had done more for the menstrual cycle. We would like to emphasize that it is important to have a medical checkup if there is persistent menstrual distress or irregularity. In Chapter I, "The Science of Bleeding," we show the scientific facts as they stand, and some serious limitations of this "medical model." In Chapter II we show how black the picture is painted for women—and how it needn't be like that at all. The first subtitle of the second chapter, "When Is a Curse not a Curse?," is a riddle the answer to which, "When It's a Blessing in Disguise!," runs through the whole book. We show how a positive attitude to menstruation, including a better sexual one, opens many doors. In Chapter III, "Animus, Animal, Anima," we show how the monthly cycle of psychological experience is known to lead to integration, and not, as is so often supposed, disintegration. In Chapter IV, "Does the Moon Menstruate?," we speculate that this much-despised menstrual cycle was the evolutionary advance that initiated human society. In Chapter V we find traces of menstrual practices that benefited the women and reflected the honor paid to them and to menstruation. In Chapter VI, "Nine Million Menstrual Murders," we speculate that the great witch persecution of the Middle Ages was one enormous menstrual persecution; in Chapter VII, "The Mirror of

purpose. Katherina Dalton's excellent book *The Menstrual Cycle* was published in 1969, but it is chiefly informative on the medical side. It gives impressive social warnings but only medical solutions.

Dracula," we find menstrual energies frankly reflected in popular culture; and in an Epilogue we speculate on further meanings that may be brought to life by a change of attitude to this intimate and essential experience.

Many think that our planet is doomed unless human nature can approach some fresh realization. In a scientific experiment, one attempts to perceive all the variables, and to find if by altering one of these, whether it is not the crucial influence. Our culture has tried many solutions to its problems, and all have failed. Then it may be that two of the variables it has not perceived could have a crucial effect. In our opinion, two of the most basic experiences in human life are two of the most neglected. Both of these belong to feminine experience. One is the experience of bearing a child, and the child's experience of its mother in being born; and the other is the woman's experience of herself during menstruation.

It is at least arguable that our children are born in modern obstetrical practice by a series of aggressive acts. The child's first experience of life in the world is a panic breath, due to cutting of the cord which is still supplying oxygenated blood, or glaring lights and noise of the hospital delivery room. The possibility that altering the conditions of birth might affect favorably the aggressive tendencies of the adults into which these babies grow, and by the same token the aggressive tendencies of those societies that practice such birth-methods, is a barely explored field. But it is at least worth a hypothesis that aggression may thus grow in people and societies by a "snowballing" or feedback effect.

Another unexplored field is the examination of how a different experience of her menstrual cycle might enhance the growth and powers of individual women, though there is much evidence, as we shall show, that such growth and powers are possible. It is up to every woman to determine for herself, so far as she is able, her wishes toward her own labor-experience, and also toward her menstrual experience.

It is only in recent years that women have begun to be able to do the former, and the effects on society may soon be seen, as the children grow up. We believe that menstrual experience may soon take its place in the total picture.

There is the great anomalous myth of the Holy Grail within Christian history. The holy male knights sought through the desolation of their wasteland for that Grail which would bring back life, and make the Wasteland bloom. The legend tells that the perfect knight, Parsifal, at last found and entered the Grail Castle, and saw the procession of dancing youths and maidens carrying the spear dripping with blood and the great chalice of the Grail brimming with blood. King Amfortas, its guardian, whose wounds bled day and night, and all the assembled company in that castle waited for Parsifal to ask the simple and natural but magical question that would put an end to the desolation that surrounded them. But Parsifal was so full of astonishment and the inappropriate kind of awe, that he forgot to ask the small necessary question.

And that question was no more than, "This Cup that bleeds, what is it for?"

We think that the mythic question has such power in the legend precisely because it can be asked in fact. The question we can ask is: "What does my bloodshed every month mean?" Women through the ages have asked this question, and the Wasteland answer they have received from the male knights (who believe that because they do not bleed they do not have to ask the question), when they have been answered at all, has been: "It is a Curse."

We do not think this is the true answer, and for some of our reasons, please read on.

P.S.
P.R.

One The Science
🌿 of Bleeding

I Odyssey of the Sperm

Halfway through the Bible is a marvelous love-poem. Some would say that the Bible is all about love, but others that the Bible is about *man*'s idea of love: self-righteous, territorial, wrathful, phallic, ambitious, chauvinist, bellicose, with man the lord of creation and a Father the lord of heaven and earth. Whatever our opinion of the whole book, at its very center, like a hinge, or a door opening onto another world, there is one of the most urgent and beautiful statements of equal love between the sexes. It is called, justly, the Song of Songs. It is like an anti-bible within the Bible.

> I am black, but comely, oh ye daughters of Jerusalem . . .
> I am the rose of Sharon,
> And the lily of the valleys . . .
> As the apple tree among the trees of the wood,
> So is my beloved among the sons . . .
> Also our bed is green . . .

Say the Lady, and the Lord has his responses:

> How beautiful are thy feet with shoes, O prince's daughter!
> The joints of thy thighs are like jewels,

9

The work of the hands of a cunning workman.
Thy navel is like a round goblet, which wanteth not liquor:
Thy belly is like an heap of wheat set about with lilies.
Thy two breasts are like two young roes
That are twins . . .
Now also thy breasts shall be as clusters of the vine,
And the smell of thy nose like apples;

That "navel is like a round goblet" spoils the picture at its most exciting part. A navel is not big enough for wine. It is no fun to play with wine and navel. We have been given a wrong translation.

The ordinary Bible commentaries are shifty about it. Peake's says that "navel" mustn't be taken literally, but poetically, as though poetry shouldn't be exactly descriptive. Clarke's says it is "too sensuous." Margoliouth, as we shall see, is accurately evocative when he translates "the bowl of the moon": where it is eclipsed (Gore 1928). "Navel" is sometimes really "body." Moffat translates "waist" instead of "navel" probably with the meaning of "pelvic basin." There is prudishness here. "Lap" is closer, and, as in Shakespeare, what the word actually means is "pudendum," "vulva," or "cunt."[1]

"Navel" is a kind of double-talk, that is, not an *actual* lie, since it can suggest "the place you were born from" since you were attached to it there, inside. Also, a woman's navel fills up in late pregnancy. The Hebrew word can also mean *border or door between the two worlds*[2] of the born and unborn. The Lover in this poem in fact is doing what anybody else in his situation would be doing: praising the lady's cunt, the birthplace.

The Revised Standard Version (1952) gives us: "Your navel is a rounded bowl that never lacks mixed wine. . . ." It is now clear that this "wine" of the "navel" is not wine either, but an even more important substance: the sexual fluid or liquors that flow and mix, and the poem is celebrating the life-giving sexuality and vivid perceptions of two people who love each other and who are about to have sex.

It is extraordinary to find this poem of Tantric vividness in a book which is dedicated to the exclusive supremacy of a male God, and which in its latter end, which Christians consider its culmination, contains statements like, "it is well for a man not to touch a woman . . ." (I Cor. vii, I). One has to say that the Truth will out, and this Bible about God is mainly about one half of God: the male half. In the New Testament the image of woman is, as it were, castrated. It is at any rate split into two halves. The two women principally important in the New Testament are Mary Magdalene, the prostitute: the woman who had sex without having a child; and Mary Virgin: the woman who had a child without having sex. This splits the power and completeness of woman into two quiescent halves, like the two harmless hemispheres of plutonium which if brought together make the atomic explosion.

In the face of another Pauline statement: that man is the glory of God and woman is only the glory of man (I Cor. xi, 7), let us look exactly at what woman does control and preside over by means of her "navel"—which is nothing other than the whole work of creation of man and woman themselves.

To the man, the "mixed wines" of the Song of Songs would mean his semen mixed with the woman's love-juices in her "lap." But every woman knows that she has two kinds of flow that come from her vagina. Ancient sources called these the River of Life and the River of Death, meaning the clear or white flow at the times when a child is more likely to be conceived; and the forbidden red flow of menstruation, when it is most *unlikely* that a child can be conceived. To the Rabbis, sex at the period when the blood is flowing was most strictly taboo. It made monsters, they said. It attracted Adam's other dark bride, Lilith. However, sex at the time when children could be conceived was quite acceptable, as if woman were breeding-stock. This is only one instance of a taboo against sex at menstruation which is spread throughout all cultures dominated by men, both historically and at the present time. It is a taboo which approves only that half of the woman's nature which is concerned with childbirth and pregnancy.

In this book we shall be looking at the other half of woman's nature, that which is concerned with love without biological issue. The creation of children is one half of human joy. The other half is the creation of love between adults, and the creation of "mental children": seminal ideas and insights. It is too much supposed that the creation of "mental children" is the sole province of men, because the creation of physical children is the exclusive ability of women. It is as though the men, unable to have physical children, insist on their exclusive ability to have mental ones. All creativity concerns both love and imagination, so why is it that women, arguably the sex more gifted with powers of loving and imagining, are not much credited with mental-creative powers?

This is one of the problems to which this book will seek to find an answer. It is as though the two kinds of love-juice, the red and the white, the childless and the child-giving, corresponded with these two aspects of woman's nature. It is the red aspect which is despised, tabooed, neglected, and which, as if in response to this spiteful treatment, in many women *hurts*. Now that modern birth-methods have shown how childbirth without fear *can* be childbirth without overwhelming pain, there is no other natural function in women which is so accompanied by pain and distress as menstruation. Perhaps menstrual pain, like labor pain, is a learned response. Can menstruation without fear be menstruation without distress? This is the subject of our next chapter.

Let's return to the warlike distillation of man's spirit, with its piles of foreskins and records of battles, the Judeo-Christian Bible. One commentator[3] notes that the full meaning of the Hebrew verses of the Song of Songs would contain these ideas: "you [the woman] rule over the lunar energy which fills the bellies of women: you control births according to your wisdom. . . ." The woman's "goblet" contains the red wine of her menstruation, and the white wine of her inter-menstruum, her between-time, to mix with the man's white. She is the Rose as well as the Lily, just as the Song says. And in what sense does woman "control birth according to her wisdom" and to what degree does man contribute to that control?

It is taught by science that the man's sperm determines the sex of "his" child. Is this not a masculine overemphasis? Certainly the sperm carry the X and Y sex chromosomes. But the sperm must get to the ovum first, and when it has got there, the ovum has to accept it; and if it is accepted, then the womb also has to accept the fertilized ovum for implantation in its wall. None of this process of selection would seem to be the male's prerogative. If a woman's lover pleases her enough, then her degree of response to him may affect the physiological processes. Only in *this* sense does he steer his sperm.

But he steers his sperm through an oceanography of currents and perils, a veritable Odysseus' voyage over which the woman's nature presides, as Athena (the root meaning of whose name is "vulva" or "lap" or "womb"[4]) presided over the voyages of Odysseus.

In order that a person can be made, the sperm has to be introduced over the border into the land of the unborn. The distance that it will have to travel to reach its treasure, the ovum, will be something between five and twelve inches, from the vagina to the upper oviduct, where fertilization normally takes place. How this distance is traveled will depend on the strength of the man's ejaculation, the vehemence of his release and commitment, and the woman's response to this. It depends on her arousal, how far she is involved in this and previous sexuality, on her orgasm, on her womb-contractions, how far down the womb reaches in orgasm, how active the cervix is, and on many other factors. Which sperm among so many millions reaches the egg depends on the woman's reception of them, and on this therefore depends the makeup of the child, if any.

All these factors vary with the woman's disposition—her whole disposition—that is, her body-mind. We shall show that every person receives and responds to a flood of information that their conscious minds are not aware of, but which may show up in many ways, including the variations of their menstrual cycle. Reception of the sperm also depends on which phase of the menstrual cycle one is in, and one's attitude to that menstrual cycle. The quality of the "mixed wines" of the vaginal and uterine juices the sperm swim in is vital. Their acidity and alkalinity vary. Semen is alkaline, but the vagina, cervix, uterus, and Fallopian tubes are usually acid, and acid kills sperm. For a particular short instant linked with ovulation, these juices become alkaline, and make the sperm's voyage easier.

There is more than that. At certain times the juices thicken, and this makes it more difficult for the sperm to swim through the cervix. Once again there is a short time in the cycle when the mucus becomes fluid, and then progress is easier for the sperm. It is like the "clashing rocks," where the boat of Odysseus has to choose its moment if it is to pass through without being crushed. It is possible that male and female sperm have different motilities under these different conditions. In what sense, then, does man determine the sex of the offspring? One sperm out of 400 thousand is selected within the woman, by the ovum. One can hardly say, then, that the male "determines" the sex of the child.

If the sperm enter the wrong oviduct, there is no chance for them. The ovum is propelled *downward* by contractions of the Fallopian tube and by ciliary current in its walls, which are covered with millions of vibrating hairs. This is *uphill* for the sperm. There are many labyrinthine crannies, in which devouring white blood cells may wait. The cervix crannies are known as the "arbor vitae": the tree of life. The actual microscopic structure of the female juice varies during the menstrual cycle. "Spinnbarkeit" develops in it at ovulation, which is its property of being drawn out in thin threads, as opposed to "tack." At the same time—ovulation—if the mucus is allowed to dry on a glass slide, you get a beautiful "ferning" pattern, as though pathways had opened up in it.

There will be no offspring without an egg, and though ovulation is usually said to occur in the middle of the menstrual cycle, halfway between one period and the next, human beings may ovulate at almost any time of the cycle under stimulus, as the presence of a desired love, or the woman's own wish for a child. Ovulation may not happen at all during an "anovular" cycle, for reasons which may be emotional, obscure, physiological, or social. A bomb explosion will do it. One's first menstrual cycles are often anovular. Menstruation may cease altogether for "unknown" reasons, or under emotional stress of many kinds, during war, during mental hospital treatment, or confinement in a concentration camp or prison.

Each sperm, then, that survives must travel the current of this inner world with as much navigational accuracy as the salmon or the eels that travel so far to mate or spawn, or the migratory turtle or flock of birds. Just as the survival of the animal species depends on their reaching the spawning grounds, so that of the human race depends on the sperm reaching the ovum within the country and oceans that are inside the woman. It is natural selection *inside* the species.

Any control for most women in these modern times is totally unconscious. Many women have no idea of the time they may expect their menstruation. Some women are aware that their menstruation is coming by a recurrent or characteristic dream (see Chapter III). For some women it comes to the hour, to the minute, that they expect. Some women, too, are conscious of their time of ovulation. They may experience a feeling difficult to put into words, or a slight pain, or a little showing of blood, or a depression, or, again, a dream. Very occasionally it seems that a woman knew when a child was conceived on a particular occasion. We all know anecdotes about this, strange tales when the woman may seem to have very great determination over her body and its offspring. A child may resemble a lover encountered when the mother was pregnant from the husband. But so far science will hardly allow or encourage any inner consciousness in women. The scientific evidence of biofeedback shows that very great participation in those bodily events which are normally thought to be out of conscious control is possible. Biofeedback control over single nerve cells is possible, and has been experimentally demonstrated. Biofeedback control of the menstrual cycle has also been demonstrated. There is no reason why Everywoman should not consciously inhabit the kingdom of her body, from which she has been exiled by male certitudes which are called "objective" but which are often rather the turning-away from unexpected powers and abilities. Yoga, for example, believes and demonstrates that great bodily control is possible and that the inner physical world can be experienced in vision-form, as tales of the heroes and heroines. Dream analysis in the Western sense shows this to be true, also—but if we have no heroine-tales told us, how shall we understand these visions and dreams?

There is evidence that colleges of women in the past, by techniques of deep introspection and dream control, were able to influence the events of conception and birth, and a likelihood that women if they wish may once again do so. This is the subject of our Chapters IV and V. The techniques of natural childbirth have shown that the one aspect of Eve's Curse—"in sorrow thou shalt bring forth children"—need not apply, when the women are conscious of what is happening within themselves, without fear. We return to this in the next chapter.

It is the other half of Eve's Curse to whose liberation in this book we wish to make a contribution. "In sorrow thou shalt bring forth children" need not be the case; "in sorrow each month thou shalt bleed" may not apply either, when the burden of fear and disgust is lifted.

II   Beneath the Surface

First of all we would like to indicate the extent of the body's participation in the menstrual rhythm. Every month, all through the month, the woman goes through a series of bodily changes of ineffable sensitivity that are a total response of her being, arguably more deeply actual and rooted in this physical world than any man can attain. Man is like the waterfly of existence, for the weight of his body-fruits do not pull him below the surface of existence. This may account for his interest in nonexperienced *eternal* events, an *unchanging* god, a science made of *invariable* experimental results.

During the menstrual cycle, there are measurable changes in most "body factors." Sex hormone levels in blood and urine follow it, as do buccal, rectal, and vaginal temperatures, basal metabolism, blood sugar, endometrial glycogen, water retention, body weight, pulmonary vital capacity, alveolar CO_2 concentration, arterial oxygen pressure, blood acidity, serum bicarbonate, heart rate, erythrocyte sedimentation rate, differential blood leucocyte counts, platelet counts, serum protein, Vitamins A, C, and E concentrations, bile pigments, blood adrenalin, urine volume, thyroid and adrenal function, electric skin resistance, pupillary size, psychic activities, pain threshold, vaginal cytology, skin color and permeability, breast changes, composition of the cervical mucus secretion and citric acid content, viscosity and gravity of the urine, work performance, electroencephalogram readings, olfactory, visual, and auditory acuity, and the ability to walk a tightrope. The cervix, as in pregnancy, can be observed to change size, position, and color.[5]

The first thing to notice is that these profound rhythmic changes are acknowledged by science to have powerful effects not only on oneself, but on other people also: children, men, other women. In fact the literature on this is quite considerable, and we shall return to it. However, *only the bad effects of the menstrual cycle have ever been systematically described.*

Again, since we often begin menstruating again while we are weaning our children, or before, our relationship to our own cycle and its changes, measurable or unguessed-at, must be a part of the influence we have on our children in those early years, for good or ill. Yet *in all the annals of child psychiatry and psychoanalysis there is no systematic treatment of this influence of the menstrual cycle on our children.*[6]

Furthermore, in all the descriptions of the bodily changes women undergo during their menstrual cycles *there is no systematic account of what they normally experience in their minds.*[7] Yet that emotional or psychic events occur in concert with the cycle is universally acknowledged by clinical writers on the subject. It is simply that all such matters are looked at in male terms, i.e., as though the menstrual cycle was not a factor in normal mental life, or as though it were merely a periodic illness only of significance as an inconvenient time-waster, irrelevant to properly lived masculine straight-line "neat" life.

Moreover, there is *no real agreement among authorities as to the actual mechanism of the menstrual cycle.* It may be argued that few mechanisms of the body are understood in detail, but on looking into the matter one can see that, as a subject, menstrual physiology is a curiously backward science. It is only since 1930 that the uncertainties about whether womb-lining was shed and when in the cycle the egg was released were more or less resolved. The changes that occur in the womb-lining were not fully described until 1950. Even now, authorities differ about many of the important details, such as the timing of "luteal" phase and of ovulation. Lest anybody think that science is rational about sex at all, it should be remembered that it was not until 1966 that there was any reliable account of what happened in people's physiology when they made love,[8] and there is still in our culture no deep and systematic account of what people may feel and experience inwardly during sexual intercourse.[9]

And again, though most women suffer to varying degrees at or around their period-time, *all that our medical technology can say about this suffering attached to the normal functioning of the female body is that it is not understood.* This is by consensus of authorities.[10] Perhaps they are not willing to look at the truth. Perhaps the suffering is a learned response to oppression, a "slave-language."

The simple account below of the physiological events of the menstrual cycle accords with a selection of authorities. It is a broad outline, and we give it because we would like the reader to see that what we are talking about is a feedback mechanism of exquisite sensitivity which links the body's roots to the mind. It is like the old allegory of the Tree of Life which has its roots in heaven and its branches and fruits within the ground. Culture ensures that so many women are not conscious of most of these changes. These body-mind links therefore, which are invisibly potent in all our lives, and potentially so important to civilization, are largely unconsciously suffered. We would like the reader to see the extent of these menstrual changes, and how they involve the whole physical being. We would also like the reader to appreciate that the cycle is a sequence of events each of which can be distinguished by an individual, if she wants, for its particular qualities. There are these events succeeding each other in the cycle in the body, so there is likely to be the experience of these stages as a part of the discriminatory experience of the mind.[11]

The menstrual cycle is often divided into four phases. We shall examine these in more detail in a moment, but they are as follows: *the preovulatory phase* (ovarian follicles ripen and mature); the *ovulatory phase* (ripe egg expelled from ovary; "corpus luteum" ripens); the *premenstrual phase* (estrogen and progesterone hormone levels drop); and the *menstrual phase* (womb-lining shed).

What is interesting is that this number four has always been important in human experience. "In all models of the universe and concepts of the divine . . . a fourfold structure dominates."[12] We must leave the reader to decide the significance of such an idea, bearing in mind that our earlier experiences are likely to be bound up, for good and ill, with the menstrual clocks of our mothers. Fourfold images are said to imply wholeness: the four seasons, the four arms of the cross, Jung's four faculties (thought, feeling, sensation, intuition), the four points of the compass, the four elements, the four humors, the four alchemical steps, the four natural forces, Einstein's four-dimensional model of the universe, and the four phases of the moon-cycle (waxing, full, waning, and dark or "new"). It is as if to attain a balanced view, we have to see the four sides of every question.

III   *Rhythm of Life*

We are suggesting that there is a structure to every woman's cycle, and that she can perceive this if she wishes. What that structure exactly is, will depend on the woman. If she is able to see it, and not close her consciousness to it, then she will be perceiving rhythms deeply rooted in her bodily experience— which science objectively confirms with its list of measurable bodily changes. Not to perceive this structure may be for many women to isolate themselves from processes which will occur anyway, and knowledge of which may very well bring balance and benefits. Even if she does not like the cycle, perhaps the only way out may be through it.

The point is that there is a *rhythm*, however one may divide it up in one's own personal experience. If mental experiences reflect, as they often seem to, bodily ones, then there are many possibilities of experience if one opens oneself to this rhythm. One is often asked or encouraged to detach oneself from them, by regarding them as an inconvenience or an illness. Detachment from the changes does of course ensure that they remain merely bodily ones, and may even force them to express themselves in the body-language of illness. Harmony with them, so far as is possible, can lead to a different form of independence: understanding of one's nature rather than repression of it. One might say that the difference is between a person who becomes independent of water by donning a heavy diving-suit, and someone who enjoys sailing and navigation through real knowledge of the tides and coastlines.

The complete rhythm may be experienced as fourfold—or otherfold with more complex menstrual cycles, which many women have. Undeniably, however, the more complicated rhythms arise from a strong basic twofold beat. The normal menstrual cycle has *two* poles, or culminations. Ovulation, when the ripe egg is shed into the Fallopian tube; and menstruation, when the thick, built-up lining of the womb is shed, and its wall becomes thin and exquisitely sensitive, like a "wound." The latter process, shedding of the womb-wall, is confined to what we regard as the more evolved animals: humans and apes. We shall return to this evolutionary point in Chapter IV.

What is not usual is to give as emphatic a value to menstruation as to ovulation. Menstruation is usually regarded as the negative pole of the process, ovulation the positive one. Menstruation is customarily seen as merely an excretory process: a simple stripping-off of the walls of the womb because the "disappointed egg" has not been fertilized: a kind of nosebleed of the womb, in which the blood-and-mucus attitudes are foremost, and not what else the experience might mean. One can see this in most encyclopedia articles, in the *Britannica*, for instance.[13]

It is a cultural attitude to favor the "values of ovulation," of childbearing, over those of menstruation, by discounting the latter experience. We can see this in dismissive expletives. A common attitude is that these "bloody women" are second-class people because they bleed one week in four. That is, if they are not breeding. That frequent expletive "bloody" is sometimes derived from the expression "By Our Lady." But we can see how shocking an unaccustomed attitude to menstruation may be if we think of the Virgin Mary menstruating. A Christian may think of her bearing her child with joy, but not of her period, or of her sexuality. Thus matronhood is separated from sexuality, the values of ovulation from—the other values.

So, in most accounts of the menstrual cycle, ovulation is regarded as the culmination, peak, and purpose of the changes. It is rare to read such a statement as that of the psychologist Esther Harding, that "the divine creative spark in man can either express itself in the creation of a human child or, alternatively, it can be assimilated into the individual himself, creating in him a spirit which is immortal" in a context, which she gives, of considering that the "alternative" is in what she calls the *yin* or dark side of women, the menstrual pole of the cycle.

It is at ovulation that the woman may dedicate herself to carrying a child for the next ten common-law months. To speak exclusively of ovulation is mentally to limit the role of women to this function. Menstruation is regarded, not only by physiologists and many doctors, but also by some feminists, as a sickness, a blank spot, a nonevent that the women must endure and would be better without, an evil time. This simply is not necessarily so. It is the time when the healthy woman may draw on abilities and capacities that are not related to the values of ovulation and childbearing, but that are instead related to that other side of her nature, of independence of thought and action. It is the exact counterpart, but in an opposite sense, of the ovulation. At ovulation she wishes to receive, accept, build, if she desires a child. But from menstruation there is a different set of energies available to her of receiving, accepting, building the child which is herself. If this is so, but she is not ready or willing to accept the possibility, then the turn or passage of change from one "pole" to the other will be difficult, and if she wishes a child or wishes to "prove" her fertility, then the appearance of the period will be disappointing. This may be because she is taught to look at herself as primarily the egg-producer, and has turned away from the interplay of the other side of her nature which is available to her at the menstrual "pole" of her cycle.

It is natural that the experiences of the women should be reflected in the folklore of a society, and the stories that are told. There is a strong twofold rhythm to feminine experience, and, again, it is interesting how many legends of duality there are. We have mentioned the two rivers, one red, and the other white; there are the twins, one divine and the other human, who often fight, and who rarely assist, each other. There are the widespread legends of the two fruits, one of enlightenment and the other of immortal life (as it might be of individual realization and of immortality in one's children), and the two trees in the Garden of Eden, of Knowledge and of Life. Then there are the almost universal legends of the two goddesses, one queen of the world and the other of the underworld. There are the two kinds of blood of the Gorgon Medusa: Asclepius the physician-god uses that from the right side for healing, and that from the left slays. The Holy Grail is said to give both red and white wine also. Jungian psychology finds that the images of alchemy arise spontaneously in the dreams of contemporary people in their quest for wholeness, which is sometimes expressed as a search for the red "philosopher's stone" which is a grail or uterus, whose touch turns the world to "gold"—that is, turns it to vivid, shining value. The search is said to succeed when it unites two or four warring opposites into one whole.

Joseph Campbell comments that it is characteristic of men-values that they set the world apart in sharply divided pairs of opposites, one of which is favored, and the other not. He says that this is like a solar mythic view, since all shadows flee from the sun. He says that in the lunar mythic view, however, which is the more naturally feminine one, "dark and light interact in the one sphere"—the interplay of the opposites creates wholeness.

This does appear to be germane to the woman's menstrual cycle. Many women are prevented from becoming whole by being regarded as two persons: the obedient, good little ovulating mother, and the fiend of menstruation:

> O Menstruating woman, thou art a fiend
> From which the whole of nature must be screened.

That screen, marked fiend, is still up, and it should be taken down.

IV   Deeper Than the Man

The menstrual rhythm with its inevitable twofold peak of ovulation on the one hand, and menstruation on the other, must have been established as a kind of clock in all of us at a very early age. Women begin to menstruate again after their pregnancies at about the time that they wean their infants: a most sensitive time for both mother and child. Thirty-three per cent of woman, however, menstruate while they are breast-feeding: the rhythm of the period with all its cyclical changes is thus established earlier. If the mother is bottle-feeding, of course it is established earlier still.[14]

It is fair, also, to say that ovulation belongs to the ovary: that the values of continuing the race through the "germ-plasm," or hereditary substance, belong to the ovary. The ovum produces ova that make ova, or DNA breeds DNA that breeds DNA, and the individual person is a mere incident. By the same token, menstruation belongs to the womb, which is part of the individuality of each woman, in exactly the same way as a man's genitalia are part of his own individuality and personal feeling, though in his case they are carried very much outside his general body, like an outward attitude as it were. In the woman, all the genitalia are deeply rooted within the body, like an inward feeling. The "female" structure is the basic embryonic structure. We are all women in the womb to begin with, until the circulation of male hormones begins enormously to enlarge the clitoris-structure and change it to a penis, while diminishing its nerve-supply and thereby externalizing it and reducing its contribution as an erotic organ to mental life.[15] It has to be realized that in erotic capacity, the ability for feeling the world and the nature of people within it in an experiential sense as opposed to an abstract or "spiritual" sense, the woman is much more gifted than the man. She has a capacity for deeper sensual experience of the actual world than man has, and a more complex nervous organization for relating bodily experience to mental experience. The superiority of the clitoris to the penis as a sensuous organ is confirmed physiologically and by experience when it is understood that by clitoral stimulation a woman is capable of many peaks of orgasmic experience in love, and a man of only one or two or a few in the same encounter. However, if a man has as his partner a woman who is capable of multiorgasmic experience, then his sexual love will be deeper, and he will be capable of many more peak-experiences than if he is with an inexperienced partner. It must be noted that for the woman who is not afraid to have sex during her period, and who has not succumbed to the frequent male taboo on intercourse at this time, her peak-experiences at menstruation are likely to have a completely different tone, and she is likely to have more of them. Pregnancy is an excellent time for sexual experience, of course, but this has also been much obscured, as we suggested above, by a desire to separate sexuality from motherhood, as the Madonna in our Western Christian myth is separated from the Magdalen.

The events of the cycle are also more deeply rooted and physically widespread than anything the male normally experiences. Though this means that the female's experience of life is deeper, it means concurrently that she is more vulnerable when she opens herself to these experiences, more vulnerable to aggression, and to derogation. The man who should be the guardian and student of these abilities in the woman has in our age become the proud and envious aggressor.

V   *Two Cycles*

Physiologically there are two cycles, the ovarian and the uterine. These two cycles are linked by a very complex system of nerve and hormone pathways that interact in a network of influences that are mutually sensitive and "feed back" the one with the other. All changes interact with all other changes, there is nothing isolated, all weaves into the fabric of a life.

Imposed conditions isolate the menstruation as something apart, like a scapegoat. Within the body of the woman this is more truly the aphelion of her body-mind's orbit, the one extremity, while the ovulation is the perihelion, the other extreme point. The orbit itself, her individuality, is, like the earth's or the moon's, maintained by an infinitely complex balance of forces both inside her and outside her skin. Each individual orbit will be determined by a balance, as it were, between neighboring gravitations.

For our present purposes we will consider the two cycles of those neighboring bodies, the uterus and the ovaries, and their interaction with a third body, the pituitary, which is attached to the human brain, and influenced by emotional, intellectual, and environmental factors that affect the brain, though of course shielded from them too; otherwise we should be at the mercy of every passing environmental influence.

Accepted scientific opinion in the name of "objectivity" likes to describe these events mechanistically. In its black-white way, its desire to discount subjective experience, it leaves out, even in its own terms, important facts. For instance, it says that "There is no recognized feedback mechanism in the human from uterus to ovary except when pregnancy occurs."[16] This is truly not letting one's left hand know what one's right hand does, because it is also accepted that the woman's emotional and sexual experience has a profound effect on her balance of hormones and her sex cycle.[17] So there *is* feedback, unless you prefer, as a good scientific extrovert, to discount subjective human experience entirely, which is also against the experimental evidence. This kind of "feedback" differs from "mechanism" in that there is clearly a large element of individual choice in it.

The situation has been described mechanistically, in this manner: "Just as the hands on the face of a clock are turned by a series of wheels with interlocking cogs, so the menstrual time-piece depends upon the events of the ovarian cycle, and these are in turn determined by the rhythmical changes of the pituitary gonadotrophic complex." The phrase "pituitary gonadotrophic complex," though you wouldn't know it, is meant to include conscious emotional experience. And again: "The ovary, unlike other endocrine glands, is endowed with a 'mirror' in which is reflected its activity. This mirror of ovarian activity is the endometrium [lining of the womb]. With the various anatomical changes occurring during the ovarian cycle, there are characteristic changes occurring synchronously in the endometrium. This sequence of changes is called the menstrual or endometrial cycle."[18] But if woman is admitted to be a sexual being, having sexual experiences reflected in her bodily reactions, then we find that for the male scientists, a frightening thing has happened. The reflection in the mirror has taken on a life of her own!

VI   *Ovary versus Womb*

The egg grows in the ovary, and it grows in a little capsule called the "follicle." The Latin means "little bag." It is an egg in a bag, like the conjuror's trick. These follicles are stimulated to grow by the first of the pituitary hormones, called the *Follicle Stimulating Hormone*: FSH for short. All these hormones act powerfully in incredibly small amounts.

The pituitary, from which FSH comes, is a part of the brain. It is associated with a portion of the underside of the brain called the hypothalamus. This hypothalamus is linked to and largely responsible for that subdivision of the nervous system called the "autonomic" nervous system, which is the part of the nervous system which is concerned with sensing and responding to normally unconscious processes, the "self-governing" processes which usually go on independently of our conscious minds. You could say that the autonomic nervous system, regulated by the hypothalamus, was the chief organ of the "unconscious mind."[19]

The pituitary is sensitive to the operations of the hypothalamus, and FSH is only one of the very many hormones it pours out directly into the bloodstream. It has been called the "leader of the endocrine orchestra," "endocrine" meaning all those glands that help to orchestrate life by secreting their responses to it inwardly into the flowing blood.

When the pituitary secretes FSH, the little capsules or follicles which contain the egg are stimulated to grow, like a kind of creative rash on the surface of the ovary. As they grow, they pour out estrogen into the blood.

This estrogen circulates and reaches the pituitary again. There it stimulates the third hormone we are concerned with, which is called the Luteinizing Hormone (LH for short) and blocks FSH. The Latin "luteus" means "yellow." When LH in its turn reaches the ovaries in the blood circulation, it causes *one* follicle to burst and to release an egg, which is picked up by the "fingers of the womb's horn," or Fallopian tube, on the appropriate side. These fingers actually grope for the released egg. After the ovum has been released, the empty follicle remaining grows larger and becomes yellow in color— hence the "luteinizing." As this happens, it acquires a new name: it is called the corpus luteum or "yellow body," and it acquires a new function, because it becomes a new kind of ductless gland, and secretes progesterone with estrogen on its own account. Progesterone circulating in the blood stimulates the lining of the womb to thicken and prepare for pregnancy, if any. Progesterone also reaches the pituitary gland, where it acts as a cut-off to LH. The consequence is that in the absence of a fertilized ovum, the corpus luteum begins to die, the levels of the hormones we have mentioned fall suddenly, and this withdrawal of estrogen and progesterone appears to be a stimulus to the shedding of the specially prepared womb-lining, then shed in menstruation.

This is a very neat pattern of interlocking feedback mechanisms. When one level rises, this stimulates the production of another substance, which regulates the first level, and initiates another process. The account is only a pattern that has been hypothesized. Why only one follicle normally grows to release an ovum, nobody knows. It is also thought that the preparation for the next ovulation happens *before* the menstruation that introduces the new cycle, and this would explain why very occasionally people become pregnant from intercourse at menstruation. Indeed at one time it used to be thought that the best time for fertile sex was during or shortly after the period, and there were figures to prove it![20] It is not so impossible that the cycle changes its rules from time to time and confounds the scientists. Doctors usually hold the view that the "normal" cycle is twenty-eight days long, and that ovulation occurs about halfway between two periods, during days fourteen to seventeen. However, most people's cycles are not exactly twenty-eight days long, and many cycles nowhere near it. To complicate matters, ovulation, with or without a detectable temperature rise, *can* occur at any time in the cycle, or even twice in the same cycle. In short, though ovulation may occur regularly at midcycle, it is sensitive to unknown rules.

A more recent view is that the variations in the lengths of people's cycles are due solely to a variation in the "follicular" stage (the run-up to ovulation), but that the "luteal" stage when the corpus luteum secretes and then, if no pregnancy, regresses, is an invariable fortnight. This opinion is not absolute either, though women, when calculating the length of a pregnancy, may use any of these rules of thumb as likelihoods, and so may their doctors. It is now thought that either phase may vary in length, as we say, according to unknown rules. The rules may be "unknown" in terms of science simply because they have to do with the emotional situation of the woman concerned, and her reactions, conscious and unconscious, to her environment. Indeed science concedes that this is so, but instead of offering techniques to enable the woman to become increasingly conscious of these unexplored possibilities, still tries to reduce them to rules. It is preferred that women should be hormone-robots, with a set of switches to press. Nobody consciously decides this, but, as we shall see, this is how it turns out. As yet, there is little sign of the rounded science of the whole human being, which can accept people as body-minds. Particularly is this so with women, whose menstrual cycle so deeply links body and mind.

By some authors, the no rules about cycle-timing are made a positive virtue, and one begins to feel an exception if one happens to have a cycle that is of the average length usually given in medical books: twenty-eight days. Authors go so far as to say that the four-week cycle is a very exceptional occurrence, and was after all only an average of a multitude of figures, and if in that multitude half were fifteen-day cycles and half forty-one-day cycles, the average would still be twenty-eight, even though nobody actually had that length of cycle.[21]

It has been pointed out also that in no age group do twenty-eight-day cycles occur more than sixteen per cent of the time, and that only thirteen percent of women have a variation of less than six days.[22] There may be wide variations too in cycles in which ovulation does not occur.

All this is of course true, but once again, only so far as it goes. Long and short cycles are part of individual experience—we are suggesting that this aspect of feminine experience may have as much of a meaning as any other aspect. What the confident figures do not say is that it is not known *why* cycle-length varies. So one must not conclude from them that the cycle *cannot* be entrained from some interior or exterior event, and beat out a regular rhythm. *We do not say this is so, merely that it can be a fruitful attitude, and we shall examine some evidence later on.* Indeed, since the woman and her whole body-mind is such a sensitive receptor of influences, there is every reason to suppose that in the presence of a wholesome stimulus, the cycle might beat out a shared rhythm among women. Indeed, it has been shown that this is possible.[23] Obviously there is no compulsion on the length of the cycle, any more than there is in the pattern of foods we eat, or our patterns of going to bed and waking up: some simply suit us more than others. But it is as unscientific to suggest that women must have irregular cycles, as to suggest that they must have regular ones, especially if science has already demonstrated that the timing of the menstrual period is very sensitively attuned to the situation of the woman's whole world. What about the fact that modern statistics are often taken from women in cities, and enormous American cities at that? And as for "age groups" it is clear that some people may be old for their years and some young. In recent years, the Pill has imposed its own rhythm which may be equivocal (see pp. 172–73). There are many different experiences and patterns that the individual can derive from her menstrual cycle, as from any natural rhythm, and all these figures are showing that there is at present *no consensus*. This doesn't mean that no consensus is possible: indeed it is highly likely that just as our whole society is broken up and alienated from nature and the body, and this is reflected in our disorderly and warlike contemporary history, that the woman's rhythms are responsive to this process also. Because the modern person feels homeless, it doesn't mean that there is no home, and if man's society does violence to woman's nature, it would be most surprising if her body didn't talk back. If it talks back in an irregular and disharmonious way, that is a just comment on contemporary history. One worker dated changes in the uterus of a woman whose period had stopped, to the exact day a bomb went off near her.

VII   *Interplay*

In the above, we have been dwelling mainly on the ovarian cycle, and not that linked cycle, the uterine. This latter is more properly called "the menstrual cycle" since the ovary does not menstruate, it ovulates.

The reader will have noticed that there are three phases to the ovarian cycle: the follicular, when the capsule containing the egg is ripening; ovulation itself, the LH peak, when the egg is released and captured by the Fallopian tube; and the luteal phase, when the newly formed remnants of the egg capsule have set up as a ductless gland on their own account and are secreting, as it were, hopefully for pregnancy, the pregnancy hormone, progesterone.

There are also three phases, in the physiological sense, to the uterine cycle. Two of these reflect the ovarian events. When estrogen is being secreted by the ovary, in the follicular phase, then the uterus is responsive to this by proliferating a new lining for itself after menstruation. At ovulation, this "proliferative phase" suddenly stops, and a new phase starts, the "secretory phase" when the womb-wall grows enormously thick in response to the secretion of the corpus luteum in the ovary. This uterine phase is called secretory, since the womb-lining develops deep glands that secrete a nutritive fluid that is presumably involved in the egg's implantation, if it is fertilized.

If it is not, then the ovarian secretions suddenly decline. For the ovary this is perhaps a nonevent; however, for the uterus it is a big event, since without these hormones the new lining does not sustain itself, its capillaries break up, and it is flushed out in the menstrual flow. Following this, "the uterine cavity resembles a large raw wound."[24]

That is two cycles, each with three phases. Two of the phases in each cycle correspond, like mirror-events. One of the phases in each cycle can be seen as its own: ovulation is the ovary's, menstruation is the womb's. Every woman has ovaries as well as a womb, so what we call her menstrual cycle in fact consists of these two cycles, ovarian and uterine, in interplay. The ovary belongs to the species. It transmits the hereditary material. Her womb is a woman's own. From time to time happily it is taken over by the species, and a child is gestated and born.

Perhaps much of the detail of the cycle is due to this interplay: two culminations of an opposite kind, separated by ovarian events which are mirrored in the womb-wall. It is not impossible that some of the confusions about timing of the cycle, and even some of the unpleasant experiences during the course of the cycle, are due to conflicts between this interplay. For instance, there is evidence that more women who conform to family roles, what we have called "the values of ovulation," tend to suffer premenstrual tensions than do women who diverge from these roles. These divergers, however, if they suffer during their cycles, tend to do so from cramping pains in the womb itself. There are indications that the premenstrual sufferers benefit from increased dreaming, which may be about family and childhood experiences; and that the womb-cramp sufferers benefit from increased sexual experience, mental and physical, that is to say, the development of genital-events including womb-events.

As Judith Bardwick remarks: "I am suggesting that there are regular and predictable changes in the personality of sexually mature women that correlate with changes in the menstrual cycle . . . The content of the change will be a function of the personality and real world of the individual, but the direction of the change will be a function of the physical state."[25] If this is true, then the menstrual cycle is only a tyranny because we (or society) make it so. If there is a pattern, then it is a pattern within which each individual woman works, just as her face and figure and brain are patterns within which her individuality expresses itself.[26] There are no rules about how to do this, and the same person may have different ideas and experiences in differing circumstances and at different times of her life. Rules about the menstrual cycle are commonly set by people who will not accept the whole woman, and instead take only one side of her. As a consequence other sides may grow ugly or distorted with neglected energies. If one chooses to acknowledge and understand one's cycle as far as possible, then one may select to emphasize from its events what one's individuality chooses as it grows, providing nothing is absolutely neglected. Similarly, one may comment on one's personality by choosing a particular hairstyle, and to do so is part of the fun of life. To shave it off altogether is a strange emphasis more suitable to the slave-camp than to fulfilled life. And anyway, it grows again.

The phases of the cycle *can* work in harmony. The effects of its rhythms can be to stimulate and to show up facets of one's nature. Menstruation is usually treated as a dustbin, in which all the unwanted bits are put by the women as well as the men. But this "rubbish," by natural law, always gets "recycled."

If one or the other facet of oneself is put aside, then it does tend to get attached to some recurring physical event in the cycle. One woman may feel very open at her period, another very vulnerable. If one hates the vulnerability for what it may show, then the change from one's usual personality to the vulnerable one may be very abrupt and painful indeed, and be strongly resisted. If one can accept what one is shown at such a time, however, one's fear is likely to diminish, and so are the physical reactions. Though the change from rejection to acceptance may look at first like buckling under to an unwelcome feminine destiny, nevertheless new gifts and startling energies are there for the taking. The destiny that has been imposed on women, not only by men and society, but by themselves, is not to accept the meaning of the cycle, or even to consider that it has one. Yet most women, deep down, and particularly while they are having their periods, know that it does. If you fight yourself, then yourself fights back—and everybody suffers. This is the subject of our next chapter.

Two The Menstrual Epidemic

(I) WHEN IS A CURSE NOT A CURSE?

I An Unexploded Bomb

The trouble is that, as everyone knows, periods hurt, or are in other ways unpleasant. Even with nothing organically wrong, nearly every woman experiences some degree of discomfort. Many women are totally incapacitated by this natural function. Moreover, during her period and shortly before it, a woman is apt to be treated by her family or intimates as, at the very least, a primed bomb, a kind of explosive package. In many cultures the woman is excluded from normal society. She is treated as a walking sickness that turns the milk sour and men's bones to jelly, she has the evil eye, she is a plague. It is a menstrual epidemic.

We have seen already how medical science is inclined to collect and interpret its results so as to favor the particular conditions of masculine physiology and psychology. We believe that the result is a picture and an atmosphere that is manipulative of women, and prejudicial to their self-realization.

First, in this section, we must look at the extent of the problem: the menstrual epidemic. Then, in the second main section of this chapter, perhaps we can begin to construct an alternative, more valid picture.

Estimates vary, but the figures appear to show that up to ninety percent of women suffer from some form of "dysmenorrhea" or "functional dysmenorrhea" or "primary dysmenorrhea" or "premenstrual syndrome" in the absence of anything organically wrong with them.[1] There is also amenorrhea, when there is no flow at all: missed periods in the absence of pregnancy. There are also the variations of cycle length, which may or may not cause distress, and the types of flow, scanty or copious, and their duration. The medical classifications vary considerably, but the simplest and most practically useful distinguishes between trouble experienced before the period flow begins, and trouble that starts actually *with* the period. You can tell the two apart by asking yourself "How do I know my period is on its way?" If your answer is an incredulous "How could I not know!" then the period discomfort or distress you feel is said to be of the "congestive" type of dysmenorrhea, and this is often regarded as a variation of the famous "premenstrual syndrome" (abbreviated PMS). If your answer is "I scarcely know until it comes . . ." then any period pain you feel will be of the type called "spasmodic dysmenorrhea." It is sometimes said that it is rare for the two kinds to be experienced by the same person, but in our experience it is not necessarily an infrequent occurrence. Katharina Dalton has coined the useful word "paramenstruum" (*para*: accessory to) to refer to the four days before the period flow, and the four days after it has begun. So the paramenstruum— what we have called the menstruation pole of the cycle—will often contain under one heading both kinds of period trouble, when they occur. Medical science, by consensus, has no explanation for distress, in the absence of organic disease, felt at the paramenstruum, and no certain cure either.[2]

Here is a short scenario which will be familiar to many women. The doctor in it is a caricature: fortunately most doctors are infinitely more intelligent and skillful. Say that every few days before her period a woman feels tense, is irritable, depressed, lethargic. She has a headache, breast pains, backache. She feels raw and sensitive. She is an unexploded bomb. She is aware that the children are playing up to her. Her husband is being far too nice, which is irritating. She explodes at him, then feels guilty. She goes to the doctor. "Why do I feel so ill, Doctor?" "You have PMS, I'm afraid. It's quite usual." "Yes, but what is the *cause*?" "Please don't excite yourself. There is an accumulation of fluid in your body which may produce these symptoms. So we'll try you on a diuretic. If this doesn't work, perhaps a mild tranquilizer will help. As a last resort, hormone treatment is usually effective." "But what is the cause?" "Ah, now I'm afraid that you trespass on medical preserves. It is your natural female functions which can produce these troubles." "But what's wrong?" "Ah . . . there's nothing *wrong*."

If one is unfortunate enough to suffer a medical encounter like this, then one finds oneself feeling much worse! It is a kind of vicious circle, or feedback loop: *I am a woman and I feel horrible so I go to the doctor who tells me I feel horrible because I am a woman and this makes me feel horrible.*

This sort of vicious circle resembles what audio engineers call "howlback." It is a common event wherever public address equipment is being used. You point the microphone at the loudspeaker, and you get a rising howl like a soul in agony. The reason for it is that the hum in the circuit is picked up by the microphone which amplifies it through the speaker which feeds it to the microphone which amplifies it through the speaker, which . . . and you get a howl like a yell of anguish rising and passing beyond tolerable limits. This phenomenon is a very good illustration of what happens in menstrual distress.

To get a three-dimensional look at the problem, one must look at it in three ways—then join them up. The result is like a howlback circuit!

First, there is how the woman feels in herself at the menstruation end of her cycle, the paramenstruum.

Secondly, there is the effect that her changes may have upon other people.

Thirdly, there is the way society may pay her back for these real or imagined disturbances.

And, finally, does this sequence bite its tail, so to speak, and does the social attitude to menstruation actually affect the way the woman feels in herself? In which case you would get howlback: *I am tabooed and this makes me feel horrible which causes me to behave unpleasantly so I am ostracized and tabooed so I continue to feel horrible and behave unpleasantly.* This of course is just an illustration, but we will find that it fits the facts. We shall also find that there are a number of ways of breaking this vicious circle. A doctor may do it by prescribing tranquilizers or hormones. But we shall find that this is only the extravert or technological way of solving the problem: effective in its own way, but as first aid is, and no real solution. The other way of breaking the circle (in the absence of actual organic disease) is to change attitude, and this is not simple either, depending on how hard one is hit each month. In fact researchers are beginning to find that a belief in the mechanistic explanation of menstrual distress is a cause of that same menstrual distress, and that "the most enduring improvement can only be achieved by introducing new insights so that the woman begins to modify her own self-image."[3]

There are many ways of changing attitude: there is the acquisition of new information about one's feminine role and the hidden actualities of the menstrual cycle—and it has been shown that such initial steps will radically ease menstrual distress. There is the detection and dissolution of hidden attitudes in oneself and others, howlbacks or knots or victimizations; and there are the ways of relaxation of physical and mental tensions, which will accompany the foregoing discoveries, and lead into the shared world of inner or subjective feminine experience which is so devalued in our "scientific" age, but which is the birthright of all. Techniques of relaxation, yoga, hypnotism, dream-recall, and just good determined imaginative thinking, all have their place here.

If we consider our model of the "howlback" circuit, not just in the individual, but howling down the generations, like the uncounted gene, from mother to daughter, father to son, son to daughter, then we shall see how serious a problem the menstrual distress of each individual woman restates for her own time. Yet the way is still open, through this very statement, made in the body-language of mental distress, if we look at it without the established prejudices.

Let's now fill out the terms in our "circuit" or vicious circle with some detail, to show how such prejudices operate, and what lies beyond them.

II *Howlback—How she feels in herself*

The *first term* in the circuit is how the woman herself feels: her individual situation. She feels horrible. If she has the "congestive" tendency then she may experience heaviness and abdominal pain and/or a tension composed of depression, irritability, and lethargy: she may get headaches, breast pains, backache, acne, asthma, hayfever, hysterical episodes, or any combination of the manifold symptoms that have been called the "premenstrual syndrome" (PMS) or "premenstrual tension" (PMT), including what has been described as "a desire to find relief by foolish and ill-considered actions." If she has the spasmodic variety, then there may be spasms of acute colicky pain in the lower belly during menstruation that every twenty minutes or so become acute again after dulling. They may resemble labor pains, and they can become severe enough to cause fainting or vomiting. They occur in the back, inner sides of the thighs and lower abdomen, but do not affect breasts, head, hands, or feet. We'll set aside for the moment all the extreme conditions that have been laid at the door of the paramenstruum: menstrual psychosis, hysteria, nymphomania, accident-proneness, kleptomania, violent crimes, air-crashes, suicides, susceptibility to viral infections of all sorts, migraine, acne, epilepsy, food fads, capillary fragility with bruising, insomnia, anorexia, dizziness, constipation, diarrhea, lack of concentration, circles around the eyes and spots before them. Moos gives a list of fifty such symptoms.

Since more or less fifty percent of humanity—the women—suffers like this, medicine has devised cures, which sometimes work. Administration of artificial hormones are recommended, progesterone or progestogen for PMS and estrogen for spasmodic dysmenorrhea. The woman may be offered the massive doses of artificial hormone contained in the Pill: if she is on the Pill this sometimes reduces menstrual troubles. It may also act as a sexual tranquilizer, this Pill, as some women find. She may be offered overt tranquilizers, which also work on her body in a fashion that medical science is not clear about. Perhaps she is luckier than she was in the nineteenth or early twentieth century: then she might be in for a removal of her ovaries, or her womb, or be treated with bolts of static electricity through her back, for persistent malaise at her period.

There is however a current in medical thought that says that perhaps these troubles, though they respond in most cases to drug or hormone therapy, are not physical in their origin at all. This is an aspect of the most hotly disputed subject in medicine, and perhaps in all science. Are human beings simply hormone-robots to be corrected in their disorders by some technologically complex but clinically simplistic pill? Or are they a webwork of psychological energies of which disease is a last resort language, or a slave language of riot after repression? No one can decide.

Again, the figures say that 140 million woman-hours are lost yearly in the U.S. alone due to mental and physical difficulties before or during the period. It is said that premenstrual tension (PMT) is "the commonest condition for which American women consult doctors." In 1973 at least twenty-six million prescriptions for tranquilizers and antidepressants were issued in the U.K. How many of these were swallowed by women at odds with their period and its tensions? The *British Medical Journal*, the foremost medical authority in the U.K., in 1967 spoke of a "continuing inability to understand" the mechanisms underlying painful menstruation. But is the only answer a pill? We are seemingly given no other by our doctors. Or is this devaluing attitude to our femininity, this encouragement to self-disgust, this eternal and inherent invalidism we are offered—is this derogation itself a cause of the trouble?[4]

Probably both views are an aspect of the same truth. If you are a gynecologist, then you will tend to see menstrual distress in physiological terms; if a psychiatrist, then in psychological terms: and your attack on the problem will vary accordingly. You can treat the menstrual distress howlback circuit at the physiological level, or at the psychological level, since the scenarios we are discussing contain interplay of both kinds of factor. Hormone levels are only the measurable, laboratory side of a body-mind unity, and they are perhaps more accessible in this age of high gadgetry.

With menstrual distress, whichever authority you consult, you find admitted some "psychogenic" component. Add up the authorities, one of whom will say dysmenorrhea has a psychological component or cure, but PMS has not, and another who will state the converse, and you get a total picture that says that both areas of menstrual distress have at least partly psychogenic origin.

For instance, Julia Sherman says that there is dysmenorrhea, amenorrhea, and the premenstrual syndrome. She inclines to the view that all except dysmenorrhea are partly psychogenic. However, Masters and Johnson say that dysmenorrhea responds very well to the psychosomatic treatment *par excellence*: genital stimulation! Again, the authoritative Kroger and Freed speak of the effectiveness of hypnotherapy for dysmenorrhea, as did the *British Medical Journal* in a leader summarizing contemporary treatment.[5] The standard works on medical hypnosis concur. The essential nature of hypnotherapy is no more than deep bodily relaxation plus convincing talk by a trusted doctor. So add this up, and you get PMS as psychogenic, and dysmenorrhea not—except that it is curable by psychosomatic procedures, such as sexual stimulation or hypnotherapy!

Ann Broadhurst, in another very comprehensive summary, refers to a "lack of uniform views" on this question, and there is a tendency for psychiatrists to recognize "a strong psychosomatic component, while many of the gynecologists considered psychogenic aspects relatively unimportant." This suggests that the distinction may be imposed by medical specialization itself.[6]

Katharina Dalton's authoritative book *The Premenstrual Syndrome* distinguishes the two entities, dysmenorrhea and premenstrual syndrome, quite sharply, saying that though they may meet and merge and be confused one with the other, they can always be diagnosed by taking case histories, and rarely occur both in the one person. She says that it is important to distinguish them since: "In fact dysmenorrhea can be induced in any woman by the administration of the wrong hormone. This invalidates any theory that dysmenorrhea is purely psychological."[7] Of course nobody would suppose that dysmenorrhea was *purely* psychological, since we are not creatures of pure mind. But it does not invalidate the supposition that a wrong hormone level can originate in a psychological disturbance. It is known that such levels are altered by mental experience, just as mental experience can be altered in its quality by any bodily change. Katharina Dalton does, however, allow a "stress" component in both clinical entities.

Paula Weideger does not find either Katharina Dalton's notions or treatment quite so clear-cut or satisfactory, and appears herself to have sought relief from both types of menstrual distress. Her informed but commonsense attitude is staking one of the sex hormones as example, as usual crisply stated: "peaks of sexual interest and heightened sexual responsiveness occur at both the estrogen output and at the points of lowest estrogen production. The pattern of sexual feeling is affected by the existing levels of estrogen, but the existence of sexual feeling and responsiveness is not *determined* by the presence of particular levels of this sex hormone." Indeed, it can be shown that the presence of sexual feeling can alter the hormone level. We shall show in a later section that the unexpected presence of sexual feeling is an important factor in menstrual distress.

A recent researcher, Julie Crabbe, takes a slightly different accent from the gynecologists, who may in fact in a busy practice be rather impatient of menstrual distress, since it is "only" a functional condition, and shows no alterations due to disease. It should, they think, give way to evidently serious conditions. She says ". . . most gynecologists generally see all menstrual difficulties, physical and emotional, as psychic configurations sailing under a gynecological flag" (Rogest, 1950). In addition, at the present time, no psychotherapy is offered the woman experiencing the distress syndrome. If indeed menstrual distress is a configuration of psychological difficulties, and if it is as widely prevalent as research indicates, then this lack of psychological treatment becomes suspect. One wonders whether negative sociocultural attitudes toward the menstruating woman are being reflected in this treatment gap.[8]

Julie Crabbe puts her finger on this rather large consideration which is now being noticed by the younger researchers in the field, many of them women. If there is, as appears by consensus of authorities, reason for believing that menstrual distress is at least partly psychogenic—then where is the psychological knowledge assembled to take care of this distress? Why must the cures always be physical ones—pills and suchlike?

It is true to say in summary of the medical attitudes that

there is a great lack of *inwardness*. If the condition of life of a woman inclines more to subjective knowledge than does the average male disposition, then this would help to suggest why menstrual distress is so mysterious to objective scientific medicine. There are on the one hand the technological cures, the tranquilization, the hormone therapy, and various treatments designed to reduce the congestion of fluid in PMS (though it has not been explained why a woman may have a great congestive increase of fluid in her body during the latter half of the cycle, and still not have PMS symptoms!).

On the other hand there are the decidedly underresearched treatments which depend on explaining the cause of the troubles in her natural cycle—that is, which depend on relieving a socially imposed ignorance. A knowledge of the cycle may actually reduce trouble in the cycle: and conversely, ignorance of the cycle may produce very serious trouble indeed. The "Samaritans," an organization in Britain that offers a telephone number for anyone in deep distress, perhaps on the point of suicide, to call, was started by a clergyman, Rev. Chad Varah. We understand that the "Samaritans" was started after Mr. Varah had attended an inquest on a young girl who had killed herself because she thought her first period was venereal disease. He swore that no one should ever be so alone again, if he could help it. Steve Reich and Morris Tiktin have researched the ways in which this social counseling can remove menstrual difficulties in the individual and in marital situations. Natalie Shainess has averred with case histories that the menstrual time is the best time for such counseling: it is a "node" for growth. It is quite certain that relaxation classes can make a radical difference to PMS sufferers, and a few psychoanalysts in addition to Natalie Shainess have made positive contributions to menstrual studies. But they are astonishingly few.[9]

We will not dwell on further negative instances at this point. It must suffice to say that it is all very well for medical science to say that the cause of the dysmenorrheas may be "hormonal," when it is not explained why the natural system should go so wrong; or "psychogenic" when the subject is consistently underresearched and avoided in all the great modern systems of psychology where, though the subjects may be female, the ignorance of the female cycle is characteristically masculine. Thus the entry to the first term of the howlback circuit is made invisible. If a cause of the immense mental and physical suffering that women undergo each month is the last term of the circuit, that is the collectively social taboo on the subject, then that collective prefers not to know about it. It prefers that the woman didn't know about it either, in case she becomes self-determining, and breaks out of the situation. Her situation may include such an extremity during her cycle that it amounts to an unconscious "change of personality."[10] Yet what this change of personality means or why it occurs has been left uninvestigated.

III Howlback—How she influences people around her

The *second* term in our "howlback" model is how one's menstrual distress may spread.

Katharina Dalton has collected much astonishing evidence of the power of the paramenstruum on our lives. We give a sample of the more outrageous figures on pp. 80–81; the effect ranges from baby-battering to kleptomania; from absenteeism to nymphomania. We ask the reader to refer to these figures and to Dr. Dalton's books to grasp the percentage magnitude of the problem; here we simply want to note that this paramenstrual effect is by no means confined to the individual who suffers menstrual distress. It *spreads*.

Dr. Dalton remarks: "Unfortunately, the menstrual influence on a woman is not confined to herself. The effect spreads to those who are in close contact with her. It is difficult to make a statistical assessment of the full effect on the male, whether he is father, husband, fiancé or son . . . Children find sudden changes in the behavior of their mothers particularly difficult to understand."

Some of the examples that are rooted in everyday life may appear at first glance trivial, but they need to be seen multiplied on a national scale, then on an international one, then on a historical scale, if one is to grasp the true extent of the "menstrual epidemic." Dr. Dalton instances the salesman whose earnings dropped from £80 a week to £20 whenever his wife was menstruating, and gives us to understand that this might be by no means an untypical occurrence. More immediately startling are the accounts of baby-battering. Mothers may, she says, "in a sudden fit of premenstrual irritation lose their control and injure their much-loved offspring. They are model mothers for the other days of the menstrual cycle."[11]

Katharina Dalton is by no means the only worker who has distinguished this paramenstrual plague, though Mary Brown Parlee has pointed out trenchantly that nobody has yet bothered to record the good things that happen rhythmically during the cycle.[12] However, the negative evidence is well-recorded, and there is no need to doubt its existence. The only thing to doubt is whether it should be regarded as a natural inevitable accompaniment of the menstrual cycle.

Family dissatisfactions flare up and escalate; a man takes them to work with him; the children react to their mother's change in temperament with psychosomatic "sniffles," or with accident-proneness to their mother's menstrual clumsiness. Dr. Dalton says that there may be a change of dominance between husband and wife at the period, and that this produces problems among all the members of the family. Herbert Modlin thinks that the precipitating factor in cases of actual paranoia is often an alteration in the relationship between husband and wife, though he does not apparently relate this to the menstrual influence; Phyllis Chesler, who quotes him disapprovingly, suggests that the deeper factor is a natural wish to be more sexually involved with the husband.[13]

Another husband in Dalton asked his bank not to post the monthly statement at the usual time; it happened to coincide with his wife's paramenstruum. A forty-year-old chef was disabled with monthly attacks of bronchitis, which nothing would cure until his wife's menstrual problems had been treated. There are these individual instances, and there are the statistical figures, to show how they are multiplied in daily living. When men seek advice about recurrent migraine, giddiness, or asthma, it might be wise, says Dalton, to record the attacks on a chart, which is then compared to the wife's menstrual chart. The two may well coincide. She says that women often wish men could have periods "just a few—for male doctors and husbands," then they would understand. We shall show in Chapter III that the experience closest to premenstrual tension for men is that of sleep-deprivation, and how this fact has significance for women also.

As far as the influence on the child is concerned, there is also much evidence, from infant sniffles to schoolteachers' punishments doled out during the paramenstruum. Dalton shows that more than half the children brought to the hospital for minor colds and suchlike were brought during their mother's paramenstruum. The effect is not confined to the home: students on teaching practice in a College of Education reported that they had great difficulties with their classes precisely when they were having their periods: "The children seemed to sense it." With these effects so apparent, it is all the more astonishing that child psychology or psycho-analysis does not appear to consider them.

The situation is reflected, however, in slang terms for the period, and in menstrual jokes. There is a fine one that goes as follows: A shopkeeper has just engaged a new supersales-man, and is watching his technique. He is amazed to see his new employee sell an entire fishing kit, waders, hunting clothes, an outdoor barbecue, a new car, a small airplane, and a country house to a customer who had simply asked about a fishing rod on display. "How do you do it?" asked the amazed shopkeeper. "Oh, I knew he was a pushover. He didn't even want the fishing rod. He had just come in to buy a box of sanitary napkins for his wife." There is every indication that these effects are very widespread, and that men *do* have menstrual cycles. There is no evidence that they have cycles of their own, but there is plenty of evidence that as adults they are influenced by the menstrual cycles of their women, and, when they are children, of their mothers. It would be very surprising if they were not so influenced, but unfortunately, for the main part the effect is made unconscious, since the subject of menstruation is simply swept under the carpet, and given no significance. It is a most unwelcome idea to many men, that in this sense they are really "one flesh" with women.

Slang terms for the period reflect social usage and individual experience. Margaret Drabble has complained that the impoverishment of common words for the period impoverishes our thinking about it.[14] In English, the two most frequent middle-class terms are "menstruation," a clinical term, or "the curse," a pejorative. "Curse" might originally have been "course"—"the courses" is still occasionally extant. Vieda Skultans has shown that in a Welsh mining community the key words are "to lose," "to see," "and natural."[15] "Period" is frequent, but it is neutral: you can have a "period" of anything. Many languages have more interesting and more friendly terms. One of the most frequent is "the moon" or "the moment of the moon"; also "the Benefit"; "Woman's Friend"; "Woman's Benefit." Menstruation is also called "Wonderful" or even "God." When did the "courses" become "the Curse"?

Less frequent terms reflect various attitudes or avoidances. Occasionally it is sexual availability, as in saying she's "in season" or "really slick." Frequently terms used by the men express disgust: "blood and sand"; "dirt red"; "gal's at the stockyards"; "ketchup"; "the rat"; or sexual unavailability: "ice- box"; "Mickey Mouse is kaput"; "manhole covers"; "she's covering the waterfront"; or sexual ambiguity: "her cherry is in sherry"; "she's out of this world." A current Americanism is OTR, meaning "on the rag," and before tampons the sanitary napkin made colloquial appearances: "riding the red rag"; "riding the cotton bicycle"; "the hammock is swinging"; "the Tailor"; "flying the mainsail."

For the women themselves, frequent euphemisms imply the visits of relatives or guests, sometimes senior ones: "Grandma is here"; "Grandma has left, thank God"; and sometimes junior: "little sister is here." "My country cousin" may visit, so may "Aunt Jane/Susie," "my redheaded Aunt from Red Bank," "Aunt Emma from Reading" or "Grandma from Red Crick." A woman may say "I'm bloody Mary today," or she may be entertaining distinguished *male* visitors, such as "Friedrich Barbarossa," "The General," "The Magnificent Marquis," "The Red King," "The Red Guard," "Little Willie," "Reggie" or even "Lachrimae Christi." Dora Carrington called it "The Fiend." A woman may say that she is "reading a book," has "come on," or that she has received her "package of troubles." She may merely be "losing blood," or she may be "swinish" or "sowish." The period may be "The Red Road," "The Woman's Way," "The Witness" or "las Reglas": the Rules. One puzzling usage is "falling off the roof"; but this is sometimes a dream-image for menstruation, roof-tiles are often red, and it could reflect the falling-off from a premenstrual "high." There is often a burst of energy late in the cycle which may replace the tension.[16]

IV   Howlback—How she affects the psychologists

The knowledge of these effects—the "paramenstrual plague"—is common knowledge, by no means confined to modern studies. Menstruation has been considered always to be energetically dangerous, and subject to complex rules of avoidance. There are the biblical rules in Leviticus about the uncleanness of people who "uncover the fountain" of the menstruous blood, and in Persian scriptures it was the fiend of menstruation, Jahi, that began all the world's disaffection and misery. Pliny's natural history lists the witchlike powers attributed to the menstruous person. Modern studies appear to bear out the age-old common opinion of menstruation.

The common knowledge of these effects should have had a radical influence on child and adult psychology. Yet we cannot find that this has happened at all. There is simply no systematic treatment of the influence of the mother's period on the mental growth of her child. Freud avoids the issue, perhaps subject to the "particularly inexorable repression" that he notes is connected with the first mother-attachment, preoedipally. Jung, we believe, disguises the issue. A younger contemporary of Freud, C. D. Daly, was an honorable exception. He wrote many complex and fascinating papers describing the universal influence of the mother's menstruation on the child, and warned that though its actuality was one of the simplest and most obvious truths in psychoanalysis, it was "the simplest truths that are often the last to be believed." Indeed, he considered the mother's menstruation the "kernel" of the famous Freudian Oedipus Complex, and terror of the mother on the part of the infant and adult the source of that celebrated engine of evolution in Freudian theory, the castration fear.[17] Alas, Daly was too committed to doctrinaire psychoanalytic therapy to develop his ideas independently, and in the effort to make them fit Freud's procrustean patriarchal bed, contradictions appeared in his arguments which enabled the more orthodox to dismiss and then neglect them. This is understandable, since had they been accepted, psychoanalysis would have worn a more feminist face.

Another Freudian, Otto Rank, fell into a similar trap among his contemporaries. He too allowed an uncomfortable amount of influence to the mother, though it was the manner of birth of the baby that concerned him, the "birth trauma." He considered that the "hero" was a person who had transcended the powerful effects of the shock of birth, the energies and pain of which he believed were repressed by society, to its great disadvantage. He would have been interested in the birth methods of our contemporary Frederick Leboyer, who above all is gentle with the baby's experience as it is born. Rank considered menstruation a similarly powerful recurring influence that had been "drawn into the general repression of the birth trauma by our civilization." He thought that the father was sought after as a refuge from the birth-trauma: hence the evolution of patriarchy. The same could apply to menstruation: providing the feminine had first been cursed by fear! Rank was thought mad by the Freudians for attributing so much influence to the mother, and did not develop his notions of menstruation.[18] Georg Groddeck had a similar opinion of the menstrual cycle, holding that we were periodically reminded of our birth-experience as infants by subliminally smelling blood each month, since blood was the first thing we smelled and tasted when we came into the world. He also considered that this was a powerfully sexual experience that one only repressed to one's damage.[19]

Two highly respected neo-Freudian schools of psychology are those founded by Anna Freud and Melanie Klein. Both appear to have bypassed the implications of the mother's menstrual rhythm, and the fact that the mother's menstruation is an integral part of almost the earliest childhood experiences. Klein describes eloquently the sufferings of the adolescent at her first period, but does not appear to consider menstruation an important experience during the early years, even though so many mothers menstruate before weaning, or feed by bottle, when the menstrual influence must apply especially early.[20] Actually this consideration would fit Kleinian theory very well, since its innovation over that of Freud, according to Paul Roazen, is to attribute "mental development, and all variations in mental disorder, to a traumatic situation occurring . . . shortly after birth," preoedipally, before conflict with the father. Anna Freud holds that "inherent potentialities of the infant are accelerated in development, or slowed up, according to her mother's involvement with them, or the absence of it . . ." but does not appear to consider the mother's menstruation. This consideration in any systematic form is also missing from the influential journal *The Psychoanalytic Study of the Child* which she coedited.

Some of the omission may be in a tendency for the Freudian-derived schools to idealize the parents, and to suppose that the child's or the adult's "intrapsychic conflict figures as the main pathogenic agent." George Devereux notes this in a strongly critical paper in which he puts forward the view that Oedipus might have had good reason for killing his father, Laius, as the latter was said to be the inventor of pederasty! Too often in psychiatry it has been that Mother and Father, Husband and Wife, can do no wrong, because they are not the patients.[21] The patient is the elected mad person, and the fault lies in him/her alone. It was with the work of Layard, Laing, Esterson, and others that the dynamics of interpersonal disturbance began to be examined, and the politics of madness in the schizophrenogenic family. The patient was then not the patient; the family is the patient. So far as we have found in the published literature, not even such workers have got around to a systematic consideration of the power for good and ill of the woman's period.

Yet it is the Freudian-based doctors that have the greatest psychiatric power in the medical profession and in the mental hospitals. When a patient is admitted into a mental ward, her menstrual status is still not usually entered on her notes— even though, when it has been, it has been shown that most mental crises occur at the paramenstruum. Nor is her experience of menstruation considered a proper subject for psychiatric investigation, any more than it was for Freud himself or his followers. The most that is allowed is that it is the woman's confirmation of her bloody castration as a "failed man" and nonpossessor of the all-desirable penis: she can, in Freudian theory, obtain one of these emblematically by having a baby. Very often a stay in a mental hospital and the treatment given there stop the periods absolutely.[22] Whether this is an effect of the treatments, or an accompaniment to mental disturbance, or a strategy for coping on the woman's part, the importance of menstruation is equally signified in this situation. How often is the period and its experiences rejected, and how often is it maltreated, and its language ignored in these hospitals, so that it goes away? Is this perhaps because menstruation in medical science is thought of solely as an excretory process, the tears of the womb disappointed of conception, rather than part of the woman's experience of herself? Twenty-six million prescriptions for tranquilizers and antidepressants were issued in the U.K. in 1973 alone, and a similar picture obtains in the U.S.[23] How many of these were given to suppress period-troubles? Mental disorder is the great prevailing disease of our time. How much of this is due to rejection and misunderstanding of the feminine experience in adult and child? In the mental hospital there is howlback at every level, including the doctor's: *Women are inclined to be crazy because of their periods but that can't be a useful approach in your case because it's not on your chart, since I didn't put it there.*

The corollary to all this is that if you systematically deny interest to the woman's period and rob her events of significance, then you will blame her, not yourself, for any unfortunate results. It is like howlback again. *I am frightened of "the curse" therefore I curse it so hard that I forget that I began it all by cursing.* Women will be treated as a dangerous virus that contaminates life, a "menstruous fiend." In politics you may argue that no woman should ever be the President of the United States, because of her "raging hormones." You may question whether the period changes have an adverse effect on the woman in authority, and her ability to make rational decisions: heads of state, Members of Parliament, directors of companies, and the like. You may be certain, as Dr. Dalton is, that the cycle makes a great difference at a much lower level, since half schoolgirls' punishments, in one study, occurred during the paramenstruum, and that prefects who gave punishments did so for the main part at this time also. She thinks it likely that this happens with magistrates and teachers and people in authority.[24]

But you will only consider that this is a social danger if you deny significance to the period, and moreover, if you believe that society as it is at present constructed is immaculate. It would be difficult to argue that there is nothing wrong with our culture, when pollution statistics tell us that we are about to poison the whole globe by our industrial effluents if not by our atomic wars. What we mean is, that there is another way of looking at the disastrous events of the period. *Suppose that society is a lie, and the period is a moment of truth which will not sustain lies.*

Thus a woman may with all goodwill and a desire for a peaceful life keep her feelings quiet about some dissatisfaction with her life, a bad habit of her lover's, some discrimination against her because she is a woman, or the necessity to study some subject which she is sure is irrelevant to her being. As a person conforming to society, she will for most of the month keep quiet about this, saying to herself, "it's all for the best . . . it's the principle of the thing . . . the greatest good for the greatest number." But then, maybe at the paramenstruum, the truth flares into her consciousness; this is an intolerable habit, she is discriminated against as a woman, she is forced to underachieve if she wants love, this examination question set by male teachers is unintelligently phrased, I will not be a punch-ball to my loved ones, this child must learn that I am not the supernatural never-failing source of maternal sympathy.

Then, in greater extremes, at the "moment of truth" of the paramenstruum, greater repressions may emerge, or may be expressed in body-language as illnesses, or accident-proneness. This is because they are given no other language in a society run by men, they cannot be expressed outwardly, so they screw women up inwardly. Her father's disappointment with her not being a boy, and the unfairness of it, her mother's jealousy at her period, of the girl's young fertility as the mother's menopause approaches, all the forgotten things that must be expressed somehow, rise to the surface. Melanie Klein writes eloquently about this when she describes the "mental upheavals" at the first period, which may persist throughout life, recurring each month in altered or unchanging form. She says that the body is at dangerous odds with itself, since menstrual blood is often identified with dangerous excreta, or with fears of being wounded itself, or her children in the womb wounded, and that she is now certain that she is no longer the boy so often preferred, and that if as she may suspect, sex is sadistic in basis, now she is in for it. Since the clitoris is active at menstruation, she may feel that by masturbating she has wounded herself. In a male-oriented society, with a psychology directed only to express the conditions of a man's life and a man's "superiority," then such suspicions are natural. In the absence of any significance given to her existence as a woman, then of course with each period these feelings may burst through! And the statistics show that the paramenstruum is the time when most women are admitted to mental hospitals for emotional crises, or commit suicide. It is the "moment of truth," which in a society which refuses woman her true place may become the moment of despair.

There is a fine Border Ballad of "True Thomas" in which Thomas the Poet is taken to the fairy underworld and initiated into the truths of the Queen of Elfland. He is returned to the world of men, and asks the Queen what gift he shall go back with. She tells him that his gift is now that he will always be compelled to tell the truth. "A gudely gift ye wad gie to me!" he protests. Indeed, men can fly from the truth, but women face the deep instinctual truth of their bodies each month. In this world of lying politics and double agents, truth-telling may well seem a disadvantage, and the bearer of truth a dangerous dissident who must be called "ill" and confined if possible to a mental ward.

We shall see that this "truth-telling" is possibly the real reason behind *the third term* of our howlback circuit-chain factors: the rewards that society returns to the menstruating woman in the form of taboos against her disturbing presence.

V   Howlback—How society rewards her

These taboos against contact with "menstruous persons" are worldwide, and occur throughout history. They are *the third term* of our howlback-circuit model. In them the woman is treated as a scientist treats a dangerous piece of radioactive material. Radioactive elements are never touched, since their power would burn. Protective clothing is needed, lead-sheathed rooms, sealed laboratories fitted with remote-control tongs. Similarly with the woman at her period. We know also of radioactivity that it is the basic, archaic power of the universe. It is terribly destructive if incorrectly handled. Nevertheless, hydrogen fusion in the solar system created the planets, and the radiation from our star, which comes from processes which are utilized in the hydrogen bomb, created life on our planet, and feeds us all day by day in the food chain beginning with photosynthesis. We would like to suggest that the analogy is worth following through, since an acknowledgment of paradoxical benefit and danger is also the characteristic of menstrual taboos.

James George Frazer, in his celebrated and influential *The Golden Bough*, brings this fact to our attention, though he by no means follows its implications. His great, flawed book is about the worldwide rites of succession by slaughter of a Divine King, and how this pattern of blood sacrifice spreads its images through legend, history, and all lands. He shows us how people have believed that the life of their community, the fertility of its crops and people, depended on the sacrificially renewed energy of this king.

All communities do in actuality depend on the blood-sacrifice of the menstruating woman, for without menstruation there is no ovulation, and therefore no people. It can be argued that all rites of blood-sacrifice including cannibalism derive from a "monstrification" of this basic fact. The menstrual blood is magic blood, and guarantees fertility, but a man does not possess this magic blood-shedding himself. If power falls into the hands of men, they cannot endure to be without this magic blood, and from this possibly effloresces imitation rites that are designed to make magic blood without need for recourse to the opposing political camp, the women: imitation rites from ritual dismemberment to subincision. It would be thus possible to argue that the whole of *The Golden Bough* investigated a deterioration of the gentler, womanly knowledge—but it would take another book of comparable size to do it. We have to content ourselves here with pointing out some fresh directions of interpretation that reveal themselves when the existence of the female fertility cycle is clearly seen in its details.

Frazer draws certain general conclusions about the Divine King. He must always be kept at the height of his bloom, to guard against the failure of the fertile powers of his world. Therefore he must be killed before this happens, and a newly potent successor take his place. But the existence of the Divine King is regulated by two important rules or taboos. The first is that he should not touch the ground with his foot, lest his magical virtue, his *mana*, drain away into the earth.

This insulation of the King was necessary not only for his own safety, and to preserve his power intact for the benefit of his community, but was also to keep this electrical holiness within safe bounds for the sake of other people too. The charge of power could easily blast the King's attendants, unless they were sufficiently holy themselves to take the charge.

The second rule was that the King should not see the sun.

Now it is remarkable that the foregoing two rules—not to touch the ground and not to see the sun—are observed either separately or conjointly by girls at puberty in many parts of the world . . . [says Frazer]. In short, the girl is viewed as charged with a powerful force which, if not kept within bounds, may prove destructive both to herself and to all with whom she comes in contact. To repress this force within the limits necessary for the safety of all concerned is the object of the taboos in question. The same explanation applies to the observance of the same rules by divine kings and priests. The uncleanness, as it is called, of girls at puberty and the sanctity of holy men do not, to the primitive mind, differ materially from each other. They are only different manifestations of the same mysterious energy which, like energy in general, is in itself neither good nor bad, but becomes beneficent or maleficent according to its application.

The reader must make her/his own decision about whether or not we have been describing the same phenomenon in contemporary terms as Frazer recounts in his. It might seem that our own taboo against the menstruating woman, and all that goes with her cycle, is one of "ignore-ance," which is perhaps kinder than the many taboo customs Frazer vividly recounts, since we have a way out by demanding and accumulating knowledge. Such a course was not open to the New Ireland girls in Frazer, who had to be kept in cages for four or five years, or the New Guinea women kept indoors out of the sun for two or three years, or the Torres Straits girls kept out of the light for three months, like sensitive photographic films. Indeed, a Cambodian girl at puberty is said to "enter into the shade." In northern New Guinea, the girls are not allowed to sit on the floor; not on the earth, in Yap, one of the

Caroline Islands. Frazer's account of the New Ireland girls, kept in small cages in the dark, is unforgettable, as is the seven-year seclusion of the eight-year-old Borneo girls who are shut up in a little cell of the house for seven years. The result of their confinement is that they are stunted in their growth, and when they emerge the skin is pale and like wax. Now the girl is shown earth, water, trees, flowers, sun, as if she were new-born. A feast is made, a slave is killed, and the girl is smeared with his blood.

The Californian Indians, says Frazer, take a more equable view of the strong supernatural power which they affirm comes on the girl at first menstruation (menarche). It is not entirely defiling or malevolent, though it does incline toward evil.

Who or what the Divine King might really have been, the "other husband" of the woman, in his various forms, will emerge in this book as we go along. We don't want to state this dogmatically, though we think that given the evidence, there is a strong presumption, which it is at least interesting to consider. It would seem to be natural if the history of consciousness progressed by the gradual externalization of instinctive processes, and by relating to them through their depiction in images and stories.

One of the most important of these would be the human fertility-cycle, without which there would be no consciousness at all: in this sense it is the original magic, and it is of the woman. And the human fertility-cycle has to do with the shedding of blood, a small individual blood-sacrifice essential to the community. It also has to do with the alteration of feelings during the cycle—and it would be natural to person- ify these alterations in dream-images and stories—which, as depictions of processes essential to life, might well take their place in community rites. If the particular rise of instinct at menstruation is powerful, then it would be natural to depict it in terms of power-politics: since it would be an opposite experience to the maternal feelings of ovulation, an overmastering Divine King might be the natural image, who is sacrificed in blood for fertility's sake, but who returns constantly. This blood king, whose image might be given horns, since the appearance of the animal and human womb is horned with its beautiful swept-back Fallopian tubes, would be a mediator between life and death.

On this hypothesis, a first stage in community evolution then might be the depiction of these events in "psychodramas," perhaps arising from the night-experiences of gifted dreamers. But if men then resented the root of these matters not being in themselves, but in women, then the former would invent imitation menstrual rites, shedding blood for bloodshed's sake. It would not be at all surprising if it turned out that such were developed to control fertility-power, or to scrutinize or depict it, which would later become instruments of political power: after all, fertility is the basic evolutionary force of any species. As Devereaux says of the menstrual taboos, "one does not bother to tie up a puppy with a steel cable"![25]

Thus one may, if one wishes, reorganize the information given in *The Golden Bough* and other such books, and see where it leads. If it leads to consciousness-raising in men and women, then it is a true direction, though much of the energy created in people by realizing that mythological rites have an actual and discernible meaning relevant to one's life lived now is usually dissipated in anger and aggressive disagreement. It is worth mentioning here a second monumental book, Joseph Campbell's *Masks of God*, which offers much supporting evidence for these views. When he is speaking of Cretan and Sumerian religion, he discusses the slain bull, who was the moon's animal, "lord of the rhythm of the womb" and equated with the moon-king in a tradition where the moon's waxing and waning is linked with ritual regicide. This would be the "other husband" of the woman, the god-husband, who, as a personification of part of the fertility-cycle, would die each month like the moon, and become the possibility in a fresh cycle of her physical child. As Campbell says: "As viewed in the pre-patriarchal age, this same goddess in whom death and life reside was herself the mythic garden wherein Death and Life—the Two Queens—were one. And to her faithful child, Dumuzi (the Minotaur), whose image of destiny is the lunar cycle, she was Paradise itself." The recurring human monthly time would become assimilated to the yearly fertility-cycle of the land, depicted by the solar events, the seasons. But in human terms, the Golden Bough was the magic of that dangerous human tree, the force of evolution itself: "But ever, as one was torn away, another branch of gleaming gold sprang in its place."[26]

Robert Briffault's *The Mothers* is like the flip side of *The Golden Bough*. It is more feminist. It has been much criticized for its evolutionary theories, which are out of date, but so far as we are aware, the *information* that it contains has never been discountenanced. There is a good abridgment, but one needs the three-volume edition to see the true force of the arguments of this book which concern us now. The direction of these is, as we have said, that the first "magic" was human fertility magic, and it was exercised by the women, who had, and have, the original power as priests, magicians, prophets, and shamans. The women are where all people came from, and the women have an approximately monthly cycle which resembles the moon's cycle so closely that the analogy between the two is a universal one in religious imagery. This, thinks Briffault, was part and parcel of the rhythm of all human life, and the first measure of human time. Thus, wherever you meet moon-imagery in religion or mythology, it has to do with the women: all moon cults are menstrual cults, he implies, and brings a massive amount of information to corroborate.

Like Frazer, Briffault shows that the person of the menstruating woman is fraught with a strange power, which is thought of in some cultures as a kind of communicable disease, and in others a kind of shamanic or magic holiness leading to prophetic fits and trances. He mentions, for example, that in Arabic the words "pure" and "impure" originally referred to menstruation, which was the source of the concept. By the same token, "Taboo" or "sacred" in Polynesian and Siouan is the same word as "menstruating." In Dakotan "Wakan" means "spiritual, wonderful, menstrual."

Briffault has a more sensitive view than Frazer, and notes, as have later writers such as Devereaux, that menstrual taboos and seclusions in many instances are for the purpose of safeguarding the woman at a receptive time, during which she may indeed go inward and produce prophetic information or dreams which are useful to the community, or on the contrary have wrong kinds of experience which can affect her badly ever afterward.[27] Miriam Van Waters, writing at about the same time, noted this also, and that the menarche or first menstruation was regarded as a time of a particular inward mental opening, as well as a physical one, during which a girl would have those dreams or other experiences that would guide her in later life, and that if she were to be a shaman or witch doctor, then this was the time at which she came into a special relationship with the powerful spirits of her menstruation. In New Britain: "It is not clear whether the wound [menstruation] has been given through love or malevolence; it inspires feelings of profound mystery, and causes the girl to be treated as a half invalid and half shaman." There is recent anthropological work which provides confirmation of the view that men envied such magical events.

For example, there is a Dogon myth that a certain woman found the fiber skirt of the Earth Mother, and it was stained with the sacred menstrual blood of this Goddess. The human woman wore the skirt, and as a consequence became a great queen, with rule over the men. Eventually the men stole the sacred skirt and established dominion. Again, the Mount Hagen native men believe they are weakened by sexual contact with women, and especially by contact of female genital blood. They are ambivalent toward bright red body-paint, since it is associated with women, and they seem to feel that to wear it is to become effeminate and to identify with loving passivity. However, if on occasions they want to exert a strong erotic appeal, or express a special friendliness toward strangers, they add red coloring to their body-paint. Among the Australian Aborigines of Arnhem Land, their creation myth tells of the men stealing the magical instruments of the women, and the women being too busy with ordinary life to worry about this. There were two Wawilak sisters, one who had just given birth, and the other who was menstruating. Blood from the latter's vagina fell into the water-hole, and woke the great snake, who turned the sisters to stone. However, they still come to the men in dreams, to tell them how to do the circumcision dances. A native man commenting on these rites said: "We have been stealing what belongs to them [women] . . . Men have nothing to do really, except copulate . . . All that belongs to the Wawilak, the baby, the blood, the yelling, their dancing, all that concerns the women . . . We have to trick them . . . In the beginning we had nothing . . . We took these things from the women."[28]

It is often said (for instance by Simone de Beauvoir) that "Society has always been male; political power has always been in the hands of men . . ." despite strong indications to the contrary. The idea of prehistoric or primitive matriarchy is often dismissed as a fable, and the historical controversy still rages. What is not in doubt, however, is that men have always feared and been fascinated by female mysteries, and have attempted to annex them, and to minimize the contribution of women. Also, whether or not there was ever a historical "Golden Age of Women" (an idea which we find is resisted with much prejudice) it is certain that the Mother came first in individual life. Whether a Goddess presided over the first stirrings of human consciousness or not, a Mother did so over yours and mine. Just as the Goddesses had two sets of attributes, as Mother of All-Living or as Queen of the Underworld, so have all mothers their procreative, breast-feeding, and providing role, and their menstrual rhythm also, which, as we will see, are connected with what Neumann calls the "mysteries of inspiration"—and the mysteries of resisted inspiration, which are those of madness.

Briffault suggests that the crueler customs of menstrual seclusion developed when the force and power of the period and its unknown qualities recoiled upon the women, and that these customs developed in the hands of the men into ways of setting the women aside for reasons of "impurity." Whatever the historical facts, we do seem to see a comparable situation around us in modern times. Briffault does seem to show how the original magic was always the woman's, and associated with a charge of power at her menstrual time. The women may have instituted the menstrual seclusions, but it is possible that the men extended and imposed them out of fear of the unknown, and of the "other": the woman's functions that they could not share, but only imitate.

Bruno Bettelheim offers convincing documentation of this in his *Symbolic Wounds*. He argues that the desire to obtain "magic blood" at puberty led to the male rites of circumcision at puberty. Men showed blood by imitation; women did by nature. He gives convincing documentation that the cruel rite of subincision, in which the urinary passage or urethra of the penis is cut into so that the organ can be opened up longways and pressed against the belly so as to resemble the lips of a bleeding vagina, was adopted by the men so that the elders could arrogate to themselves female wisdom. "Look! I have a menstruating vagina," they could say. The blood of the men would also be used for magical rites. This book opens with some memorable observations of disturbed children. The girls wish the boys could bleed a little, as they do. A secret society is formed, which the boys can join by shedding a little blood.

In the Freudian view, the man jealous of his father fears

that he may be deprived of that which makes him his father's rival, the precious penis. He fears castration, and the woman's genital, especially when it is bleeding, frightens because it seems like the site of a castration. Freud supposes that the woman herself shares these terrors, but in her case, the castration has already occurred, so she is at once a second-rate man, and somebody to whom the worst possible thing has happened, so she is free of male fears and male responsibilities. So, on this view, one of the chief energies in male life is avoiding in himself what appears to have happened to his womenfolk!

There is important work by W. N. Stephens which looks at this in terms of the menstrual taboos of seventy-two cultures. He measures this "castration anxiety" on various scales, which include whether the father is or is not the main disciplinarian, whether masturbation is punished severely or not, the general strictness of the father, the relative severity of the punishments, whether they are physical or not, whether or not the sex training is of a severe kind, and whether or not the children are trained to be aggressive.[29]

Stephens concludes that the societies exercising these anxious restraints on their children also had strong menstrual taboos against knowledge of or coming in contact with the women's natural functions. It is particularly interesting to find that "training for aggression" is linked with a strong menstrual taboo. It is perhaps not legitimate to reason from Stephens's demonstration that those peoples who hate and avoid the feminine in life become the most bellicose—that if there is no acknowledgment of the women's natural shedding of blood, then blood still has to be shed somehow, in warfare if necessary—but with all the considerations that are accumulating, it certainly begins to look this way. It is certainly true of our contemporary culture that the two go together: Western Protestant Capitalist culture is arguably the most woman-hating that has ever existed, and it is certainly the most bellicose. But it is not unique: Ruth Benedict quotes the example of the Amerindian Kwakiutl, for whom "menstrual blood was polluting to a degree hardly excelled in the world" and who were megalomaniac, self-glorifying, egotistical bullies dedicated to economic display, "recognizing only one gamut of emotion, that which swings between victory and shame." This description resembles the women-fearing Greeks of classical times, superbly described in Philip Slater's *The Glory of Hera*, whose behavior resembles so closely and depressingly that of American society, in his opinion: "The systems are alike in depriving women of contact with and participation in the total culture, and in creating a domestic pattern peculiarly confining and unfulfilling."[30]

Contemporary studies confirm this male avoidance and fear of the woman's menstruation in interpersonal relationships, and now our cultural feedback snake has bitten its tail. We have come full circle from the woman's personal experience, through her effect on others around her, through a hypothesis of the way societies have formed around these fears, back to what custom means to the woman's own relationships. Among our contemporaries Paula Weideger shows how the fear of menstruation is felt more insistently among American men than any self-disgust of one's own period is felt among the women. She suggests that the common taboo against sexual intercourse during menstruation, which still persists at the present day, comes from the man's dislike or fear of blood on his penis, rather than from any discomfort the woman may experience. She implies that the male is usually so vociferous about this that the woman gives in and does not have sex at this time—even though it may be sexually a very sensitive time for her.[31]

It's all very well calling this a "castration fear"—but the term is a remarkably elastic one. Psychoanalytic documentation suggests very strongly that men do indeed fear menstruation as a kind of castration. Freud said that *women* feared menstruation for this reason. His assumption was that women did not experience the vagina as a valued thing—and he did his persuasive best to persuade them that it was a very inferior organ—and that they felt that the clitoris did not give sufficiently powerful sexual feelings in comparison with the penis, which is not true either. It has been shown that Freud's theories about women have little to do with female experience, but have to do with men's fears of women instead. This makes him an inadequate guide to female psychology, except insofar as Freud has persuaded women to act as if what he says is true. On this view "castration" was Freud's word for his fear of losing command. It really means a loss of one's well-being, a damage to one's ego, or loss of "ontological security."[32]

What does this "losing command" involve? One thing, it has been suggested, is feminine identification. The man cannot bear to become like a woman. He is not "the other," he is himself. But what a magical thing it would be if he could safely cross this bridge, become for a while "the other" and return safely! Briffault and others have shown that if a man wants to become "holy" and adventure into another world, a "zone of magnified power," then he dresses as a priest, that is to say, in women's clothes! Frazer also says this, and Crawley gives as his view of the origin of taboo that it originates in the fear of, or the control of, the process of "becoming the other"—of extending one's sympathies in unexpected directions.[33]

But this is what happens in sexual love anyway! As Ferenczi, Freud's younger colleague, puts it: "The acts preparatory to coitus likewise have as their function the bringing about of an identification with the sexual partner through intimate contact and embraces. Kissing, stroking, biting, embracing serve to efface the boundaries between the egos of the sexual partners."[34] We shall find that menstruation is a very powerful site in the sexual landscape, and this sexual power may be the source of the trouble. It may appear that the genital bleeding works as a kind of doorway in human nature, both female and male, beyond which there are both dangers and prizes.

VI   *A Surge of Response*

Another way of putting this is that there is a powerful surge of response in men to the woman's rhythms. It can be a resisted response, in which case it turns to distress and illness, or it can be a sympathetic response, in which the man becomes something more of "the other" than he otherwise would be. To a stiff and unyielding masculine spirit, this change would be classified among all the other assaults on his ego as a "castration"; to the sensitive man, however, it will be full of experience. In most cultures this has been recognized, by virtue of the powerful customs of taboo by which the women's rhythms have been isolated and controlled. One manner in which instinctual forces are controlled without repression is by the enactment of rites and legends—what we would now call "psychodramas." However, in our age the body has become so secularized by medical technology and other political forces, that this manner of imagining participation in natural processes has been neglected. A consequence of this is that these powerful menstrual influences are found to be alien to society. This does not, however, eradicate them. Instead they influence people almost totally unconsciously. The result, with repression, is disturbance and sickness among both men and women, the latter most so, as it is their own inner rhythms which are without name or relationship to them—merely "hormones." There is an unknown and hitherto almost unexamined effect on our children. The situation howls down the generations like the uncounted gene. Our submission is that at least a proportion of menstrual distress, "the paramenstrual plague," is due to the interplay of these factors, and that it is not merely a medical problem, but a psychological and social one also.

In an exaggerated form, this is the scenario of escalation:

your period frightens me because it is beyond my experience therefore I shall keep quiet about it, so quiet that not even your goodself will realize fully what is happening, but the children will notice it as the chief people with whom you communicate, since I have reduced the area of communication between us by pretending that your period does not exist. I shall claim to protect these children from your influence by not discussing the subject which will therefore act on them inarticulately in the strongest possible manner, by the body-language of your menstrual distress. This will demonstrate how unfit you are to be a mother, therefore, having created this ignorance I will remove the children from your menstrual influence by educating them on nonmenstruating principles in my schools and universities and religions. The children's ignorance of themselves will make them far worse menstruees and menstruators when they grow up which will further darken their relationships with each other and with their children, and they with each other and their children, and their children's children, ad infinitum. The word "meme" has been coined for a body of opinions or ideas that are inheritable, just as a "gene" is the means by which a bundle of inherited characteristics are transmitted by the DNA code. The idea "God" is a meme; so is the idea "Marxism." Both memes have had demonstrable evolutionary effects.[35] So does the meme "menstrual secrecy," in our opinion.

There is a certain amount of information that suggests how we may begin to make these adjustments to the most powerful rhythm that exists among human communities, which is controlled in their manner by most of them, but which by our culture has been so neglected that we do not even systematically assemble such data as there is. Paula Weideger's helpful book closes with a plea for such information, in order that women may begin to shape their destiny according to their nature, and not according to stereotypes imposed by ignore-ance. All the authorities we have consulted who do not regard the period as an illness pure and simple agree on this: it is astonishingly underresearched.

This statement ranges in modern times, for example, from Havelock Ellis (1935) to Pistilli (1976).

In such of the literature as is open-minded, there are fascinating suggestions concerning these sensitive and unexplored areas, some of them stern and difficult in their implications. One analyst, Poul Faergeman, writes about the notion of "psychological castration"—which may mean anything from "loss of well-being" to "fear of woman," from "fear of love" to "fear of loss of love." Faergeman suggests, using case histories in illustration, that a man who is "psychologically castrated"—and the presenting symptom may be anything from profound depression to schizophrenic hallucination—is not simply an inadequate man. He is a different creature altogether. It is as if he "has been turned into a woman and bleeds as the woman does; he menstruates, is deflowered, gives birth . . ." In other words, the woman's pattern of rhythm is what is behind his overt symptoms; they are the basic scenario of his disturbance, which is a disturbance because they are a knowledge or observation of these rhythms which has erupted after long repression. Faergeman believes, from his observations, that what the psychoanalysts call castration is a "bloody bridge that leads from masculinity to femininity" and that this is a concealed and repressed response to menstruation.

This suggestion accords in a most interesting way with one of Bettelheim's, which depends on the anthropological documentation, that is, of cultures rather than individuals.[36] He implies that menstruation can be seen as the gate of blood that leads back to childhood, that is, to the time when we were not psychologically *neuter* as infants, but *deuter* that is, comprising the underdeveloped qualities of both sexes, like a complete being "trailing clouds of glory," like Plato's bisexual being whom God split into male and female.

Indeed, every person, by physiology and society, is at puberty given his/her sexual role—but this does not mean that the potentialities of the "other" have been eradicated;

they have, as it were, gone underground. It is possible that this gate of blood opens every month in the woman's menstruation, and can be valued as the way open to these areas of potential development—which are also the places where all the damaged childhood things are kept, and these are inclined to present themselves in a strong form during menstrual distress.

For the man, the gate to past time and therefore to his feminine side either does not open at all or is given a chance to open by his acquiring a "symbolic wound" at his puberty initiation. This wound is not only like a touchstone of his masculinity (and some cultures mark the ceremonies by awarding a stone as a kind of mnemonic to the successful graduate to manhood: he only has to touch it to remember his courage) but also a gateway to his "other" powers, which may have come to him in the form of dreams or visions during the initiation.

Bettelheim describes these notions in several ways, and there is a case for the idea of a man's being forced by these customs to acquire a sympathy for the woman's bleeding, by bleeding himself, before he can be regarded as a complete person. He may then unfortunately decide that he is by virtue of his "symbolic wound" plus his masculinity a better person altogether than the woman; indeed there is a body of opinion which says that the purpose of circumcision in both man and woman is to extinguish the countersexual side and its inner influence, and to monstrify, as it were, the conventional roles. It is interesting that Karen Paige has found a greater incidence of premenstrual tension among women who have allegiances to conventional roles, and Peter Sheldrake that "convergers" may have a similar tendency (see p. 99). It may very well be, then, that in the puberty customs, the door to underdeveloped abilities is either opened wide or slammed shut.

Bettelheim's vivid description of the children for whom the shedding of blood—menstruation in the girls or a "symbolic wound" in the boys—was a prerequisite for the joining of a secret society that would accomplish great things, has already been noted. The analyst Landauer reports the case of a boy who envied and hated his sister's menstruation because it separated men and women and through it he had lost his sister as a harmless comrade. Phyllis Chesler brings many instances to bear upon a similar argument, which she states thus: *"What we consider 'madness' whether it appears in women or in men, is either the acting out of the devalued female role or the total or partial rejection of one's sex-role stereotype . . .* Women who reject or are ambivalent about the female role frighten both themselves and society so much that their ostracism and self-destructiveness probably begin very early. Such women are also assured of a psychiatric label and, if they are hospitalized, it is for less 'female' behaviors, such as 'schizophrenia,' 'lesbianism,' or 'promiscuity.'"[37] It is, of course, the function of the shaman or witch doctor to frighten and instruct their societies. Phyllis Chesler says that women who fully act out the stereotyped "conditioned female role" will find themselves in an artificial, compulsive situation which is when hospitalized also given psychiatric labels. This would correspond, in our view, with the pattern of two extremes of the menstrual rhythm: what we have called "the values of ovulation"—the conventional or tribal role—and the "values of menstruation," the unexplored values, distressing in a culture which is stereotyped for "ovulation values" in the woman. Of course women have the ability of both sides—unlike men, who can have the ability only by a kind of synchrony and sympathy—and each set of qualities is appropriate to different events and times in her life. The sickness comes when she is stuck in one or the other role, of which the interplay of menstrual events may be the basic pattern. As the feedback is so sensitive, disturbance of one is likely to show up in the other. On this view, the feminine rhythm is a kind of mandala or code of possibilities which should as far as possible have symmetrical proportions.

C. D. Daly says that "due to the menstruation, the son goes through a phase of pure femininity, identifying with the mother . . ."[38] In Faergeman's paper there is a little boy of ten, who dreamed that he "was a lady, and it felt so good." A male blood donor said, "I don't understand why more people don't give blood. I have to do it regularly; otherwise I get to taste it in my mouth. It makes me feel better." Passing from the individual experience in analysis to the anthropological observation once again, Margaret Mead speaks of "synthetic male menstruation, bloodletting for males in which they also can rid themselves of their 'bad blood' and so be as healthy as females . . ."; and with regard to the "menstruating men" of the cruel puberty rites, Bettelheim remarks that ". . . men were willing to and ready to make themselves into females in order to share women's superior powers."

Faergeman also remarks on the universal fantasy that connects the moon not only with sex and menstruation but with insanity or "lunacy" also. He implies that the child has observed the menstrual rhythms of his mother either sublim-inally or overtly, and that his adult interests might form themselves about the patterns of these interesting rhythms. He asks himself, even, "How frequently do astronomers in choosing their profession recognize the impetus from an unconscious interest in cycles based on infantile observa-tions?" Turning his telescope into the sky may also help to increase his infantile anxiety about these events on the earth: in past ages and other cultures it is surely worth speculation that people found intelligible and reassuring images of these rhythms in, for example, moon-cults based on observation, and attempted to reconcile human rhythms with celestial and tidal ones (see Chapter IV) in order to respond to them both as fully as possible. By contrast our age is very insulated from both environments: that of the female rhythms and by extension the world of nature too.

Perhaps we should seek again for reconciling images. Perhaps one day there will be a "field theory" of natural rhythms, among which the menstrual rhythm is clearly one of the most immediately important.

In the meantime, we have little more than the data of sickness. Mary Brown Parlee has trenchantly argued that menstrual studies are incomplete while we only chart the sickness of the cycle, and not its peaks and inspirations, its valued acts. Berta Bornstein says of a boy patient that "since bleeding women aroused his fears and distrust he retaliated by attacking all the women in his house" and that in the boy's mind the bleeding woman meant the "crazy woman." But who was crazy, the woman who menstruated naturally, or the boy who attacked her for so doing? The American usage is an apt pun: "mad" also means "angry." Thus the bleeding woman is not just "crazy" she is both "mad" and "angry." One should ask, what angers a woman most? Is it neglect? Then she is human.

Another of Faergeman's patients told of the smell of his mother's menstruation, and how he hated his wife when she smelled the same, and how this led to homosexual episodes.

"Vicarious menstruation" by bleeding from the nose or elsewhere is not all that uncommon in men. Georg Groddeck is very forthright about the "monthly" rhythm: he says that it is powerful on three most important counts: the first is that menstruation is the most exquisite time to have sexual intercourse, which is precisely the reason why it is so dangerous and fascinating: people both desire and fear such deep experiences. The second power, he says, comes from the re-collection of our childhood: indeed we respond to the interesting changes in our mothers, and they may be the terrifying changes if the mother has learned to hate them (which is to say, fear and desire them at once). When we are little children, all our senses are sharp, and since we are little our noses just come up to our mothers' laps, where every month she bears an interesting smell. This is not just an ordinary smell, though, it is the first smell that we ever experienced, since it is like the smell of our birth-blood, the first time we drew a breath of the air into which we were born. It was in our first breath, and taste too. No wonder it is a very powerful imprint: the suggestion is that the smell can carry with it, for good or ill, that total experience of ourselves and of woman which was in the turmoil of our birth. Perfumes bring scenes back: it is for this reason that Freud argues that with our two-legged posture we have surmounted a primitive stage of evolution, carrying our noses proudly in the air. Therefore this archaic sense of smell will carry all the primitive dangers and energies with it, as the perfume manufacturers know very well. Vieda Skultans wisely points out that in this Freud is saying that "woman is at her most attractive during menstruation." Is this, then, the "phase of development that has been surmounted"—women's sexuality? For the rigid patriarchal ego, perhaps that is so.

Then, on Groddeck's view, menstruation is like a little birth, in which we learn something about ourselves, and about our attitudes to our origins. This will be so for the one undergoing menstruation, in her own person, and for the man who instead responds to all its profound bodily changes, which comprise much complex body-language, including olfactory stimuli. We both fear and desire this knowledge, as Mary Chadwick points out also. We have noted Rank on the birth-trauma earlier; it is also interesting to recall how Groddeck attributes his psychological insight to "the black, the white and the red" of his mother taking him to bath with her,[39] and how these three colors recur universally as the sacred colors of human life. Even J. G. Frazer in his peroration to *The Golden Bough*, "Farewell to Nemi," finds it necessary to describe the fabric of his thought thus: "while the black and white chequer still runs through it, there rests on the middle portion of the web, where religion has entered most deeply into its texture, a dark crimson stain, which shades off insensibly into a lighter tint as the white thread of science is woven more and more into the tissue."[40] The black thread is "magic." In fact many primitive cultures, such as the

Mandari and Ndembu, weave these three basic colors into the patterns of their self-interpretive "psychodramas," and the red is often explicitly "menstrual blood," which is the color of danger and life-energy.[41]

Groddeck's third power to be attributed to the menstrual rhythm is that it arouses the man's fear of becoming a woman, and his desire of it. We have already touched on this. If the period is for the mother her "moment of truth" and her most profoundly sensitive time, and perhaps her most sensuous time, then it is natural that her attitude to her child will be an intense one. If, however, she hates or is suspicious of her feelings of menstruation, as a result of male domination and ignorance or rejection of all that is "not-male," then she will suffer a split of sympathies. She will love her male child intensely, but also hate his maleness as a representative of those powers that have deprived her of the full rights of citizenship. This at least is the view of classical Greek society that Philip E. Slater persuasively expresses in a book we have already mentioned, *The Glory of Hera*. Slater does not examine the menstrual situation except in passing, but his patterns are consistent with the "howlback" that we have described.

The women, Slater believes, exercised their political power in the nursery. The atmosphere there was seductive, and reproachful. Slater shows how it is possible to see the great interpretive myths or "psychodramas" of the male Greeks as a way of expressing and conquering the terrifying self-contradictions that disturbed their childhood as a consequence of their own act of depriving women of actual political power. Thus—to simplify disgracefully his fascinating argument—the Greek God heroes included bland Apollo, who denied the power; frenzied Dionysos, who beat them by joining them in the Maenad rites of blood, drunkenness, and dismemberment; Perseus, who used the petrifying influence of the fearsome female genitals, imaged as the Medusa's head, to turn his enemies to stone; and laboring Hercules, whose name means "glory of Hera," who found numerous ways of conquering female mysteries, including spending some years in women's dress spinning for Queen Omphale as a punishment for a murder.

Philip E. Slater says that "menstrual taboos will arise wherever there is a fear of the mature woman" and quotes instances of tribes in which the glance of "a menstruating woman will, like the glance of the Medusa, turn a man to stone." He compares the Greek culture with contemporary America, but argues that since the Greeks did not have menstrual taboos, they were not concerned. We do not think so: the Greeks, like ourselves, tabooed by avoidance and ignore-ance.

Many cultures believe that the first menstruation is a crucially important time. The woman is seen as though she were a sensitive photographic film, and what she undergoes at the menarche will be permanently imprinted on her psyche. Therefore great pains are taken to see that she undergoes experiences that will be of what is considered the most benefit to her, or which best fits her to her role in society. Most girls will in such ceremonies be related to "tribal" values of childbirth and rearing—"values of ovulation"—and menstruation will be seen as a sign of fertility in fresh blood. There are women who are exceptions to this, however, and in whom the menarche is the time of dedication to imaginative values, such as the psychodramas of the shaman—it is at this time that a woman may commonly become a shamaness or a witch, which we see as the "values of menstruation"—in which the imaginative and interpretive energies are released in body language and symbolic form. In a healthy situation, these become art and magic, even insight and healing perhaps; in an unhealthy one, madness. As a contemporary medical statement puts it, modern girls would benefit very greatly from a "ritualization of menarche." There is, evidently, an "emotional moment" among young American women that "more primitive societies have met with familial and social rituals." Simone de Beauvoir has said how powerfully girls feel the disappointment if they sense that "nothing has changed."[42]

Some of the primitive menstrual rites appear to help the girls realize a new body-image: that which belongs to the mature woman, not the child. There is a great emphasis on the skin, its ornamentation, and the emphasizing of the body's shape by smearing with earth, plunging in water, sleeping in soft ashes, and reclothing it. There appear opportunities for the woman to adopt as a custom some form of secluded meditation, to learn to enter deep within herself, like a descent into the underworld, or into the dream-world, during her menstrual time. Later we shall show that a characteristic of premenstrual tension is a need for dreaming and meditation. In some cultures, of course, as we have said, these customs of seclusion, which may at first have been adopted by the women for their own benefit, to take advantage of a "moment of truth" in their bodies, have hardened into cruel and stereotyped practices.

If indeed the ego changes and reforms at puberty and adolescence, as it seems to, then in the woman her menstruation is the time at which these deep changes will have begun, and during which on future occasions any unfinished business is dealt with, for development in the individual need never cease. Esther Harding suggests that this is an important part of a woman's birthright that she should never surrender in order to pattern herself on an unchanging male ego. She has the inestimable advantage, in the right situation, of a monthly rebirth of the ego: which can be, Dr. Harding avers, a conscious going with instinctual happenings, and therefore a conscious drawing-upon instinctual powers and renewals. Ideally, the men should be able to share in the experience of this rhythm too. If the men do not bend, as the women have to, then they will break, and carry our world down with them.

VII   Slum Records

If the subject "menstruation" is a slum, a tenement neglected by absentee landlords, then it is hardly surprising that we find there disease, riots, sickness, bad repair, antique sanitation. The records of this slum make grim reading, and the following is a sample. We ask the reader who wishes to know the method of sampling and the validity of the statistics to consult the works referred to in the notes, particularly Katharina Dalton's excellent *The Premenstrual Syndrome*.

Now for a selection from the statistical archives of the most terrible slum in the world:

84% of crimes of violence committed by women were during the premenstruum; most rapes are committed while the victim is menstruating; suicides increase during the premenstruum and menstruation; nineteen out of twenty-two Hindu women who committed suicide by pouring kerosene over themselves and lighting it, were menstruating; five billion dollars are lost annually in the U.S. due to menstrual absenteeism; 45% of 276 acute psychiatric patients were admitted to hospital during the paramenstruum; of 185 admitted for depression, 47% were in the paramenstruum; 50% of 156 newly convicted prisoners' crimes were in the paramenstruum; 54% of alcoholics and 56% of thefts were in the paramenstruum; of 94 disorderly prisoners studied, 35 were menstruating; the law of many countries treats menstruation during the commission of a crime as an extenuating circumstance; Marion Coyle, who with Eddie Gallagher in 1976 kidnapped the Dutch industrialist Dr. Herrema, was menstruating during the police siege, and sanitary napkins were sent in: shortly after her period was over the kidnappers surrendered; acute admissions to general hospitals are greatest during the paramenstruum; sickness in industry is greatest during menstruation; of 91 children who attended surgery with minor coughs and colds, 53% were brought by mother during her paramenstruum; in a survey of accidents in four London hospitals, 52% occurred during the paramenstruum; of twenty-three women who were autopsied after they had committed suicide, twenty had ovaries that showed they were

about to menstruate; school prefects are more strict in their punish-
ments during menstruation; girls during the "A" and "O" level
examinations gain fewer passes, less distinction marks, and a lower
average mark; women are more accident-prone during the paramen-
struum; viral infections are increased during the premenstruum,
bacterial infections during menstruation; 76% of paralytic poliomy-
elitis occurred during the paramenstruum; burial in consecrated
ground was only granted to a suicide if she had been menstruating at
the time of death.[43]

(II)   WHEN IT'S A BLESSING IN DISGUISE

I   *Lifting the Curse*

It was not so very long ago that all copulation was thought a
sin even for married people. Women were thought not to
have sexual feelings in the way men did, and the notion of a
"female orgasm" was unthinkable. There was a double standard, since it was thought quite all right for men to seek
pleasure in sex, to the point of promiscuity, but a woman who
did so was utterly outside the pale. It was only in the early
1960s that the first objective investigations were made into
the physiology of the female sexual experience, by William
Masters and Virginia Johnson.

Something very similar a blanket censorship or ignorance—went on with both childbirth and breast-feeding.
Professor Niles Newton has recently used the phrase "The
Trebly Sensuous Woman" to point out that just as recent
knowledge of sexuality has "permitted" women to enjoy
intercourse, so new knowledge shows that it is no sin for
women to enjoy (indeed it benefits profoundly both mother
and infant) breast-feeding their infant, and that the pain and
terror traditionally associated with childbirth is in many cases
quite unnecessary and indeed the opposite to the natural
process. Professor Newton shows how childbearing resembles

no physiological process so much as it does orgasm. Erna Wright[44] tells us that with "psychoprophylaxis" that is, knowledge of what is happening inside them during labor, and with relaxation techniques, 35% of "trained mothers" experienced *painless* childbirth, and in the remaining 65% of mothers the following was a representative remark: "I had pain during the latter part of my labor . . . but as long as I carried on doing what you had taught me to do, I remained in control. The pain never overwhelmed me." Notice the emphasis on *having learned knowledge* appropriate to childbirth. In the Erna Wright classes there is also emphasis on unlearning culturally conditioned habits, such as the habit of fighting a contraction by tensing all the body in fear. This only leads to unnecessary pain. The revolution in women's experience of childbirth really began with Dr. Grantly Dick-Read's *Childbirth without Fear*. His work emphasized an attitude to labor in which joy replaced pain. He said: "There is no physiological function in the body which gives rise to pain in the normal course of health . . . All fear in a human being is acquired either by suggestion or association."[45] He noted a fear-tension-pain-fear howlback loop in childbirth. Millions of women have cause to be grateful to this recent attitude, and it seems that birth for many women can be a profound experience to be looked forward to and not dreaded.

The familiar "howlback" pattern repeats itself. It has done so with intercourse, childbearing, and breast-feeding: *it is wrong to enjoy this natural function and you are a good woman so you cannot be enjoying it as you appear so I shall try to take that enjoyment of your body away from you by finding reasons why you cannot be enjoying it.* And since one of the excellences of femininity is that the body and the mind are not as divided up as they are in masculine existence, then under this onslaught of suggestion of course the pleasure does disappear.

Fashion plays a big part. Breast-feeding becomes unfashionable. It is dirty and sexually suspect. Bottle-feeding becomes the rage, to the great profit of the dried-milk companies. Now however scientific fashion has changed, and it becomes evident that breast-feeding is not only pleasurable to mother and infant, and a natural erotic process, but also the woman's whole recovery from the processes of childbirth is initiated and accelerated by breast-feeding. The womb recovers its place more quickly, the body its shape, and intercourse its interest. A cry from the baby or the sight of it starts the milk flowing, and so does a loving gesture from the father. Milk is a love-juice.

Scientific fashion in a revelatory mood has now noticed that childbirth itself is a natural erotic process analogous to a great orgasm. Niles Newton lists breathing, vocalization, facial expression, action of the womb, the cervix, the abdominal muscles, the reaction of the central nervous system, sensory perceptions, and emotional response in childbirth as all comparable to what occurs in sexual orgasm: "After birth, there is a flood of joyful emotion, which Dick-Read describes as 'complete and careless ecstasy.'"

Follow-up work has now shown that such practices and attitudes to birth benefit not only the mother but the infant also. The Leboyer method combines training for relaxation and conventional "natural childbirth" with a delivery suite which is softly lit and has soft music playing. The cord is not cut before it has stopped pulsing, so the baby's first breath is not a panic fight for oxygen. The muted lights and sounds that make the first impact of the baby's new world are not an aggression, to which it is supposed the baby may react with aggression in later life. The infant is placed on the mother's tummy and then given a warm bath so that the change of environment from womb to air is not so absolute and shocking. Danielle Rapoport in France has done a follow-up study of 120 children delivered by the Leboyer method. They appear to have better total coordination, sometimes of left and right sides to the point of ambidexterity. They are happier, better adjusted. There were no toilet-training problems, and no trouble with sleeping or colic, and few tantrums.

However, the children did not lack liveliness or curiosity. Mothers did not seem to need psychologists' advice on dealing with their children. The mothers enjoyed the birth: "64 percent whose first birth it was, and 60 percent of the remainder, described the conditions as 'remarkable, wonderful and extraordinary.'" All, with only three exceptions, described the delivery experience as "very deep."[46]

Dick-Read stated that there is no physiological function in the body which gives rise to pain in the normal course of health. In the experience of very many women, this change of attitude has led to the exploration of new fields of experience, which at first have seemed unfamiliar, even shocking. Sheila Kitzinger is very straight about this: "The feeling is very acute and some women hate it; they find it what can only be described as 'shocking.' It is a sensation so vivid that they do not know whether it is pleasure or pain, whether to welcome or retreat from it. For some it is almost as if they are being violated . . ." she says in her book *The Experience of Childbirth*. One must note that a man's habitual reaction to pain is to fight it. In child-bearing this is just the wrong reaction: it leads to more pain.

Readers of the previous section will have seen that there is indeed another "physiological function in the body which gives rise to pain in the normal course of health," and not only pain but apparently disease and mental disturbance also. This natural process is menstruation. We want to suggest that it is at least worth a try to see what a change of attitude toward menstruation will uncover, on the analogy that progressive relaxation toward feminine sexuality, childbirth, and breast-feeding liberated new areas of experience for Everywoman to occupy. We would expect the area concealed by the idea of a "curse" or the experience of an "epidemic" to be characterized—and dismissed—by the word "erotic" which would include as a blanket term such natural sensuous pleasures as enjoyment of one's own body, intensity (possibly of a variant kind) of sexual experience, an altered set of perceptions together with such natural adaptations to these as dreaming or imaginative exploration—in all the emergence of a new dimension of individuality in the same way as we expect a nursing mother to be an altered kind of individual from the same person when a virgin.

Instead of a "menstrual epidemic" stalking the nations, we would have the "Quadruply Sensuous Woman" capable of enjoying without fear (and therefore on this hypothesis without pain) not only her orgasm, her childbirth, and her breast-feeding as deep erotic experiences, but her menstruation also for what it can give. Perhaps, just as there are classes all over the country for "Natural Childbirth" there will one day be classes that include "Natural Menstruation" in their approach to feminine experience.

An appendix to Erna Wright's book *The New Childbirth* is called "Lifting the 'curse'" and in it Ms. Wright describes how the same kind of relaxation techniques, knowledge of the natural processes, and training as are applied to childbirth are effective in relieving the period pain of young girls, who may say, "'If this helps me during a period, isn't it possible that it might also help me when I have a baby?'" Ms. Wright says, "I have divided the course into lessons just like the course for labor" and the teaching includes "The story of reproduction," "decontraction-drill," "disassociation-drill," and "conscious controlled breathing." ". . . she should handle the pain as a Labor Diagram (2) contraction, which is what it really is"; she likes the girl to have a warm bath and go to bed. Ms. Wright does not mention that we may take pleasure in this contraction, as one may, with proper training and good luck, take pleasure in a labor contraction; nor does she mention that a girl's clitoris is often particularly sensitive during the period, and that masturbation will turn the painful cramps into a pleasurable experience. Masters and Johnson confirm this: subjects of theirs found both masturbation and intercourse a decided relief for dysmenorrhea.[47]

Another change of attitude is suggested by Mary Brown

Parlee in a hard-hitting article (1973) that points out that it is all very well to collect data to show what a curse the period is but that doesn't mean to say that there is a "curse" there. If you look for the stereotype of the menstruating woman, you will find her. She shows how narrowly conceived and inefficiently interpreted many of the "scientific" studies have been. If you ask people (men or women) whether they have periodically recurring headaches during, say, a period of a. month, they will usually oblige you by finding them, and discussing them. Ms. Parlee shows that the field is dominated by the *assumption* of finding a premenstrual syndrome. She says: "To take a hypothetical example, if female performance on a digit-symbol substitution task should be found to fluctuate with the menstrual cycle, it would seem incomplete and therefore misleading to say only that females' performance is worse at certain times in the cycle than at others, since it may at all times be better than the average performance of males on this task." She implies that the possibility of positive events at menstruation is rarely considered by researchers, who appear to be in search of the inferior stereotype. "Rarely is it suggested that it is the behavioral events that affect the menstrual cycle . . ." rather, the usual suggestion is that the menstrual cycle affects behavior: "although gynecology texts state that psychological stress may delay menstruation . . . or precipitate its onset . . ." She says that, "From knowing, for example, that crimes are likely to *have been committed* during certain phases of the cycle, it is not possible to assume the truth of the inverse—that women in these phases of the menstrual cycle are more likely to commit crimes . . . It is possible that studies of different populations of women might reveal correlations between the premenstrual and menstrual phases of the cycle and more positively valued acts such as, for example, bursts of creative energy . . ." In other words, the researchers in their pursuit of that stereotype, the Cursed Woman, have always asked the question, "Do you feel ill? Have you committed Evil?" rather than, "Tell me what good experiences you have had in your paramenstruum." Women have been asked to tell whether they have been depressed during their periods, *but they have never been asked whether they have been inspired during their periods.* On the contrary, as Julia Sherman points out, what is found is "three monthly peaks of disturbance. The maximum psychological disturbance is early in menstruation; the second greatest peak is premenstrually, and the smallest rise is at mid-cycle."

Since nobody has researched for "inspiration" as opposed to illness in the menstrual cycle, it might at first appear that we are initially short of evidence that menstruation, on the analogy of labor pains, might turn out sometimes to be at least an erotic experience in disguise. But when we start to look for positives rather than negatives in the feminine rhythm we discover a very remarkable thing, which many women will confirm from their own experience. *There is widespread evidence of a rise in sexuality associated with the paramenstruum.*

How remarkable if this is so! What a strange coincidence that the very same time in the cycle of the "paramenstrual plague"—the time when intercourse is almost universally tabooed—should also be the time of a rise in that very inconvenient commodity, feminine sexuality! Could it be that the "curse" or menstruation is that very same old serpent, the "curse" of sex? Just as the "curse" of Eve "thou shalt bring forth children in pain and fear" turned out also to be that serpent too, orgasmic sexual experience, disguised by custom and distorted by ignorance. There will still be people to whom sexuality is always a "curse," but not the majority of them women.

It really does seem too much of a coincidence that the "menstrual epidemic" should be located just at the time when a woman's sexual abilities may rise. Paula Weideger has put it crisply: "It seems preposterous to say that menstruation is a sexual experience. But it is." And she is firm about the "magical" power of menstrual blood, and its status as a tabooed thing: "menstrual blood . . . contains an element capable of enormous power. It is a sexual element . . ."

Before reviewing the evidence that convinces that this is a widespread phenomenon and not merely the isolated experience of a few people, let us be clear about what we mean by sexual or erotic experience. We intend to imply a wholeness about erotic experience, and we are not just talking—when we speak of an increased orgasmic ability at menstruation—of a heightened ability to "have it off." When we say "erotic" we are speaking of the ability of the mind to merge with the body in felt experience, when the perceptions of one's own self, the world, and of course any partners that might be involved, becomes heightened and, it may be, more meaningful. The range of sexual experience goes from a simple discharge of tension to a complex act of sensuous relationship to people and things in the outer world.

It may include acts of love apparently as distinct as loving involvement with one's partners and children, and sensuous involvement with the world: the kind of love affair that results in works of art. It may, on its dangerous side, include such cruel complex acts as rape or sexual murder. We presume that often what may first show itself as a simple sex appetite may with luck develop into a complex and meaningful erotic experience, that is, one that arouses one's passions and creativity. This is the true magic, and we think that a lot of it is hidden under the heavy disguise of the "menstrual epidemic."

II *Another Dimension of Sexuality*

Many researchers have shown that there are rises in sexuality during the course of the menstrual cycle. Some have plumped for the chief peak's occurring at midcycle, at the ovulation, when you would expect it to occur if the purpose of that sexual rise were to impregnate the egg in order to produce offspring. Others have found that the chief rise is during the paramenstruum, or at the opposite end of the cycle, with an increase of desire immediately before, during, or immediately after the bleeding.

At first it was acknowledged freely by the earlier writers that this paramenstrual peak occurred. There was no conflict with the idea that desire could not occur because sex was for reproduction and not for pleasure, since it was not under-stood until the early nineteen-hundreds that women were not commonly fertile during the bleeding, and that it was not analogous to the "heat" of animals. So it seemed natural to the observers quoted by Havelock Ellis writing in 1910 that there would be a rise of desire at the period time: these included Krafft-Ebing, Adler, Kossman, Guyot, and Campbell. Dr. Mary Putnam denied that there was a rhythmic alternation of desire comparable to an estrus cycle, as Helene Deutsch does today. However, Dr. Elizabeth Blackwell compared the menstrual flow to nocturnal emissions in men, and said that afforded equal relief. Havelock Ellis himself considered it an important time for erotic experience, particular imaginative autoerotic experience and erotic dreams. He says that "there can be no doubt whatever that immediately before and immediately after, very commonly at both times—this vary-ing slightly in different women—there is usually a marked heightening of actual desire. It is at this period (and some-times during the menstrual flow) that masturbation may take place in women who at other times have no strong autoerotic impulse." He regards the blood as a love-juice, that flows with sexual excitement. He also considered that the statistics of his time showed a considerable menstrual problem, with, for instance, a 75 percent incidence of menstrual troubles in two thousand girls in New England schools. He agreed that this situation might well be improved by better sexual education for women: "The time may come when we must even change the divisions of the year for women, leaving to man his week and giving to her the same number of Sabbaths per year, but in groups of four successive days per month. When woman asserts her true physiological rights she will begin here, and will glory in what, in an age of ignorance, man made her think to be her shame." He gives impressive accounts of a woman in whom menstrual tension and release of sexual desire were reflected in her dreaming in bold acts, such as plunging into dangerous waters fully clothed.[48]

To some later observers the menstrual peak has apparently disappeared, as though once one had understood that impregnation usually happened at midcycle, then one would find most desire there also. Studies that found desire only at ovulation and did not seem to want to find the one at menstruation have been criticized on two grounds: one that you do not in science necessarily find things that theory tells you you ought to find; and secondly that the quality of desire may be of a different kind at the period, and therefore not noticed by the ordinary questionnaire.

Thus Fluhmann says: "From Havelock Ellis to Kinsey most investigators have not been able to implicate an intensified sexual responsiveness with the time of ovulation in women . . . On the contrary it appears that maximum sexual interest is manifested most often just before or sometimes just after menstruation."[49] Kinsey remarks: "Evidently the human female, in the course of evolution, has departed from her mammalian ancestors and developed new characteristics which have relocated the period of maximum sexual arousal near the time of menstruation," and cites fourteen studies that support his own painstakingly gathered data. Incidentally, Kinsey confirms separately Havelock Ellis's observation that if a woman masturbates at no other time during her cycle, she will most often do so near her period.[50]

And Money and Ehrhardt say the confusing or contradictory results of some of the studies that only found ovulation-peaks were because the questioners did not distinguish between the two poles of experience. Such questionnaires asked about sexual desire, but not about the quality of sexual desire. They say that at the ovulatory time, the woman may tend to experience a desire to "surrender" or to be "occupied" sexually. At the menstrual period, it is, they say, more likely to be a desire to capture and envelop: in other words she is more likely to take the erotic initiative at her period.[51] This could be disturbing to men reared on the idea that it is the male prerogative to initiate sex. The combination of bleeding and increased sexual capacity is a formidable one to the conventional view.

Jung talks about "the sexual heat appearing with the period,"[52] and C. D. Daly makes it the cornerstone of his evolutionary theory, as does Mary Jane Sherfey. Masters and Johnson found that "many women are interested in and desire sexual activity during their menstrual periods," and that a proportion of their subjects "described the frequent use of automanipulative techniques with the onset of menstrual flow as a personal method contrived for relieving minor to major degrees of dysmenorrhea. These study subjects stated that severe orgasmic experience shortly after menstruation increased the rate of flow, reduced pelvic cramping when present, and frequently relieved their menstrually associated backache."[53]

Alex Comfort in one of his notable love-books, *The Joy of Sex*, notes that "the height of a period may be a girl's randiest time" and suggests that nature programmed the period for experiment and versatility. Seymour Fisher, reviewing much recent work, appears to accept a dual peak, but sensibly suggests that each woman "may have a fairly unique pattern of her own"—obviously it is to her advantage to know it if she has one, and if her "randiest times" happen to occur during her period then she should not be put off using it by custom or taboo.[54] Paula Weideger is very strong about it: she says that women need to be aware of when they themselves feel sexy, and not be told when they should feel sexy by other people, particularly men. If women are told that it is wrong or somehow "dirty" to have sex at the period, then they suffer doubly: "they experience a recurring period in which they think poorly of themselves, and, because of the generally common increase in sexual feeling, they are also likely to experience increased sexual frustration." She is quite definite that "the peaks of female sexual feeling fall around the time of flow and at mid-cycle," and also that there are often in any cycle a day or two of sexual lows, a temporary anesthesia.[55]

Judith Bardwick says that with only one exception, "every woman I have ever interviewed could recall the circumstances of her first menstrual period and how she felt about it," and Natalie Shainess and others that such experiences are recalled with each subsequent period. Thus the primitive tribes seem to be right when they guard against untoward influences at this time—and ourselves wrong who do nothing about it. But Elizabeth Douvain tells us that the experience of the first period, though it may in our society be associated with hurts and wounds and body waste, is nevertheless of "the essence of primary process—the vivid, concrete, imagistic, prelogical thought process shared by dreams and poetry."[56] Therese Benedek concurs in this when she says, "it is as though the woman were exposed to every stimulus through an increased sensitiveness. The whole psychosomatic personality seems to regress to a deeper level of hormone and psychic integration."[57] There is unfortunately a sad story here, for when Benedek, a psychoanalyst, combined with Rubenstein, a clinician, and published in 1939 they produced together a powerful but seriously flawed study that has held the field ever since. Benedek was a psychoanalyst, and she studied the dreams of fifteen women. Rubenstein was a clinician, and she took vaginal smears of the women to establish the exact phase of the cycle. The two parallel pieces of work were done independently, and at the end of the study, put together without previous consultation. Thus there was no prejudging. Benedek offered to predict from the dreams exactly what phase of the cycle was being undergone at the time of a given dream. She was absolutely right. Thus it seemed established that particular dreams with particular sexual meanings and feelings can be associated with the phases of the menstrual cycle.

This immaculate work seemed an important advance in knowledge, a proof of the interdependence of psyche and soma, body and mind. Unfortunately it was approached with completely stereotyped prejudgment. The women subjects said they felt most desire during or around their menstrual flow. Benedek, however, insisted they were actually most sexual at their ovulation time, for the reason that the feelings they expressed at menstruation and the dreams they dreamed were not acceptable to a Freudian-trained Benedek as the kinds of sexual feelings or dreams women *ought* to have. Consequently she concluded that because the women felt most "loving" and "receptive" (i.e., passive) at the time of ovulation, and this was the highest form of female sexuality, then their "real" sexual peak was at ovulation or midcycle. The menstrual feelings were really an expression of a lower kind of sexuality, because they were not "womanly," they were "masculine." The menstrual feelings were of an "impatient demand" for sex, and this time is full of an "extroverted activity and urgency" and therefore this peak of sexuality is more "masculine" in character. But this is the very essence of stereotype! Weideger puts it well when she says: "Surely this conclusion is laden with value judgments we would be reluctant to accept. Why should we agree that receptivity is of higher value than extroverted activity? It is not higher or lower, but rather *another dimension of female sexuality*. To place a value judgment on types of sexual feeling and to call those around the time of ovulation 'better' reflects the prejudices of an investigator who has started out with a view of what the female ought to be and assumes that when women are conforming to this vision, they are at the highest level of psychosexual development." Weideger concludes: "The menstrual taboo . . . has been one of the most successful methods devised to undermine the self-acceptance and confidence of women."

Mary Brown Parlee appears to believe that with the assignment of proper values to menstruation and other aspects of feminine experience, that phantom we know as the premenstrual tension syndrome would simply dissolve, since we would see that it is "the result of complex psychological processes arising from an interaction between physiological changes and environmental factors specifically related to femininity and sexuality. As such, it would be associated with other aspects of the personality to the extent that these also are related to sexuality, and considerable individual differences might be expected." C. D. Daly considers the sexual power of the menstrual experience and its outward and visible manifestation, the blood, so powerful that we should argue against Freud's view that it is the Oedipal situation that is society's evolutionary force, and replace it with the notion of the Menstruation Trauma.

This appears to echo the observation that there are broadly two aspects to the "menstrual plague": painful bleeding, or spasmodic dysmenorrhea (that Masters and Johnson say can be relieved by orgasmic experience); and premenstrual syndrome, or congestive dysmenorrhea. While Daly favors the bleeding itself as the powerful sexual influence, Mary Jane Sherfey says that the premenstrual congestion is a sexual power of such terrific force that human society could not have developed without limiting and controlling it severely.

To her, the congestion *is* the sexuality, or rather unused sexuality, and it is in these last fourteen days, or "luteal" phase of the cycle, when swelling or edema is produced by the fluid-controlling hormones, that multiorgasmic sexuality is natural to the woman. According to male standards, the woman would be "oversexed" at this time. Dr. Sherfey believes, however, that this hypersexuality is normal for the woman, and it was in response to it that society developed its controls over sexuality.

Dr. Sherfey's work developed from her experience of her

first period. As a little girl, she was told that her period was the remains of her dead baby. This, understandably, distressed her terribly. She collected all her napkins from her period and buried them in a little funeral with coffin and all for her dead baby. She concluded that God was wrong so as to afflict women by killing their babies with menstruation. Later on she found that the error was not God's but science's in giving no consideration at all to *why* women had periods, and what actually happened during them. She embarked on her own research, through medicine, psychology, and primate zoology, and produced an important book on the subject (see bibliography).

Where we believe her conclusions still fall foul of the inimical cultural climate we have sketched, is that she believes that women must, because of their physiology, forever remain unsatisfied, since each orgasm only leads to greater congestion and greater desire. This is certainly true if the experience remains solely at the genital level, and does not proceed to the erotic level, and begin to involve the totality of one's life and relationships.

The principal technique required, by both sexes, is a change of attitude. We cannot approach our problem if we behave as though we were creatures of pure mind, or of only body. Joseph Campbell in his great mythographical history speaks of the Odyssey of "the long return . . . to the realm of those powers and knowledges which . . . had been waiting unattended, undeveloped, even unknown, in that 'other mind' which is woman . . ." and the desirability of knowing "the reality from both sides that each sex experiences shadowlike from its own side." The Odyssey recounts psychological adventures, in which "the male must *experience* the import of the female before he can meet her perfectly in life."[58] He says that "The image of the 'Meeting of Sun and Moon' is everywhere symbolic of this instant" of understanding of identity, which at present we feel as an inchoate nightmare of uncoordinated and unconscious response to unknown tides and currents. This image of meeting of Sun and Moon was also in antiquity the image of menstruation, the dark of the moon, the New Moon, when the sky was dark at night because the moon was elsewhere, in conjunction with the sun, and rose with the sun. What can this image mean? We cannot find an answer to such questions, or our own dis-ease, merely mythologically, any more than we can merely physiologically. The reason for this is that mythology and physiology are only the two sides of the same thing, which is alive.

Three Animus, Animal, Anima

Women sometimes wish that men could feel what premenstrual tension is like. It is a feeling like nothing else, they say. It is a scratchy, jumpy state, your energy is gone, all the life drains out of the world, which becomes a "sour apple," you have no friends, your nerves seem to stick out six feet from your body, you feel bloated and heavy, but at the same time exquisitely nervous, your eyelids and navel itch, you misjudge distances, you knock things over, you are clumsy as if to provide more occasions for the just-underground rages that you already feel.

But there is one way in which men can feel exactly what it is like to experience premenstrual tension: that is to stay awake for a few nights without sleep. After this, any man is likely to experience all the symptoms.

There have been many important experiments in sleep deprivation. People have been kept awake to discover what happens. One result of these experiments has been to find that it is not *sleep* deprivation as such that matters, it is *dream* deprivation. Volunteers in these experiments were awakened just when their sleeping eyes started to move in the characteristic to-and-fro manner that is called REM (rapid eye movement) and which signifies the occurrence in a sleeper of the main type of dreaming. After a night or two of these interruptions the subjects were in a bad way, with irritability, depression, and lethargy, just the signs of PMT. With continued dream deprivation, there were hallucinations and mild psychotic episodes, just like the paramenstruum, again.

The likeness between PMT and dream deprivation was first pointed out by Ernest Hartmann in his *The Biology of Dreaming*. He found that premenstrual symptoms are worse when women can't sleep enough and improve when they are allowed to sleep more than usual. Perhaps, he says, "treatment for premenstrual tension should include a prescription for more sleep." D-time, which is what he calls REM dreaming sleep, increases toward the end of the cycle, around days twenty-five to thirty. He suggests that the changes of the menstrual cycle produce an increased "need for D" late in the cycle, and this need shows itself as higher D-time at night and as premenstrual tension in the daytime. There is greater D-pressure during the premenstruum. Indeed, two women in the studies when asked what their premenstrual tension felt like, said that it reminded them of how they felt after a sleepless night.

Since dreams are the "royal road to the unconscious" and to our unrealized selves, what perilous matter do these premenstrual dreams contain that produces strong physical and nervous reactions during the day, when dreams are not being dreamed, and which when given more chance to be dreamed, reduces these waking symptoms of premenstrual tension? It looks as though the women's changes may show either as premenstrual symptoms during the day, when she is awake, or as dreams without these physical symptoms during the night. The need for D-time was most evident in those women who had the most severe PMT symptoms. Evidently, PMT women are powerful dreamers.

Once again, there has been no extensive study of what happens during the dream-life of the menstrual cycle, even though we have here, in Hartmann, a strong indication of a way to cure a whole section of disorders belonging to the "menstrual epidemic." Why do women not enter this dream-state naturally, dream these dreams, and by thorough dreaming avoid entirely the premenstrual symptoms? Is it not likely that the dreaming has been made frightening, just as the menstrual taboo has made the period itself frightening? Is it perhaps that women have particular dreams at this time that are special to women, and the study of which is therefore neglected? Is it because too few women are allowed to believe that dreams themselves are important, and therefore when they have dreams they do not consider them much, all the less so if they are strange and frightening?

These are further indications that it is bad science to approach the "menstrual epidemic" as though it were merely a technological matter of adjusting potassium or hormone levels. Rather, it is a range of neglected experiences.

Recent scientific work confirms that inner experience and the menstrual cycle are interrelated in important ways, and that further study would be fruitful.

One possible line of thought is indicated by a recent study by Peter Sheldrake and Margaret Cormack which suggests that the menstrual experience may be of a different kind depending whether you are a "converger," that is, good at conventional IQ tests, or a "diverger," creatively good at imaginatively open-ended tests. It appears that some "convergers" show more anxious dreaming before menstruation, and "divergers" more anxious dreaming before mid-cycle ovulation. The study says that the recall patterns of dreams "for divergers is similar to that for estrogen secretion during the menstrual cycle, and that for convergers parallels the progesterone secretion curve." This opens the way up for further studies, perhaps on our own hypothesis that "divergers" are better dreamers, and therefore suffer less from menstrual troubles, just as it has been shown by Winget and Kapp that people who dream about labor tend to suffer less at childbirth. Work by Constance Berry and Frederick McGuire purports to show that sufferers from spasmodic dysmenorrhea, which is sometimes associated with a relative estrogen-lack, are not adapted to the conventional "female role," while PMT sufferers are, and PMT is associated with a relative progesterone-lack. Katharina Dalton also distinguishes a more "female" PMT type who blooms particularly at pregnancy. If this is so, then it suggests that PMT could have to do with conventional "converging" or "tribal" adaptations tied to "Kinder, Küche, und Kirche," while the divergers associate with the more independently imaginative values of the "menstrual pole." One finds cases, like those cited by Ian C. A. Martin, in which candidates for hysterectomy due to profuse uterine bleeding were women with histories of psychosomatic illness who "while strongly wanting to fulfill their maternal role, considered that there was more to life." The suggestion is that the bleeding was a defense against pregnancy. Dr. Martin, commenting on a MIND conference delegate's reference to "bloody neurotic women," concludes that it "seems possible that a lot of women are being maneuvered (quite literally) into a lot more bloodiness than is necessary." Isidor Siberman gives extraordinary case histories of how women he has known as analysands gain a control over their own lives and those of others by knowledgeable manipulation of male fear and desire at the menstrual bleeding. One passed the frontier-customs by these means, and made a man fall in love by showing that she was bleeding while she was bathing. Erickson shows how training can impart this ability (p. 186). Then again, Karen Paige finds that the more Jewish and Catholic women lived out their prescribed feminine roles, the more often they suffered from premenstrual troubles. Shader *et al.* found in their sample that rise of libido went together with PMT in women with college-educated fathers.

One might emerge with a picture of women convergers interested in pregnancy but apprehensive of menstruation, and women divergers interested in what menstruation will bring, but balked of the experience by society's howlback avoidance of it. We apply no stereotypes: a woman may choose to fulfill more than one role in her lifetime, and her resources include what she chooses to take from her menstrual cycle—if she is allowed feminine knowledge without "howlback." The result of withheld knowledge is usually depression and pain.

Two interesting pieces of information already mentioned come in here. Miriam Van Waters, among others, shows that if a woman becomes a shaman or priestess in a culture that recognizes such functionaries, she is able to do so because she has developed a special relationship to the "spirits" of her menstruation. It appears also from W. N. Stephens's work that anxiety and aggression are tied cross-culturally to strong menstrual taboos. We cannot forget that our own society practices systematic menstrual ignorance, and is one of the most bellicose in human history.

The modern European or American woman has little opportunity to develop her "shamanism" though she may feel "witchy" at her period—no mere figure of speech, as we will show. Even her dreams are guarded about by taboos of custom, particularly when they appear to discharge aggressive energies. However, everybody can develop as a "diverger," that is, someone who looks at facts without conventional prejudice, and does not plump for anybody's "role" without thinking freely first: a creative person.

Benedek and Rubenstein showed long ago that particular dreams were dreamed at particular times of the menstrual cycle. More recent research has confirmed this. They found there were tense heterosexual dreams during the run-up to ovulation, relaxed and contented dreams during the event of ovulation, passive and receptive dreams associated with pregnancy and nursing during the luteal phase after ovulation, and then a confused and energetic dreaming time beginning with heterosexual dreams during the run-up to menstruation, with a kind of climax of terrifying dreams in their subjects near menstruation itself, which Benedek disapproved of as "regressive."

"Some huge fossil belonging to the reptile family, mounted, standing upright in the museum. Some remark or other brought it to life and it began to crawl over the land. People fled before it in terror. Very slimy and shining and ugly green . . ." That is a dream of preovulatory tension, the awakening of sexual energy, fascinating, repellant, green with growth. "Of a head that was cut off or hanging connected with a holiday candle." That is another tense preovulation dream. Benedek says merely that this is "destructive-aggressive," but we must look at this positively also. It is like the womb so energized that it feels like the head of a separate person. The candle is like the shaft of the vagina, ready for the flame of sensation at the clitoris that will turn the whole shaft into fire.

In the ovulating state there were dreams of babies and fears of having babies. One woman was going to play poker, and was afraid to be alone. Her brother's wife was going to bring the baby, but would only give it milk. "So I asked the hostess if she had any eggs and she said they don't eat eggs in her home." The mother-in-law had eggs, however. Dreams of conflict with the mother, rivalry of motherhood, and envy of other mothers tend to occur at this time, but also of yielding, say, to an operation. We have found that dreams of eggs, jewels, round, fragile, or precious things, occur at the ovulation-time. It is interesting that the above dream echoes an African taboo in which women who wish to be fertile are forbidden to eat eggs. Witches are said to sail on broken eggshells; a menstrual image.

In the premenstrual phase there is a rise in sexuality and anger, and dreams of change: "I changed my profession and got into school teaching . . . I went down the corridor and saw my own son who did not belong here . . . I became very angry because you [the analyst] did not give me a chance to express myself. A man and a woman came in and you were angry at their coming . . . Then I decided I did not need to be scared because another man was there too." Benedek does not say so, but this appearance of "inner people" in response to some disagreement with the outer world, such as a misunderstanding analyst, is characteristic of paramenstrual dreams, as is also the appearance of a man who is a "comforter" with whose help one does not need to be "scared." Given this kind of dream, premenstrual tension or "fear" may very well leave one, with the help of the "inner man," or "inner woman." No help may be needed, as in Havelock Ellis's brave premenstrual dreamer, who said: ". . . I have to *decide* to walk through deep water, fully clothed. I have a fear of deep water . . ."

The strange thing about this Benedek and Rubenstein study, however, is that they offer rather sparse dreams experienced during menstruation itself. The notation "no analytic material" for that time is frequent. There are plenty of increasingly aggressive (or attackingly vigorous) premenstrual dreams, involving difficult journeys with much luggage, shooting, scratching a man's hand so that blood comes, sex with the analyst, syphilis, the father making her take castor oil, two jolly young men, murder, dirty water that nevertheless cleans a pail, and a dream of wished-for rebirth in which the woman's mother presses a child down in water. She associated her own birth with this: "I was dead when I was born. The doctor put me in hot water. This is what my mother told me." This is like rebirth through the period, not permitted by the mother, but perhaps allowed by the analyst. "Some children sliding down a big marble stairway. Part of the marble was red stone"; and in another premenstrual dream: "I saw a girl dying in bed, in her hand a rose tree, a religious figure—symbol of death of the Savior. I wanted one of the roses and I wondered if anyone would see if I picked it . . . I was afraid, something was going to injure me . . ." Benedek comments: "Heterosexual wish, but narcissistic defense." Another way of looking at it is that the woman sees herself as undergoing a death and resurrection, and wishes to pluck this "rose" but is afraid of the pleasurable part of doing so. Briffault tells us that in other cultures the period is naturally seen in this way, and that the girl is sacrificed or belongs to the god, the "other husband," at the period. This "other husband" himself is sacrificed in blood as the cycle proceeds on its course. Both are aspects of the one woman. It is not really surprising that this attitude should arise from the natural source of a modern woman's dream, only that an analyst should give it such a pejorative terminology. In another dream there is a headless body, with a hideous bloody gash. The dreamer kept repeating, "It's all so hopeless," but then she goes over to the hideous corpse. "Suddenly the girl was standing on the sidewalk. She was smiling happily. Her head was on her body again and she appeared to be more cheerful, as though she didn't *fear* that it would be detached again" (our italics). Something has given this woman permission or confidence to approach her period, so that she is no longer afraid of the threshold of blood, that her dream sees it as a renewal. The next stage would be conversation with this dream-figure.

No wonder that the dreams are difficult to recall if they contain such taboo material. Or is it that the dreams are difficult for an analyst to accept, particularly if he or she is dedicated to a stereotype of femininity directed to the values of ovulation, as we have shown with Benedek. But how much of the *danger* of the material is due to the dreamer's knowledge that, because she is a woman, it will not be accepted? Is the violence of menstrual dream-imagery due to its place as a factor in the "howlback" circuit, once again? Patricia Garfield, in her book *Creative Dreaming*, accepts the menstrual changes in dreaming as a basis for creative dreamwork, but finds dreams of the menses themselves difficult to recall. Hartmann finds least D-time during the menstruation. Our own observation is that menstruation is a time of vivid dreaming, and Van de Castle also finds no deficiency in dreaming during the period. He says that menstrual dreams are characterized by *more active social roles toward males.* Ovulation involves dreams of more passive roles. This reflects what we have already shown, that there is a type of sexuality not usually allowed women, another dimension of their sexuality of an active or initiating kind, that reaches a peak during the paramenstruum, and is experienced either in external reality, or in dreams. Ethel Swanson and David Foulkes confirm this most interestingly when they find that the sexiest dreams happened during the menses, but that seems to be because the waking expression of sexuality in their subjects was at its lowest. Is this because the women in their study sought to go inward to meet the sexuality of their inner "dream-husband," or because something in their circumstances (not related in the paper) forbade them having sex during the period— perhaps the prejudice of their lover in the outer world? At any rate the dreams of these people were also at their most unpleasant and hostile during the period. If you play record- ings of their own voices to dreamers, say Castaldo and Holzman, you help create in them active figures. Seymour Fisher thinks this could happen naturally during menstrua- tion, which produces "a series of specific, novel, and yet periodically familiar patterns of physiological arousal during sleep that cannot find expression and therefore increase fantasy activity." Lee Porach relates sex identification to the four phases of the menstrual cycle, and shows how they may activate or resolve conflicts. Patricia Garfield remarks: "By allowing open sexual expression in dreams, it seems to me, we may actually be freeing creative thinking on all levels of consciousness." She reviews the startling difference in sexual dreams between creative and noncreative women: the former seemed to have escaped sexual stereotypes even in their dreams. Evelyn Reynolds also shows how menstruation- reveries may assist personal integration. Van Waters shows how in many tribes the dreams of first menstruation are regarded as a guide to life; Devereaux gives some detail about this among the Mohave Indians. All this suggests that menstruation contributes to the formation of an aware dream-personality, with all the part this can play in self-integration.

Another working analyst found that he could increase dream recall associated with the menstrual cycle, but when he did so there was acute "dream-shock." Dreams came flooding in, but so did "fatigue, exhaustion, increased ingestions of water, increased carbohydrate intake, *increased feelings of creativity*, increased sexual feelings, and a strong desire to sleep" (our italics). He had trained his patient to use "auto-suggestive techniques," a kind of self-hypnosis, and appears to have created a kind of Frankenstein monster! So power-fully did the dreams come, that recalling them instead of just dreaming them produced sleep-deprivation symptoms. The dream shock was so noticeable that this worker, Richard Frenkel, thought that it might be a contributory cause of heart attacks. The woman's cycle changed in complex ways during the year's study, in correlation with the dream-changes. Resistance to the autosuggestive technique was greatest during or slightly after the menses, except for one "dream spiking" during the bleeding. The strongest effects occurred during the ovulation. It is a pity the study is not more detailed. The analytic *resistance* is likely to point to the most significant material.

We have mentioned that many cultures believe that the moon is the dream or "other husband" of the woman, and has sexual intercourse with her at the period. For instance, the Lepcha of India believe that a "divinity peculiar to women makes love to them in their dreams each month." It is interesting that this is reflected in another recent study by Dan Herz and Mogens Jensen in which "menstruating women are likewise shown to be more preoccupied with male adult figures, other than husbands and fathers, in their dreams then than at other times. A classic study by Stone and Barker finds increased daydreaming almost the only consis-

tent characteristic of postmenarcheal girls. Another paper by
Michael Billiard and others describes the case of a girl who
would sleep for more than fourteen hours a day during her
menstruation, and wonders whether it is a new clinical entity
of the cycle. It perhaps seems more like an old one, since in
all times and places other than our own, the menstruating
woman has chosen rest and seclusion, or these things have
been forced upon her. Perhaps she has meditations to do,
dream-battles in the dream-country to fight on behalf of us
all. Perhaps her natural power is resisted by the male culture.
The Rabbis tell us that a characteristic of the Niddah, or
menstruous woman, is that her neck muscles are weak, and
she nods off. Yet does the Jewish Lord not thunder against a
stiff-necked generation that will not bend the head as a
woman has to, each month? In Hindu culture, so Sarasi Lal
Sarkar reporting in a psychoanalytic journal tells us,
"Through a dream a mental state can be attained within a
short time, for which lengthy mystic practices would otherwise be necessary . . ." Here, the purpose is sexual abstinence and sublimation of the instincts, but in a man: the
withdrawal inward of the penis so that it resembles a vagina.
This is obtained "through worship at the Asana of the Divine
Mother, a seat of red earth symbolical of her menstruation."
Thus it is no wonder that there is so great a "dream-shock"
when male analysts approach, after thousands of years of
neglect, the mysteries and powers of the woman's menstruation.

But what happens when the analysts are women? Not
much, if they are Freudian-trained, and dedicated to Freudian ideas of the "second sex," woman as a failed man,
deprived of penis, or to notions that a woman is only truly
and fully fulfilled by motherhood. As dangerously, little
happens if the analyst is possessed by the idea that the only
sexual sensations that are allowed are genital sensations, and
that it is genital fulfillment that crowns the human sensuality.
It is not: it is that the whole body is illuminated. Even

Benedek and Rubenstein speak of the "erotization of the body" at the premenstrual phase, without seeing that the suppression of that erotization will have serious consequences. We have quoted Judith Bardwick on the menarche as "vivid, concrete, imagistic, prelogical thought" like dreams and poetry—Elizabeth Sewell might call this "postlogical"—going further into truth than can logic, in which there are no surprises. An honorable exception to the more repressive Freudians is Judith Kestenberg, who realizes that in the little girl, "The multitude of stimuli of various rhythmical qualities act upon each other . . . Oral, anal, urethral, clitoral, secretory, and skin discharges are used sometimes in wholesale fashion, with the resulting feeling of being flooded with stimuli and flooding the world in response . . ." These multitudes she believes are subordinated to the sexual vaginal-discharge rhythm, which is emphasized by the beginning of periods, and integrated by menstrual experience, even in the shaping definitions of pain. She says: "Although a certain amount of inhibition of other excitation waves is operative in this subordination, the principal achievement of feminine genital maturity is the coordination and integration of various rhythms to a point where unity and continuity of the sexual experience are accomplished." This is surely good feminine sense seriously qualifying Freudian vaginal politics. Whatever happens, everything must take part! Unfortunately, so many of these other experiences, the "anal, urethral, clitoral," etc. are bound up with the rejected parts of woman's experience, in the menstrual pole of her cycle, while the ovulating vagina holds sway at the other pole. Woman is and must be a unity! Judith Kestenberg says, "Attempts to hypercathect one organ to counteract free-flowing shifts of cathexis often produce conversion phenomena,"[1] which is Freudian jargon for "If you don't let it all work, it hurts."

One of the chief differences between Jungian and Freudian theory, however, is that the former considers that the desire to *create* and *transform* is not just a civilized accident, but *a basic human instinct*. This renders Jungian psychology more open to the menstrual experience of transformation and mental creation. We shall show first, briefly, that this view is a consequence of Jung's partial and disguised acceptance of menstruation—as opposed to Freud's outright rejection of it as a "castrating" force—and that consequently certain of Jung's associates or followers *who are women* have drawn maps that are practical guides to menstrual experience, though this extension of women's powers is still in its first stages. Among such women are Jung's wife, Emma Jung; Barbara Hannah; Marie-Louise Von Franz; Ann Ulanov; and Esther Harding.

In his autobiography, *Memories, Dreams and Reflections*, C. G. Jung recounts certain important childhood events that had a powerful effect on his future psychological work. These included dreams and visions. During his schooldays his parents started to sleep apart, and he slept in his father's room. "From the door to my mother's room came frightening influences. At night Mother was strange and mysterious." In one vision he saw a luminous figure coming from that door. It had a head that detached itself and floated on ahead "like a little moon. Immediately another head was produced and again detached itself. This process was repeated six or seven times."

Earlier, when he was about three or four years old, he had a dream which was "to preoccupy me all my life." The dreamer often cannot understand his own dream, and in this case though his own interpretation led Jung to important work, he certainly did not interpret the dream with the inevitable fact that his mother at times menstruated, in mind. Yet this is perhaps the most important thing about it.

He is in a meadow. He discovers a rectangular stone-lined hole in the ground. In it is a stone stairway which he fearfully descends. There is a round arch at the bottom, closed with a sumptuous green curtainlike brocade. Behind this is a rectangular chamber of hewn stone, with an arched ceiling. From the entrance, across the flagstones, runs a red carpet to a low platform, on which is standing a rich gold throne, "a real king's throne." There is perhaps a red cushion on the seat, but standing on that is something like a tree trunk, huge, reaching almost to the ceiling, made of flesh with a rounded faceless, hairless head. There is a single eye on the very top of the head, unmovingly gazing upward.

Above this head is a brightness, like an aura. The thing is motionless, yet Jung feels it might crawl off the throne at any moment toward him. He is paralyzed with terror. Then he hears from outside and above his mother's voice calling out: "Yes, just look at him. That is the man-eater!" He awakes sweating with terror, and for many nights after that is afraid to go to sleep.

Jung says that it was not until years later that he realized that what he had seen was "a ritual phallus," and that the dream was alerting him to "the motif of cannibalism that underlies the symbolism of the mass."

Yet was it quite that? Why the blood-red cushion, and the blood-red carpet leading up to the object? To go underground is to go into the tomb and womb of earth, and this is in truth the man-eater. Besides, it is more usual to say "man-eater" of a woman, or of a woman's demanding womb. Is it not likely, then, that the dream is of entering a womb-place? Then what of the phallus? There is some fertile confusion in the dreamer's waking mind here, because Jung says "I do not know where the anatomically correct phallus can have come from" as though the small boy had never seen the little phallus between his legs. And again, a phallus does not have a "round head"; it has a urethral groove, though this might not have been made visible in the dream-setting. That "round head" is much more like the heads like "little moons" that came off another luminous figure: that which emerged from the mysteriously charged door of his mother's room. The Maoris worship the Moon as a menstruating Goddess, incidentally, under the title "Round-head." The cervix of the womb has a round head, like the Cornish Witch's Cross—the *Crows an Wragh*.

So he goes into the earth, through the green curtain, and this is like going back into the mother he was born from, and he hears her voice from above him and outside him, which is where the child would hear the mother from, if he could hear in the womb, say "That is the man-eater!" Inside he finds a thing like a phallus. What is most like a phallus inside the woman is the cervix of the womb, particularly at menstruation, when it ejaculates blood, like a blood-red carpet, or a cushion it stands on. Yet it is too fanciful to suppose that the small Jung could have known this, even though he was crowned by it as he was born; yet not so fanciful if one accepts his own conclusion, that the dream was so wise that it "talked of problems far beyond my knowledge." If one does not accept that conclusion, one may suppose that what he saw in the atmosphere of his mother's menstruation was his own incestuous sexual excitation: his first knowledge of his own sexual being. It is the "man-eater" because the period stimulates sexuality, and then passes; because the mother is aware of sexual excitement, but inhibited by the incest prohibition; because sexual discharge leads to detumescence and passivity. It is the man-eater too because menstruation means that no baby is to be born, that the baby's flesh has been mysteriously eaten, and yet there is to be a renewal of the next cycle. Perhaps that is where the "cannibalistic" symbolism of the mass came from in the first place. Layard would compare this vision of the phallic great mother with the tall Malekulan standing stone initiator to the world of men; she is perhaps the archetype too behind the monolithic round-headed Cornish crosses marked with knobs that in a downward light show the moon's phases by shadowing, surrounding a single central "birth-cone."

Then it is the "man-eater" too because of the dangerous aspect of the change in the mother's personality, if that occurs at her period. And here Jung testifies that he was haunted by the strange figure of the man in black, the man in women's clothes, the "Jesuit": "my first conscious trauma." There is a "phallus" here too: the other dimension of the woman's sexuality perceived as "masculine" because repressed and active, black as a shadow because thought evil and made guilty, and dressed in women's clothes because that is how women dress, however menstruous they are feeling. Jung tells us also how his mother used to speak to him in two completely different personalities.

Yet from this dream may have come very much of Jung's mature work. Every child experiences his mother's menstruation, whether he knows it or not. It was Jung's ability to dream this experience in vivid and memorable images, which then he *trusted*, so that they gave up their riches during his life. He would have been the first to admit that such a dream is not exhausted by a single interpretation.

Throughout Jung's creative life he was completely receptive and open to what the women gave him. This giving was often unconscious, and the debt was often too great to be the kind that can be acknowledged consciously by the recipient. It was the mad and distressed women that gave him these gifts. His mother was ill and the marriage in difficulties at about the time of the "great dream" above. This made Jung distrustful when the word "love" was used. "The feeling that I associated with 'woman' was for a long time that of innate unreliability. 'Father,' on the other hand, meant reliability and—powerlessness." Of course, with an illness, which is likely to be exacerbated by her periods even if it is not actually gynecological, a woman will seem "unreliable" and her "love" will ebb and flow, which in the physical sense it does naturally, anyway. Jung records how interested he was in "blood and water trickling out" of a drain in a washhouse where a corpse found by fishermen had been laid out. The red tincture of alchemy, celebrated in Jung's later work, that turns the world to erotic gold, like the gold throne touched by the red cushion of his dream, must have begun its transforming work as early as this, as perhaps it does in all of us if its origin is our mother's menstruation and birth-blood. The latter is sometimes called "lochial blood" and it is from this that we get the notion of "location" as "active place."

Joseph Campbell tells an amusing story that highlights this reactivity between Jung and the women.[2] Once during a lecture, Jung, then a young doctor, hypnotized a woman paralyzed in her left leg. She fell into a deep trance, while continuing to talk ceaselessly of her remarkable dreams. The young instructor could not waken her, and became increasingly alarmed. After ten minutes he succeeded, but she was giddy and confused. Jung said to her, "I am the doctor; everything is all right!" At this she cried out, "But I am cured!" flung her crutch away, and left the lecture-theater able to walk without any assistance for the first time in seventeen years. Jung, blushing with embarrassment, said to his students, "Now you've seen what can be done with hypnosis!" In fact he hadn't the slightest idea what had happened. He had done nothing, yet the woman proclaimed far and wide the miracle cure, and from that moment Jung's private practice grew.

Then there is the case of the Miller Fantasies. These were the diary experiences of a woman journalist whom Jung had never met, written while she was beginning to fall ill from schizophrenia. They had such a powerful effect when he read them that out of them he wrote his own "improvisation" in the form of a burgeoning interpretation, *Symbols of Transformation*, which was his first truly "Jungian" book. It was an "explosion of all those psychic contents which could find no room, no breathing space, in the constricting atmosphere of Freudian psychology." All from a few pages of the journal of a half-mad American woman. "They operated like a catalyst upon the stored-up and still disorderly ideas within me." "Menstruation" is not indexed in the book, but there are many chapters that take on fresh life if they are read with the woman's experience consciously in mind: "The Sacrifice";

"The Dual Mother"; "The Battle for Deliverance from the Mother"; "Symbols of the Mother and of Rebirth." In the last there are fascinating accounts of the "night-sea journey" in the womb-belly of a fish, or in an ark, chest, barrel, ship, etc., each of which is "an analogy of the womb." The journey is sometimes brought to an end by cutting out the heart of the fish, slitting its belly so that the hero may emerge from the dead animal. What should not be forgotten is that the nonpregnant womb menstruates, and the woman goes on her night-sea journey through whatever her individual menstruation reveals to her of pain or vision; and often, with the flow of blood, there is a renewal of feeling: the hero (hera) emerges. This is the cycle of individuation (Jung's word) or of "integration of her rhythms" (Kestenberg) that a woman goes through each month, and in which she learns, if she will, all that can be learned. The hero, the man, can be her companion, as a child or adult, who learns what as a man he cannot directly know, but yet which is true, from the woman's changes. This is, as we have seen, how Jung learned, from the women.

Thus it would be surprising in this psychologist, whose great achievement is to alert us to what is to be learned from the world of the Mothers (as Freud showed us something of the world of the Fathers), if we did not find the themes of menstruation running through and through. We have mentioned alchemy. In this medieval and Renaissance "magical" discipline, Jung believed that he had "stumbled upon the historical counterpart of the unconscious." In these strange magical texts Jung saw the ancient counterpart to his own "real magic" of becoming one's true self, uniting all four sides of one's nature to become a true individual, by a laborious process of uniting the opposites, of dissolving and crystallizing, or watching through the ritual processes of the blackening (nigredo), the whitening (albedo), for the redness (rubedo), and for the red tincture that turns the world to value, or gold; the search for the stone (lapis) that was a womb also by the mixing of principles in the feminine *krater* (mixing vessel): the vessel of spiritual transformation; assisted by versatile and tricky spirits, such as Mercurius, who is also in some way the work itself, and the fountain that "within its basin completes a circle . . . because he [Mercurius] is also the serpent that fertilizes, kills, and devours itself and brings itself to birth again." The process starts with the *prima materia*, the substance that, transformed, becomes the magical stone or tincture. This *prima materia* is the most despised substance, that is nevertheless found everywhere, that is neglected because nobody thinks about it: "Take the foul deposit (*fecum*) that remains in the cooking-vessel and preserve it, for it is the crown of the heart," and the royal diadem appears "in menstruo meretricis," in whore's blood. We have said that the whore, the Magdalen, is the woman who has sex without having a child. And the glorification proceeds from the red; "And when my beloved has drunk from the red rock sepulchre and tasted the maternal fount in matrimony, and has drunk with me of my red wine and lain with me in my bed in friendship . . ." then will there be resurrection of the purified corpse.

This is the system of symbols that in Jungian psychology illuminate the troubles of modern people, and which provide a map of a healing quest, the experience of which sends people on an inner journey that brings riches. There is no space to illustrate as fully as we would wish how closely linked with the menstrual experience this imagery is. If it is seen in this way, then these Jungian writings acquire fresh life and insight that can be seen by any woman to be the psychological experience of her feminine changes, and which can provide exactly those images that interpret and stimulate her dreams in a way that is specific to her femininity. And since female experience is root-experience, these images are not less healing for men.

Jung apparently was never conscious of this application of his studies. He makes no comment, for example, when the "arcane substance" is likened to an egg, expresses no physical correlative when he comments on the old alchemical text, "Therefore pull down the house, destroy the walls, extract therefrom the purest juice with the blood . . ." even when he equates this bloody moon-juice with the spirit of vital participation without which no real therapeutic effect can be achieved, or says that the moon-bitch carries in her belly an essential part of the personality, which is tender bleeding flesh, which is "the 'one thing' on which the whole work turns." This dog is sickest at the New Moon, can affect others, and this dog, lapis, stone, or womb reappears in its dark, feminine form as the Shulamite in the Song of Songs. Jung even expresses surprise that the conjunction of the sun and moon is accompanied by the shedding of blood, though this is among the earliest and most pervasive imagery for the menstrual moment. Daly would say that about such deep childhood experiences there is always "hysterical amnesia" and that our mother's menstruation is the most deeply suppressed of all such experiences. Nevertheless Jung, by trusting his dreams and visions, preserved enough of such origins to be practically useful to people. Though women may be irritated by the way all these experiences are attributed to *masculine* alchemists, with the honorable exceptions of Alexandrian Cleopatra, and Maria Prophetissa, whose mysterious numerical axioms can be seen in terms of menstrual timing within the month.[3]

Not all Jungians have so neglected the physical facts of women's lives. Robert Grinnell speaks of the "dirty meal" or "pork" which is tabooed and sacred, in which "Mercurius menstrualis" is active in producing a "renewed virginity," an idea which Layard has echoed, without, however, referring it to menstruation: his *The Lady of the Hare* turns upon recognition of a dream-hare as "willing sacrifice," and a young girl apparently recovers from mental retardation. Also his *A Celtic Quest* studies the mythology of "the terror of the hag, whose jealous greed is the worst thing on earth, but whose blood is the most precious." Grinnell also considers the demonic masculine component that may possess a woman at her period, reflecting back the "basilisk stare and menstrual poison." The "dirty meal" is in a dream. It is Palestine, and by accident the dreamer has killed a youth, the son of a chief. "In a fit of rage I go out and arrive at an abandoned house by the sea where an old servant woman brings me rotted pork or bacon to eat. Before she does so, however, a hydraulic engineer takes it and washes it off."

Grinnell observes that "the 'dirty meal,' the 'hatred of femininity and fight with sexuality,' the 'release of tension through menstrual flow,' and the 'early pubertal feelings'" associated with his patient's compulsive eating "seem to me to center primarily on the activity of *Mercurius menstrualis*,' which is to say, on a transformational activity which is bisexual and more profound" than either the masculine or feminine forms alone of this Mercurius spirit. Early pubertal feelings enter like "renewed virginity." He says that "Resonances strike out from this symbol, which belongs to the 'pregnancy diet' in which 'Queen Luna' dissolves the old and sterile 'King Sol' in a sort of 'uterine bath'"—here he refers to the Jungian alchemical symbolism as a pattern for what is happening within the woman, as Jung did, who took less note of menstruation. Robert Grinnell says that this "corruption" is Mercurius in his menstrual and seminal aspect, and while the "old king" is disintegrating, the "patient's feminine lunar side has been reawakened." This recalls what we have said in connection with *The Golden Bough* and the cult of sacrifice of the old king, as a psychodrama depicting an ever-recurring inward process that only women possess, but that both men and women may, and probably have, enacted, to give social meaning to these processes. Esther Harding says in *Women's Mysteries* that this "dark of the moon" is when a woman has her "*yin*-power" over men, and, if she is wise, uses it sparingly, for it is immensely powerful—on herself as well as on the man.

Ann Ulanov is a Jungian who has produced a very interesting study that implicitly compares the events of the menstrual cycle and the love of women, with the bleeding of Christ, his death, and his resurrection. She says that it is particularly the feminine mode of being that has been too long neglected, and how confused a Christian woman may be by a dream in which she approaches a goddesslike being if she sees this as a throwback to a "primitive pre-Christian idolatry." Such a goddess would symbolize "potential transformative powers."

Ann Ulanov quotes a dream in which a girl has done a hatchet-murder in an asylum. The dreamer is living with this murderer and reasoning with her to confess, but is very scared. Nevertheless the hatchet-murderer has a mysterious all-knowing quality about her: it is the "shadow" or split-off part which is a shock to cherished notions. She says: "As we begin to give some attention and care to channeling these neglected aspects of ourselves, they become less threatening and more and more helpful to us." She is speaking generally, and does not mention the period here. She does say later, however, that for the "feminine style of consciousness" time is periodic and rhythmic, waxing and waning, and the moon symbolizes this fact. "Each woman experiences this in the blood tides of her menstrual cycle and its attendant psychological effects".

She then goes on: "At ovulation, a woman's body is receptive and fertile. She may then feel an emotional expansiveness, an abundance of sexual energy, a new potency in her creative ideas and insights. If her ego is not in touch with this phase of her cycle, she often squanders her energy in increased busyness or talkativeness, or perhaps in nervous flirtations. If she is related to what is happening in her body and psyche, this time of the month can give her increased confidence and new certainty in her own capacities. Because this sense of herself is rooted in psychosomatic reality, it does not lead to inflation or a drive for power but to stabilization, and a real sense of her own strength. At menstruation, when the body passes its blood-food, a woman often feels an ingathering of her energy and feelings to a deeper center below the threshold of consciousness. If estranged from that center, a woman experiences this phase as a 'curse,' as moodiness, as oversensitivity and pain and irritability. If she is in accord with herself, this phase can be a time of developing fertile insights, new relationships, or creative possibilities suddenly opened to her during ovulation." If these talents are unrelated in a woman to her whole self, then a keen intellect becomes strident, a heart that should be warm becomes cloying, and the ability of feeling becomes maudlin.

She points out that the accented rhythms of dance and music, as for instance they were performed in ancient mystery rites, played an important part in activating the "feminine style of consciousness" as it put women in touch with their own bodily rhythms. In feminine time, events seem like a series of unique births and rebirths with a sense of the authority of the present moment. In masculine time, she says, they are like a series of equal or similar moments. She says that time is *kairos* in feminine consciousness rather than the *chronos* of masculine consciousness: both of which, of course, may be experienced within the same person.

Again, Ann Ulanov says that because women are guided by cyclical processes, the feminine is characteristically dual: waxing and waning. If they are not in tune with their own rhythm, then it shows itself in sharp and inappropriate breaks or alternations rather than as a cyclical steady unfolding. This certainly accords with the medical evidence we have adduced.

She notes that some religious art depicts these human facts in the form of a moon-goddess who is half light and half dark. There are, too, the black virgins of medieval Monserrat and Einsiedeln, where they call Mary "The Moon of the Church." She quotes Jung's remark that the female element in the deity shines in the dark side of that deity: as he also said of the feminine, it stands directly within the shadow of most men. She emphasizes that a woman must not relate exclusively to eros, since logos lives in her too, as part of the duality—and one certainly must not associate logos exclusively with what is masculine: doing so is a great mistake, as Emma Jung also remarks in *Animus and Anima.*

Ann Ulanov also insists that in her belief Christianity is incomplete without some reemphasis on the feminine elements of the Bible. Not only Mary Virgin, she says, but Ruth, and the ancestresses of Jesus, and the apocalyptic woman "clothed with the sun, with the moon under her feet." She quotes a saying of the Baal Shan: "When the Moon shall shine bright as the Sun, the Messiah will come." Layard also says this about the ancestresses of Jesus, the counter-bible of women who insisted on their power as "virgin": this word not meaning "without sexual experience" but rather "uncontaminated in their feminine integrity" by men's laws. In Ulanov's system, it is Jesus who has "The Wise Wound," but she believes that in women "dyings and the risings up of love" should be related to the Christian myth, and achieve their perspective in the context of the Passion. We applaud Ulanov when she says that it is not of nonbeing that man is afraid, but rather of the truth—which is an avalanche of being!

This is confirmed in Seymour Fisher's well-documented book *Body Consciousness.* He says that women are on average much more aware of their bodies than men are, but that by the stereotypes of our society "the woman's greater sensitivity to body cues is given a negative significance." She is not allowed to know what she knows, even though "She keeps tuning in on her body to a greater extent" than men do. She relates more flexibly to her body than men do, and she probably has these advantages because of the menstrual cycle, "That is, she repeatedly experiences rather profound changes in the feel of her body as her menstrual cycle waxes and wanes . . . there is no comparable set of experiences for the male."[4]

You can look at feminine preoccupations in two ways, he suggests, as vanity and narcissism, a "vain" attempt at "mastery of body events that are disturbing," or in a more developed and positive way, that "women direct their creativity into the body world." In comparison, the male "feels less unified with his body. He is perhaps more likely to experience it as a shadow tagging along. He is less sure what to do with it . . ." But a man can be fascinated and instructed by a woman's bodily changes: "he can, without any threat to his own frame, watch the ways in which the body can be transformed," and with the body, of course, the personality itself. "Body alteration is a universal problem and challenge. It . . . has to do with the unavoidable changes in the body that accompany the normal life cycle," that is in its relationships to nature: it teaches life.

Esther Harding, similarly, in her *Women's Mysteries*, speaks of how complex the feminine rhythm is, as complex as the moon-with-the-tides "whose larger monthly cycle works itself out concurrently with the diurnal changes, sometimes increasing the swing of the tide and at others working against the tidal movement . . ." She says that "To consider menstruation as 'the curse' . . . means to lose the deeper experience of an essential part of feminine nature. . . ." She considers the many customs in the past and present which accreted around the particularly feminine experience, drawing on Briffault for some of her information and emphasizing the moon-analogy with the ebb and flow of women's experiences. Such realizations symbolically expressed are still essential, she says. She reproduces a very beautiful dream-drawing of a woman clothed as a mermaid with fish-scales up to her bosom, which, as the moon waxes, draw down off her body. At the full moon, she is nude, completely human. Then her nonhuman features reassert themselves, her face gets older too as the moon wanes. She is not shown at the dark of the moon, but a Goddess holding the looped Egyptian ankh-cross presides at one side, seated on the throne. The picture was also called by the dreamer "The Phases of the Goddess." Dr. Harding comments: "In the picture the dark moon, the dark woman, would stand behind the Sun Goddess, Sekhet, Goddess of Life." Sekhet, in Egyptian mythology, was formidable. She was a form of Hathor, and presided over women's "toilet." Once she nearly destroyed humankind, but she drank red beer mixed with pomegranate juice put out for her instead of the human blood she thirsted for. The fish-skin garment means someone who inhabits the unconscious mind.

On symptoms of women's illness, Esther Harding remarks: "The realization that her symptoms indicate that her conscious attitude is not in harmony with the deeper needs of her own nature would enable her to approach the problem in a more intelligent and constructive way. The significance of the old taboo customs is to be sought . . . ," for these too express in symbolic form certain needs, though they may have become distorted or misinterpreted. "So the woman also has an opportunity at the dark of the moon to get in touch with a deeper and more fundamental layer of her own psychic life. Symptoms of physical or emotional disturbance at that time indicate that there is a conflict between her conscious attitude and the demands of her own nature, and if she recognizes them as an indication of her need to be by herself, because an inner necessity is calling her to introvert, to withdraw psychologically from the demands of her external life and live for a little while in the secret places of her own heart, she may be able to re-establish her contact with the deeper part of her own nature." These are very good words from a much-respected Jungian, but we would say that quietude is not for all women at all times, the inevitable deepest desire at their periods, nor should it be laid down as such. While every person is different, each should be aware of these rhythms, whatever effect these may have within the individual personality. Preferably, one should not be taken by surprise, or be subject to Ulanov's "breaks or alternations." In many people, "To withdraw in this way and give attention to that other side, so commonly sacrificed in the struggle to achieve an adequate and conventionally correct adaptation, produces a strangely healing effect."

Emma Jung's great study is of the Grail, that feminine *krater*, or vessel of spiritual transformation.[5] Once again, it takes fresh life if we refer its scholarly minutiae to experience as lived by Everywoman, thought its author does not emphasize physical experience. These are the figures of her experience and inner encounters, separated from day-to-day living maybe; but it is within women's power to relate these symbolical events to their physical nature. Doing so not only honors it as it should be honored but the power of the symbols initiates a healing process in which the despised feminine functions are recovered. "When a myth is enacted in a ritual performance or, in more general, simpler and profaner fashion, when a fairy tale is told, the healing factor within it acts on whoever has taken an interest in it and allowed himself to be removed by it in such a way that through this participation he will be brought in connection with the archetypal form of the situation and by this means enabled to put himself 'into order.'" That "himself" in partial perhaps, and the reader will be exasperated by the way in which all the Grail events seem to occur in a remote never-never world. In fact it is a dreamland, but what is being talked about is something which is happening everywhere here and now: half the world menstruates and all the world dreams. These stories meditated, once their significance is realized, energize. Enjoyed for their vivid energy, then they begin to bring the healing realizations, healing sleep-experiences. Everywoman may be put off by the very masculine settings of the Grail stories. However, Everywoman may take another look when she reads in Emma Jung of the arrival of the red knight who spills his goblet on the skirts of the Queen, who retires in anger; who is like the "red man" of the alchemists who is the personification of the mysterious *prima materia*; of man's own "inherent femininity"; of the blood which "flowed happily" into the Grail, and it is "in the blood that the essentially atoning power inheres" which stirs "men's feelings to their depths"; that hot poison is drawn from the sick king's wound with two silver knives, like crescent moons; that the table in the Grail Castle is in Latin *mensa* which Emma Jung relates to *mensis*, month, and on this table meat is carved on a silver plate like the moon; and that the Grail full of blood "forms a bridge to the as yet unsolved problem of the material world and evil . . ." and is a "mediator whenever the individual hears the voice of God directly and personally, whereby a connection more suitable to the new age between man and the divine is made possible, as well as a continuing realization of God's challenge to man." Should one not say the new age in which woman gains her rights, in which a new connection between woman and the divine is made possible, and speak of "Goddess's challenge," or as Dame Juliana has it, "Mother God"?

We have a story here too of a red-robed nature-being who is the anima, man's essential feminine being, in whom blood, or feeling, has flowed over from the shadow, the opponent. Her red dress is covered with stars and blood-red "refers to the unsolved feeling problem." This is the Melusine, who dwells in human blood, where she possesses "the capacity to cure diseases and to change her shape" and should become again what she was from the beginning in man "a part of his wholeness."

So throughout Emma Jung's Grail book we have hints that this is not merely story-telling, but something actually applicable to day-to-day feminine experience. But what technique is there for relating such stories to one's own experience? To accept the idea of the Grail as an allegory of the feminine womb and vagina, the "goblet" full of blood, the menstruation that contains many redeeming secrets, is one step.

Another is in the acceptance of the reality of the figures in these stories as powers in the life within. This is particularly true of the figure which Jung called the "Animus," by which he meant the energy that seizes the woman in certain circumstances, often personified in her dreams as a man, dark, mysterious, criminal, or in her feelings appearing as a masculine-tinged energy. We have shown that such an energy often appears during the woman's paramenstruum, and represents the "other dimension" of female sexuality.

This is certainly not to say that a woman is really a man within, or anything like it. This would be a profound misunderstanding. It is best to say that the "animus" of the woman may symbolize her relationships between herself and her unconscious mind, the unknown countries within. There are other figures male and female who may do this, but that known as "animus" is the most active, and usually the most transforming.

But why a *man* within the woman? You could answer this and say that because the problem of the world was a masculine problem, then in the inner world its answer appears in a masculine form. Or you could say that because nature polarizes the sexes into male and female, then the unknown quantity in a woman will be represented, likely as not, by a male figure. You could put this in another way by following Bettelheim, and saying that as infants we were "deuter," both male and female in one, and at puberty in women, the male component went underground, as it were. If this last model approaches the truth, then we can say that as each menstruation recalls the circumstances of the first one, the menarche, the occasion of one's other self going underground is recalled. That other self therefore, usually with unwanted energies, is particularly available at the period. Perhaps because men do not have this, is a reason for their "cursing" it. If that other self were integrated, then he would not "possess" with his energies, but would cooperate instead. It is possible to conjecture that a woman who has a good relationship with the period imaged in mental or dream-form, who is able to reapproach an integration with another side of herself each month, will not have such severe that other side which the world commonly regards as "male" menopausal problems. It is possible that at the menopause, becomes part of the whole character of the woman who therefore acquires new energies. If, however, that other self has been a monthly alien visitor, then there will not be such an integration, and he will be more severely what he always was before, a devil in her life. Vieda Skultans has found that the women in her study regard the "change" often as structural or anatomical change. One seventy-year-old told her that at the menopause "women turn into men inside." This lady had experienced this change herself as a "turning and tightening" in the muscles of the thigh.

Perhaps a chief contribution of these women Jungians is to show the way to contacting this "masculine" principle in women, and to integrating it into the whole life, so that its abilities are not lost, or by repression cause illness, particularly menstrual illness.[6]

Barbara Hannah, in an important little booklet, *The Problem of Contact with Animus,* quotes Jung speaking from the opposite point of view, the man's. His task is to contact *anima,* his "feminine" dimension within, personified as the mysterious unknown woman of fantasies, waking life, or dreams. Jung says, "A man would be singularly right to treat the anima as an autonomous personality and to put direct personal questions to her" and adds: *"I mean this as an actual technique."*

For the woman approaching her new dimension there are certain important distinctions and problems that have to be grasped. First, her psychological structure is exactly comparable to the man's in the respect that her relationship with her "unknown self," her unconscious resources, are likely to make contact with her in personal form. In a man, this personal contact may be made by his *anima.* In a woman, this principle is likely to take a man's face and body to contact her, as her *animus*. The unknown is always personified as the opposite to oneself. Thus it is not because she is "really" a man inside, but because her relationship with things undiscovered, in so far as they are not her integrated possession, are personified by the "other" which she is consciously not. In fact, she certainly incorporates both principles, those of woman and man too, as everybody does, but we have seen how her "masculine" side becomes polarized by social and other conditions. In reapproaching this division in herself, it will often present itself in terms of this polarization. Thus, if society tells her that what she would best like to possess is really a man's prerogative, then as her nature approaches this prerogative, it is likely to take a masculine form. And if it has been forbidden, then it will possibly have a forbidding masculine form. Such a mechanism seems to be keeping women under; in fact it simply means that they have to approach their unused abilities with courage. Most important, the bogeyman is not to be destroyed, but related to.

This brings us to a most important point. Many writers, Emma Jung among them, appear to think that the psychological structure of a woman's relationship with her animus is different in kind from that of a man's relationship with his anima. She rightly says that as a man's task is to lose pride, so a woman's is to acquire self-confidence. But we have seen that Jungians, though open to images of natural events, tend not to acknowledge the roots of these images in external realities, particularly physiological ones. Thus Emma Jung testifies by inescapable implication to the power and value of menstruation in her Grail book, without relating it to feminine experience of monthly bloodshed and self-sacrifice. We ourselves believe that this structure of relationship is identical in the woman as in the man, except *in so far as it is altered by the monthly period and by the menstrual taboo.*

Thus, images of the inspiring Muse or anima of the men are manifold, but in the same way as the woman's period is tabooed, so are the personal images of woman's inspiration by her animus. Think of all the simpering madonnas painted by the men! But how frequent are the images of woman's "other side"? Heathcliffe, who beats his head against a tree until it bleeds? The Wounded King of the Grail story, who presides over the sterile Wasteland until some knight asks what use is this cup of blood?

This means that when the resource of the animus is uncovered, it often operates with extraordinary power. Sometimes indeed with ugliness as well as power, since it, as representative of the "other dimension" of femininity locked up in the period, has been so long outlawed. Sometimes this power is destructive, as in the possession of Jeanne Fery described by Barbara Hannah, which echoes extraordinarily that film parable of possession-in-our-own-time *The Exorcist*. This gifted nun was possessed by extraordinary abilities that spoke in many men's and women's voices, but, as in *The Exorcist*, her gifts were betrayed and quenched by the rough use of exorcism. Thus her intelligence took a man's form, but the priest forbade it to her, calling it a Devil. Then it took the form of Mary Magdalen. Unfortunately, this Christian image of womanhood did not seem sufficiently developed to guide Jeanne to her fulfillment, and she returned to childishness, her surprising abilities discarded. It is an early record of feminine underachievement. Barbara Hannah implies that had the priest conversed with the "devilish" animus, Jeanne Fery would have been in a better way to understand herself. As Marie-Louise Von Franz says, talking about the meaning of "the devil" in *Problems of the Feminine in Fairy-Tales*: "In such cases, renewal can only come by discussion with the other principle—the devil, or the principle of evil—whatever was hitherto excluded."[7]

Another most important point is that the animus-energy may operate in a strange way not only because it has been outlawed for so long and made so violently "masculine," but also because of our own unfamiliarity with instinctual processes. For the menstruation *is* an instinctive process: a natural wound, which heals naturally—and it energizes at the very deepest level all the humanly tinged natural processes of the body: we have seen how radical the physiological process is. Now our natural image for instinctive processes, things which happen accurately, or themselves—is that of the animals and plants: the natural living world outside us. It is hardly surprising then, if our awareness of these processes within, especially at the period, takes animal form.

Jung has noted that a characteristic dream during an illness is that of a visit by helpful animals, or by animal-headed people. This is a sign that the healing processes are operating. It is probably the desire to evoke these helpful powers that has led so many cultures—the Egyptians, for example—to depict gods with animal heads: the so-called theriomorphic gods. So the woman who is developing techniques of reverie or dream-recall of approaching her unknown country in her periods must not be surprised if she encounters, as in the fairy tales, speaking animals, or a man with a beast's head whom it is her task to turn into a man, as in the tale of Beauty and the Beast. Here animal matures into animus.

A friend of ours began to hallucinate red ants on doorposts. She was asked whether she was menstruating. She was. The ants, she concluded, were an image of the busy instinctual elements, archaic, unconscious, of her period. The idea fascinated her, and she lost her fear in her interest, and began dreaming instead of hallucinating. She dreamed of little ratlike animals entering the house, and outside, many auburn-furred monkeys swinging like fire through the trees. She decided that these were also images of the instincts of her period, and now they were warm-blooded and more nearly human. Could she, in dream or imagination, speak and listen to one of these animals, as an articulate representative? She did so, and at the same time her whole outer life changed. She was able to make a decision which took her to another country and more promising prospects.

In anthropological or folkloristic terms, she had acquired a helpful animal spirit, or familiar. This is a natural process—perhaps it is why people like to have pets, on one level, and young girls bloom if they have animals to take care of. They are taking care of a side of their own natures as well! It is the case that the healing yoga postures that are so popular now in the West are copied from animal postures, after which they are often named; as are the Kung Fu fighting attitudes. It is the intention of these disciplines to learn instinctual grace and harmony and unreflecting accuracy, from the animals. Yoga, and dancing, are also among the psychophysiological cures for menstrual distress. As one starts Yoga, one is often visited by powerful dreams. One should write these down, and use their images for meditation. This will give rise to other dreams: a sequence will often develop. Menstrual distress can be mastered in this way, if the meditations are directed toward the period, and not away from it.

The acquisition of a helpful animal spirit is a feature of puberty rites in many cultures other than our own. The young candidate may go out into the wilderness, build a sweat-lodge, and fast until he has a dream of an animal who speaks to him, and sometimes a hallucination of this without dreaming: a vision. This is his animal ally, a spirit who will ever afterward assist and guide him when called upon. He will only have to close his eyes and think of this helper for his courage to rise, or for him to have an insight that will take him out of a tight corner. There is much documentation about the male rites of this kind. The shaman will go through more rigorous, but related training.[8]

What is not so fully realized is that the dreaming of a guiding dream or the acquiring of an animal spirit are features of the training of *women* of power, that these events are looked for at or around the first period, and are much prized in the ordinary woman if they occur at this time. Miriam Van Waters gives many instances, and Devereaux's close study of the Mohaves confirms this. Dreams that come at the first period in any woman are usually regarded as invaluable guides to future life.

A spirit-animal, once encountered, may be one's counselor for the rest of one's life. Carmen Blacker shows how modern spiritualist practices in Japan stem from ancient shamanistic practices in one unbroken line. It seems from her account that there is a likelihood that the original shamans were women, and Briffault is certainly of this opinion. Shamanistic colleges certainly would not have neglected the menstrual period, and their image of it seems always to have been the cyclic phases of the moon. It is possible that shamanistic practices of possession by articulate and helpful spirits originally came from the upsurge of energies at the period. There are indications that these spirits were sometimes seen not only as animals, but as the spirits of unborn children. That is, the blood of the period would come instead of the pregnancy, and the blood spoke with the spirit of the unconceived child. A distressing development of this would be in the rumored cults where children were aborted for magical purposes: there would be no need for this in a menstrual cult where the natural energies were listened to by women aware of their existence. Vieda Skultans shows how modern spiritualistic practices in a mining village in Wales may be organized round or related to menstrual events that define and extend the women's roles. The men may act as teachers or healers, but there is a sense of election to this role by the women's energies, as there is in C. G. Jung's life. It is possible that the ancient Sibylline colleges were organized round the monthly "descent" and we consider this possibility in Chapter V.

Emma Jung wisely comments in *Animus and Anima* that in approaching these personifications, the problem in a man is to put down his pride; but in a woman, to acquire self-confidence. For a woman, she says "the idea that what is masculine is in itself more valuable than what is feminine is born in her blood" [*sic*]. Therefore, she should listen, but very critically, to what the animus tells her.

Barbara Hannah speaks of how a modern woman may hold conversations with her personified animus: "the art consists in allowing one's 'opponent' a voice, in placing the means of expression at his . . . disposal. This technique requires a lot of practice." Naturally practice is acquired, but once the premises are accepted, the natural ability unfolds. In fact, all the arts are means of holding such conversations. When they become art, it merely means that the artist has left traces of his/her encounters accurate enough for us to follow; they affect our own processes of integration. And this is one of the clues to developing technique, by "active imagination," by writing stories, poems, painting pictures of these conversations, by recording dreams and extending them into waking life by allowing one's fantasy to play—critically. But, as in art, there is not necessarily any need for cumbersome interpretations. The Rabbis knew that "the dream follows the interpretation." This means that if you answer a dream by interpreting it, it will respond with further information. This is why you get the apparently comical feedback effect of Freudian analysts getting classical Freudian dreams from their patients, and Jungians getting Jungian dreams. In fact, both these psychological techniques are only *languages* so formulated that the dreaming-powers can use them, unlike the threadbare language of ordinary life. Freud and Jung and the rest have only contrived ways of conversing with the dream, the unknown self. They have no claim to objective truth except *in so far as their systems work*.

Often it is helpful to have a professional analyst forming such a language when one has not been able to form it for oneself. But one must not believe that because the analyst is a competent linguist, he/she necessarily has a special insight into truth. We have in fact seen what an important segment of human experience—the menstrual cycle—most psychological interpreters have been concerned to leave out.

But there are many languages. Modern psychology has returned with its specialized languages in an attempt to cure the disorders produced by contemporary alienation from nature and woman, but it may have a certain interest vested in perpetuating features of this alienation. In the world of unconscious abilities seeking to converse and integrate into individuality, every occurrence is a sentence of meaning. One does not necessarily have to translate this into psychologisms to understand it, since it is the natural language of *oneself*. It is a kind of body-language, that needs no specialists. All it needs is sensitivity, a willingness to change, trust in something greater than oneself. With dreams, one does not necessarily have to interpret them; *the important thing is to experience them.*

As we have suggested, this study of femininity is in its infancy, for the reason that the authors and practitioners concerned with it have not realized the source of the dangerous *negative animus,* the destructive masculine spirit in women that so besets their analyses. If the woman's menstruation is despised, that is, a deep instinctual process in her is ignored or hated, then its spirit will return with all the evolutionary power of those instinctual processes that grew us and continue to energize our physical being. You could say in this way that the Christian Devil was a representation of the animus of the menstruating woman, in so far as the Christian ethic has Satanized woman and her natural powers. In former times, this kindly horned god, Cernunnos to the Celts, who wore horns as a sign of conscious knowledge of the horned womb, with its splendid sweeping trumpeting "uteri tuba," was a symbol of instinctual life brought to consciousness. When that life was exiled by the development of a masculine hegemony, he became the dark shadow of the woman and deteriorated into "raging hormones."

But many of the Jungians are open, if they would have the courage to approach nature in physical fact. Symbols are physical realities, as well as mental ones. Esther Harding shows how the moon-transformation in a dream of woman's sense of herself is a smooth sequence of change, each part conscious of the other. She shows how women may take the period as a psychological opportunity of contact with her deeper self. Unfortunately Dr. Harding seems a little too mild or indefinite about the actual happenings in physical reality, perhaps a little too fastidious. Emma Jung is most definite about the role of the animus in her helpful *Animus and Anima,* but again she does not relate the opportunities of negotiation with the animus to actual physical rhythms. In the Grail book, however, she testifies: "In the dreams and fantasies of even happily married women, a mysteriously fascinating masculine figure often appears, a demonic or divine dream or shadow lover . . . a kind of inherent primal phenomenon." She suggests that women often cherish "a more or less conscious secret idea that one of her children, preferably the eldest or youngest, was fathered by this psychic lover."

This is the "other husband" of the woman, in so many cultures the Moon, or a Moon serpent, that is, an allegory of the monthly period, or blood-tide. But if the woman regards the abilities of this lover as not transferred to her physical son, but rather as her own possession, a "divine child" which is her own self, in the round of the periods, like the Moon, giving birth to herself, what happens? Rivkah Kluger, who traces the biblical story of the Queen of Sheba, and shows that this person, the Wisdom of Solomon, like the Shulamite in the Song of Songs, is the spirit of woman disentangling herself from her imposed demonic role without forgetting her instinctual side, tells us: "If a woman is freed from the animus possession, by uniting as a woman with the animus, instead of *being him,* i.e., *by relating with her feminine feeling to the spirit,* she becomes both more consciously masculine, by accepting and developing her masculinity, and at the same time more feminine, because the accepted animus does not sit any more on her femininity, twisting or destroying it." This to us means accepting the instinctual riches of the period, also.

One of the legends of Solomon says that he knew the Queen when he saw her *reflected in a looking-glass floor,* and saw her animal foot, her cloven hoof. She is said to have got this cloven hoof when a drop of dragon-blood fell on her foot! A cleft? An animal cloven place? We think Solomon saw up her skirt, and wisely acknowledged the blood he saw there. Rivkah Kluger gives us reason for believing that Sheba was once Lilith, the first wife of Adam, exiled like menstruation as a demon and returning as the black Shulamite of the Song of Songs: so does Raphael Patai.

Marie-Louise Von Franz (1972) shows us how much we can learn about our neglected selves from the language of fairy and folk tales. Such tales arose in a moment of integration in a gifted teller, and speak natural picture language. Grimm is a kind of Bible of the Goddess, a book of epiphanies, fantasies with a hard core of experience, pictured in inward terms. "Renewal can only come by discussion with the other principle—the devil, or the principle of evil—whatever was hitherto excluded . . . (a) one has to enter into discussion with the unconscious; and (b) to promise that life in the future will be conducted on new lines." This "devil" may at first be so polarized against the "good" side that his appearance and his conditions seem one-sided, untrustworthy, and unrealistic. But this can mean that one should go into seclusion, sink down, and find a totally new solution. Solutions can come in the form of dreams, visions, or sudden insights in reverie. The self-renewal of the period's sequence is in itself an insight, if consciously entered with the aid of a disciplined imagination, such as an artist develops, but which is everybody's birthright.

Premenstrual tension may show all the opposites, good-bad, light-dark, love-hate. Impossibilities and alternatives may revolve with enormous energy and rapidity; then the period comes with its terrific discharge of tension and the whole matter is different. If this is done with conscious purpose, and not in the body alone, then the monthly struggle is not mere repetition of a forced situation. Experienced growth, creative turmoil and resolution, the anguish of choices, and the solution that comes of itself are all possible. "Do nothing" is sometimes the best advice, but above all, not to fear.

We conclude with more testimony of Emma Jung. She records a series of dreams and fantasies of the "differentiation of the animus," and though she avoids mentioning menstruation itself, how can we doubt after reading them that the teller must have come into a healing relationship with her physical nature?

The instinctual animus-energy appears first as a bird-headed monster with a wind-filled bladder-body, like a balloon. This represents an energy she had detached from a lover, on whom it was projected. She is by this image beginning to acknowledge it as her own power and possession. A fire spirit appears also, as a demonic energy, the instigator of "feminine devils' or witches' arts," according to the teller. He becomes "Urgo, the Magic Dragon" in a dream. There he has a girl in his power, and is able to prevent the girl's escape by stretching out in any direction.

Now this patient of Emma Jung's fantasizes a dance, set in India: "A dance of transformations, in which, throwing off one veil after another, she impersonates a motley succession of figures, both animals and men . . . she dances on and on, till finally, as though throwing off her body like a last veil, she falls to earth, a skeleton. The remains are buried; out of the grave a flower grows, out of the flower, in turn, a white woman." This meditation brings about a real transformation, "not just a representation of one. An important function of the higher, that is, the personal animus, is that as a true psychopompos it initiates and accompanies the soul's transformation." In this case, the "fantasies" are true "meditations." One of the guarantees that they are, that realization is actually occurring, is that a vivid spontaneous dream supports the "fantasy."

The dream is that the girl has "a ghostly lover who lives in the moon, and who comes regularly in the shallop of the new moon to receive a blood sacrifice which she has to make to him." The girl is an ordinary human being at other times, but as the new moon approaches she turns into a rapacious beast. She is impelled to climb a height and make lonely sacrifice. This sacrifice in the dream transforms the moon-lover, and he himself becomes instead a sacrificial vessel, "which consumes itself but is again renewed, and the smoking blood is turned into a plant-like form out of which spring many-colored leaves and flowers."

On another occasion, there is a murderer, called "Amandus." He is like Bluebeard, and lures the girl into an underground chamber after giving her wine to drink, to kill her. On a sudden loving impulse, the girl embraces the murderer. He is "immediately robbed of his power and dissolves in air, after promising to stand by her side in the future as a helpful spirit."

These are not fairy tales, or the remote rites of a savage society, but the experienced images of integration of a modern woman, who only needed the courage of that "lonely sacrifice," that "loving impulse" to possess the unacknowledged part of herself after it had appeared in its form of the awakened, perhaps sinister, animus. The ghostly spell of the moon-bridegroom—the menstrual epidemic—was broken by the willing offer of blood, and by the giving to the blood value and meaning: "by embracing the terrifying monster, the girl destroys his power through love" and gains his help instead.

Marie-Louise Von Franz (1970) gives her interpretation of the Grimm fairy tale "The Three Feathers" in which an ugly toad is transformed, and proves to be the rightful queen of the kingdom. Oddly enough, she gives this a masculine interpretation, but we believe that her words are just as apposite to the woman. She says that the meaning of the toad turning into a beautiful woman is, *practically* "that if a man has the patience and the courage to accept and bring to light his nocturnal sex fantasies, to look at what they carry and to let them continue, developing them and writing them down (which allows for further amplification), then his whole anima will come up into the light. If, when doodling, he says: 'Now what am I doing here?' and develops the sex fantasy he has expressed in his drawing, then often the whole anima problem comes up and the anima is then much less inhuman and cold-blooded. The repressed feminine world comes with it . . ." But this repressed feminine world must include the problem of menstruation, its shape and form, for man as well as woman. What should never have been forgotten is that *the anima menstruates*.

This eminent Jungian implies that all the tales of treasure found in the fairy tales, those psychodramas, refer to the buried, despised, neglected faculty, the withered ugly one in the makeup of the human being. The ugly witch terrifies the knight, but he sleeps with her, and in the morning he awakes to find the most beautiful woman in the world in his bed. It is the neglected faculty of the four that, recovered, transforms life. Jungians often say that the faculties of intellect and observation are the most used in our world, the faculties of intuition and feeling most neglected. One may look at this in a different way, and redress the balance by being physiological: the most neglected phase of Everywoman's rhythmical fertility cycle is the experience of the bleeding. It is despised, and thought of as a "wound." But the only wound that is given, the dolorous blow, is given by those who despise and fear it. Jung has said "The inferior function . . . there we have an open wound . . . through which anything might enter."[9]

Jung says also there is a fifth faculty. He calls it the "transcendent function" because it emerges from, and unites, the other four in balance. This function is no other than the disciplined or creative imagination. Elizabeth Sewell calls it the "postlogical" ability that satisfies logic yet goes beyond it, as all good art does, fairy tales included.

Bruno Bettelheim's most recent book to date (*Symbolic Wounds* was his first) is called *The Uses of Enchantment* and is about the practically integrative power of fairy tales, as Von Franz's is. In a middle chapter he discusses the meaning of the witch's curse in "The Sleeping Beauty." Twelve fairies are invited to the christening of the child, and bring their gifts. The thirteenth, evil, fairy is left out of the invitations, so she brings her curse on the child instead. The curse is that she shall prick her finger on a distaff and bleed. The King, her father, removes all distaffs from the land in an attempt to forestall the bleeding. But the girl enters a secret chamber in the castle where an old woman is spinning and pricks her finger here, and falls into a deep slumber. Everybody in the castle sleeps as she does, for a century. A high wall of thorns protects the castle, until the magic prince cuts a way with his sword, wakening the Princess with a kiss.

Bettelheim shows how, called so from its biblical origins, menstruation is the female, or fairy's "curse"; and it is plain that had the King her Father not tried to keep her from puberty, the bleeding would have been no curse at all. Why thirteen fairies? Because the solar, Father's year, is divided into twelve months, while the woman's year of experience is divided into thirteen periods, since twenty-eight days is the traditional length of a menstrual cycle. To forget this, to forget the thirteenth fairy, is to bring on a curse. Bettelheim believes that "The story of Sleeping Beauty impresses every child that a traumatic event—such as the girl's bleeding at the beginning of puberty, and later, in first intercourse—does have the happiest consequences. The story implants the idea that such events must be taken very seriously, but that one need not be afraid of them. The 'curse' is a blessing in disguise."

Four Does the Moon Menstruate?

I

In our modern age intellect is so divided from body that we look at the moon and marvel at its aesthetic qualities as it rides the night like a white queen, and at the same time wonder whether there can be any truth in the old legends that the moon's growth and dwindling influence us and our destinies. If it is a new moon and nobody's watching, we may bow to it three times, and turn the money over in our pockets, hoping that our finances may increase as the moon waxes. If we catch sight of it through glass, we wonder what misfortune will follow. In fact, the misfortune will follow if we catch sight of it reversed in a glass, that is, a mirror, and mistake the waxing for a waning moon. Why, will appear.

Then, if we read our newspapers, we find that new discoveries are being made about ancient history and the moon. Recent controversy developed about the function of the Aubrey holes at Stonehenge, when Gerald Hawkins, working with a computer, claimed that Stonehenge— megalithic monument of a culture we tend to think of as merely that of savages—was a sophisticated computer for calculating, among other things, eclipses and lunar phases.

Why were these "savages" so interested in the moon? Why did they roll these immense stones from Wales, a task which it has been calculated would have taken the entire labor force of that area in those times seven years to complete, just to know about the moon? A Professor of Surveying, Alexander Thom, clinched the matter by showing, even to the satisfaction of much of the scientific community, that not only Stonehenge, but many other monumental remains dating from the Stone Age, at the very least 4000 years B.C., were lunar calculators. Even before this, there had been indications that early peoples carved notches on animal bones to mark the phases of the moon, and colored these markings with red ochre.[1]

Why the interest? If we read mythology we learn that the moon always, to all peoples, times, and cultures apart from our own (and *we* send Apollo in the form of a rocket and shining men to moon-walk) has been a focus of that degree of passionate interest that we call religious. Time itself was probably first measured by the moon's phases, the months, and one of the troubles about the calendar is that the months will not fit exactly into the solar year. In our current system, the months have been made to fit by Gregory XIII who gave them an arbitrary number of days unrelated to what the moon is doing. So our calendar puts us out of sync with the moon, though in past ages people appear to have been concerned to live in harmony with it.[2]

But why? What event in human lives corresponds in any way to the moon's events? Is there any connection between human fertility and the moon? It seems a strange coincidence, if coincidence it is, that most of the medical books say that the average length of a woman's menstrual cycle is twenty-eight days. This might be no more than a coincidence, since, as Paula Weideger has pointed out, the figure is only an average one composed of the cycle-length of thousands of women added together and divided by the number of women. She says that it is quite possible in the statistical samples that no woman had a twenty-eight-day cycle, since it is quite normal to have fifteen-day cycles or forty-one-day cycles. What she says is true—nevertheless it is also true that the vast majority of cycles cluster round this figure of twenty-eight. Around four weeks is a very usual length of cycle. The coincidence is that the length of the moon's cycle from new moon to new moon also averages out at about four weeks, or 29·53 days (mean synodic month). Even the name of the cycle, the *menstrual* cycle, according to the OED, comes from the Latin *mens, mensis,* meaning "month," and the same authority also reminds us that "month" means "moon."

Partridge's dictionary goes further. If you look up "month" there, you will be referred to "measure." He tells us that the changes of the moon afforded the earliest measure of time longer than a day. Under "Menstruation" we are referred also to "measure." The paragraphs tell us that "menstruation" does come from "month" which comes from "moon." More-over, he tells us that the following words for ideas come from the measurement that the moon makes in the sky: *measurement, mensurable, mensuration, commensurate, dimension, immensity, meter, metric, diameter, parameter, perimeter, meal,* and many others. A suspicion grows that perhaps many of our ideas come from the moon-measure. All the words for "reason" certainly come from "ratus," meaning to count, calculate, reckon; and all the words for mind, reminder, mental, comment, monitor, admonish, mania, maenad, automatic, and even money appear to be associated with this Latin word *mens,* or Greek *menos,* which both mean "mind" or "spirit"; or the Latin for "moon" or "monthly." The Greek word for "moon" is *mene.*

The Greeks also had three words for "womb": *hustera, dephus,* and *metra.* This last word, *metra,* was used to denote the cervix including the orifice of the womb. Thus in Galen the term "mouth of the womb" using *metras* was translated into early Latin as *cervix uteri.* It is the cycle of the womb which is the measurement of the human cycle, and even the Greeks called it the *meter* of the woman. This is the same word used for the moon's cycles. The cervix of a woman's womb, the *metra* in effect counts out the menstrual month by changing color, size, and position. Looked at with a speculum, it resembles a globe resting in a crescent.

What we are trying to show is that basic to our language and our thought is an idea of measurement or proportion, originally associated with the measured return of the moon each month, and that many of the words we use for rational science and its measurements are "lunatic" words. It is possible that these ideas of measurement and ratio in human society originated not solely from the moon in the sky, but also in the emerging rhythm of the woman's cycle as civilization grew, and the effects of women's cycle on the people among whom she lived, which includes men and children as well as herself. We are trying to show, as a starting point, that this is recorded in the language.

Briffault accumulates remarkable testimony to this theory. He says that the moon has always been associated with women's menstruation, and has often been thought to be the cause of it. Transition from one moon-phase to the next always was a time of power and consideration. It is a vital rhythm in many human societies that is watched and obeyed. "Menstruation" means "moon-change." German peasants call the periods "the moon" and the French term is "le moment de la lune." Sabbatu was the "sabbath" or menstruation of the Babylonian goddesses: a taboo time at which no work was done. The Mandingo, the Susus, and the Congo tribes call menstruation "the moon." A European judge in court in India was puzzled that a female witness was unable to attend "because of the moon." In British East Africa menstruation is "caused" by the new moon, and in Aristotle's works women are said to menstruate at the new moon. The Papuans believe that the moon has intercourse with girls and that this is the cause of their period. Maori call the period "moon sickness." An old Maori woman said that "a woman is always affected at the same stage of each moon" and another Maori stated that the moon was the true or permanent husband of all women and that "the marriage of man and wife is a matter of no moment; the moon is the real husband." The Fuegians call the moon "The Lord of the Women."

Calling the moon the "true husband of women," says Briffault, is one statement of the relationship of women with the moon in their menstrual cycles, which is "fundamental." Another statement is when the moon, from being the "Lord of the Ladies," becomes an image of the woman herself in her changes, the Great Mother. Then she is the chief goddess in the pantheons: "The Queen of Heaven": Isis, Ishtar, Demeter, Artemis, and she has the moon's attributes. She is said, as Mary, to have made the world, to have made God. Her worship relates to the moon's phases, and evidently to the analogous women's phases of the menstrual cycle.

Not only her phases, but her eclipses are noted, as may have been at Stonehenge. Among the Ibo of Nigeria the Sabbath observed is "The Woman's Day," which is the day of the new moon. The same in the Congo. The Wemba women whiten their faces when the new moon appears. The Aleutian women have particular rites and dances in the moonlight at the full moon, and the Trobriand Islanders use their understanding of the moon's changes in a calendar of festivals of courtship and mating. Briffault says that these lunar observances are found in the advanced religions of Western Asia, Egypt, and Europe. Aubrey tells us that in the north of England in his time "women doe worship the new moon on their bare knees, kneeling upon an earth-fast stone." In Zennor, Cornwall, there remains a stone which, according to the locals, will make a woman a witch if she circles around it like the moon and worships the moon upon it. In Ireland there was the custom of the women falling on their knees at the new moon and saying to it "O Moon! Leave us as well as you found us." There are many such survivals of feminine practices to do with the moon. We call them "superstitions," a word that means "*to stand over*" from a former religion. It also needs noting that the devils of a current religion are usually the "stood-over" gods and goddesses of a former one. Erich Neumann, in "Fathers and Mothers,"[3] using other dictionaries, takes us further. He says that etymologists—the ones he quotes are all four of them men—have tried to separate off the word-root meaning "spirit" from the word-root meaning "moon" though in fact the two are identical. Thus *men* (moon) and *mensis* (month) belong to the root *ma* and the Sanskrit *mas*. On the other hand the idea of "spirit" is related to the Sanskrit root *manas*, *menos* (Greek) and Latin *mens*. According to Partridge the Polynesian word *mana* meaning "the nonphysical immanent controlling power of the universe" is akin to this same Sanskrit *manas*, which he thinks was introduced by ancient traders from India. We have seen in our Chapter II what personal *mana* or charisma a menstruating or premenstrual woman has! and we have suggested that this spirit or energy causes her terrors and pain when it is frustrated.

In addition, the Greeks used the word *noumenon* for the New Moon at festivals. This is the word Kant uses in his philosophy to indicate the metaphysical nonobservable immanent controlling power behind the things we commonly observe, the phenomena. Kant, coming in the middle of a line of male-controlled philosophy, naturally could not observe such feminine or intuited things as *noumena*.

Neumann shows us that these two meanings of "spirit" and "moon" have been separated on no grounds whatsoever. From the spirit-root stems *menos*: heart, soul, spirit, courage, ardor; *menoinan*: to meditate, wish, consider; *memona*: to intend or to have in mind; *mainomai*: to be so lost in one's thoughts as to rave, or to think ardently; and from this comes *mania*, which means "possession" as well as "madness" and also *manteia*: prophesy. Other words arising are those for "anger," "reveal," "learn," "remember," and "lie."

For no good reason, it would appear, this root has been opposed to the moon-root *men*: moon; *mensis*: month; *mas* and *ma*: to measure. There is *metis*: cleverness, wisdom; *metiesthai*: to dream, meditate, also.

Both sets of words, that is moon-root and spirit-root, are derived also from Sanskrit *mati-h*, meaning both "measure" and "knowing."

Neumann's conclusion is that the single meaning underlying all these ideas is that of "moon-spirit" which has two emotional movements to it, just as he says the unconscious mind has, and as (in our opinion) the menstrual cycle has, in its two poles of ovulation and menstruation. As we have said, the degree of separation of the poles, polarization, depends on society's and the individual's attitude to these two extremes of woman's menstrual experience. In Neumann's moon-terms, in active eruption, there is a fiery spirit: of anger, courage, possession, rage. This spirit is "fiery productivity," it leads to lying, crime, cogitation, prophecy, and poetry. There is, however, a more "measured" emotional movement that goes along with these moon-words: it waits and wishes, meditates, dreams, lingers, hesitates, obeys; it has to do with learning, memory, moderation, and explicit meaning.

An older source, Gerald Massey, accumulates a quite remarkable amount of information to show what seems quite natural that "the female nature has been the primary teacher of periodicity." Cottie Burland in *Feathered Serpent and Smoking Mirror* gives a very clear example. Aztec culture was absolutely male-dominated: men were the priests, leaders, and kings. The aspect of the moon-goddess that was favored was the ovulating goddess of pregnant harmony and the blessings of married life. But this was only her short-lived third aspect: she had before this been an unreliable, cruel, and brilliant adolescent, succeeded by a gambling phase (just as it's a gamble whether the egg is fertilized, and if it is, then the woman is out of the moon-cycle for a while). Then finally there were the fiery Hecate energies of the fourth phase, that the men cannot experience, and can find no use for. They were therefore exiled and feared, and used as scapegoat: as we do in our society. This culture's separation from feminine things had evidently polarized the fertility-cycle into its beneficent ovulation aspect and, to the men, its maleficent aspect. However, the analogy moon-cycle, woman-cycle had been kept, and extended on the pattern of the month, to the entire life-cycle, through youth to marriage and death.

This is only one example of such a goddess. It was this culture that developed the terrible rite of dressing a sacrificing priest in the skin of his human sacrifice. It was a fertility-rite. He would burst from the bleeding human skin as the germinating shoot from the husk of the grain. As it was men who performed this rite, it is possible that it had developed as a "psychodrama" of the bloodshed and renewal that women normally undergo in their fertility-cycle, and which the man had to imitate to perform their fertility-rite.

Erich Neumann in his *magnum opus* of that name traces the structure of the archetype of "The Great Mother" whenever or wherever she occurs. All her manifestations are discernibly linked to this moon-analogy; indeed one can say that "moon-thinking" and lunar matters are characteristic of cultures interested in the feminine, and solar matters of the patriarchy. Neumann finds a fourfold structure in the totality of these appearances of the feminine archetype, though in a different sense to the Aztec example just given. He says that wherever the image of the feminine is valued or feared, it is so either as Mother or Muse. The latter he calls "transformative character." There is the Good Mother of the mysteries of birth and vegetation, who is bearing and releasing. In polar opposition to her is the negative Terrible Mother, who holds fast, devours, and who is mistress of death mysteries. There are Demeter and Isis—"Good Mothers"—and Hecate, Kali, Gorgon—"Terrible Mothers."

Crossing this life-death line, as it were, is its mental or spiritual counterpart, the two poles of inspiration on the one hand, and madness on the other. Astarte, Lilith, Circe, the

Witch, according to Neumann, represent the lower, negative pole of this transforming character, and the mysteries of drunkenness and madness. On the positive side are the mysteries of inspiration and vision, which Neumann attributes to Mary, Sophia, and the Muse. The four aspects operate like dynamic currents or electromagnetic fields urging to rebirth and spiritual transformation, or degeneration and death, with resorption into the Great Mother. All these figures are linked to the moon-image.

In our own terms, once again we see the ovulation-menstruation polarity. The Mother is concerned with the life and death of the ovum, she will bear if she can, and she will take into herself her dead offspring, which is her other side, the Terrible Mother. The Transformative Feminine is concerned, however, with spiritual children, which she will either bear, as the Muse, or destroy and reabsorb in the ecstasy of madness: it is her own transformation by which she transforms others—just as the Mother by her pregnancy and labor evolves the abilities of fatherhood in the man. All the aspects are contained in the great round of the feminine, which has always been understood in terms of the moon's cycle, the phases and the tides, and the fertility of the earth mediated to it by moon-animals who reflect in some way the moon's or the woman's changes.

According to Mircea Eliade's *Patterns in Comparative Religion,* the moon-animal par excellence has been the snake because it "changes" by shedding its skin—though of course many other animals are involved with the symbolism as moon-familiars, such as the hare, dog, lizard, pig, etc. Eliade's documentation of the fact that the moon-woman analogy is universal is also copious, and the snake is often invoked as a moon creature, coiling in spirals as the moon travels around the world, casting off its skin, changing as the moon does. He says: "There is a great deal of ethnological evidence to show that witchcraft is a thing bestowed by the moon (either directly, or through the intermediary of snakes). To the

Chinese, for instance, snakes are at the bottom of all magic power, while the Hebrew and Arabic words for magic come from words that mean 'snake.'" And again: "All over the East it was believed that a woman's first sexual contact was with a snake . . . A Persian tradition says that after the first woman had been seduced by the serpent, she immediately began to menstruate. And it was said by the rabbis that menstruation was the result of Eve's relations with the serpent in the Garden of Eden . . . Certainly the menstrual cycle helps to explain the spread of the belief that the moon is the first mate of all women. The Papoos thought menstruation was a proof that women and girls were connected with the moon, but in their iconography . . . they pictured reptiles emerging from their genital organs, which confirms that snakes and the moon are identified."

II

In this chapter we have to see what the mountain of corroborative evidence that exists can mean to us if we are concerned to restore to the feminine cycle its lost respect. It is to be noted that it is only in the woman-hating religions that the Garden was the place of a "Fall," and the serpent was an evil creature whispering bad advice. In the majority of religions which express the idea, the garden is an enclave of blessedness, yes, but it is haunted by *beneficent* and oracular serpents, tended by wise priestesses interested in imparting the gifts of wisdom to people who are willing to accept them.[4] It is also worth noting again that the gods of the former religion become the demons of the next.

If we survey all the evidence, we do seem to enter on considerations that are both worrying and exhilarating to every woman and to every man interested in women. It seems for instance undoubted that our words for "mind" and "civilization" came from words which mean "moon-experience." But what was this "moon-experience"? Did it come from humankind's observation of the remote moon? Or did it come, as seems more likely, from humankind's much more intimate experience—the most intimate experience that individuals can have—of their relationships with women and women's changes in the menstrual cycle. The history of words—let alone images—reflects psychological realities: that is the history of our relationships to the universe. In this history, the root-meaning of "spirit" and "holy spirit" and "mind" and "mentality" appears to be "that which is promoted by the moon's and the women's changes." This is the psychological truth. But if it is truth, then it is a one thing, and it is physical truth also. So what does the physical truth of science say about the role of the menstrual cycle in the evolutionary development of human society?

It is received opinion in zoological science that the development of the menstrual cycle was responsible for the evolution of primate and eventually human societies. We are now talking of our roots in time not merely of thousands of years, as with Stonehenge or native customs or the origin of words, but back in time many millions of years, when the beings that eventually became human began to separate from the other warm-blooded animals and developed a different order of being.

The fact is this: most of the animals, right upward in the evolutionary series through the mammals, have specific breeding-times and seasons, and these are the only times that they are inspired with sexual energy to beget offspring. At other times animals are not interested in mating. This is because the majority of the mammals have an *estrus* cycle, and they come "in heat" at specific times.

With the Old World Monkeys, the Apes and the human being, an immense evolutionary change occurred. This was the development of the *menstrual cycle*, in which the wall of the womb is shed, with bleeding, and the animal can be sexually aroused at almost any time in its cycle. Moreover, the menstrual cycle is continuous—unlike the estrus cycle of many animals, which have longish resting-phases with no discernible ovarian activity at all. Another difference is that in most *estrus* cycles a little blood is shed at the *ovulation*, and this is a powerful mating-signal. In the menstrual cycle, the blood is shed with the womb-wall, which becomes thin, raw, and responsive, though a little blood is sometimes shed at ovulation also. It is as though the mating-signal of genital blood has been wrenched from its former position at ovulation, to a new position at menstruation, when it is very unlikely that ovulation can occur, or offspring can be conceived. It is as though what this evolutionary step meant was that sex was now to be used for something other than reproduction, since sexual libido was also wrenched from its former exclusive attachment to the ripening of the egg, and spread over most of the cycle, with another concentration of sexual interest at or around menstruation. Yet how, ask the evolutionists, can this be of benefit to the species, since menstruation is a "safe" period, and offspring cannot usually result at this time? The answer must be that the sexual experience in primates (monkeys and humans) must have become of benefit and importance to the individual (and thence to the race) as well as to the species by breeding.

Thus a difference between humans and most mammals is that humans are interested in sex almost all the time! This is the "Fall," according to Judeo-Christian religions, the free-will of choice given to the individual. The Bible says that this capacity for sexual choice was given to Eve by the serpent. As we have said, in many other religions this was a prized gift. It is to be noted that the Biblical translation "the tree of the knowledge of good and evil" is a little slanted. It can be: "the tree of the knowledge of all things."[5] The Biblical two trees were originally the moon-tree of the Babylonians and others. As we have shown, on the analogy "moon-woman," then this moon-tree becomes the lovely swooping branches of the tubes and ovarian fruit within. In the Bible, the Trees may possibly be the "Tree of Life" of the species, life transmitted by offspring; and the "Tree of the knowledge of all things" from which, so to speak, Adam and Eve plucked the menstrual fruit. The God of the Bible was angry at this and prevented them getting at the Tree of Life because if they had done so, then they could have transmitted their knowledge down the generations. As it was, the Biblical God did the job by separating the two trees, ovulation from menstruation, exiling womanhood and menstruation, and creating the "howlback" circuit by devaluing both women and her natural cycle. He did his job by separating the two trees *in our minds*. The Biblical myth states our dilemma, like a riddle that has to be solved before we can proceed out of the Judeo-Christian situation.

To summarize: *The evolutionary change from estrus cycle to menstrual cycle implies that sexual libido became available for something other than the perpetuation of the species by the reproduction of offspring. That "something other" is the enhancement of life produced by shared sexual experience between individuals. An act of sex became this, rather than simple impregnation of the female. From the appearance of the menstrual cycle therefore dates all the evolutionary developments which have been seen as specifically human: viz., the development of mentality, symbolism (a "mental child" is a symbolic child), recognition and valuing of the individual, and social organization.*

This may seem like a tall story, but let us have a look at scientific opinion. For example, a standard text by J. Z. Young states: "The situation is different in humans from that of most mammals in that there is no well-defined sexual signal at the time of ovulation, though this can be detected by various signs, including changes of temperature. Copulation is acceptable at all times, and this is part of the pair formation that is one of the many human biological characteristics." "Pair formation" is zoologese for "sexual affection" or "love" or "physical attraction" or "carnal knowledge" or "elective affinity." It is the story of love and war. Recently, Benjamin Beck's experiments on baboons at the Chicago Zoo have given fresh evidence that "humans' non-stop libido is an evolutionary adaptation that favored the development of social and economic co-operation in developing hominids" (reported in *New Scientist*, 15 November 1973). In Zubin and Money we have the following statements: "The continual sexuality of man contrasts sharply with the seasonal sexuality of most nonhuman primates. We do not have a sexual season . . ." and, under the heading of "The Evolution of Mammalian Sexual Autonomy": "Outstanding here is the gradual separation of the sexual drive from the reproductive function. In subprimates, sexual drive is for the most part limited to the time of estrus, and estrus coincides with ovulation . . . In the higher, nonhuman primates (apes) which menstruate, sexual drive begins to separate from reproduction . . . Finally, in humans, sexual activity as such becomes independent of reproduction . . ." Theo Lang says: "The year-round sexual urge can therefore be seen as the dominant factor in forming human society."

Again, Eayrs and Glass writing in Zuckerman's *The Ovary*: "In primates, the social implications of the continuous sexual receptivity of the female are of considerable interest, for this imposes a pattern on group behavior and organization." They quote Zuckerman, who says: "Both male and female primates are always sexually active, their heterosexual interests providing the bonds that hold them together in permanent bisexual association . . . The primate family consists of male, female or females, and young, but the family of the lower mammals consists only of the female and her young." Eayrs and Glass continue by pointing out that the social function of an almost-continuous state of sexual receptivity fosters stable reproductive structures in which both males and females are participants. They point out that "Out of this, and outside this primary stable reproductive unit, elaborate non-reproductive organizations have grown," i.e., the sublimated apparitions of worldwide human culture. They suggest also that the effect of the sex-hormone play, "a generalized hormonal effect," is increased alertness in the brain as measured by its electrical activity and "an increase in exploratory behavior, thereby creating a potential increase in social and sexual contact." Their suggestion is that people, unlike animals, are largely emancipated from the tyranny of short and abrupt hormone-bursts in the estrus cycle, and are able therefore to form larger and more stable social structures.

Similarly, Paula Weideger, reviewing the position up to 1975, states that the difference between animals that have estrus and those that have menstruation is not simply that the latter have menstrual flows. The big difference is that sexual behavior is not limited to the time of ovulation. She says that: "Within this context it would appear that sexual behavior has become independent of reproductive potential." Eve plucked the menstrual fruit from the estrus tree. The estrus tree— what is this? Estrus implies egg, so it is the egg-tree. In humans, the egg-tree fruits at about monthly intervals. Therefore it is a moon-tree. Many cultures have depicted it as the moon-tree: Persian, Arabian, Turkish, Indian, Assyrian, Phoenician. Why an apple as the fruit Eve plucked and ate? Cut the apple across, and you will see a five-pointed star at its core. If you are a woman, and stretch your arms and legs wide, you make a five-pointed star. A man, with his extra external point, the penis, makes in the same attitude a six-pointed star, the patriarchal star of David. The apple, then, is an emblem of woman's nature. When she plucked the red apple from the estrus tree, Eve separated her sexuality, that is, her whole pentagram nature, her witch-nature, her magic, from the estrus tree. She plucked the menstrual fruit, and gave it to Adam to participate in, consciously eating, from choice not breeding-season. A. E. Waite in *The Holy Kabbalah* infers that, according to Rabbinical lore, it cannot be decided whether the plucking of the fruit is a glory, since it separates us from the animals, or a shame, because it led to Eve's curse of menstruation, that is to say, of sexuality apart from breeding.

As Mary Jane Sherfey points out, the new things that are brought into evolution by the menstrual cycle are caused by a shifting of hormonal action—which we have called "plucking the menstruous fruit"—and these new things are, she confirms: "Interest or continuous sexuality of a greater or lesser degree" and a build-up of the uterine wall in preparation for possible pregnancy. This build-up is so great that it "cannot be reabsorbed whether or not the embryo implants: it must be shed." And this too is like the exposing of a new inner skin as a snake sloughs into newness; mythically, like the plucking of a red apple, or in the Greek myth, the tasting or experiencing of the red pomegranate, womb-shaped fruit of many seeds. The entrance to the underworld, mined out, as it were, by menstruation, opens periodically to Persephone, where she is wedded to no human husband, but to her inner husband, Pluto, the god of the riches of the earth and the body, to whom she must always return, for he is herself.

Dr. Sherfey also gives us the idea that the menstrual cycle could have been involved in the development of androgenic-sensitive structures that enhanced the sexual capacity of the female. Androgens are said to be the hormonal substances that stimulate masculine structures and behavior, and embryology now tells us that the male embryo is to begin with anatomically female until fetal androgens begin to circulate. It appears that progesterone is strongly androgenic, and though during the period itself both progesterone and estrogen levels decline sharply, androgens still circulate. Sherfey associates these facts with "the marked development of the clitoral system" and that of skin erotism in the primates, together with sexual swelling or edema, common before the period. On her theory, this would correspond to the "other dimension" of sexuality at the period, which in a male-oriented society might be seen not as the natural possession of the woman, but be polarized into "unnaturally" masculine behavior, or be seen as the inner "other husband" of the woman in her dreams and visions. What has not been usually acknowledged is that this "other dimension" of sexuality is plainly a guide to extended experience, and might appear as such in dreams and visions. If this were the case, it would be natural that this "other husband" would be projected on the woman's male companion, and this would tend to form his behavior during the course of the evolution of masculine consciousness, which we suggest can be seen as a later development than that of the feminine. The woman not only forms the masculine in her womb from originally feminine structures, but also, on this hypothesis, inspires the man through her "animus," her "other dimension." Of course, this would be a complex feedback process between two individuals, and within a social structure, and it is interesting as it has been pointed out as far back as Freud that what we see as "characteristically masculine" behavior does not obtain through the animal kingdom among males. Perhaps this is another way in which the menstrual rhythm operates in an evolutionary sense. Jung has noted the mutual animus–anima feedback and individuation in the figure known as the "double pelican" known to the alchemists: in the ancient world the pelican was also thought to feed its young on blood it gashed from its own chest. On this view, *masculine consciousness originated with the woman's menstrual period,* as did specifically human sexuality.

Thus a further difference between human and other animals is that most animals have wombs which are comparatively thick-walled and entirely specialized for reproduction. After and during estrus there is a thickening of the womb-wall, but this wall never becomes very thin since it is engaged in and specialized for either pregnancy itself, or for reabsorbing its own growth.

The human womb, as we have said, is not like this. Every month it sheds the lining it has built up for a possible pregnancy, and this shedding leaves the womb-wall raw, like a continuous wound. This means that the womb is intensely sensitive, just as the lining of the eye is sensitive, being lined with brain fibers—the retina—and exposed to light. The uterus is strongly supplied with consciously sensory nerves, but also with many filaments whose function is not clearly known to anatomy, as though these supplied an unconscious component—it is probable that all that the tissues of the body experience is in some manner accessible to our consciousness. The womb, particularly at menstruation, is like a sense organ, raw and very very responsive. It is as though in animals other than the primates the womb is not thus a generalized sense organ, but a structure solely for making children. In the human, or so it appears, the womb has become an organ particularly open to stimulation through the genital organs, and this is why if there is intercourse during menstruation it can be exceptionally deep. Without practice, the rawly open womb may react with pain and irritation; and as it is immensely alive to all that goes on in the individual, if she is told that she is disgusting at that time, it writhes and cramps in anger and disgust. If the truth is told, however, and sexual stimulation is gentle and gradual, sex at menstruation can build up to an experience with completely different dimensions from that of sex at other times of the cycle, as for instance at the child-offering time, the ovulation, a fortnight earlier.

If the sexual experience is not offered, the desire is there still, and the womb seems to cramp in unsuccessful attempts at orgasmic experience, and the result is spasmodic dysmenorrhea. The orgasm cures. An orgasm at this time causes an ejaculation of blood into the vagina from the cervix. Of course this ejaculatory capacity must also give sex at menstruation a different tone of experience. It is interesting in this connection that Epiphanius mentions a lost gospel of Eve, in which Eve is instructed by a man bleeding from the genitals. We believe that this is an emblem of the knowledge of oneself and one's lover to be gained at the period. The man of blood is Eve's "true husband," the Moon. He recalls the Fisher King, guardian of the Grail, who is also wounded in the genitals.

Weideger remarks: "As a menstruating species we are free from the constraint of sexual behavior which is completely determined by the time of ovulation." This is true, providing that we do not follow the tribal taboos which try to keep the woman in her role of continual pregnancy as must have been the condition of primitive species. Menstruation must have emerged as a permanent human possession, when the female *learned not to become pregnant*, and this was her emancipation toward the experience which a sexuality not geared ·to reproduction would give her. How this came about we do not know. There are persistent legends of magic drinks that give wisdom—*soma* from the Moon in India, *lygos* in Greece. One might guess that plants containing steroid substances related to human sex hormones may have been drunk as magic potions, which aborted the uterine lining and gave this new, magical experience of a particular sexual sensitivity, a particular dreamy quality of meditation, an independence from the men, a descent within. Many menstrual taboos of seclusion reflect a woman's desire to be alone at this time with her own body, to the present day. As we know that sexual experience can affect hormone levels, it is possible that a feedback that induced strong menstrual flow was established first by custom, then by evolutionary selection. Could it be that clitoral experience hinted that the womb could be deciduous?

III

Now we must look at the facts that enable us to conjecture that in this state of emancipation, which involved the development of menstruation, the woman's meditations or potions opened her to the effects of the tides, and the sight of the moon. Perhaps she felt the tides in her body, as all water-diviners do. Perhaps she felt the moon-tide as the great 81,000,000,000,000,000,000-ton body passed only a quarter of a million miles overhead, the tidal vibration that is greatest at new moon and solar eclipse when the sun's force and the moon's force are in line and their gravitation is added together (the sun adds some thirty percent to the tidal peaks at new or full moon). Perhaps she felt this tidal vibration in her body as it is felt throughout the whole earth, in her body made of water and solids as the earth is, of spaces of fluid acting over hard bones, and opened herself in a kind of yoga-tuning to this experience. Then in her excitement these fluids at the focus of tautness and sensitivity at her premenstrual time, burst through their membranes in a flood of tidal communion with the moon and its waters, and the blood flowed in excitement and sympathy. We know that there are these tidal peaks and dynamisms in the earth's progress through its month and through its year, like a breathing of the continents, and it has been conjectured by Theodor Schwenk that these times correspond to the great yearly festivals: "All naturally flowing waters have their rhythms perhaps following the course of the day, perhaps keeping time with longer seasonal rhythms . . . Everywhere liquids move in rhythms. Countless rhythms permeate the processes of nature. Not only are the great currents and tides of the oceans subject to the rhythms of the seasons; every lake, every pond, every well with its ground water level has its movements that fluctuate with high and low tide or according to other laws." There is really nothing mystical in this, or in the idea that an enhanced body-consciousness would be capable of perceiving and responding to these tides. Perhaps this is a rationale of the lunar bowl meditations described by E. A. S. Butterworth in his *The Tree at the Navel of the Earth*: descending into the body to perceive the environmental harmonies, and drawing upon their strength.

It actually seems more surprising that the human being is in present times consciously so blind to these influences! There is no doubt at all that they occur. One of the standard books on the subject is Sollberger's *Biological Rhythm Research*.

In this book he summarizes the evidence for the influence on biological organisms of the great natural rhythms, the "synchronizers." He says, for instance, that "In view of the gravitational effect of the moon, the lunar day [24.8 hours] may be as real a period for the living organism as the solar day." The rhythm of the two combine in a particular beat, which will vary through the lunar month. There are two daily tides, and the moon's passage and its tidal effects will travel through the solar day at a different rate at different times of the month. The two will "beat together" once a month.

The lunar tides act on the earth's crust as well as on the waters. The lunar half-day of 12.4 hours makes beats with the twenty-four-hour cycle, forming an approximately half-month period. Big beats in the earth twice a month. It would be surprising if the human body did not feel this through the tides as do the creatures on the seashore. We have the salt of the sea in our blood, in the proportions that obtained there many millions of years ago, when we crawled up the littoral enclosing our own salt self-environment in our bodies. Many sea animals swarm with the lunation, herrings, for instance, eels, and the famous palolo worms. Grunions spawn on the flood tides of full moon. When pilchards were fished from the Cornish coasts, they appeared at the tide-time as a red stain in the sea, perceived by watchers on the cliffs, who signaled to the fishing-boats. It was like watching for the sea's period. The sea floods with light that answers the full moon when the Atlantic fireworm swarms and breeds along the Bermuda coast. Sexual activity at the full moon in the animal kingdom is the rule rather than the exception.

Sollberger remarks that it is a fact that the human menstrual alleged twenty-eight-day period lies between the sidereal month (when the moon returns to the same position among the stars) of twenty-seven and a half days and the synodic month (the time during which it returns to line up with the sun) of twenty-nine and a half days. He will not commit himself on the significance of this, though he notes that the length of certain mammalian cycles could be treated as harmonics of the lunar period, and that the human sexual cycle was possibly once synchronized with the lunar period. A much earlier theory quoted by Havelock Ellis does maintain that the menstrual period originated in the excitement generated during full-moon festivals of aggressive courtship, which were also hunting seasons. This he says originated in the tropics, when one might not hunt during the heat of the day. At the time of this theory, it was not understood that menstruation was distinct from ovulation-time. Malinowski shows the importance of these full-moon festivals in tribal life. Observing such festivals might enhance the monthly rhythm as well as originating in it, in a feedback.

Accordingly, then, Sollberger only goes so far as to say that this lunar coincidence "suggests a connection," and that in the statistical material the information is "usually very noisy and statistical proof difficult." We shall later examine one of the more thoughtful of these accounts.

Where the lunar effect is undoubted, as in nonhuman animals, it is not, apparently, known what the external agent of control is, whether it is the moonlight, the gravitational changes, or other factors. There is a twenty-seven-day solar rotation cycle with a fluctuation of the sun's radiation which could beat out patterns also. However, there are hundreds of examples of exact lunar cycles also being sexual cycles in the lower animals: mayflies, mosquitoes, and algae are involved as well as fish.

But in humans the whole matter has proved difficult to settle statistically one way or the other. There may be many components to the influence, many lunar synchronizers: the length of the period of moonlight, the spectral composition of the light, influence on the ionic composition of the atmosphere, as well as atmospheric and terrestrial tides and geographical position. Is the menstrual rhythm a "genetic memory of an earlier entrainment to the lunar period, though not, any more, phase-locked" or is it purely coincidental? There are *huge* statistics claiming that menstruation is more common at new and full moon, and equally authoritative papers that pooh-pooh the idea.

We ought to summarize the position so far. Menstruation, moon-caused or not, is, without any doubt, involved in primate evolution. This is an entirely respectable zoological position, and up-to-date research supports it. For instance, Beck has recently claimed that studies of apes show evidence that "humans' non-stop libido is an evolutionary adaptation that favored the development of social and economic co-operation in developing hominids" and that "insight" during problem-solving was promoted by sexual receptivity, and not when the hamadryad baboons he was studying were at the one time in their cycle when they do not have sex: the run-up for ovulation. It seemed that the condition for problem-solving was "continuous libido" or sexual brightness—carnal knowledge. It is interesting that Freud echoed this, when he said: "At about the same time as the sexual life of children reaches its first peak, between the ages of three and five, they also begin to show signs of the activity which may be ascribed to the instinct for knowledge or research . . . concentration on an intellectual task and intellectual strain in general produce a concomitant sexual excitation in many young people as well as adults." It is also interesting that the Jewish Kabbalah uses the word "Daath" for *insight*, or knowledge that comes from union of the conscious and unconscious minds, and that this kind of knowledge is affirmed to be a deeply erotic experience.[6] It is interesting also that when we dream, when we are experiencing this form of body-consciousness by contemplating our dreams in REM sleep, there is always concomitant sexual excitement. Contemporary workers believe that the development of the ability to dream had survival value, and assisted in the development of our species.[7] So we have menstruation leading to sexuality leading to dreaming and other inner experience leading to the development of humanity. In the Kabbalah, Daath is said to be the union of God with his Bride, or Sabbath. This is another way of saying the same thing.

Moreover, we have shown that menstrual experience, in both the history of cultures and of our own cultures' languages, has been associated with moon-experience, with the phases and experiences of the moon. Moon and menstrual experience are referred to in language, science, and mythology in terms which suppose them to be linked as the founders of civilizations and mental experience.

IV

What science cannot seem to tell us, however, is whether the woman's menstrual period is *or can be* linked in any but a coincidental manner with the moon's phases. Whether or not there is a relation of effect and cause between the experience in the woman and the phases of the moon in the sky. It is undoubted that the two have been associated in the minds of people all over the world and from the earliest times, but is the connection in any objective sense true, and if it is, what use can we make of this truth? Were the old religions expressive of objective scientific truth as well as of a truth of female experience, psychological truths? Since they were certainly the expression of psychological truths, then they can still perhaps be of intimate use to women today who wish to recover their feminine instincts in a patriarchal secular world.

This boils down to a personal question: if I feel an affinity with the moon, can I trust the feeling to mean anything, or is it just fantasy? If I feel the pull of the tides on me, if I feel that my period is related to the moon's phases, and arrives with the glory of the full moon and the high tide, or with the tide when the moon is hidden so that one can believe it will never come again—and then that thin scythe and sliver is suddenly noticed; if I feel more restless at the full moon than at other times of the month, if I dream more, if I dream of moons, or white horses, or white cats, or magpies, or hares, or other "moon-creatures"—then am I to trust these things, or am I "lunatic"? What does it mean, if the moon attracts me, how can I use it in my life?

The first answer is that if you respond to the moon, then you are in good company. The whole of humanity is behind you, from the earliest time, nearly to the present day. Just as people have enjoyed and responded to the plain light of the sun and felt the confident reality of it warm on their skins, so women in particular have, since the very beginning and even before we were human (for many animals respond to the full moon: cats howl in the street, dogs hunt), responded to the moon's light. It is as though the hard light of the sun divides and discriminates in their actuality objects one from the other; it is like the logical intellect that insists on clear sunlit spaces between ideas or observations; while the moon with her soft light appears to unite everything, like love or intuition. Objects merge one into the other, ghosts and visions walk, daylight decisions and discriminations melt into each other and are reseen in a light that feels rather than states. We need both lights: it is said to be the purpose of Yoga to bring both into the conscious body. As the old alchemists said also: *solve et coagula*; for the work of individuality we must both unite and discriminate. It is perhaps (as Jung hints) characteristically feminine to unite: to be interested in what is complete rather than what is perfect; and characteristic of the man-spirit to separate, to be more interested in what is perfect than what is complete. Moonlight seems to belong to the woman and sunlight to the perfecting patriarch: too much of solar intellect in society, with atomic bomb technology, brighter than a thousand suns, is likely to reduce the world to a dust-ball if unchecked, just as the sun would if there were no nights. Subjective truths change, as humans change, and as the moon changes, are not sun-established, but balance, as the moon balances its aspects in natural rhythm.

And people have used these subjective moon-feelings and

abilities, which may or may not be corroborated by objective science, to structure their lives and to take their experience deeper into their own particular universes. We have seen how the development of the menstrual cycle appears to have been responsible for the establishment of the human universe during the course of evolution. We have also seen how the majority of peoples at all times have responded to the moon as if it held in itself the secret and pattern of that evolutionary change: Goddess, the creatrix. But is there objective evidence that a woman's cycle is actually geared to the moon's cycle?

We must give our short answer to this, and then explain and expand our conclusions. *The evidence is that the woman's cycle is probably naturally related to the moon's cycle, but even if it were not, there are indications that she has the ability so to relate it, if she wishes.*

As Sollberger explained, the statistics are full of noise. We have examined many assertions that the moon's phases are related to the period, and otherwise. In medieval times it was taken for granted that they were, and that women naturally menstruated in the dark of the moon. Aristotle's books were the standard texts, and the statement is to be found there. Further back, in Babylon, the Sabbatu of the moon-goddess was at the full moon, and it was then that she was thought to be menstruating. This was Ishtar, and we shall show that it is *possible* that her colleges of priestesses menstruated in synchrony with each other and in sympathy with the moon. It is almost certain that the moon-colleges of Hera in preclassical Greece were institutions for studying the moon's phases and relating them to the change within one's own body. We shall return to the evidence for the action of the moon's light on the period, and for menstrual synchrony among female colleagues, in the next chapter.

It is possible too that the Sibylline colleges watched their menstrual cycles for the time when they would be "possessed" or in the state of intense menstrual sensitivity that we have noted in these pages, but this sensitivity would be put to use and turned into a creative or political statement. The Sibyls prophesied once a month, and no political action was ever taken even in classical Greece without consultation with the Sibylline oracle. By this token, Apollo, the flaming inner sun, might be integrated as the animus of the bleeding womb and its energies, turned into "mental fire," uterine light. The colleges were originally lunar, and presided over by the Moon-Goddess. As Briffault shows us, originally all shamans that guided early societies were women; Eliade and Carmen Blacker concur. One cannot believe that their shamanism was unrelated to their menstrual periods, particularly as their own statements speak of possession by lunar spirits. Among the Sibyls, the tripod might originally have been a speculum for watching the cervix of the womb for its first seep of blood.

This is a particularly powerful image that we shall return to. One can imagine the effect of a religious system that insisted on the analogy between the phases of one's periods and the phases of the moon. If, then, one was shown with a metal speculum the appearance of things inside the vagina, then the sense of conviction would be remarkable indeed. For, in a sense, every woman can look into herself and see the crescent moon shining there. If you use a speculum, such as is used for inspecting the cervix of the womb, and a mirror and a flashlight, so that you can see for yourself, you will see inside an appearance rather like a globe resting in a crescent, all of which shines and glistens. This is the cervix of the womb, that projects into the vagina whose tissues curve around it and on which it rests: the exact appearance will depend on the time of the month when you look at it, since color, shape, and size vary with the menstrual cycle.

Then the first seep of blood would be a particularly sacred inner moment, particularly combined with a religious teaching. If it happened that by some kind of training, a yogic training or self-hypnosis, or even naturally or by menstrual synchrony, that this event occurred at the new moon, when it rises invisibly with the dawn of the sun, then that would be a powerful inner feeling corresponding to a beautiful outer event. Again, if this event occurred, again at the new moon, in the kind of conjunction that leads to a solar eclipse, then the event would be terrific indeed, and ripe for trance conditions and shamanism. It would be especially potent if it occurred when the new moon and the sun's winter solstice coincided. This was certainly an important Greek Festival, called the "Meeting of Sun and Moon." It happens every nineteen years, and it is the moment at which lunar and solar calendars coincide in Meton's Grand Cycle. It has been said that this meeting of the two lights after voyages is the true subject of Homer's *Odyssey*, and this idea of sun and moon meeting inwardly is certainly also central to Tantric yoga.[8] One can imagine a Festival at which these inner and outer events were caused to coincide.

It is said that the dog-headed ape was sacred to the Egyptians because of its capacity to menstruate exactly at the new moon, and the temples therefore bred them. McClintock quotes a modern opinion that monkeys on the equator menstruate in synchrony with the new moon. The three–four days monthly when the moon does not appear in the night sky, like the days of the full moon, would be considered important taboo days or Sabbaths. These would be times unpropitious for secular work, and potent for magic. There are reports that the Sibyls, just as they allowed temple snakes to lick into their ears to clear them for prophecy, allowed each snake their first seep of blood at the cervix. This intimate and to us almost inconceivable event would have had a religious and probably shumanistic, that is, a creative purpose. Perhaps later it was replaced by blood-sacrifice at the so-called *ompha-los* or navel-stone, which we believe it is more natural to see as the cervix of the earth-mother's womb.

Franz Joseph Gall in the eighteenth century made a study of women's menstruation, and concluded that there were two types of women, those who tended to have their periods on the full moon, and those who tended to have them on the new moon. Gall is best known for "phrenology" but also contributed to the foundation of psychoneurology as a science, particularly in America. Perhaps an individual woman might move from one tidal peak to the other during her life, if his observations were true.

The great Arrhenius at the turn of the century took the cycle-statistics of thousands of women and found in his samples that there was a definite tendency to menstruate on the new moon. Sollberger quotes eight studies, one of which, by Gunn and others, concludes quite definitely that there is no relationship at all of the menstrual cycle to the lunar events. Sollberger himself is unconvinced either way, but sensibly points out that our calendar is organized into weeks, and we have a pronounced weekly cycle of activity in industry and commerce, dying down at the weekend and resuming on Monday. He says one may speculate whether this may be a harmonic of the lunar monthly cycle, or a "spontaneous rhythm entrained by a harmonic of the lunar cycle" for as he counts up the visible effects of the moon's changes one has to conclude and agree that the moon *does* influence biological processes, as it does weather, and it would be surprising if human beings were not affected.[9]

The most convincing recent examination of the question we have read is by Walter and Abraham Menaker. They show that the mean length of the cycle is 29.5 days, which is also the length of the mean synodic month, "providing the data of earlier workers is not carelessly arranged." They also show that the mean duration of pregnancy from last menses is precisely 9.5 synodic lunar months, not the "ten lunar months" of twenty-eight days of the textbooks. In view of this "constellation of coincidences" it seems churlish not to postulate "some connection between these astronomical and biological phenomena."

Moreover, since the mean duration of pregnancy from *conception* is nine synodic lunar months, then it is likely that a child conceived on a given day of the lunar month would be born on a corresponding day nine months later. The common law lunar month of twenty-eight days cannot be used in this computation; it is the exact synodic month of 29.53 days which adds up to the average 266 days of gestation. Most doctors count pregnancy in weeks to avoid confusion.

Accordingly, these workers counted more than 120,000 births during thirteen lunar months. Fewer births occurred on the day of the new moon than on any other day. This is what you would expect on the hypothesis that more women tended to have their periods at this time than another. Full moon days, however, had more births, which is also what you would expect if people tended to ovulate on the full moon.

Gunn *et al.* were critical of existing statistics because of cultural factors, such as Sundays and holidays, and noted that during the time they took, legal holidays had a slight tendency to fall on new moon days. This would affect the statistical drift. Consequently, the Menakers studied 250,000 births at private hospitals with physicians in attendance even on holidays. Once again, the new moon was associated with fewer births (over its three-day period) and the full moon with an increase of them. After a further study of over 250,000 births to determine whether the difference they observed between the two halves of the lunar cycle, new moon half and full moon half, could possibly be due to chance, they concluded that "the difference just noted could occur by chance less than once in 10,000 times." If the studies were combined, then probability against chance was once in 30,000 times. Day fourteen, the full moon, when we hypothesize a likelihood of ovulation occurring, deviated "to an extraordinary extent" above the mean for 112 cycles. However, after all standard statistical corrections are made, guarding against any misinterpretation of the data (the interested reader should look at the original paper, with the remarkable graphs that show with visual impact this rise in births—and hypothetically conceptions—at the full moon), these cautious workers give their conclusions as follows:

> The evidence presented here shows a small but statistically significant synodic lunar (or sun-moon) influence on the human birth-rate, and presumably on the conception rate and, perhaps, on the ovulation rate . . . The peak of conception and probably ovulation appears to occur at full moon or a day before it . . . The lunar cycle of births . . . seems to be a prototype of the human ovulatory or menstrual cycle, with new moon being associated with decreased ovulation (and conception) and increased menstrual bleeding, as suggested by the menstrual studies of Gudd and associates, and full moon with increased ovulation and conception.

This, it must be remembered, was done with New York City births: one of the environments most removed from nature in the world! The lunar influence (if it exists) on human beings in their cities must be rather small, otherwise it would be easier to demonstrate with smaller samples: there are studies with small numbers that do not find these correlations. But the indications point to the synodic lunar month as a kind of module or time unit of human reproduction and prenatal growth.

The study could not be clinched without (a) allowing for environmental differences: whether or not the cities showed these rhythms less or more than, say, seaside towns; (b) studying whether the menstrual cycle actually varied over a statistical average as the synodic month itself varies, which it does by plus or minus six hours. If it was found that the menstrual cycles of a statistical proportion of women varied in the same manner as the synodic month varies, then the matter would be clinched. Perhaps, the Menakers remark, living things follow lunar time to a significant extent, and nonliving things—processes such as the swing of a pendulum or atomic vibrations, such as are used in atomic clocks—

follow a sidereal time. We should not time our living processes by nonliving clocks. The study suggests that there
could be a quantum theory of living processes, with "quanta"
of biological time. It would be more use to us than the
quantum theory that has given us atomic physics. And even
though in city life the lunar influence may look small, "the
course of scientific progress has been greatly influenced by
discoveries of small differences." It was after all the bending
of light through less than one hundred-thousandth of a right
angle that indicated that Einstein's relativity theory would
work in practice. This, incidentally, was determined at the
moment of a solar eclipse.

We have deliberately refrained from mentioning in any
detail the astonishing work of Jonas in Czechoslovakia and
his followers on "astrological birth control" in this country
and America. The reason is that though we know people who
practice his method successfully, numerical information is
difficult to obtain, and the published work in English does
not seem to concern itself with statistical proof. The reader
has to decide from her own practice. Jonas's method says that
if a woman determines the angle of the sun with the moon
that obtained in the heavens at her moment of birth, then she
will know her moment of fertility and ovulation, and can plan
accordingly. Also the sex of her child can be determined by
the position of the sun and moon in relation to this angle
when she conceives. We urge interested people to investigate
this for themselves. Jonas claims a birth-control rate better
than the Pill's.

Art Rosenblum's and Leah Jackson's *The Natural Birth
Control Book* deals principally with Jonas's method, and its
implications. It may be that it is an important way to be in
touch with one's environmental and personal rhythms. A
recent report (*The Guardian,* 19 November 1976) suggests
that it is so, and tells of a Canadian woman, Meredy Benson,
who has been teaching the method in England for some
years. She says that the Pill gave her headaches and depres-

sion, but that after one year of practicing the "astrological" method of natural birth control: "I wasn't pregnant and I felt marvelous. Aside from the fact that it works, I was in tune with my body, and knew what it was doing and when; I knew when my astrological fertility times were coming up and could sense them . . ." There is, according to the article, no scientific evidence to prove this, or theory to explain it, just personal experience. Meredy Benson is aware of the need to collect data, since there are as yet no reliable figures. This is a familiar situation with any study that concerns women's self-determination: scientists do not bother to research, thus ensuring long neglect.

The usual "rhythm" method, that is practiced unsuccessfully by many Catholics, is the measurement of body-temperature, which goes up a little at ovulation. A rhythm can be established and the times to avoid intercourse rather roughly known. An improvement of this time-honored method is being investigated by John Bonnar, Professor of Gynaecology at Rotunda Hospital, Dublin, in which electrical changes on the skin at ovulation-time are detected by means of a simple apparatus. Normally, it is said, the charge is minute, only a few millivolts, but at ovulation it leaps up to roughly half a volt. Long ago, in 1936, Burr and Musselman proposed research on a bioelectrical effect they had measured through the index fingers, that fluctuated rather precisely during the menstrual cycle with the hormone changes. It is very likely that these bioelectrical fields fluctuate with the environmental electrical fields, as Frank Brown, quoted below, points out. But research on them is also still in its infancy.

What of the Pill itself? It is possible that the contraceptive pill, though its cycle is a far from natural one, does not entirely quench one's personal rhythm, but may assist one to establish at least a simulacrum of one. There does not appear to be any substantial research on this at present, but we have noticed that characteristic ovulation-dreams do not necessarily disappear from the pill's cycle, though ovulation itself is suppressed. There may be a psychological rhythm that is maintained or even entrained by the use of the pill, even though a person on it neither ovulates nor, according to some doctors, menstruates properly. Karen Paige has shown that the type of pill used may influence the emotional rhythm. Again, whatever the status of this particular kind of menstruation, the inner menstrual experience is not necessarily denatured.

There are reports from individual women that though taking the Pill gives them the boost of added sexual confidence, after that they tend to worry about not ovulating or menstruating naturally. Some women find that coming off the Pill gives them an impression that they were previously somewhat muted by the evenness of the Pill's influence. One conclusion that can be drawn is that if a woman's cycle starts out in a very irregular and unpredictable way, and if this worries, then the Pill can help give her confidence. Later on, with this confidence, that will include sexual experience, she may decide to become more self-determining, off the Pill.

The contraceptive pill is still something of an unknown quantity—and was of course invented out of a social situation which has diminished woman's access to her natural rhythms, while appearing to increase her self-determination. Coming out of a situation which had possibly created its need, it seemed a step forward. However, there is evidence that in some women their cycles do not return when they are off the Pill. Nor is it a panacea for either dysmenorrhea or PMT. The effect of the contraceptive pill on the natural interplay of hormones must be gross. It used to be said of the condom worn by the male for contraception that it is "like playing the piano in gloves." For a woman, the Pill may be like retuning her "hormone orchestra"—with a tone-deaf leader.

So if a person feels that she has a moon-affinity, then she should certainly investigate it, as she may indeed be timed by this, or another, natural clock, and may have enough body-consciousness to feel it without special study or training, just her inbuilt intuitions. Indeed, one may see the menstrual cycle as an opportunity of contacting natural energies.

V

The extraordinary work in zoology on animal "biological clocks" has as yet scarcely been applied to humans. Properly controlled experiments have been applied to the influence of the moon on the natural flow of small currents on trees, but it is only in the "fringe" sciences that this kind of observation has been applied to human conditions. There is, for instance, a work called "Moon and Plant" which purports to show that mistletoe—according to Frazer, "The Golden Bough"—cures cancerous conditions when it is collected at certain lunar times, and paper chromatography shows up a lunar variation in the composition of the mistletoe sap. The doyen of biological clock research, Dr. Frank Brown, right at the beginning of his work was able to show that oysters removed from their native beds opened just at the time when the tide was passing over those beds, though they were hundreds of miles away. After a while the oysters regeared themselves so that they were opening at the time of the passage of the moon overhead in the laboratory, though they were in tanks with hardly any tidal action. These oysters saw the moon, with their bodies.

This is not "fringe science," but proper experimentation. There are many examples of these "mysterious senses" in animals—bird migration, for instance, which may depend on the bird being able to sense the earth's magnetic flux.[10] Frank Brown (1972) has this to say about the moon's influence: ". . . information concerning the synodic month is steadily available as fluctuations in the atmospheric electromagnetic fields . . . the rhythmic physical environment steadily contributing to the internal environment of the organism. No clear boundary exists between the organism's metabolically maintained electromagnetic fields and those of its geophysical environment." The direction of evolution of the human species has been toward independence of the environment. But now, a measure of that having been achieved, is perhaps the time to learn to tune in on environmental rhythms at choice. The Menakers' work seem to suggest that the body of the pregnant mother can, apparently, "see" the moon passing overhead. Michel Gauquelin's work using statistical methods appears to show that people's eventual professions are linked with whatever planet is rising at their births: doctors and scientists when Mars is rising, soldiers and politicians with a rising Jupiter, and so on. The authenticity of this work is now generally accepted, though there is no explanation in orthodox terms. The facts are simply there.[11]

Giorgio Piccardi, a scientist quoted by Gauquelin, wrote: "We are powerless in face of external phenomena. We cannot prevent very-low-frequency electromagnetic waves from piercing through the walls of our laboratories, factories, homes, and bodies." No doubt we screen ourselves or select the influences to which we respond by our society, our customs, and our habits of attention from the influx of these "great synchronizers." But we can open ourselves consciously to unconventional influences, and the most immediate natural rhythm which is sensitive to all discernible influences, from male deprecation to excitement at travel or a wedding, is the menstrual cycle. The womb and its nervous system is the receiver of so much influential information on so many unexplored wavebands that investigation of the cycle will surely bring surprises.

Gauquelin's hypothesis of the possible means of lunar influence comes from the work of Piccardi and others that shows that the structure of water, a crystal lattice, is actually altered by the passing of the moon overhead. This can be measured statistically in the laboratory by the alternation in speed of certain chemical reactions, repeated in long series. If we consider that we are two-thirds this crystalline pattern of water ourselves, it would be surprising if we did not pick up from our body some conscious trace of these events, if we elect to tune into them. In this sense, the water in our bodies can be said to "see" the moon. Water-divining must surely be a sensitivity to patterns of water in the neighborhood of the diviner perceived through alterations it makes in the patterns of his or her own body. Water-divining is a proved fact, both in the laboratory, and by the existence of professional diviners who earn their livings by finding water for commercial concerns.

Some recent Czech workers quoted by Gay Gaer Luce have found in a study of 800 girls that the menstrual periods usually began between four and six o'clock in the morning, with fewer between eight in the morning and noon, and still fewer in afternoon or evening. The indications are that healthy childbirths are timed roughly in the same way, so that the timing and regularity of menstruation may be related to the timing of labor and delivery. It is possible that the time-structure of healthy menstruation may be related to the potential ease of delivery of children.

Edmond Dewan is another distinguished worker in biological rhythms, who is an exception in that he has extended his work to practical suggestions for people who wish to regularize their periods. This is exciting work, which we have found is actually useful, or at least worth trying, for individual women.

Dewan began his work by shining light on marine worms in the laboratory in an attempt artificially to synchronize their sexual cycles with the moon-cycle, and he found that they would so synchronize. Then in 1965 he asked a young woman with a history of irregular menstrual cycles to sleep with the light on during the fourteenth, fifteenth, and sixteenth days of her cycle: the time when ovulation would be expected, in the hope that indirect lighting like the moon's, reflected from walls and ceilings, would promote ovulation. Indeed, the cycle shortened to twenty-nine days. Another woman found that she could distinguish the time of her ovulation after the treatment by a slight pain in the fourteenth night. Dewan's work is very simple to repeat, and we have found ourselves in two cases of irregularity that it had the desired result. One of our subjects used moonlight of the full moon, as the weather was clear.

Dewan's work has been repeated by a clinic in Boston with excellent, but not invariably successful, results. The samples are as yet small, but the possibility is evidentially there. We believe that when a moon-religion operated, that it is likely that this "Dewan effect" was used practically to entrain the cycle to the Moon, to point the analogy both for religious reasons, and for all the practical advantages that come from physical self-knowledge. Great feminine mental power may also have been the result. There may be a survival of this practice in modern witchcraft, in the ceremony called "Bringing Down the Moon," which may have this practical and literal meaning.

Concerning light generally, it is probably "the most important exteroceptive signaling or controlling mechanism to which man and other animals are exposed." There is evidence that constant light increases, via the hypothalamus and pituitary, FSH levels (follicle-stimulating hormone) in experimental laboratory animals, so this "Dewan effect" would not be inconsonant with known mechanisms. Curiously enough, the pineal gland appears to be implicated. This gland is thought to affect sexual development: in its absence people may become sexually mature while they are still young children. It has been postulated that the pineal gland in animals reacts to seasonal light-changes and thereby regulates reproductive development, and there is good evidence that this is so. The interesting thing here is that the pineal— which is like a small pine cone buried deep in the brain—has always been referred to in occult science as the "third eye." Descartes thought it the seat of the soul. In modern times Stan Gooch has made a scientific case for regarding the pineal as the eye-mechanism of the older part of the brain, which is a set of structures anatomically distinct from the "new brain." The new brain is a proliferation of cerebral cortex in human beings that has folded over these older structures. In some lizards and birds, this pineal eye can be shown to react to light shone on the top of the skulls.

Gooch thinks that the pineal is indeed the "third eye," and that it is responsible for turning sensory input from the body into visual images, such as those we see in dreams and recount in folklore. Just as our visible eyes obtain visual information from the outer world, so does our invisible third eye, the pineal, convert into visual images experiences from within the body. This argument is supported by painstaking evidence.

If we put the two notions together: that the pineal is the eye of the body, and that it regulates sexual maturity, then we have a fascinating hypothesis whereby one can imagine "seeing" sexual rhythms. Moreover, that sexual fantasy and vision can have objective and verifiable meaning. To elect to "see" such events could be to increase their influence. Again, since the body has many sensory channels the data of which does not ordinarily appear to enter consciousness, perhaps the channel by which such information does so enter is the dream or vision. So in this sense the body may "see" and respond to the moon's phases, among many other subliminal seeings. This may be the mechanism by which sensitive people like clairvoyants, mind-readers, or shamans obtain their information, or talented diagnosticians obtain their intuitions. It may be that the events of the menstrual period, especially by suitable training, can be "seen" in this manner, and that the body's inner information is more available at some times of the cycle than at others. It has been shown that the external senses: sight, color-vision, hearing, smell, all decline at menstruation, and we have shown that the body's interior sensations correspondingly increase. Perhaps for a full knowledge of this interior information the channel is by

symbols and images experienced in "hysteria" or trance or
deep meditation particularly during the period itself. Perhaps this is the reason for the universal customs of menstrual
seclusion: to enable the woman to draw upon this information.

One footnote to the scientific work is that Japanese workers quoted by Gay Gaer Luce have shown, by painting the
heads of quail with pigment that sent green light into the
skulls of some birds, orange light into those of others, that
the orange-painted birds developed sexually, but the green-
painted ones did not! Red has always been considered the
color of life, the whore's color, the Babylonian color, ever
since the cavemen painted the bones of the dead with red
ochre, it is thought in token of the hoped-for resurrection. It
has been pointed out that though it is known that light has a
powerful effect on many metabolic functions, at present we
use it haphazardly. One scientist who has been concerned in
pineal research, Richard Wurtman, predicted that "light
would someday be considered as potent as any drug, and that
we would use both wavelength and timing deliberately," says
Luce. Our own submission will be that it is at least worth a
hypothesis that people in past ages, particularly women, did
so: not only with ritual colors and lighting in their ceremonies
and psychodramas, but very directly by training people's
sensitivity to the moon, and allowing it to exercise its known
potency on their sexual lives. The facts, we believe, are being
rediscovered now, and await their reapplication.

VI

This reapplication could be by some form of biofeedback
training. "Biofeedback" is the name for any technique,
whether assisted by gadgets or not, of perceiving some event
in the body that is signaled in some manner not normally
noticed, and by "feeding back" an amplified signal, increasing
one's sensitivity to this event and one's control of it.

Thus, when we think or experience we have patterns of

slight electrical changes chasing each other in waves all over our scalps, from the brain inside, and indeed a kind of electrical skin-talk going on all the time over our bodies. If we are tense, it has one kind of pattern; if we are relaxed, another. So we can find our way to relaxation by observing by means of a gadget whether our skin is tense electrically, and whether, for example, certain relaxing thoughts or symbolic images improve the picture. If they do, we can pursue them, and *increase the pattern on our skins which relaxes which increases the pattern which increases the relaxation, etc.* This is feedback but not howlback.

When we pick up these wave-forms from the scalp, we find that one of the slower rhythms called "alpha-rhythm" starts up with closed eyes and relaxation. We do not directly feel this rhythm, but an electroencephalogram and electrodes attached to our scalp will pick it up and turn it through an amplifier and speaker into a sound. If by meditation we produce more of this amplified sound, we know we are going the right way to relaxation. Eventually the sound itself produces the relaxation. Eventually we do not even need the sound-image. Merely the thought of it will produce alpha-rhythm on the external meters and relaxation and reverie inwardly, just as though one were using a mantra for meditation. In due course the mere intention to relax will produce these results.

So, whether or not our wombs are or ever were naturally entrained to the moon's phases, it is possible that by introducing a rhythm of moon-lighted nights into the month we can help our wombs "notice," as it were, any natural rhythm it might possess of this order. If they exist, then by noticing them, they may gather conviction, as it were, and a consciously experienced cycle of regular rhythm can result. Since this has been shown to happen in modern times at least among some women, it helps us guess some of the reasons for the ancients' interest in the processes of moonlight. We shall offer some more historical evidence for this view in the next chapter.

It has also been shown in modern times that there is a rhythm of change of electrical potential over the skin, and between head and body, that varies with the menstrual cycle. So there is no reason why a woman should not, if she wishes, pick up her regular rhythm by using feedback with a skin-resistance monitor, sometimes called a relaxometer. If we notice such a change beginning to happen, then we can go with it: the instrument merely observes and amplifies a change that with practice we can detect by our own means, and thus become more responsive to our body's rhythms. Thus Barbara Brown in her book on biofeedback remarks: "If there were a simple way for women to monitor one of the physiologic activities of the body that accompany the varying amounts of female hormone released during the estrus cycle (such as monitoring skin-talk or even body temperature, and learning to control it), then there may be the possibility that learning to control these slow monthly rhythms might lead to a natural and simplified method for birth control. This possibility may not be such a long shot as it seems at first glance."

One of the simplest ways of monitoring such changes is, we believe, not only to train one's awareness of body-sensations, but also to dream experience which, if we are right, reflects and images actual knowledge: of bodily processes as well as memories and mental imprints that may go back to the earliest times. This kind of knowledge needs development.

There is also another simple way of inquiring after and establishing these rhythms, and that is by the techniques sometimes known as "autohypnosis," "autogenic training," "patterned relaxation," or "meditation." It is sometimes said that "meditation" differs from these other procedures in that a "command" or "suggestion" is introduced into the so-called hypnotic state. However, meditation is usually *about* something and whether that something is a sound-pattern or mantra or a god-image, it is still an organizing "suggestion."

We should not be scared by the word "hypnosis" if it conjures up pictures of Svengali-like compulsion. This is not it at all. The important point is that the practitioner—one may need an external hypnotist at first to show one what it feels like—merely calls up a capacity which everyone possesses. And this is a very familiar and desirable capacity. It is the ability to spend time in that moment between sleep and· waking when the body is blissfully relaxed, when images arise of their own accord, and when words become pictures and sounds images. At some time or another everybody has had this pleasing experience as they drift off to sleep, or as they are waking up. The images and feelings that come are sometimes called "hypnagogic" or "hypnopompic." The word "hypnosis" itself merely means sleep, and by giving it an overspecialized application, we have restricted our access to an important means of communication between mind and body.

In this state, suggestions given by the mind to the body can have an extraordinary influence. Bad habits may be broken, phobias cured, psychosomatic complaints may disappear, dangerous blood-pressure may be reduced. In deep trance, the subject is not conscious, but in the light and medium trance states, which is what most people can reach in auto-hypnosis, consciousness is enhanced to include profound and delightful body-consciousness. One slight danger is that one may slip into deep trance and remain asleep—but one usually wakes naturally from this without intervention, and anyway one can introduce a suggestion not to slip off like this. The best safeguard is to get training and advice from a qualified hypnotherapist. The other danger is that a powerful suggestion may mask symptoms of illness. The important safeguard here is that one is trying to listen to oneself as well as to command, and one must notice if there are things wrong, and not wish them away, but rather assess them. If there are any signs of illness, then of course one must check with one's medical practitioner.

Menstrual distress in many of its forms is one of the conditions best alleviated in the "hypnotic trance." "Surprisingly effective," said the *BMJ* in one of its leaders summarizing recent work. Eysenck's summary agrees, and so do Kroger and Freed. Is this fact, that hypnosis is one of the best treatments for the dysmenorrheas, really surprising? The feminine body-mind is a sensitive unity and menstruation is among its most significant rhythms. It would be surprising if a cooperative reverie between mind and body could not be established when it is known that such a reverie has strong physiological effects. Once the meaning and value of the menstruation has been reestablished in a person's mind, then by the use of such a reverie, and perhaps with the help also of such strong images of meaning as this book may provide, then a new relationship with oneself may be established.

VII

You can look upon hypnosis as a biofeedback procedure also. The relaxation and then the reverie give you practice in assessing and exploring the sensations of the body. One may "tune into" and turn up to a fuller volume, if one wishes, whatever is happening within. It is a form of concentration which is more like a lover's caress than anything else, and just as a caress will tune one into any part of the body, so will these practiced reveries. If one wishes the body to behave in a certain way, for the period to come, for example, one will signal a strong image of this event. The body will respond to the image with a memory of the sensation of the event, at first perhaps faint. The relaxed mind will notice this sensation, which will increase the strength of its image, which will increase the sensation, which will strengthen the image, and so on, in positive feedback. This is no longer "howlback" though it can be "purrback." With practice, one can pick up what the body wants, in this way, and one's natural images; one can request, and the request be granted. If in past ages the moon's phases were studied as a powerful image of the woman's changes, and the analogy of the "inner moon," the cervix, were taken, then these would be potent reinforcing ideas for hypnotic reverie—but why, except for religious prejudice, should we call this "hypnosis"? In such moon-cults—if they did in fact exist as we have suggested, and there is more evidence to come—this would be called "meditation" or even "prayer." Whether they did ever exist or not, they can exist now, if they seem suitable: a woman who combines the practice of disciplined imagination with reverie with the "Dewan effect" of increased indirect lighting at the time of her anticipated ovulation (moonlight or shaded lamplight on walls or ceiling) will be unlikely to suffer from functional menstrual distress, and her self-awareness and individual power are likely to develop remarkably.[12]

We must again note in passing the analogy with natural childbirth: Erna Wright in fact says that the deep inner concentration with which one handles contractions in the first stage of labor is more like "prayer" than anything else, and should not be disturbed by doctor or nurse. In the "fourth-level" breathing, natural rhythmical breath is restored after the patterned breaths of the other levels, by a practice sometimes called "dissociation," which is concentration on a potent and familiar mental image—a rhyme, a picture, a mandala. This takes up the mind harmoniously so that the body can work in its natural way. There is no difference in kind between this and what we have been suggesting, and women trained in natural childbirth will find entry into disciplined reverie as natural as it always was in a less fraught age, and their breathing an appropriate relaxation technique. We emphasize again that we are suggesting natural proce-dures leading to a natural result, one which many people will have discovered for themselves whether to handle their menstrual distress or for another purpose. Natural childbirth techniques on the one hand; but we must not forget techniques of sexual relaxation and postcoital reverie. Reveries in enhanced body-consciousness after one's sexual intercourse are probably the deepest of all—with second stage labor possibly the only exception, when the woman is overwhelmingly "suggestible"—and what is called "sexual magic" is often no other than introducing images into such a reverie.

VIII

The procedures are no more in essence than what we have described above: perfectly natural, but involving the imagination. The more trained and precise the imagination, trained whether by the practice or perusal of art, or by some religious or meditative procedure, then the more effective this biofeedback or hypnotic procedure. In fact, the hypnotist is a kind of poet. But one should not use the word "hypnotic" since that to the popular mind implies a kind of stunned repose, Svengali presiding. Our society, having neglected such natural techniques, has no real words for this, any more than they have a humane word for "menstruation": only the medical term or the loaded words like "curse." Instead of "hypnosis" one should say "directed reverie," "psychosynthesis," "contemplation," "daydream," "creative visualization," "active imagination," "symbolic manipulation," or some word not yet coined. Such a word should perhaps combine the two ideas "body" and "prayer"—ideas which are to our age such complete and absolute opposites. Body-prayer.

Bernard Gindes in his book remarks: "Imagination is the integrating factor which welds belief and expectation into an irresistible force." And: "Every organ of the body seems to respond to a certain colloquial language." In the section on "Menstrual Conditions" Gindes is confident of the benefit of these procedures with any state of irregularity or pain in the cycle, provided a physical examination has been given to ensure that the hypnosis does not interfere with any possible pregnancy or cover up any physical abnormality. Moreover he says: "Some sexually-adjusted women who are free of inner fears and complexes concerning the state find that the menstrual period brings them increased mental power and sensitivity. They so arrange their lives as to ease down on physical activities at that time, using the stimulated mind for reading, writing, letters, or study. I have one patient, a motion picture actress, who reserves this period for memorization of scripts in their entirety instead of the customary piecemeal preparations through the month for 'morning scenes.' When instituting suggestions, this possibility should be kept in mind, that the patient, instead of being negatively free of pain, can learn to use and enjoy all the days of each month."

One of the most distinguished doctors working in the field of hypnosis is the American Milton H. Erickson. Among his remarkable publications is his 1960 paper describing the case histories of three women trained in "autohypnosis" or "autogenic" techniques. It consists of "three separate clinical accounts of an intentional purposeful interference with the menstrual cycle." Two of the women deliberately employed hypnotic experience to effect special personal purposes, one to switch her period on to repel a man she disliked; another to stop it so she could do her job as a model; a third to simulate pregnancy and to punish herself for a sexual misdemeanor, as she saw it, bringing her period on when she felt she had been punished enough. There are a few case histories in the scanty psychoanalytic literature on menstruation in which it is shown that the patients are using their periods to manipulate themselves or their analysts: notably the sexually gifted woman described by Silbermann who used her period to gain lovers and pass frontier guards. In one of the "Studies in Hysteria" a woman's period, under Freud's hypnosis, was set like a watch at twenty-eight days. But "hypnotic" techniques when properly applied are a means for going inward with one's self-possession reasonably intact.

Indeed, analytical techniques have this characteristic also: Jung's "active imagination" and Assagioli's "psychosynthesis" are based on the natural abilities of reverie that we have been describing—the therapeutic and self-developmental use of imaginative play. Most techniques of psychoanalysis, using as they do dream and reverie, can be seen in terms of feedback of traditional or newly discovered symbols. The analyst discerns an image important to the patient in dream or free-association material, and feeds it back by dwelling on and interpreting it. The psyche of the patient digests the image, and, if it is important, it will return in developed form in new material, with probably an accompanying insight or some other development in the situation. The psyche will in good conditions take up whatever competent language is presented to it: that is why with a Freudian you get Freudian dreams and with a Jungian, Jungian ones. There is as yet hardly offered a competent language for the feminine psyche to speak of its menstruation.

Hartland's book on medical hypnosis also shows how menstruation can often be induced or arrested by hypnotic suggestion, and suggests its use in functional uterine bleeding, amenorrhea, and functional dysmenorrhea, and stresses the value of starting the treatment of all menstrual disorders with the standard ego-strengthening procedures. This is quite a starchy medical book, in our opinion, so we wonder quite what direction a male doctor prefers the woman's ego strengthened. On p. 196 the writer says the procedures are intended to restore the patient's confidence in "himself." In the case of a powerful woman patient, this could mean strengthening of the doctor's ego in competition! Ambrose and Newbold's *Handbook* describes the "control of menstruation" by their methods of hypnosis, and gives case histories of the cures of menstrual disorders. What is important to realize in reading these books is that for the ordinary person, all these techniques of "directed reverie" can be exercised on oneself, by oneself, with practice and a suitable introduction to the techniques by one experienced in them. In other words, it looks as though every woman under normal conditions can be mistress of her cycle, providing she accepts it as a friend. In fact, according to Gerald Massey, "The Woman's Friend" is the oldest term for the menstrual period in all languages. To "make a friend of the Goddess" is to say that one is "making a friend" of one's womb inwardly—for all the traditional Goddess-names, as we have reported, mean at root, "womb" or "vulva"—and making a friend of the outward rhythms and tides also, if they happen to correspond with one's own, or rouse one's emotions in this way. This is simply an endeavor to harmonize oneself with nature—hardly an outrageous desire—and is evidently a possibility. A kind of natural magic of response, uniting inner and outer.

IX

We cannot tell whether these reports of ancient women-religions full of knowledge are fact or fantasy, though we examine the factual basis more closely in our next chapter. What we can be sure of is that in so far as it corresponds to external fact, or evokes objective realities, then the fantasy— if that is what it is—is useful. It is the competent language of the psyche, and the inner language for woman's experience has been neglected and must again be developed.

As far as the moon-fables used in such cults are concerned, we have seen that they are, at the least, an effective analogy, and they may correspond to objective environmental reality: there is evidence, but no proof. However that may be, they are surely *effective* analogies, since by their means a woman may find the symbolic language that can develop her nature. There is evidence that her nature may respond to natural environmental rhythms: in that case, she is the interpreter of these rhythms to human society, which is alienated without them.

There is a Slav fairy tale in which the Prince Redeemer is obliged to answer correctly six riddles posed to him by the Princess. The fifth of these is: "I existed before the creation of Adam. I am always changing in succession the two colors of my dress. Thousands of years have gone by, but I have remained unaltered both in color and form."[13] Briffault tells us that the Virgin Mary, identified with the moon, was asserted to have created the world. Said St. Alphonse: "At the command of Mary all obey, even God." In Portugal the moon is called "Mother of God," in parts of France "Notre Dame."[14] We have shown a possibility that if the menstrual period developed in response to the moon's rhythm, then there is a factual basis for saying that the moon created human society through the evolution of the menstrual period, and this could have happened through woman's conscious acquiescence in the tidal feelings produced by the moon: "My soul magnifies the Lord." Briffault describes the moon as Lord of the Ladies— says the first measurement of time was menstrual time. If menstruation follows the moon, if the tidal rhythm of the moon established the menstrual rhythm, then the moon was the creatrix. And if the menstrual rhythm has nothing to do with the moon's rhythm, then this does not affect the essence of the argument, since the moon and its Goddesses have always at all times and in all cultures been regarded as the image par excellence through which a woman may strengthen her sense of her own nature. Whether it may or should do so again depends on the testimony and experience of modern woman. As Esther Harding says: "Yet when she recognizes that this all-powerful fate is *not* wielded by some outside power, by an inaccessible deity of the moon, but is instead the expression of the essential nature of her own being, she will feel very differently about it. For the rhythmic life within her is determinant of her own life, while her conscious wishes and impulses do not necessarily coincide with her deepest needs . . . For woman, at all events, the moon goddess that is, the feminine principle within her, plays a hand and she usually holds the trump cards." Or as Paula Weideger remarks: "Ishtar . . . Could I invoke her name? Certainly to do so is to acknowledge the real existence of internal changes of feeling and to acknowledge, as well, certain limitations of the 'mind.'"

When we are musing on the evolutionary origins of human society, we could also go back far before the creation of the human and monkey sexual cycle. We could go back to the first days of creation when the earth was wrapped in cloud, and its surface concealed by the boiling vapors raised by the sun. It is said that the reactions that started life in the warm lagoons where protoplasm grew from a "primordial soup" would never have started had the moon in its tidal circling not cleared pathways in the clouds for radiation to reach the earth's surface. It is remarkable that the only planet in the solar system that has on it a life-form we can recognize as such is our own earth; and it is also the only planet in the solar system which has a moon of such effective dimensions, so that it is almost like a double-planet. Then again, in ancient legend, the moon was called "the funnel of the earth," and it was believed that if the moon were to vanish, all mental activity on earth would cease.[15]

Five Did the Ancients Have Wisdom?

Freud was a great man. He was a great *man*, however. And he was great enough to admit that in the history of the individual everything connected with the mother was "so elusive, lost in a past so dim and shadowy, so hard to resuscitate, that it seemed as though it had undergone some specially inexorable repression." Here he is talking of the woman's past, in the 1931 essay on "Female Sexuality." He knows there is something "pre-Oedipal," that is, before the intervention of the father, that is at the root of experience and of evolution, and that this factor is specifically "maternal" and of the woman. One of these specifically maternal influences was thought by Otto Rank to be the influence of the manner of a person's birth on their lives: the birth-trauma. Rank was, by his psychoanalytic colleagues, believed psychotic to have thought up such a thing. But the other specifically feminine influence that was around these Viennese doctors all the time they were talking and writing, and growing up, was not noticed by them. And this was the effect of the changes of the menstrual cycle.

Our question is, whether any past ages were wiser. In meeting this query, we must expect to find many traces of that "specially inexorable repression" with which man has treated feminine experience, and worsened the lot of women.

It is in the Greek colleges of Hera that we find some initial clues. In discussing them, perhaps we can ask the reader to recall what was shown in the previous chapter about moon-colleges: that there is a strong presumption in any womanly cult that menstruation will be a feature of interest, that it will be linked with fertility on earth on the one hand, and the phases of the moon in the sky on the other. That there is good evidence from many quarters that the majority of cultures find the situation of a full-moon festival a great stimulator of sexuality, and that there is good reason for assuming at the very least that the moon, to somebody who is open to its doctrine, is a very powerful "hypnotic" image indeed to which a woman by choice or training may link her menstrual cycle. In addition modern work shows that the moon's light, or any other indirect nighttime lighting at midcycle, may actually stimulate ovulation physiologically.

With these linked ideas in mind, what evidence is there that these capacities have actually been used in the past, as they may be used in the future?

The name "Hera" means "Womb." If, as has sometimes been said, "Hera" means "Mistress," this is because she gives the laws, and the women's laws are the ways of the womb. "Thesmophoria," the great Greek women's fertility festival, means "law-bearing." These laws include *las reglas*, or the "way of all women," the menstrual rhythm. A reasonable derivation from Hesiod and Homer of the name "Hera" is "womb," and this interpretation is backed by the fact that she is called *panton genethla*, "origin of all things," which is the "womb." The great Goddess's name in most cultures in derivation means "womb" or "vulva": the Goddess is Gene-trix. The womb gives birth, and it also menstruates.

"Astarte" or "Ashtaroth" means "womb," or "that which issues from the womb." "Pallas Athena" means literally "Vulva-vulva." The name of the Greek Goddess of childbirth is Eileithyia, and her name means "fluid of generation" which in this context is "menses," which was thought to enter into the composition of the child and the milk.

The original home, or dwelling-place, was the womb of the woman, so cities may be called by the name of a goddess. Thus, the capital city of the ancient land of Og was called "Ashtaroth-Qarnaim" which means "Womb of the Two Horns," since the human (and divine) womb is two-horned with its Fallopian tubes. It is the emblem of fertility and containment, and the sacred bucranium or ox-head decorating Greek and Roman temples was a womb-emblem. A *locality* is where you lie in childbed (Gk. lokhos) and produce the child and the magical lochial blood of childbirth: the blood of the person's first place of arrival. The Queen is *cwen* or wife with the *quim*, which is a *combe* or *cwm*, the *gune* (woman) is a goddess when she is *gana* and *jani* (woman) with a *yoni*, or cunt. *Gens* is wife, as in generation, or "great tribe." This is all natural, as all human beings are born from a womb, and without this first "magic" there would be no consciousness and therefore no human religion, or anything else. So Hera's *womb* is literally *panton genethla*.[1]

The Heraion, the temple of Hera, the cunt-place, was for centuries in Ancient Greece "the sanctuary of the whole country, originally in the same way as the temple of Jerusalem, for instance, was a unique temple of Israel," says Carl Kerényi. When you have an altar, you have to have a facing-partner: that is, an emblem of the deity whose rites are celebrated at this place. On the Christian altar this is a crucifix. A Poseidon altar would have the sea "in its incalculable mobility." An altar of Helios might have the sun's ecliptic. The terrace of the Argive Heraion was an immense cult stage for viewing the moon, and Hera herself was a single goddess in "three phases." Her myth in later times, as in Homer, is associated with Hera's "sulks," but in the true cult sense this was a descent of Hera into the underworld, the low point (or, as we might say, PMT) being associated with the new moon. Hera is sometimes shown with a pomegranate, the red fruit full of seeds which associates her with the Queen of the Underworld, Persephone. Pausanias says the story of the pomegranate is "rather secret." These goddesses guided through the underworld. Prosymne is the new moon, and Prosymnos was Dionysos' guide to the underworld, as, according to Graves, Eurydice was the guide of Orpheus. Prosymne was Demeter's epithet, the earth-mother in her underworld aspect. The Goddess Prosymna was summoned in the name of the new moon when it lingered in the darkness. In Athens, Pallas Athena ("Vulva-vulva") was reborn with the new moon, just as Hera was reborn from a bath in which she had her virginity restored, in the same manner as the womb is restored after the menstruation for a fresh cycle, with a fresh womb-lining. There was a ceremony of the washing of Athena's "laundry." In the Hera cult there would similarly be a procession of "freed" women after the purification of a wooden figure of the goddess, shortly after the new moon had appeared, following "the low point of Hera's periodic being."

It is possible that the original temple on the Acropolis at Athens belonged to such a cult. Hera was worshipped in her "great part-secret, part-public cult . . . in her transformations according to the Moon's phases" and so was Athena. That is to say, that the Acropolis was dedicated to Vulva. This is as shocking as supposing that where St. Paul's great dome now stands in London was originally the site of moon-worship, and that the name "London" was originally "Laundon" in Celtic, or Moon-Town. There is, however, evidence for this also.[2]

Hera's three phase names were: virgin "Pais"; "Teleia," as wife of Zeus; and "Chera" or widow, after falling out with Zeus. There is a tradition that as Parthenos or Pais, "virgin," and "girl" she was not without a man, but enjoyed "secret love-making" with her brother-husband, and these dark nuptials would have taken place at the new moon, when the moon cannot be seen because it is in conjunction with Zeus, the "bright sky."

"Widowhood" in its literal meaning cannot be justifiably applied to the wife of an immortal god, so we should take its meaning in the most natural sense, as menstruation, says Kerényi, particularly as the Romans "openly assigned the periodicity measured by the lunar month to the woman's nature—*provinciam fluorum menstrorum*—of their Juno" who corresponds to the Greek Hera. They name her "Ionu Fluonia" and speak of her menstrual seclusion and the "Abstinence of Jupiter," *castus Iovis*, which would be the "widowhood"—though no doubt there was "secret love-making" at this special time also.

That the periodicity of Greek women corresponded with the moon's phases, or was believed to so correspond, is attested by Aristotle, Empedokles, and Diokles. The period was known as the "katamenia," or the "monthly going-down." Kore, the lost daughter of Demeter, experienced a Kathodos or going down, and an Anodos or return, and the showing in cult spectacle of this was the basis for the Eleusinian Mysteries, which were originally monthly, and for the women.[3] We shall return to Eleusis later. There exist beautiful anodos-vases, showing the return of the earth-mother via an omphalos, or birth-cone, which is properly a representation of the cervix of the womb; with fruits and flowers, and a child emerging from a horn of plenty.

It is interesting in this question as to whether the periods were synchronized by training or some other means, that weddings in a given city could be held on a definite predetermined day. The pattern of rite would be that the brides were all *parthenos*, which would not necessarily mean that they were without sexual experience, but would mean that they had come from their purification bath of the new moon, that is, they had their period and were "newly virgin" once more. In fact, the original meaning of "virgin"[4] had the sense of a "woman belonging to herself" rather than to any man, and in the menstrual sense, a woman who renewed herself and was not pregnant and therefore not dedicated to bearing a child. Thus the word "spinster" very likely comes not from the idea that the unmarried woman spins to pass the time, but that she spins through her months as the moon spins. This spinning-moon image is found in most cultures that weave cloth, says Eliade. The woman could be spinning the inner cloth of the soul's shirt, if she is pregnant; the outer cloth as a sign of her capacity to become pregnant, and of her ability to weave her dowry. Homer's Penelope spins, in Odysseus' absence, "like the Moon." The temple of Hera Chera in Stymphalos was probably by the waterside, where a bathing ceremony signifying the end of the period could be carried out. Hera would rise "from her bath of purification a virgin once more, for her wedding," says Kerényi.

The month for weddings was Gamelion, which approximated to our January, the month that looks forward and backward, the gate-month. Gamelion was originally determined by the date of the new moon, and the feast was the Gamelia, which was sacred to the Hera of Weddings. At this time, Zeus belonged to Hera, and not the other way around, so he was called "Heraios" and the rites and ceremonies were called "Hieros Gamos." This term has been degraded into the term "sacred marriage" implying a union of gods, but it did not originally mean this. It meant a marriage of human beings sanctified by the observances of the moon-rites of Hera. The dark moon time of the women was only once a year linked up in this manner with the solar year which was the large unit of time for the Greek man. Excavations in the Argive Heraion have turned up two principal kinds of goddess figurines: the crescent figurine, associated therefore with the virgin goddess of menstruation, and her rule of the underworld, her "sulks" and her *agon* or contest in darkness there (from the word comes our "agony"); and the full-moon figure, associated with physical fertility, ovulation, and pregnancy. Kerényi summarizes the position by saying that we possess this evidence of "a prehistoric moon religion which, as an outline *filled with female human content*, became the Hera religion" (our italics).

We have also evidence of the practice of a deliberate withdrawal into menstrual experience as something which can be learned, and which it is important to undertake. There are even legends of the prehistoric plant which women first took to cause their menstruation and the experience it gave them: it was called *lygos*.

Lygos flowered in three colors by the river Imbrasos, also called "Parthenios," on an island "Parthenia" whose other name was "Anthemoussa," "rich in flowers." With *lygos* was associated a "highly archaic experience" connected with a withdrawal and a checking of the ordinary sexual urge, but the plant also "stimulated women's katamenia." Branches of it made bowers at the great women's autumn festival, the Thesmophoria, from which men were excluded, though there are indications that they might be admitted in women's attire. The Thesmophoria took three days, and the first one was called kathodos and anodos: this was when the women went down into caves in which pigs had been thrown early in the summer, and recovered the remains which they mixed with the seed grain, on the third day scattered on the fields. It is probable that the origin of this festival was a specifically menstrual mystery. The women, who according to some authorities, invented agriculture, did so because only they had the secret of the strong fertility of the seed corn. The reason for this was that originally the women mixed the seed corn with menstrual blood, which was the best possible fertilizer, before planting it. Since the men had no magic blood of this kind, they could not grow corn as well as the women could, any more than they could grow babies. No doubt the men discovered somehow that the magic of fertility was in the menstrual blood, and tried to obtain magic blood themselves from their own genitals.

We may conjecture that the fertility-magic of menstrual

blood did not stop there. Uterine blood would be a very potent "drag" for laying scent-trails. This might have figured in the development of hunting-disciplines. Huntresses could use their powerfully magic menstrual blood as a trail— perhaps as a bundle with secret contents, dragged on an ambush-track. The uninstructed hunters would not have been able to match the women's results! Artemis, the Goddess of the New Moon, was also the patroness of hunters.

This may be the origin of the emblem of the bundle of In-Anna described in Gertrude Levy's *The Gate of Horn*, who shows us that the Goddess's presence was indicated by knotting a scarf or bandage on a peg on the wall of the hut. If this "sacred knot" were in fact the belt with which she fastened the towels that caught the "magical" blood of her menstruation, this would account for its appearance on the wall of the hut when she was not menstruating, was fertile and "newly virgin." At other times it would be around her waist. Some writers, including Gerald Massey, have gone so far as to say that this is the derivation of the "key of life" or looped Ankh cross of the Egyptians, which is nowadays in current vogue as a personal ornament, and also the "garter" of the witches. Hargrave Jennings in *The Rosicrucians* has the amusing suggestion that the "Most Noble the Order of the Garter," a particular distinction of British knighthood, orig- inated when Queen Eleanor dropped her menstrual napkin while she was dancing. The nervous dancers, the men, laughed at this, but the King picked the whole thing up, belt and all, and tied it around his own thigh (and "thigh" is a biblical euphemism for "penis") saying that they should honor the place whence they came, the womb, and he would therefore establish a high order of knights to do this. Jennings says that the motto of the order "Honi soit qui mal y pense," "Evil be to him who evil thinks," was actually, "Yoni soit qui mal y pense," "Cunt be to him who evil thinks." This is not quite crazy, since the Sanskrit word *jani* is an origin of the word "Queen." The whole story could refer to a ritual psychodrama rather than to a historical event, whatever the truth of the details. Francis King in *Sexuality, Magic and Perversions* thinks this is a silly story—we think it is an excellent parable.

It is possible that the estrus cycles of wild animals can be shortened to the more frequent cycling which is the fertile value of domestic animals, by feeding them the hormone-rich menstrual blood. It would be interesting to perform an experiment to test whether this is so, as an exercise in speculative archaeology. If it were so, then we might suppose that it was the means by which the *women* domesticated animals at the beginnings of human culture. However, animals in captivity naturally shorten their bleeding-cycles.

To return to the Thesmophoria: this plant, the *lygos*, which was reputed by Greek medicine to bring on the "monthlies," was used to make a bower, or menstrual seclusion hut. "The Thesmophoria were nothing else but the periods of the Greek women elevated to an annual festival," as Kerényi remarks. Apparently among the Greeks, as in innumerable other cultures, the women withdrew at these times, ceased all intercourse with men, and meditated, sometimes with the aid of rite of blood-shedding and animal sacrifice. The woman is held to be taboo at this time, and in many cultures there are tales that the moon herself withdraws for the same reason as other women, that is, to have her period. However, among the Greeks we know that it was thought that women independently of men were able during these days to promote the earth's fertility. The rites were developed for this purpose. It was perhaps a certainty about themselves, and their own femininity, that they retired to refuel all over again, in concert with the earth's renewal and fertility. In their seclusion, freed from immediate worries, energy could flow inward again.

We may also conjecture that rites of blood-sacrifice repeat in external and visible form the fertility-secrets of the menstrual blood-shedding that only women truly possess. The sacrificed animals, then, would represent the womb, the womb's instincts of fertility sacrificed at the period. The sacrifice inwardly brings renewal, as sacrifice has always been held to do. In the Thesmophoria the animals were pigs, as they were at the Eleusinian Mysteries. The pig is a womb-animal and a moon-animal, and is part of the great chain of sacred animals, i.e., serpent-pig-bull, associated with the moon's sacrifice and renewal apparently since Mesolithic times. The consistency of these equations is very remarkable, and has been much documented. We are suggesting that these rites, whatever the function of their outer language in denoting custom, taboo, and kinship, had an inner meaning also as "psychodramas" based on the natural menstrual sacrifice. Perhaps it was some whim of generosity, or the wish for male companionship, that led women to admit men to these rites, or to devise rites in which the men could take part, that involved "symbolic wounds" to the man's person, or dances in imitation of the animals, followed by animal (or human) sacrifice.

Neumann, in *The Great Mother*, conjectures that the benefit to the man would be a sense of identity with the women, with his own feminine side, his anima. Kerényi concurs: "Men, too, entered into the figure of Demeter and became one with the *goddess* . . . There is historical evidence to show that the initiate regarded himself as a goddess and not as a god." We have seen that a disturbance of this inner countersexual relationship can be thought to be at the root of some forms of madness. We have seen too that "there is no bloodless myth will hold": that it seems as though the shedding of blood in secret by the women gives rise to aggression and anxiety in the men. The indication to this is that societies with menstrual taboos appear to be the most aggressively anxious. The shedding of blood, somehow, releases great power. If such psychodramas include birth-imitations, ceremonies of adult rebirth, then the presence of menstrual or other blood would lead to a more complete anamnesis, or therapeutic recall. This abstract terminology needs to be translated into the excitement of the chase, the death, and the rising again. Perhaps the modern impulse to "mock-suicide" is an impulse to recover these meaningful rites of self-development. In Homer, the Goddess Circe turned men into pigs, but when Ulysses persuaded her to change them back again, they rose "goodlier than before." The pig was a center of the mystery of life, not only because of its immense fertility, but because every part of the pig can be used in the domestic economy, and it eats all refuse, including dung, and therefore renews the world's waste. It will also eat its farrow, like the earth taking back into itself its progeny.

"But these unconscious elements," says Joseph Campbell, "do not simply rest in the psyche, inert. As unrealized potentialities, they are invested with a certain readiness for activation in compensatory counterplay to the conscious attitude; so that whenever in the sphere of conscious attention a relaxation of demand occurs . . . the released, disposable energies turn back, as it were, and flow to the waiting centers of potential experience and development." What Campbell does not say is that such an experience, as does dreaming, has a strongly erotic element in it. Just as it is said in yoga that the rise of the spinal energy and the opening of the "flower-centers" is an exquisite and secret pleasure, so such journeys within, when they touch those centers of potentiality, give rise to a sense of "secret love-making." It is as Sheila Kitzinger said of the experience of childbirth without fear; and the raptures of St. Teresa bear witness to such a journey to a center: she found herself pierced in her womb by a fiery spear borne by cherubs. Ouspensky says that all true "supersensuous" experience is accompanied by strongly erotic feeling. The sexual emotion is joy; joy is the sexual emotion.

In the menstrual seclusion of the Greek woman during her *katamenia* or widowhood, a sense of "secret love-making" is said to have taken place. One could see this as a figure of speech for intense withdrawal into oneself, or perhaps this withdrawal was accompanied with ritual erotic experiences that in this inner world of seclusion were more appropriate to the "other dimension" of sexuality. There might be love-making with one's own sex, that is, countersexual identification, as is said to be a part of witch-beliefs, with a wand made magic by being used as a dildo. Morton Smith believes there is a case for homosexual initiation being used by the inner disciples of Jesus. With the women, this might be with members of one's sisterhood, or with the "other husband," the dark self in the underworld encountered and found, a friend and lover. Cecil Williamson says that Rhodesian native witches have menstrual seclusion huts in which there is an image of a god with an animal's horn as a phallus. The practice is sexual meditation during the period by intercourse with this god.[5] Or there might be a visionary encounter with half-human instincts, striving to turn their energies to human use, like the great hog of Venus, with his lunar-crescent tusks. We shall return to such stories, but say now that we believe they have application to the subjective experience of the menstrual cycle, and have such power because they are the mind's way of digesting and using the new power made available for human development by the evolutionary step of the menstrual cycle.

Imagery of scourging and binding is pervasive also. The gray myth of Ishtar of the Babylonians was that she descended to the underworld. At the successive gates of Hell, the goddess put off layers of finery and jewels, so that she entered the presence of the Queen of the Underworld Erishkigal naked as the day she was born. The Queen ordered the demon Namtar to bind Ishtar and torment her with miseries. But the earth above was left desolate, so the gods ordered the messenger Asushunamir ("He whose appearance is brilliant") to intervene, and Ishtar was released. At this the plague-demon became a friend, and sprinkled Ishtar with the water of life. Then he led her back through the seven gates where her clothes and jewels were restored to her, and she came into the world again "goodlier than before." This myth has been adopted as a psychodrama of rebirth in modern witchcraft, and similar psychodramas are used in psychiatric group-work: "birthing" and psychosynthesis.

Among the Greeks, the goddess's bonds, with which she was tied up to be released by the priestess, were made of that same *lygos,* the plant which stimulated katamenia. In menarche ceremonies all over the world, there are corresponding ceremonies of binding and release. This binding was carried out upon Hera, and also upon Artemis, who in Sparta was called "Orthia," "she who arouses," and "Lygodesma," "she who is bound with *lygos* withies." Scholars have confessed themselves puzzled by this custom, yet there is a rationale in that it provides a structuring and a valuing to the menstrual experience. For a woman, there is scourging and binding, descent and return, kathodos and anodos, initially painful initiation into the mysteries of an inner universe of instinctive thriving life, of her other sexuality, her threshold of blood into life-understanding, her crown of thorns, her monthly "resurrection."

What may happen when women combine into sisterhoods, colleges, or societies? There have always been these women's societies associated with the moon, and with the menstrual cycle. Some of them show advanced knowledge, as with the Greeks, others cruel survivals, as one may see in the menstrual seclusions lasting for years of imprisonment in darkness and wooden cages, which Frazer describes.

We have seen something of the way the Greek women became mistresses of themselves (though in the history of Greece, this too became a survival), and we have, we hope, given some sense of the power of the moon-emblem, whether or not one decides that the moons and the tides can actually be perceived and responded to directly by the human body. Clearly, by the systemization of this knowledge, and the identification of oneself with natural processes, consciously, by vivid stories and actual "psychodramas," interior development will take place. Is there, however, any modern evidence that such women's colleges could beat out, as it were, the menstrual pulse in synchrony, with its associated mental and sexual power? We have heard a nun say of her convent, it was like "a powerhouse of prayer." Would there be a physical component of this, even in a convent?

One of the important features of American feminist life is the "consciousness-raising group" which is sometimes centered around the visit of a medically informed feminist, or even a woman nurse. Her concern is that women should know more about themselves from the point of view of feminine experience, not from that of the prevailing masculine stereotype. She forms, with her helpers, a discussion group, to part of which men are welcome. Everything germane is discussed, from social rights to the workings of the reproductive system.

There is, however, one meeting to which men are not allowed. This is the meeting that introduces the use of the speculum. The speculum is a simple apparatus for dilating the vagina so that the cervix of the womb can be inspected, by the woman herself, if she holds her mirror at the right angle. In this way she can monitor herself for such troubles as erosion of the cervix or polyps without having to submit herself to a doctor's examination. In the group we attended there was much complaint of being treated like a parcel, and of unwarmed metal specula, which must have been as cold as the "penis of the Devil" reported in witch trials!

The men were allowed back into the room after this instruction and demonstration. It was not surprising that there was a very palpable feeling of sisterhood in the room among the women. It was of course equivalent to, though more mature than, a group of males comparing penises. The feeling was there, in the air like a perfume or an agreeable conspiracy. They had of course been showing each other their deep femininity, the birth-cone of the womb in its place of entry at the top of the vaginal passage. Looking through the speculum one sees a cone, with the tip missing, and an aperture, like the pupil of an eye. This cone is contained in the rounded vaginal passage, on which it rests, making the shape of a globe resting in a crescent-like moon, "the old moon in the new moon's arms."

This birth-cone was much imaged in the ancient world as a naturally sacred object. Its appearance is widespread on ornaments, architecture, and pottery, but male scholarship has forgotten what it represents, and calls it "omphalos" or "navel," thus cleverly diverting attention from the women's exclusive possession without actually telling a lie: since it is "navel," in the sense that it is the place we were all born from. Sometimes it was called the god's penis or phallus, but one can always tell when the flagrant male takeover of this sacred object has occurred because a penis has a urethral groove and a frenum, or tucking-in of the glans, and few of the so-called omphaloi have this. The Penis of Shiva worshipped at Elephanta has, by the photographs, none of the appearance of a penis, but it does look like the cervix or birth-cone, which it would be more natural to make an object of veneration in a culture that was at a stage when fatherhood was unimportant.[6] If, then, fathers rose to the kind of dominance they have in our own society, then the valued cult-objects would be renamed within credible limits, much as the Christian fathers in their takeover of pagan places of worship christened the indigenous goddess with the names of male saints. Any woman who can use a speculum can see for herself what we mean: men are advised to take an opportunity to view one of the "consciousness-raising" films on the use of the speculum; they will then have no doubt that when the learned books discuss and illustrate the famous ancient cults of the "world-navel" or omphalos at, say, the Oracle of Delphi (delphus is one of the Greek words for womb), then they are using male double-talk for a natural woman's cult of the birth-cone of the womb. Its resemblance to an inner moon must have greatly increased the emotional force of contemplating the phases of the outer moon.

The single eye as an emblem of the goddess is widespread in ancient cultures, and it may originate from this single-eye appearance of the inner vagina. The mysterious cup-marks on stone-age monuments may have this meaning also, particularly in their conical form. Silbury Hill in Wiltshire is an immense conical mound, dating from Stone Age times, that resembles the birth-cone. Sacred mountains in general are of this form, with the tip missing, which is supposed to be the place where the earthly meets the other world. This can have a literal meaning if one takes the "other world" to be the place where everyone was grown through the stages of gestation, up from the single cell through the animal series to the human baby. Everyone is then born through the birth-cone, or "axis of the universe." In the emblems the sacred mountain is accompanied by a world tree haunted by serpents, and a spring of water. The shaman may climb such a tree to meet the gods. It is interesting that the os or aperture of the cervix is lined with a complex branching corrugation which is called *arbor vitae* or tree of life. We think, however, that "tree" more reasonably refers to the fruiting tree of the ovaries, and is figured as the "moon-tree" which bears full-moon globes or even human heads, and is often seen in association with a birth-cone. Emblems of this kind can be found on cylinder-seals of the fourth millennium B.C. in Mesopotamia, and later in Palestine, Syria, and Cyprus on seals, coins, and reliefs. The birth-cone is very widespread, and was often the center of cults, for instance in Greece, where it was clothed in a net or tunic. Hitherto this image has not been given this meaning, which is clearly appropriate. Jane Harrison shows how the birth-cone resembles the tumulus, and we interpret this as a return of the dead to await resurrection through the cervix of the earth-mother. Bones were often coated with red ochre to signify, we believe, lochial blood. The Hindu "yoni-lingam," from which *puja* of blood or milk is made, is more naturally seen as inner vagina. The "lingam" does not usually have either urethral groove or frenum.

It is not of course possible to prove any of this, though it seems churlish to resist so evident and powerful an emblem. The Celtic Cross shows a central cone, and four others arranged on the crossarms in such a manner as to indicate by shadowing from sunlight above four phases of the moon, from dark moon through the quarters to full. This effect which is easy to observe need be no accident. Leroi-Gourhan's book is full of the mysterious Stone Age language cut on the walls of caves: many can very fittingly be read as vulva-emblems. One puzzling figure carved on a baton could be read as a nether-eye seeing a bear-totem in a sexual vision: an experience we have no right to deny to Stone Age lovers, particularly as no other explanation for the carving is offered, and a baton might easily be a magic wand. Some authors have interpreted these emblems as "flying saucers." Jung says that it matters less whether there *are* flying saucers than that people *see* them. We would rather suggest that the markings in question—circles with a raised conical center—more closely resemble the source of all life, the inner vagina. Visions of flying saucers might well be a projected hallucination of this archetypal shape, and their meaning be "return of the feminine."

Alexander Marshack argues that notations scratched on Upper Paleolithic reindeer bones are lunar counts, and Peter Lancaster Brown commenting on this says: "Human and animal birth *must* have been one of the great mysteries of Upper Paleolithic man. The Venus female images might be expected to reflect the biological miracle of birth. Neither can it have escaped notice that the lunar and menstrual cycle of women had a similar time span. It is not unreasonable to expect to read symbolic meanings of birth and rebirth in the Venus Figurines and seminal connections with lunar and solar seasonal rites which were gradually elaborated and later became very important in the Neolithic cultus." Janowsky *et al.*, discussing these evolutionary possibilities, remark that "It is possible that Pleistocene women, like related primate and other mammalian females, may have had seasonal rather than monthly cycles. Perhaps the greater frequency and regularity of menstrual function which we observe in modern women may have evolved as improved conditions of life became predominant." We have suggested that the subjective side of any such development would be important also, and this evolutionary process might well have been assisted by rites and psychodramas of powerfully emotional or "hypnotic" effect, in much the same way as a modern doctor might establish a powerful uterine rhythm from scanty or irregular bleeding using hypnotic relaxation and imagery, or in the same way Dewan established a rhythm by increasing exposure to indirect light, as it might be in a full-moon festival coinciding with people's midcycle and therefore stimulating ovulation. That such a synchrony is possible, and observed in modern times, we shall shortly show.

On this subject, Peter Lancaster Brown, writing of this most ancient history, is of a similar opinion to our own. He says: "Whether *Homo sapiens* has retained a biological vestige of a lunar-tidal rhythm inherited from his distant fish ancestors is conjectural . . . It seems more than coincidence that the female menstrual cycle, on average, follows the monthly interval of the lunar cycle. It is true, however, that this menstrual range is *now* extended either side of the interval (in extremes of 20 to 120 days), and the female cycle as such does not any longer follow the phases of the Moon, but this in no way invalidates its likely evolutionary time-structured origins." We have evidence, though, that the Greeks thought that the fertility cycle did, or could, follow the moon's phases, and they held their festivals accordingly, and their group-marriages. Of course this may have been only a token-rite, but there are indications that it need not have been. The Stone Age origins of Greek culture among the great Mother-Goddesses have been well described by several scholars.

The single-eye symbolism has also been described. It is interesting that the celestial vision of ultimate reality at the end of Dante's *The Divine Comedy* is of such a single-eye shape: "In the deep light three circles appeared to me of three hues bound into one dimension, one by the other reflected as Iris by Iris" ("Iris" is usually translated "rainbow"). This beautiful image can combine into itself the idea of the fast bonding glimpse of the mother's look, the Kabbalistic idea of the refraction of pure god-light into the varying colors of creation, and the source of all life from the womb-center, which is as aware as the eye itself, if not more so. There is a Taoist emblem precisely similar of three enameled colors denoting earth, water, and sky. Erica Jong in her *Fear of Flying* recounts a jocular dream in which her diaphragm is a contact lens and her womb-cervix is the eye. Ulysses pierced to the center of the single eye of the giant Polyphemus, converting it into a blinded grail of blood that bubbled with the heat of the stake he used: he had to blind the giant to escape out of the mother-cave, calling himself "Noman" as he did so. In much the same spirit he forced the Goddess Circe to return his companions to their human form. Joseph Campbell believes that the meaning of his voyages is that the male spirit was seeking a workable relationship with the power of the feminine. At the end he comes to Penelope's bed, which is made of a great tree that is alive.

To return to the possibility of menstrual synchronous rhythm among sisterhoods of women, the possible "powerhouse" of "body-prayer" that would be amplified by community living, there is modern work that shows that this is not only possible, but that it often occurs. Martha McClintock has shown, in an important article in *Nature*, that women living together can beat out a strong co-operative menstrual rhythm. One's cycle becomes adapted to one's friend's or colleague's cycle, so that one is menstruating or ovulating at the same time, just as we have suggested for the ancient women's colleges of the Sybils or the women prepar-

ing for the group marriages of the Gamelion. We suppose
that it would be surprising if this didn't happen among
communities of women associating for a purpose, whether
they were medieval convents or nurses' hostels, the Young
Women's Christian Association, or the women's Devil Bush
Society of Nigeria, or a college of women poets in ancient
Greece dedicated to Sibylline prophecy.

McClintock says that both direct and anecdotal observations indicate that the menstrual cycle is affected by social
groupings. Menstrual synchrony is a matter of frequent
report by "all-female living groups" and by sisters, mothers,
or daughters who live together. She quotes a case of seven
female lifeguards whose cycles synchronized after three
summer months spent together. She thinks that the greater
number of cycles without ovulation that occur among college
women may be due not to some immaturity inherent in the
college situation, but to this "interpersonal factor" as well.
McClintock worked with 135 women, and allowing for other
possibilities, such as a similar life pattern, repeated stress
periods, and seasonal variations in commonly eaten foods,
found undoubted menstrual synchrony that took about four
months to establish itself among people who spent time
together.

She quotes Dewan's suggestion that the menstrual cycles of
monkeys around the equator are synchronized because they
are locked in phase with the moon. She tests whether the
synchrony can come from common light-dark patterns, but
finds that "roommates" were less synchronized in that particular environment than "closest friends." Nor was it the
presence of males at the weekends, or the conscious knowledge that their friends were menstruating. It was the women
spending time together that gave this effect of menstrual
synchrony.

It must be a complex interaction of factors which, if
consciously applied, would surely increase the menstrual
synchrony. The study shows that there must be factors in the

environment that these women are responding to without being aware of doing so. McClintock suggests that one of the mechanisms could be pheromonal. Pheromones are substances which are given off in minute amounts by the body, and which act physiologically, usually without conscious awareness. They are very powerful chemical substances, as powerful as the internal chemical messengers which circulate in the blood and control the menstrual cycle, and which are called "hormones" or "internal chemical messengers." These "pheromones" are also known as ECMs or external chemical messengers, and there is very good evidence that these could influence the menstrual cycle, and other bodily processes, by transmission externally, between people. This is just to say that the air we breathe carries information that we are not usually aware of, but which our body is. Pheromone mechanisms have been plentifully demonstrated in the laboratory, possibly because it is easier to identify these substances than to isolate, say, the complex subsonic, ionic, electromagnetic, or gravitational influences that our bodies are certainly subject to, and which we may very likely "see" in symbolic form, and interpret by rites and stories, or perceive in dreams.

There is in fact a whole theory in this connection on the genesis of schizophrenia. A schizophrenic is a person whose "primitive" senses are most acute, including the sense of smell. The schizophrenic's illness comes from the shearing contradiction between what people tell him/her is true, and what he/she smells from them that is the truth. We say in common parlance "a nose for news," meaning an intuition. All nonhuman animals have this kind of sensitivity, including domestic animals such as the dog, where it has been shown that the animal's nose can discriminate between substances presented in astronomical dilution; more than 500 times more information is available to the nose of the dog than to human beings. Freud believes that the change from four legs to two diminished or repressed this sense, with our corresponding enhancement of the visual capabilities, but removed us from the powerfully sexual signals generated through the olfactory sense. It has been shown that infants in the cradle respond both by means of a language of body-gestures, which the mother responds to also, and also by the emission of "perfumes." What could be more natural? We know how deep into our memories the waft of a perfume associated with some past romance will take us. We know that when we smoke we calm ourselves but also diminish our sensitivity to odors. We know the effect of women's perfumes on themselves and as a sexual language between people. It is possible that tranquilizers interfere with olfactory response. It has been shown that women's olfactory sensitivity varies throughout the menstrual cycle, with a high in sensitivity at about ovulation, when the desire for impregnation may be at its height, and a low in external sensitivity at menstruation, when the desire may be to go inward. Perhaps this is one of the reasons for a taboo of menstrual seclusion, when it occurs, so that the process is not altered by intrusive male perfumes.[7]

The Tantric art of love involves the conscious use of perfumes to alter inward response to sexuality and to redefine it. Note "the fragrance of being," the "odor of sanctity," and there is an Indian saying: "That the fragrance of a flower travels with the wind, but the odor of sanctity travels against the wind." "Olfactory mating-calls" between moths, which are pheromones, will travel and attract suitors from miles around. It is a language that perfumers and Tantrics know. The Tantrics will anoint their hands with jasmine, their cheeks and breasts with patchouli, their hair with spikenard, their vulva with musk, their thighs with sandalwood, and their feet with saffron.[8] This is a part of their body-language, learned in their temples or societies for their Maithuna or ceremonial sex union. Each part of the body has its language.

Associated with these discriminations of a body-language practically unknown to the West is a valuing of the menstrual power in Tantrism. We shall return to this, as it is an extant practice of ancient origin which concerns itself with the special sensitivity of the menstrual time. So there is a countryside of sensuous experience that, in our culture's suspicion of the senses, we have repressed and not explored. How is this extension of the senses to be exercised? Did the ancients know how to do this too?

It has long been known that in the condition called "hysteria" as in "hypnosis" the power of sensuous response is enormously increased. It is possible, on the evidence, that what we call "hysteria" is the repression of a state in which body-consciousness is naturally extended. It is possible that what we call "states of possession" or "Shamanism" are such states of "hysteria" but controlled and extended in such a manner that the information from the extended senses can be usefully employed.

Even in the classical era, the Greeks would not make a political move without consulting the inspired utterances of a Pythoness, or oracle spoken by a priestess. Jung demonstrated in his M.D. thesis that in a hysterical subject "occult phenomena" could be attributed to an excited state of the senses that were fifty times, he estimated, more sensitive than was normal. Eliade and de Martino say that shamans, or witch doctors, in their state of possession, are able to detect real changes in the external environment, weather changes and migration patterns can be "seen," and sickness can be detected and cured, perhaps through sensitivity to pheromone and other body-language. It is just as a psychiatrist or a physician can read an expression and feel an atmosphere. We have quoted evidence that Shamanism was originally a female practice, linked to moon, and therefore menstrual, cults. This emerges in modern times, ironically, with the foundation of Freudian psychoanalysis, which was a study of hysteria. Freud and his colleague Breuer showed that hysteria with bodily symptoms was a meaningful language that expressed some conflict or uncongenial memory. If this information was brought into consciousness by "hypnotism" or other techniques and expressed verbally, the need for expression-as-an-illness vanished. The word "hysteria" comes from another Greek word for "womb" (hustera) and thus was in effect a Goddess-name! The womb was said to wander through the body, and cause hysteria. But of course body-consciousness, like any other attention, can wander, and it can be tuned in to concentrate on any part of the body, just as the trained memory can recall a variety of specific facts. "Hysteria" might then be a pejorative word for "womb-consciousness" in a culture that does not elect to cultivate any kind of body-consciousness. So many magical, yogic, and religious disciplines concentrate on the idea of rebirth—of the recalling and overcoming of past traumas, including the birth-trauma. R. D. Laing gives recent witness to this idea—in himself, experience—and traces imagery in phobias and dreams back to the conditions of life in the womb, which he calls "a bed of crimson joy or a battlefield . . . The original template for all reception . . ." It is difficult to resist the conclusion that the overcoming of such traumas releases new energy for living into one's ordinary consciousness, and changes it. Experiences that were dark and anonymous may become flooded with light—light, as it were, through the body—as though the whole body *saw*: the Hindus say that the senses became divided one from the other out of the one original sense, which combined them all. In moments of great emotion, we may see touch, hear smells; much poetry is explicitly "synesthetic," and during an intense artistic experience one may seem to hear the sounds of painted landscape, or touch the textures of music. The accounts of mystical experience also tell of similar phenomena, and floods of light and color in the body and in the senses. This is very likely what we experience as very young babies or in the womb, and it is this that our growing minds are trained to forget. These are, one might suppose, the rainbow skin and the lights of the Great Work in alchemy and Tantric yoga, the "tail of the peacock" and the "flower-strewn yoni."

Stan Gooch offers us the notion, from scientific evidence, of the consciousness in sleep as a traveler down from the great convoluted cortex of the new brain, through the mirror-reversal of the crossing nerve-pathways at its base, into the old brain, which is haunted by the symbols and energies which are described in folklore, but which we suggest are the images of body-consciousness, right down to the history of our gestations. Dreams, it has been said, are a replay of the genetic code. We recall the Greek god of sleep—Hypnos, a winged head. We remember also the great traveling, feasting heads of Celtic mythology; the sign of holiness to many Mediterranean peoples, the horned bucranium; and the horned god of the Celts and witches, and wonder whether the traveling head, like that of Orpheus, is not the natural symbol of prophecy, and whether, when it is horned, like the moon or like the womb with its Fallopian tubes, this signifies the overwhelming of ego-consciousness with greater consciousness that transforms. The cool unchanged observer calls this womb-recall "hysteria," "possession," "the Mother."

One of the pheromones that has been identified, in the curiously negative way of Western science, is that which appears to reduce male desire during the luteal phase of the cycle. It is a fact, according to this work, that men have fewer erections during this time. This could be adaptive, as it is the phase during which the womb-wall is preparing for the possible implantation of a fertilized egg, and it is presumed that male sexual importunity could interfere with this process. It would also contribute to premenstrual sexual tension and "witchiness." We shall examine later the notion of the menstruating woman as witch: is it possible that this observed pheromone effect contributed to the fables of witches stealing men's penises? Such a fable would be a tribute to the woman's sexual power, and fear would exaggerate it in a negative sense. It is to reduce fear that these things should be known consciously as attributes of the personality, each with its use. This effect—and the pheromone component must be the one identifiable factor in a complex of them—would have a profound influence on the emotions in a family: its coming, and its passing as well with the period's arrival.

A German pejorative for the period is "swinishness." But now this looks different: the pig is the "uterine animal" of the earth. In the Eleusinian Mysteries, the pig was a part of the drama, which concerned the search of the earth-mother Demeter for her lost daughter Persephone, their meeting and recognition, or "heuresis," "happiness," and the birth of a young God in a blaze of light, probably by the opening of a birth-cone: "Brimo has born Brimos!" These mysteries stood behind Greek life for 1,500 years and many of the greatest Greeks were initiates. The mysteries were so secret that initiates were killed for hinting at their nature. They persisted into Christian times, but did not fit there, and gradually dwindled away with the rise of the new religion. When Eleusis made its own coinage, the pig was the symbol on it of the Mysteries. George Thomson says that they were originally monthly, and originated as fertility mysteries having to do with the old menstruating goddesses.[9]

Whatever happened at Eleusis, our modern age may yet have to reconstruct. It is certain that whatever it was, it flooded the initiate with a new consciousness, and changed him or her. A flood of body-consciousness might look to an outsider like frenzy or hysteria; to an insider it might look like Whitsun, where the Apostles seemed drunk, wore flames of fire on their heads, and babbled in tongues so that every man seemed to be speaking in the language of the hearer, a pentecostal universal language. Such communications, when respected and studied, may give not only joy, but information. There may be reconciliation. In the Freudian case histories, hysterical babbling by free association led to the discovery in a woman of repressed desires, and with their acknowledgment, the ending of an illness. Neumann in his *The Origins and History of Consciousness* tells us of the feast of Aphrodite at Argos "when women appeared as men, and men as women wearing veils," that was called "the 'Hysteria' after the pig-sacrifices associated with it." He quotes Hastings, who says: "In the celebration of these anniversaries, the priestesses of Aphrodite worked themselves up into a wild state of frenzy, and the term Hysteria became identified with the state of emotional derangement associated with such orgies . . . The word Hysteria was used in the same sense as Aphrodisia, that is, as a synonym for the festivals of the goddess." Such a festival swept medieval Europe like a menstrual plague, in the shape of the Witch-Persecutions, the subject of our Chapter VI. It is interesting that Frank Lake, in his *Clinical Theology*, gives Mary Magdalen the typology of "hysteria"—we have already suggested that she represents the other side of womanhood in the Christian myth. But we have seen that if such phenomena are produced by the pressure of withheld information, their solution is likely to lead to increased consciousness, and that indeed this was the purpose of such rites and ceremonies of "possession." The initiate is being possessed by Nature herself, and only through nature is true harmony possible. Perhaps among the other visions people were brought to realize that unnamed force on their infancy that was the power of the menstruation, and perhaps they saw that this was only a harmonic of natural rhythms, like the death and rebirth of the moon, and the seasons.

Perhaps the ceremonies brought men and women alive to the baptism of blood at the birth-trauma, the pain of birth to the human baby which stands between it and the natural bliss of the womb, like an angel with a flaming sword, turning every way. Perhaps in a "birthing" they saw their own creation by body-light, womb-light. Perhaps in this way the men came into understanding of what a woman is, just as a rite of menarche (which Thomson believes the Mysteries began in) for the woman shows her that she is now beginning to be what her mother was, and there is a recognition, if possible a "heuresis." Both men and women know that they have the power to feel death and be reborn, since they were once unborn, and recall passing this threshold. Having passed into life successfully once, there might seem no reason why they should ever really die, and one of the Eleusinian hymns praises the initiates for their awareness when all other shades after death are without existence or consciousness. Kerényi speaks of "the vision into the 'abyss of the nucleus.' Every grain of wheat and every maiden contains, as it were, all its descendants and all her descendants—an infinite series of mothers and daughters in one . . ." and concerning entering into the drama versus discursive knowledge, "there is a vast difference between 'knowing of' something and *knowing it and being it.*"

If the rhythms which make up our bodies are the same rhythms that make the great festivals of the sky in the external world, then if we feel the two as one, we know we are a part of nature. Is this why Stonehenge is marked out as a lunar computer, and were festivals of "Hysteria" and "Aphrodisia" held there in celebration of the knowledge that what is happening in the sky, I feel in my deepest body? It would be an awesome experience to watch the sun rise at the winter solstice at the new moon, and feel the blood flow that meant life to come, as the sunrise at the turn of winter means life to come. The flood of poetry would come, and life would be talking back to itself in its own language. Or at the solar eclipse, predicted at Stonehenge, the shadow of the moon on the sun can make bright golden horns, like an animal's, or the hull of a boat made of light, or a bright grail containing a dark drink. The sun's halo, in an annular eclipse which is totally central, can look like the white of an immense eye and the shadow-disk of the moon covering it like a great dilated pupil. Yet this appearance does not terrify the shamaness, who feels the flood of body-consciousness and poetry come, who has predicted the eclipse, and who has seen the dark sun shining within her.

The great non-Christian legend of the Middle Ages was that of the Quest of the Grail. The Christian Knights of King Arthur's Table were tormented by a vision of the cup used at the Last Supper that contained blood from the wounds of the crucified Jesus. Only the pure Knight without stain, Parsifal, was admitted into the Grail Castle, where the genitally maimed Fisher King sat awaiting the question that would bring life back into the Wasteland. Parsifal watched the show of knights and maidens carrying the lance dripping blood into the cup of the Grail, and he was thunderstruck. He was speechless. Being speechless, he did not ask the question that would have redeemed the Wasteland. He showed no curiosity. The show came and went—and the Castle vanished. Parsifal had failed.

The terrible fact is that the question was a very simple one. It was "And Whom Does this Grail Serve?" What is this Grail, containing blood, for? It must now be obvious to readers of this book what the meaning of the Grail is in a society that had forgotten its roots in feminine experience. The Grail is the buried feminine secret. And the question which nobody answers is, "Why does the woman bleed in menstruation?" What is this cup full of blood for? That "navel" full of wine? The Christian Knights tried to be good without the feminine principle, yet the knowledge of it came in this vision. Before Christianity it was there, in the Celtic caldron of Cerridwen, which also stood for the maternal all-bleeding woman.[10]

In the *Parzival* of Wolfram von Eschenbach we get more than a hint that not only is the blood a blood of sexuality, but that the whole rite is connected with the rhythms of the sun and moon: "A squire suddenly stepped over the threshold carrying a spear from the point of which blood spurted . . . there followed eight other ladies, four of whom bore great torches, while the others effortlessly held up a precious stone pierced by the rays of the sun, its name

derived from its brightness. Two deliciously adorned prin-
cesses arrived in their turn, their palms supporting two sharp
knives of extraordinarily white silver . . . The queen followed them, her face so brilliant that everyone thought dawn
had broken . . ."[11] That picture of the queen glowing with
fulfillment is amazing! Is the procession not like the spring-
ing of the blood to the solar eclipse we have just described?
That white silver of the knives is like the two slender crescents
of the moon, like the tusks or horns of all moon-animals
signifying the full career of the moon's phases, as Eliade
notes.

We have been grateful to the writings of C. G. Jung's wife
Emma Jung, in a previous chapter. In her book on the Grail
for instance, she relates the Grail legends to medieval alchemy, which was dedicated to producing a precious stone,
red in color, that sweats blood, and which turns the world to
gold. Jung's own work was to relate this medieval "fantasy" to
modern psychology, and to show how powerfully relevant it
was. The Grail can also be a stone, in the legends. We are led
to suggest that a precious stone which sweats blood is the
moon; both inner moon, the womb; and outer womb to
which the inner is related either by inherent rhythm or
obvious analogy. Emma Jung, for example, speaks as
follows: "'The soul . . . dwells in the life-spirit of the pure
blood' . . . Gerald Dorn describes the arcane substance of
the alchemists as 'blessed rose-colored blood' . . . the alchemists spoke of their stone as possessing a soul 'because at the
final operations, by virtue of the power of this most noble
fiery mystery, a dark (obscurus) red liquid, like blood, sweats
out drop by drop from their material and their vessel.'"
Surely this is male double-talk for the spirit of sexuality that
is reborn or alters at the menstrual period? Emma Jung,
however, though she relates the alchemist's Philosopher's
Stone to the Grail of the legends, and speaks of the Quest of
both as the same process, treats the blood as a spiritualized
symbol, and does not relate it in any way to an event which

happens in a person's actual life, except as a purely spiritual influence without concrete meaning on the physical level.

Jean Markale's researches in *Women of the Celts* come much much closer to natural life. He too describes the legend of a drop of magical blood that turns to a torrent, and he tells us absolutely that "the Grail-chalice is the uterus of the mother goddess . . . but since the Fisher-King has been wounded in his genitals, the Land of the Grail is waste and arid . . . This simple equation of the Grail-chalice with the maternal womb furnishes a conclusive argument in favor of the femininity of the Grail."

But even Markale underplays the fact that women menstruate, and that this menstruation has a meaning to the women, including the mothers. Perhaps the Wasteland will be redeemed if the men share with the women. If the reader looks at these books, without forgetting the simple facts of feminine physiology, then he/she will be amazed at the way the learned or Christianized or masculinized "double-talk" falls into place.

Rather than go over these authors' ground in this book, let us instead attempt to answer the three famous Grail-riddles that are supposed by tradition to lead to the secret that is no secret, for everybody knows it really.

The first is: "Whom does this Grail serve?" The answer is: "Humanity, which would not exist in the evolutionary series without it."

The second riddle goes like this: "The world is in the Grail and the Grail is in the world: what is the Grail?" The answer to this is that the world is within the Moon-Grail's influence ("frail air-chalice" in the Anglo-Saxon riddle) and women may respond to its influence by having periods; if they do they have "brought down the moon" and they are the Grail which walks about the World. A subsidiary answer is that every woman has been born from a womb, which is what she herself possesses.

The final riddle is about the Grail Castle. "Where is the

Grail Castle, that is surrounded with water, that is every-where at once, and which is invisible?" The correct answer to this riddle is to point to the woman's belly or groin. The answer is the birth-cone, which is surrounded by watery secretions, which exists in all women invisibly as the cervix of the womb, and which contains wonders of experience. In ancient times one might also point, perhaps, to the cone-shaped sacrificial helestone of one's neighborhood computer moon-temple. "Mother Holle" or Hele was the German Death-Life, Life-Death Goddess.

But is there any extant tradition of ancient origin in which these practices can be proved? In fact there is: it is Tantrism. Tantrism is an ancient yoga practice which is a way of affirming the excellent things of life, that is, it is not a way of negation, or asceticism. One of its central mysteries is called *Maithuna* or sacred sexual intercourse and its visionary aftermath, or reverie, in which one's body-consciousness, all one's perceptions, including the mental and spiritual ones, are stimulated. Philip Rawson remarks of Maithuna: "The most powerful sexual rite of re-integration requires intercourse with the female partner when she is men-struating, and her 'red' sexual energy is at its peak." Again, Hindu Tantra does "cultivate activities aimed espe-cially at arousing the libido, dedicating it, and ensuring that the mind is not indulging in mere fantasy . . . All the concrete enjoyments and imagery are supposed to awaken dormant energies . . . [which] once aroused, is harnessed to rituals, meditations, and yoga . . . [the altar is equated with] the vagina of the female companion, who should . . . be menstruating so that her own vital energies are at what is believed to be their dangerous peak." The Tantrists call these energies "the red goddess" or "Dakini," and she is the Inspiratrix, the Muse.

Alas, the study of these matters has been relegated to what is called black magic, and is supposed to be destructive. It may be destructive—to the male operator, and to his partner not prepared for the intensest experiences, or renewal. In magic, however, the sexuality is not usually *maithuna*, dedicated to the mutual pleasure or illumination of both partners, but is often a coldly deliberated and willed action designed to obtain some specified benefit. Yet even this is effective, and even permissible, for one may ask one's sexual reverie questions, or formulate wishes within it, and obtain ideas and images in answer: it is the time par excellence for creative contemplation, which need not be solely the person of one's partner. It is the coldness, though, in magical practice, which destroys, not the furor, or the heat.

According to Kenneth Grant's illuminating study of sexual magic, "red substance of female source" is "the prime menstruum of magical energy," and the destructive aspect of lunar or black magic. This is of The Scarlet Woman, who is also the Goddess Kali. C. D. Daly wrote a fascinating paper on the black goddess Kali's cult as a menstrual cult. He says that the destructive aspect comes from the great evolutionary energy, but even more from men's fear of it. In due time the hideous Kali, when she is loved as she deserves, will reveal her beauties hidden patiently for centuries, he says. Aleister Crowley says "the best blood is of the moon, monthly" in the Scarlet Women who are the "sweet-smelling ladies," the *suvasinis* of the temple. At the period the "cup" or "chalice" of the woman would be full of a special *kalas* or energy that by intercourse could be turned to visionary or magical purposes: she would be "the gate of the sun" (Babylon). The male and female secretions are the alchemical substances that combined initiate transformations: "the blood of the lion" and the "gluten of the eagle." Grant quotes Gerald Massey, who describes a Gnostic rite that corresponds to a Hindu Tantric one in which a certain cup of wine is turned red and into blood by a "miracle (one that could be wrought monthly)" so that Charis, the female savior, "should be thought to effuse her own blood into the cup . . . and the grace of Charis flow into those who tasted of her cup." The

Gnostic Marcus then "handed cups to the women who represented Charis in person and in presence. These women then consecrated the cup with an effusion of Charis proceeding from themselves . . ." One cannot say whether the hormone-rich menstruum would have had any physiological action, or whether the act was a purely sacramental one. An ancient remedy says: "For cessation of the menses. Take internally pulverized menses, and wear a chemise smeared with human blood"—like a primitive kind of estrogen-replacement therapy. One may conjecture that survivals of these non-Christian practices would have led to the charge of cannibalism and "eating children" ascribed to the witches: one is said to be using matter that would go to make up the flesh of the child. Massey in *The Natural Genesis* says that to such a cult "The blood of Charis preceded the blood of Christ, and there would have been no doctrine of cleansing by the blood of Christ but for the purification by the blood of Charis. The male Messiah or word of God would not have come arrayed in a garment dipped in blood, if blood had not been the feminine manifestor of the Word of Wisdom." Massey goes on: "Moreover, the change of sex did not turn the typical mystery into meaningless mystification." We have said that the change of sex and the taking-over of female mysteries can mean more positively an emergence of masculine consciousness by testing itself on the female realities. The morbidity comes when it *separates* itself from those basic realities. "This consecration of the cup of Charis and of the Hindu Sakteya had a natural genesis in the most mystical nature of the feminine logos."

As Crowley says, "the womb 'sees things' in the glamour of physiological upset" and is the Eye of Set or "blind" Horus who can see in the dark of this underworld. The annular total solar eclipse we described above was known as the "Eye of Horus." Grant says that the Witches' *Vinum Sabbati* (Wine of the Sabbath) was "the mystical effusion of the Scarlet Woman, the ever-virgin Whore . . ." Kenneth Grant writes eloquently on the number *five*, which is still given by medical texts as the approximate number of days of the usual menstrual period. "Five was the primal number of woman as the genetrix long before the stellar seven and the lunar twenty-eight. For five days woman was engulfed in darkness and eclipsed; from her issued the deluge that primitive man rightly identified as the substance which would later congeal and flesh forth progeny. Blood was recognized as liquid flesh and the female expressed (through the number five) her nubility, which was the archetypal *nobility* because the only known lineage was of the blood of the mother alone. The male's role in the procreative process was at that time unknown. The five-day eclipse was the seal of woman's nobility, the nobility that wears the scarlet mantle of nature herself, the one unimpeachable rubric of her sovereignty. And because she was seen to renew life upon earth woman was likened to the goddess in the sky, who renewed herself through celestial cycles as a type of resurrection, a return to unity and ultimate perfection in the heaven and the hells. The number five thus became the seal of authority in the world of spirits; it was represented by the pentagram or five-pointed star, still used by magicians for establishing contact with and controlling transmundane entities. The origin of the magical pentagram can thus be traced to the first observed facts of elemental nature."

This makes an unexpected gloss on John Donne's beautiful poem "The Primrose," and in our opinion adds a dimension of meaning. Knowledge does not diminish a true mystery: the poet Gerard Manley Hopkins said that to most, a mystery was "an interesting uncertainty," but he meant "an incomprehensible certainty . . . the clearer the formulation the greater the interest." However, we doubt if, receptacle and transmitter of evolutionary forces, woman would wish ever to be merely "content." The primrose flower, of course, has five petals.

> Live, Primrose! then, and thrive
> With thy true number five;
> And women, whom this flower doth represent,
> With this mysterious number be content.

Six Witchcraft: Nine Million Menstrual Murders

What is a witch? A witch is a woman with strange powers. These powers can be used for good or evil, cursing or blessing. She rides to the Sabbath on a broomstick, she has spirit lovers, she has animal familiars. She worships the goddess of the Moon, she operates in covens of thirteen persons, and these may comprise men. To her "fair is foul and foul is fair" so she is concerned with turning ordinary ideas upside-down.

Here is a list of some of the events witches were supposed to be able to bring about with their special powers, their spells and incantations. Gardens, crops, and fruit-trees blighted and withered. Horses ridden nearly to death by witches on their way to the Sabbaths; "hag-ridden," Nightmares sent. Mares miscarrying. Cows drying up: no milk. A witch could curse the owner of a fine dairy herd and his cows would henceforth give no milk. A test for a witch was to bring her into contact with a churn of fresh milk, which would sour. If she churned cream it would not become butter.

Witches were also supposed to be able to cause storms by

shaking their hair, by combing it out. They could if they wished cause drought. They were rain-makers also: by whipping the water or by urinating they would bring rain. If they were floated in water they could not sink. They went off and left their husbands in bed with a broomstick or a bundle of old clothes for company while they went off to their wild orgies, to seek out a lover of supernormal sexual energies. The witch is the woman a man may marry in the belief that she is a beautiful young girl. She suddenly transforms into a menacing creature, an old, ugly woman, a fox, a snake. Yet thinking about witches gives us a tingling sense of excited terror; witchcraft is one of the ideas, like ghosts and sex, that are inexhaustibly interesting.

In this chapter we want to disentangle some of the misconceptions, and, we hope, show you that what is called witchcraft is the natural concern of all women. We want to sort out what witchcraft is to witches, and what it is to men afraid of witches. We intend to deal with the facts about witches that come to us from past history, from legend, and with contemporary evidence. By the end of this chapter we hope that you will see how natural witchcraft is, how important to all women and to men also, and how a great natural ability of human beings has been suppressed by Church and State for centuries.

Let us summarize our argument: witchcraft is the natural craft of the woman. It is this because witchcraft is the subjective experience of the menstrual cycle. Witchcraft gives names and activities to the cycle; by means of witchcraft women have been able to structure their cycle and know it. Because it is a woman's reality, and because women can fulfill themselves and come into their proper powers by understanding their menstrual cycles, it has been denigrated ceaselessly by men, who fear women and who wish them to underachieve. This is the reason for our title: *Nine Million Menstrual Murders*. In the Middle Ages it has been estimated that nine million women were burned as witches for exercising their natural crafts of midwifery, hypnotism, healing, dowsing, dream-study, and sexual fulfillment. They were persecuted and burned by the Christian Church of that time, who wished only men to have power and ability, by men worshipping a male trinity.

This persecution is not over yet: we shall show, with Thomas Szasz, how the language of the indictments of women as witches through the years of persecution uses the same forms and diagnostic approach as does the medical jargon of modern mental hospitals that arrest and condemn women in the name of their male psychoanalysts who worship male psychology, and have no knowledge of the special events that belong to women.

We write this on Saturday, November 1st, the day after Hallowe'en. Hallowe'en, all Hallows Eve, is one of the four great Sabbats, held on October 31st. The others are Candlemas, on February 2nd, May Eve, on April 30th, and Lammas, on August 1st.

In England we now take little account of the weekly "Sabbaths," the Sunday, the Day of Rest, though there is still the Lord's Day Observance Society to keep it in the calendar. We take some account of Hallowe'en. On television last night there were tiny unsatisfying bits of ghost-stories: "Date with Danton" tried to reinstate a new "most haunted house in England" now that Borley Rectory is burned down. There was a slight chiller from Australia that linked the ghost of a murderous boy with flying saucers and aboriginal star devils. At one time, Hallowe'en was a great public holiday of the dying year in the Celtic Calendar, with huge bonfires to cook feasts in the open air, and to warm the people who came from miles around to join in the fun, which would include dancing and games.

In Cornwall we celebrate May Eve in one of the few surviving hobby-horse rituals: a drama of death and joyful resurrection, a celebration of the approaching summer. The great 'Oss dances in the streets of Padstow like a horse and rider in one, led by his "teaser" and his master of ceremonies, and all the young people follow the 'Oss, who is "my dear" to them, the dancer in the great mask of god. This is a full celebration of one of the great Sabbaths, but apart from this and the increasingly Americanized "trick or treat" Hallow-e'en, and the obsessive observance or nonobservance of Sunday (though orthodox Jewish communities will still keep the Saturday holy) we do not in this country much keep the Sabbath.

Unless we are witches. Then in past ages we would have observed the passing and renewal of the year on our great Sabbaths; and on our lesser Sabbaths, which are the quarter-days, and sun-festivals: the Summer and Winter Solstices, and the Spring and Autumn Equinoxes. It is said that these observances began to come to an end as public holidays with the Peasants' Revolt in 1381 in England; but how far back they go, how long they have been observed before this opens up terrifying perspectives of time. It is possible that Stone-henge and Avebury and the whole complex of Neolithic monuments and temples were computers of considerable sophistication that were used to establish these days of festival, and the movements of the sun and moon that determined them.

So something has been lost and disregarded, and one of its names is "Sabbath." What is the origin of this word "Sabbath"? Perhaps discovering the meaning of this word will give us a clue in human terms to exactly what is being celebrated as the "Sabbaths." This is one of the questions we hope will be resolved by the end of the chapter. Another question we will seek to answer is one that has been asked by all anthro-pologists, and never until now answered: why is it that all peoples at all times believe in witches, and why are these beliefs so remarkably similar all over the world? And, what is Magic?

II

O she looked out of the window,
 As white as any milk;
But he looked into the window,
 As black as any silk,

Hulloa, hulloa, hulloa, hulloa, you coal black smith!
 O what is your silly song?
You shall never change my maiden name
 That I have kept so long;
I'd rather die a maid, yes, but then she said,
And be buried all in my grave,
That I'd have such a nasty, husky, dusky, musty, fusky,
 Coal black smith
 A maiden I will die.

Then she became a duck,
 A duck all on the stream;
And he became a water dog,
 And fetched her back again.

Then she became a hare,
 A hare all on the plain;
And he became a greyhound dog,
 And fetched her back again.

Then she became a fly,
 A fly all in the air;
And he became a spider,
 And fetched her to his lair.

Robert Graves believes that this poem is one of the few
surviving witch-liturgies. He tells us in *The White Goddess* that
a Northumbrian witch called Anne Armstrong performed a
dramatic dance to these verses at a well-attended Sabbath,
mimicking the cries and actions of the animals. This psychodrama had the meaning of a holy (*selig*, origin of "silly")

celebration of the passing seasons. Thus the hare represented autumn coursing, and the water, winter rains.

Graves reconstructs other liturgies which give the sequence complete. The pursuer may in some versions be the woman, in urgent fertility pursuing the sluggish man to stock the world anew. Graves's is one view of witchcraft: that it is the recurringly organized fertility religion of the Great Goddess, who has presided over our welfare since human origins before the Stone Age, and whose rites we neglect to our cost.

An alternative view to this is that there never was any organized cult or society of witches, and that the great witch persecutions of the Middle Ages, in which it is fairly certain that up to *nine million* people died, were the result of political moves by the ecclesiastical authorities in which scapegoats were manufactured and responsibility for society's troubles— famine, plague—shifted. Norman Cohn expounds this view in his *Europe's Inner Demons*. The historian Hugh Trevor-Roper is another exponent, and tells us that there never were any witches.

On this view the witch persecution in the Middle Ages is comparable to the persecution of the Jews by the Nazis. The latter crystallized all undesirable qualities in the notion "Jew," and by purging their Reich of "Jews" gave the illusion that the community was now improved, and fit for all tasks. The common enemy united the persecutors. It is interesting that among the ancient propaganda against Jews is the charge that the men, as well as the women, menstruate. What the Nazis said about Jews was invented out of fear and hatred and political expediency, and was untrue propaganda. We do not for that reason conclude that there were never any Jews.

Similarly, the evidence is too strong that there always have been associations of women (*Weiberbünde*) who have met to celebrate the "Mysteries of the Woman," just as there have always been societies of the men (*Männerbünde*) who meet to celebrate men's mysteries, which include Christian or Jewish religions.[1] What were the Bacchanalia or Thesmophoria but organized "witching" in ancient Greece? Since anthropological and historical science are predominantly masculine, information about women's societies has come to us often by highly colored rumor, though there is still plenty of sound evidence for the existence of *Weiberbünde* throughout the world.

Just as one central feature of men's societies is their initiation into sexual manhood at puberty, so a central feature of women's societies is their initiation into womanhood at their first menstruation. Because it has been men anthropologists, mostly, who have studied societies in which this happens, and the ceremonies are reserved to women, it is hardly surprising that, for instance, Eliade has to say "we are still poorly informed regarding the content of the feminine initiations." However, Miriam van Waters analyzes in feminine terms the considerable amount that was known even in 1910: how important the dreams of first menstruation are to some cultures, or divination by first menstrual blood, or the acquisition of a guardian spirit at menarche.

Edwin Ardener also in the *festschrift* to one of today's great woman anthropologists, A. I. Richards, says that "The problem of women has not been solved by social anthropologists . . . Those trained in ethnography evidently have a bias towards the kinds of model that men are ready to provide . . . Lévi-Strauss . . . expressed no more than the truth of all those models when he saw women as items of exchange inexplicably and inappropriately giving tongue . . . a model in which women and nature are outside men and society . . . the failure to include half the people in the total analysis . . . the female model of the world which has been lacking . . . a male model of the universe in which female reproductive powers do not fall under male control . . . It is . . . men who usually come to face this problem, and, because their model for *mankind* is based on that for *man*, their opposites, *woman* and *non-mankind* (the wild), tend to be ambiguously placed. Hence . . . come their sacred and polluting aspects."[2]

To accept this argument is to accept that whenever we use the word "witch" we mean a certain aspect of "woman," and when we say there were no witches, it is almost like saying "we wish there were no women." When we say "there were no societies of witches" we are saying "there were no societies of women."

This is still not to say that the medieval Church persecuted a "society of witches." What we are saying is that it certainly persecuted women. As Savramis, to give only one such author, points out in his splendidly titled *The Satanizing of Women*, the Christian Western world identified women with sin. She was an "advance-guard of hell," she was "a frightening worm in the heart of man." She was "the devil's gate." The witch-hunters saw themselves "as representatives of a theology that satanizes sexuality as such, equates women with sexuality, and seeks to destroy the female sex in order to eliminate 'wicked' sexuality in favor of a man-ruled Christian world." The infamous manual for inquisitors that was written for use at witch-trials, *The Hammer of Witches* or *Malleus Maleficarum*, is distinguished from other works on heresy in that it is "solely and exclusively devoted to the persecution and destruction of the female sex."

In 1484 a Bull of Pope Innocent VIII authorized two Dominicans, Heinrich Krämer and Jacob Sprenger, to write the *Malleus Maleficarum*, one of the most infamous instruments ever fashioned of persecution of a class. The class being women, and the instrument a handbook defining what witches did, how they were alleged to do it, how to try them, and how to sentence them.

One might argue, though figures are hard to pin down, that this book was responsible for nine million deaths from the date of this Papal Bull until the end of the seventeenth century. The people executed—we are speaking principally of the Continent of Europe—were mostly burned, and they were burned for being witches. Some were men, but the persecution was chiefly a genocide, since the proportion of women to men executed was somewhere in the region of one hundred to one.

The *Malleus*, written by these two monks, was explicitly and chiefly against women, since they were those of God's creatures who were chiefly liable to this recurring disease and sin of witchcraft. According to the *Malleus* they had certain characteristics which made them thus susceptible: "And the first is, that they are more credulous . . . The second reason is, that women are naturally more impressionable and more ready to receive the influence of a disembodied spirit . . . The third reason is that they have slippery tongues, and unable to conceal from their fellow-women those things which by evil arts they know . . . Since they are feebler both in mind and body, it is not surprising that they should come under the spell of witchcraft." Men of course are more fortunate, since Jesus died "to preserve the male sex from so great a crime."

Moreover "All witchcraft comes from carnal lust, which is in women insatiable . . . there are three things which are never satisfied [misquoting Proverbs xxx] yea a fourth thing which says not, it is enough, that is the mouth of the womb."

And if it is the mouth of the womb that is the devil of the witches, then it is not surprising that the powers attributed to the witches are those that have been attributed from immemorial time to the natural monthly functioning of that devil, the menstruating vagina.

III

The reader will by now have noticed a familiar pattern. There is a terrible plague. Men don't know much about it, but they fear it and persecute it. It makes women "witchy" or secretive. They do things which men cannot see a reason for, together. It somehow has to do with sex. It can turn a good companion of the day into a sinister night-rider. Men try to get rid of it, either by calling it heresy, and giving good intellectual reasons why it should be expunged, or by calling it a plague of madness.

With nine million or so women killed in the Middle Ages for these reasons we are by no means approaching the modern figures of "90 percent dysmenorrhea," but we are getting close to it. The persecution continues, and is current. The popular American journal *Redbook*[3] wrote about women who are "once-a-month witches" and suggested that there were about thirty-six million out of forty million American women who might be so described. *Time* in 1956 wrote about Dr. Erle Henrickson who, with his colleagues, classified these "part-time witches" as grades one, two, and three, the last "to be avoided on her bad days unless she gets effective treatment." The treatment in this case is not burning at the stake but "the turquoise miracle pill," a mercurial diuretic.[4] It must be mere coincidence that modern witch-covens have three grades of initiation!

We have made a connection here between the obvious aspect of femininity that men fear and hate, and witchcraft. It is also becoming clear that "witchcraft" means "woman-craft." Now the question whether the witches were organized into groups with political power in the Middle Ages is seen as almost a side-issue. Women may have been so organized in such movements. They often have been so organized, historically, as we showed in the last two chapters; and from the evidence of anthropology, they are still so organized.

In the Middle Ages, it scarcely mattered whether you were an organized dissident or not. You were a dissident by being a woman. One aspect of women's dissidence, so far as men are concerned, is that they magically menstruate, and produce magical blood. As they menstruate, particularly if they are in a society which is suspicious of them, by the "howlback effect," they may change personality, or speak direct truth in an uprush of instinctual reaction. They may fall into a hysterical trance in which their dream-life comes rushing to their lips: the judicial "witch-confessions" which may or may not have meant an organized religion. This happened when the witch-finders persecuted them in prurient curiosity about woman's dream-life: indeed the practice of witch-pricking with pins to find the numb spot was one of the earliest demonstrations of hysterical symptoms, Freud's earliest study. They might masturbate with a carved stick, or do other "mad" things such as meet together for trance-experience, or act out in body-language and psychodrama their unease in society. Vieda Skultans has shown this last effect in a Welsh working-class spiritualist community. Again, one of the earliest organized groups of witches of which we have knowledge would be in this view the "Colleges of Hera" described in the last chapter. Cohn begs the question by calling all the confessions of Sabbats, wild night rides, attendance at covens presided over by monstrous goats or tomcats, animal transformations, and the rest, "fantasy." We know, however, that all over the world such "fantasies" have been acted out in totem-dances and in shamanism for reasons that seemed good to the communities that did so. We know also from the documents of psychoanalysis that such fantasies recur in archetypal form in the reveries, dreams, and visions of modern people uninstructed in the anthropology of witchcraft. It is reasonable therefore to regard ceremonies and rites as objectified inner events: tales of them told by people under torture may either be accounts of such rites confessed; or fantasies stimulated by torture, either in shamanic ecstasy, or in a desire to give the inquisitor something to content him.

With what we have said in the last chapter the benefits of studying at a moon-college of Hera become clear. To a young woman, regularity of the cycle. Knowledge of her moods and abilities through the cycle. Knowledge of changes such as suggestibility (the "credulity" and "more impressionable nature" of the *Malleus*) leading to skill in hypnosis and autohypnosis and the yoga-control of bodily functions.

Knowledge of her feelings of ovulation and therefore her fertile periods. Knowledge of her dark time of the moon, her menstrual period, and of the interior images that this brings (which include, as we show in our chapter "Animus, Animal, Anima," the appearance of the man-figure of her unconscious-side, her demon-lover of the witches). Knowledge of her increased sexual ability at these times, including autoeroticism, and the flying of a broomstick or dildo to a Sabbath of hearts-ease by her own sexuality applied to herself for her own self-knowledge (Love thy neighbor *as thyself*).

A graduate of this college would be a knowledgeable woman. She would be in full possession of herself and of her changes during her period. She would have a knowledge of plants and animals, she would have explored her animal affinities and sympathies: as for instance in a totemic dream of some animal speaking to her in an initiatory menstrual dream. This animal would be the mouthpiece of her instincts. She would have a knowledge of her male side, her interior lover. This other person would have come to her in an erotic dream, and she would know that her true lover in the outer world would have to bear this image for her, and develop it in himself for her.

By her dream-yoga and her symbolization of her changes with the moon she would have a deep knowledge of her body's changes and abilities, and she would when it came to her time to bear children, stand a good chance of doing this consciously and with less trouble or pain than a woman not so initiated, and having this knowledge she would have the power to communicate it, as a midwife. Who knows what powers of ESP and telepathy which may be inherent in the human condition and yet not developed in this scientific age of paralyzing skepticism, might be aroused by these studies? One power which is not understood by science but which is certain in the world, that of water-divining, might well be developed by these studies, which are the studies of the tides in all things, brought about by the moon and the sun. This may be no more than a fantasy of the past; but it could also be an image of the future.

So it is moon-knowing and womb-knowing and woman-knowing that these two infamous monks of the *Malleus* wished to expunge from the face of the earth. What they most persecuted and distinguished "witches" by, were those same taboos that have been imposed on women in all ages. It seems likely that the persecution of the witches in the Middle Ages was one enormous menstrual taboo. How strange and pitiful it is that of all the ways it is possible to execute a person those that were chosen by the witch-persecutors observe the one law: *thou shalt not spill a witch's blood.* The reason? The power was in the blood. Frazer shows that this is also universally true of royal blood.

The strange fact about this moon-knowledge that study in the college of Hera would inevitably give, is that it is knowledge that is recoverable from age to age wherever women menstruate and wonder how their own interior changes are related to the changes of the moon and the tides. It is not like masculine knowledge, that is built up from painful generation to generation, and which can be lost utterly if the chain is broken. Women's knowledge is available to them if they will only look inward and give themselves trust, and not be afraid to personify with (for example) goddesses' names, those forces greater than their own selves that move them; and not be afraid to learn from themselves rather than from men who abuse their "credulity" which is their openness, and their "impressionability" which is their ability to take what is happening and what is communicated to them, even by men, deep within. Woe to them if what they learn from the men in the outer world is not true! Clearly it is of advantage if there is a strong tradition of taught knowledge passed from woman to woman, but so strong is the menstrual taboo imposed by the patriarchs who call their fear of castration "self-possession" (one of the loaded *Malleus* words for the qualities of men) that nowadays not even mothers communicate a trust in the period within the family circle.

When this knowledge was trusted and communicated, we have suggested, then witch-matters, including rituals derived from the subjective experience of the woman's nature, flourished, but when it flourished, the men soon wished to imitate, and grew jealous, and persecuted. Thomas Szasz, in his *The Manufacture of Madness*, gives a very moving and terrifying account of the type of mental blindness that could afflict communities to the skills that were exercised within it, to the extent of persecuting "white witches" most ferociously precisely on account of the benefits they brought. Michelet writes that the Church "declares, in the fourteenth century, that if a woman dare to cure *without having studied*, she is a witch and must die," and Szasz comments: "But the wise woman had 'studied.' Her teacher, however, was Nature, not the Scriptures! In the age of Religion, to have 'studied' meant to learn what the Church defined and taught as the true principles and correct practices of various disciplines, just as today it means to have learned what Science so defines."

It was in the Middle Ages the poor people, the exploited classes, that were succored by the witch, and the persecutions partly arose from class struggle in these terms: "Only the mighty leaders are supposed to 'get knowledge' and so enrich themselves; when the lowly individual tries to do the same, he is castigated for selfishness, thinking only of his 'own lucre' and offending against 'God's law' . . . Affecting the rhetoric of selfless collectivism, the authorities declare that only the 'Realm' (the Ecclesiastic State) can rightly own knowledge and riches; for the individual, to have such possessions is theft—a sin against God and a crime against Society."

Szasz's *The Manufacture of Madness* is concerned to show how classes of people are persecuted by first calling them something bad and then finding out bad things about them: "give a dog a bad name and hang it." He implies throughout that thus we throw away riches by discriminating against those who are unlike the powerful classes, who are "the other", and that the idea of the mentally ill is a myth of this kind. Witches appear evil because the persecutors of evil must justify their persecutions, just as psychiatrists must justify their own professions by finding people who need treatment, according to Szasz.

We have shown, to give only one example, how C.G. Jung owes his achievement to translating into acceptable form the utterances of "mad people": even his first medical practice to a woman curing herself of hysterical paralysis without his intervention or wish even. He learned throughout from the inspired utterances of women, who had been isolated, and called "mad." But it was in a similar way that the ancient Greeks learned from their Sibylline oracles, their Pythias. The Greeks would take no move in political or personal life without consulting the Oracle. Neither members of government nor private individuals. Yet the Greeks, as we have indicated, despised women nevertheless, and resented them. It is not recorded how the oracular colleges of women were trained, but it is at least worth a guess that they were trained similarly to the graduates of the colleges of Hera, since inspired speech by possession was the characteristic of the oracles. And it is worth note that the oracles were delivered monthly.

Thus throughout recorded history we have accounts of movements of women toward self-realization and service to the community which have been regularly frustrated but which have as regularly returned, whether in the guise of oracles, witches, or Jungian psychology. This recurrence is due to the eternal facts of woman's nature, which are that she has the first original magic in her, which is that without her there would be no persons to consider magic; and that in her cycle is a nature that rhythmically dies to be reborn again in blood and through a descent into the underworld, a process which has been recorded in myths and rituals all over the world, and distorted into surrogate myths in which it is the man, hero, not the woman, hera, who bleeds and resurrects. But this may be the woman's gift to the man, to show him how to sacrifice and return, and he has forgotten the giver.

In the Middle Ages there is evidence that woman's knowledge flourished, but was then especially persecuted. Norman Cohn, in his *Europe's Inner Demons,* denies that there was any organized witch religion, but his book is curiously unconvincing, principally, we think, because he does not find himself able to admit that the universality of witch beliefs makes it likely that there was something *really* there, whether it was organized on a large scale or not. He seems unable to look at the nature of women from this point of view.

Thomas Szasz, also with considerable documentation, and being a medical doctor, is much closer to the realities of existence: "Because of the nature of the human bond between suffering peasant and trusted sorceress, the good witch becomes endowed with great powers of healing: she is the forerunner, the mother, of the mesmeric healer, the hypnotist, and the (private) psychiatrist. In addition because she is actually a combination of magician and empiricist, the sorceress acquires, by experimenting with drugs extracted from plants, a genuine knowledge of some powerful pharmacological agents. So advanced is her knowledge that, in 1527, Paracelsus, considered one of the greatest physicians of his time, burns his official pharmacopoeia declaring that 'he had learned from the Sorceresses all that he knew.'"

IV

Let us add to our description of the characteristics of witches, as given in the folklore or in history books. "When the Devil first appeared to a future witch he was clad in flesh and blood; sometimes his shape was that of an animal . . . Almost always he appeared at moments of acute distress . . . A witch was able to perform *maleficium,* i.e., to harm her neighbors by occult means . . . She could bring sudden illness, or mental disorder, or maiming accidents, or death, on man, woman, and child. She could bedevil a marriage by producing sterility or miscarriages in the woman, or impotence in the man. She could make cattle sicken and die, or cause hailstorms or unseasonable rain to ruin the crops."

That is one description of witches, one deriving from historical sources, taken from Norman Cohn. Now read the following: "If . . . they happen to approach or go over a vessell of wine, be it never so new, it will presently soure; if they touch any standing corn in the field, it will wither and come to no good. Also, let them . . . handle any grasses, they will die upon it; the herbes and young buds in a garden, if they do but passe by, will catch a blast, and burne away to nothing. Sit they upon or under trees . . . , the fruit which hangeth upon them will fall. Doe they but see themselves in a looking glasse, the clear brightnesse thereof turneth into dimnesse, upon their very sight. Look they upon a sword, knife, or any edged toole, be it never so bright, it waxeth duskish, so doth also the lively hue of yvoric. The very bees in the hive die. Yron and steele presently take rust, yea, and brasse likewise, with a filthy, strong, and poysoned stynke, if they but lay hand thereupon." Is this a description of a witch? It might well be, but it is in fact Pliny's description in his *Natural History* of the powers for evil of a menstruating woman. "Hardly can there be found," he says "a thing more monstrous than is that flux and course of theirs."

This simple observation of the likeness between reputed witchcraft and the menstrual taboo solves a very old query in anthropology. Margaret Mead, for example, has said, "The extraordinary thing is that the image of the witch is remarkably consistent all over the world. In one place and time the idea may be like a simple sketch while elsewhere—as in 16th and 17th century Europe—it may be tremendously elaborated. This indicates that the essential conception of the witch is one that is very, very old in human history, or alternatively, that it is a conception that can very readily spring up among both men and women." Indeed it can, and does, and is both of those things. The best explanation of the constant presence of witchcraft everywhere is the simplest one, the secret that is no secret, for it is so close that it remains a secret because nobody thinks of looking at it. The image of the witch is consistent because it is an image of the transforming and changing menstrual cycle; it occurs all over the world because women occur all over the world, and if they didn't we wouldn't be here; it is very, very old in human history because menstruation is as old as Eve; it is thought to be evil because men fear the power and abilities of women. This fear travels the spectrum from her possession of her fertility, the original magic, the creation of persons; through the castration-fear of the bleeding vagina which might swallow a penis as it swallowed this month's possible baby (which is the explanation of why witches were thought to cannibalize babies, a propagandist rumor which started with Zoroastrianism); to the other end of the scale—the jealous fear of the sexual, mental, and spiritual abilities of a fully evolved woman in full accord with the consciousness of her body.[5]

The men who were not so afraid might have been allowed to wear the horns of the Devil on their head, the sexual man with womb-horn knowledge, horns which the institution of marriage considered the mark of a cuckold: a sad deterioration when that may mean that the man does not (as in marriage) treat the woman as a possession like breeding-stock, but as a person with her own varying sexuality that may demand more than one partner.

If we are right about all this, then the historical documents about witches will confirm us. The evidence usually considered by historians is that taken at those infamous medieval witch trials. Irrespective of whether they reflect the fantasies of the judges about femininity, or are the actual confessions of members of a feminine witch-cult, they should reflect the truth behind either standpoint. Norman Cohn calls it a "stereotype." We have already had some discussion about what Mary Parlee calls the "stereotype" masculine picture of the menstrual cycle, in which investigators ask themselves whether they can find anything *bad* about the effects of the cycle, but never, never whether there is something *good* about it.

A witch was usually a woman bound to the Devil by a pact or contract. "Wash your Devil" says that black slave-mother to her daughter in A. Swartz-Bart's *A Woman Called Solitude*, meaning "wash your cunt." The Ifaluk woman sings of the "devil" beneath her skirt. Woman is "Janua diaboli," says Tertullian, "the gate of the devil." The pact with the devil is popularly signed in blood. When the blood of a woman's menstruation comes, it means that a pact is signed: she is committed to her femininity. If she doesn't like being a woman, then she is contracted to a devil. If her man dislikes the female sex, then she is in league with the devil of sexuality. So you could say that the "Devil"—fallen angel—is an image of woman's sexuality, and that he deflowers her from within.

"Among psychotic patients the menstrual disturbances are particularly severe and many of the symptoms can be seen more clearly . . . Now as a punishment for her sins the Devil had taken possession of her. He was inside her now and would probably come out of her somewhere . . . During the Sunday night she was still more restless, and seemed to be disturbed particularly by the bright light of the moon, which was full. Every twenty minutes she held a conversation with the Devil, using first her own voice and then one which was supposed to be his . . ." This was a menstruation disorder which had continued over into menopause in a patient of Mary Chadwick's. The analogy of a Lord of the Women who lives in the moon and takes possession of all women at their menstruation is an instinctive universal analogy: "There is a great deal of ethnological evidence that witchcraft is a thing bestowed by the moon," says Eliade in his *Patterns in Comparative Religion*, and that "the moon is the source of all fertility, and also governs the menstrual cycle." "Woman can practice witchcraft only once a month, at the new moon," says Briffault, of the Tartars. In India witchcraft can be practiced only by moonlight, and the moon "is the cause of time, just as it is the cause of menstruation." "The moon is the real husband of all women," say the Maoris, and the Papuans ascribe menstruation to the moon's embraces. When a Jewish husband has intercourse with his wife he embraces her in the "moon" or "foundation" (*yesod*). The Australian aborigines say that the moon claims all women by right.

Hekate is the moon-goddess, and the special patroness of witches. On the Gold Coast the same word meant both "moon" and "witchcraft." In the Shetlands witches will lie in the moonlight to strengthen their powers; we have shown that a modern worker, Dewan, indicates that the woman's menstrual cycle can be entrained to indirect light, such as moonlight, if she lies in it at ovulation-time.

In Brittany if a woman exposes the lower part of her body to the moon when it is "horned" it is likely to make her pregnant. The Devil is often represented as horned: his two horns could represent, besides the horned appearance of the womb, the crescents of the moon in its first and last quarters. Osiris was in all probability a moon god, and he was worshipped at Mendes as a goat; this is the traditional representation of the Devil at alleged witch-sabbaths.

There is an ancient Egyptian liturgy which speaks of Osiris as waxing and coming into the house each month, and dying too. His legend is one of sacrifice and dismemberment. The word "witch" is close to "cunning sacrificer," according to Partridge. If you look at well-drawn anatomical pictures of the womb, you will be able to see in it the appearance of a wise goat-head bent forward with magnificent sweeping horns, which are the Fallopian tubes. Authorities say that this appearance of horns may be "propriocepted," that is, felt inwardly with the body's own perceptions. Menstruation, in which the horned womb becomes a "wise wound," the lining is shed and the womb-wall is raw, may give "horned" or "winged" pains in the back. It signs the menstrual napkins with its renewed contract.

The goat is often depicted with a lighted candle between the horns. A candle may represent the phallic shaft, the woman's other dimension at menstruation, her clitoris, sexual use of which will carry her through her menstrual period by giving her a sense of sexual identity and help cure dysmenorrhea by producing orgasmic contractions of the womb which spurt blood into the vagina in a phallic way.

The Devil's contract then is that these feelings, with their gifts or curses, depending how you look at them, will return each month or "moon." Men are outraged by this specifically female resource, and are jealous of the woman's competent "Devil." The Papuans say that the Moon-God's embraces always have aroused the husbands' jealousies. Pliny says that "if this female force should issue when the moon or sun is in eclipse, it will cause irremediable harm; no less so when there is no moon. At such seasons sexual intercourse brings death and disease on the man." Recent work on such stone circles as Stonehenge shows that they were used as computers to predict such times: is this not witchcraft? The brides of Orkney, for whom these Stone Age circles are still "temples of the Moon," would visit them and pray there to the moon.

So the moon, by a worldwide instinctual analogy, which seems to be built in to the feminine physical condition, is regarded both as a source of menstruation and a source of magical power. Van Waters shows how first menstruation was widely regarded as the time to acquire special deities. The Torres Straits Saibai woman, for instance, believes that the moon embraces her, and that its halo is her blood. Men by diligent study of moon-practices may become witches: among the Thonga of South Africa, the male candidate for power drinks the blood of a sacrificial victim. He is then *thwaza*, which is the same word as is employed *for the renewal of the moon*. Similarly, in a Vedic treatise on magic, a woman's beauty comes from the moon, that is, it changes its character with the side of her menstrual personality which is upper-most in her. It is promoted by eating the flesh of the moon-hare.

"Hare" is a frequent witch-animal in folklore. The usual story is that a hunter shoots a hare, and follows its bloody spoor to a cottage, in which he finds a woman lying with a bleeding wound. "The hare" is also a word for the period, and the animal as a representation of the "willing sacrifice" or "conscious sacrifice"—which seems from Partridge an origin of the word "witch"—is a worldwide symbol, as Layard shows us. "Hare" or "baby-fat," that is, hormone-rich menstrual blood was also supposed to be mixed with drugs like hyo-scyamus or belladonna to make the witch's ointment which if rubbed on the body gave sexual feelings and illusions of "flying." Often a broomstick, which seems to have been a dildo, was used in conjunction with flying ointment. The result was an ecstatic trance-experience. The hare is extraor-dinarily fertile, and is one of the few mammals capable of "superfetation," that is, of bearing several litters at once. But in hard times, its womb can resorb the fetus. Its "March-madness" is like seasonal shamanism of ecstatic sex-play!

Another constituent of the witch's ointment was rumored to be soot, which may also be a metaphor for menstrual blood (as the traditional joke has it: "I know a whore who smokes so much she has a fall of soot each month instead of a period"). However, changing the color of one's skin, becoming covered with clay or mud, which is then washed off in a pageant of renewal, is said to be not only a feature of witches' rites, but of women's menstrual initiations also. In such rites a cele-brant may be seized by an ecstatic trance-experience of possession, the actions and speech of which are taken seri-ously by the congregation and priest, as instruction.

Voodoo, for example, is a religion of Haiti which runs in parallel with the official Catholicism of the island, and is like a mirror-image of Christianity. Such may have been the relation of witchcraft to the medieval Church. In Voodoo, possession and prophecy by wise ancestors is one of the purposes of the meetings, "dream-husbands" and "dream-wives" are provided for therapeutic purposes, and the Voodoo rites contain techniques for supplying these dream-lovers, who are gods, to the sexual imagination. This is very close to the "incubi" and "succubi" of medieval witchcraft. The menstruating woman in Voodoo is a particular source of magical power. She is very liable to possession by loups-garou, which are werewolves, that is, animal changes or possessions.

The witch is often said to perform her rites naked, as well as by moonlight. This simply means shamanism, or consciously induced trance-experience for practical psychological or social purposes. The old prophets of the Bible became much more interesting when one realizes that they were naked dancing shamans uttering the scriptures: "And he stripped off his clothes also, and prophesied before Samuel in like manner, and lay down naked all that day and all that night. Wherefore they say, Is Saul also among the prophets?" (1 Samuel xix, 24). Nakedness and prophecy go together, says Butterworth: "We see that the offense of Adam and Eve was, in all likelihood, that they had cultivated a practice, at least akin to shamanizing, in which they had attained a condition of ecstatic vision or consciousness, called eating of the tree of life, or of the tree of knowledge of good and evil. When their eyes were opened and they knew that they were naked, Adam and Eve knew that they were seers and persons of power and sacred quality in their own right." This must have exasperated any Deity dedicated to any authoritarian or hierarchical rule, or any church derived from a repressive interpretation of the legend, like the medieval Christian Church.

We have shown that the "Fall," the evolutionary step that made humankind, can be seen as menstruation itself. There is much evidence that the original shamans were women, from whom the men learned ecstatic techniques, perhaps at first more controlled, because not natural, like the women's, then later stolen enviously, and the female origins ignored. If the women were the shamans, and the shamans relied on the moon, this is to say that the shamans relied on the natural descents into body-consciousness that the menstrual period brings about monthly. This Apple was offered to Adam. A feature of this in the circumstances we have described might be the reappearance of the animus and his animals in association with the "other dimension" of femininity, as we have suggested in previous pages. Of course this would look magical and cursed to the men, in so far as they did not have the talents to participate in some measure. But it is the very stuff of feminine experience. And it is real magic too, in so far as it provides images that can arouse and make use of the undiscovered energies of the human personality. Magic is the play-method of investigating interior consciousness.

Many of the witches killed were old women, since "the devil walks in a dry place." Of course, menstruation is only one of the particularly feminine experiences. It is known that menstrual blood was used as a medicine to help women in the menopause—was this a use of "witch ointment"? The wearing of a chemise stained with menstrual blood freely shed was also recommended. Menopausal difficulties may not only still show cyclical manifestations, but can also show the accumulated difficulties of a life of unsatisfactory menstrual experiences, healed perhaps by witch-rites.

The only time a woman might not be a witch was when she was bearing a child (though experience shows that a menses-like rhythm goes through the pregnancy). Natural wisdom is needed whether women are bearing physical offspring, or mental progeny. In the modern "psychoprophylaxis" techniques of childbirth, trance and "dissociation" techniques play an important part. At other feminine times—let us again quote a modern authority—Elizabeth Douvan says: "Genital maturity in girls is marked most obviously by the menarche, a development that lends itself to mixed and primitive fantasy. Associated with hurts and wounds and body waste, it is the essence of primary process—the vivid, concrete, imagistic, prelogical thought process shared by dreams and poetry." How we value such a process depends on what value we give the natural spontaneous activities of the mind, what we consider they can reveal by the discourse of images of the world of nature. When we enter the feminine sphere, we enter deeply into the subjective body-experiences which make us all kin. We all have bodies, but those of us who have feminine bodies have the ability of a deep inward awareness which is commonly denied men. In fear, men may substitute for this a flight from the body; instead of deep subjectivity, a high objectivity that explores the universe. Yet there is a universe within, and the facts of that world are as actual as those of the universe outside.

What has modern psychology to say of "pacts with the Devil"? In a good sense Freud gave a "nether face" to the modern alienated psyche, just like the nether face kissed by the witches that was the Sabbath devil's hind parts. Jung agreed that Freud had given an unexampled anatomy to the shadow of modern man, and in Jung's terminology, the Shadow is the Devil, seen beneficently. Mephistopheles, with red cloak, and horns and cloven foot, and all, whose name means "stinker" (as though he were exuding the pheromones of menstruation), is a Jungian "shadow," intercourse with whom brought development to the soul of Faust. Freud himself, as Bakan showed, knew that "The pact with the Devil is therefore really a pact with the super-ego [or conscience] not to help human beings in getting these things but to stop preventing them in doing so." In other words, to let Nature in. Eliot echoes this when he is describing the nature of "inspiration": it is as though something that is the barrier to inspiration has been taken away, rather than that something new is imparted. Then this is truly natural magic.

Freud in his *New Introductory Lectures* said outright that if one wanted to know about women one must go to the poets.

Why not to the women? Or the women poets? As our quotation from Elizabeth Douvan above said, first-menstruation and poetry are very alike. If we let it be so. Perhaps the witches did. It seems so.

We saw in the Pliny another faculty attributed to witches, the evil eye. In modern terms, we have already described the medical effect of the "menstrual epidemic," and how the menstruating woman, segregated as a fiend, may produce apparently fiendish effects because of the neglect of her powers. The Ancient Persians thought this too, and attributed the evil eye to the menstruating woman: "for a fiend so violent is that fiend of menstruation that, where another fiend does not smite anything with a look, it smites with a look."

This fiend, the Devil, is (in Cohn) described by his opponents as presiding over the Sabbat as a "monstrous being, half man and half goat: a hideous black man with enormous horns, a goat's beard and goat's legs, sometimes also with bird's claws instead of hands and feet. He sat on a high ebony throne; light streamed from his horns, flames spouted from his huge eyes. The expression of his face was one of immense gloom, his voice was harsh and terrible to hear." A Jungian would regard this as a perfect picture of negative animus. If this is a monk's description, maybe he remembers what his home felt like when his mothers or sisters had PMT. Perhaps this decided him to join Mother Church, who does not menstruate, except in so far as wounded Jesus bleeds and resurrects.

To sum up: witches, according to Norman Cohn, had the following unreal characteristics: a pact with the devil; a familiar; a habit of riding to Sabbaths; the power of causing mysterious illness or ill-luck, "maleficium"; were killers and eaters of babies. We interpret thus: the blood-pact is with that dark animus-devil, menstruation; the familiar is an animal image, theriomorphic instinct; "flying" is Sabbath sexuality;

"maleficium" is the Menstrual Plague; and you slander menstrual blood by calling it "wasted babies."

Another, smaller puzzle among witch-experts is the *meaning* of the word "sabbat" or "sabbath." Esther Harding and Briffault tell us that the original "Sabbath" was the time of pause, the dangerous day of the moon, usually at its full, when the Babylonian Goddess was thought to be menstruating, or at the new moon, which in other societies was thought to be the moon's time of menstrual seclusion. Cohn lays great emphasis on the idea of this witches' meeting: "But the witch-hunt would never have taken on such massive dimensions without the notion of the witches' sabbat." The derivation of the word "sabbat" has troubled several authorities.

It is strange how little this word has been looked at, even though its true meaning is so obvious. Margaret Murray is one of the great writers on Witchcraft, though her chief contention, that it was an ancient and universal religion, has been criticized on this particular ground by Norman Cohn. Even she could not look at this word. She says in her *Witch-Cult in Western Europe* that "The derivation of the word Sabbath in this connection is quite unknown. It has clearly nothing to do with the number seven, and equally clearly it is not connected with the Jewish ceremonial. It is possibly a derivative of *s'ébattre*, 'to frolic'; a very suitable description of the joyous gaiety of the meetings." Lucy Mair follows this in her *Witchcraft* with: "The name Sabbath was not given, as most writers suppose, as an offensive reference to Jewish practices; it came from *s'ébattre*, to be gay."

"Sabbath" means "Goddess." It is the name of a Goddess. It signifies that Goddess, and it signifies Goddess-things, that is to say, woman-things.

In Orthodox Jewish law, when a man makes love with his wife, the Shekinah, the female spirit of god, descends into the house and dwells there. Another name for the Shekinah is "Sabbath." While she dwells there, no man-things may be done. No commercial work, no willful doings or manipulations, no materialistic pursuits. This is why the Sabbath is holy. It is a day, not merely of rest, but of reverie, of imagination. And of reverie and imagination of a particular kind. For by Orthodox Jewish tradition, the man makes love with his wife on *Friday night*. Therefore the Saturday is given over to the postcoital reverie, the beauty of the afterglow is allowed to develop, it must not be disturbed by doings or materialism. It is the day of love, of poetry, of inner discoveries. This is the Sabbath, the day sacred to the Goddess, to love: that is the religious way of putting it. In human terms, it is safeguard against "wham, bam, thank you ma'am" which is the ultimate perversion and denaturing of humanity. It is the reverie and the dreaming which brings the good things, the contact one with the other with rinsed perceptions, the leisurely thoughts and feelings in the warmth and understanding that sex should and does bring, which is why it is a holy thing, setting aside the magic of creating a person which it is also. So it is a very useful and practical Law. Unfortunately, as the world grew less interested in the love between men and women, and more interested in the monolithic masculine Will, this Sabbath became a mere law, an obsessive observance, though if it is observed in an orthodox manner, the reason for the Law will become plain in the feelings of the Day.

The whole sad story of the exile of the womanly spirit of God, the Shekinah, the Lady, Queen or Matronit in the history of the Jews is given in Raphael Patai's authoritative book *The Hebrew Goddess*: a surprising title, it may be thought, since few appear to know that the Jews ever acknowledged such a Person. Yet she "assumed the form of a divine queen and bride, who joined them every Friday at dusk to bring them joy and happiness on the Sacred Sabbath."

Alas, the Goddess of Sabbath went underground. It is possible that she reappeared in the Gnostic and witch-cults; and naturally she would reappear wherever a religion of equal love between woman and man was celebrated, particularly where moon-rhythms of sexuality and fertility were associated with the religion in festivals known by the moon-goddess's name or her menstrual condition: originally in Babylon the sabattu or monthly rest-day of Ishtar. The history of the Western world for the last 2,500 years has been concerned with a religion or religions that have men's faces: it is the God, the Man who is supreme. But whenever revolution against the holy things being merely men's things has appeared, then the Goddess has appeared also. We are here concerned with the Witches' Sabbath, that is to say, the Witches' Goddess.

The Goddess of the Jews, originally the Babylonian Goddess, went underground. In Jewish tradition, her nature is celebrated in the Kabbalah, a body of doctrine that is a gadfly to the orthodox, being a persistent source of wisdom to Jewish teachers in exile yet difficult for the orthodox person dedicated to the supremacy of the male to swallow. The Kabbalah has in fact been the source of most modern magical discipline. It is the source of the disciplines of reverie of the Golden Dawn, to which the great poet Yeats belonged, the most famous of magic lodges; it was the source of Crowley's Magick, together with ancient Egyptian ritual; and it is the discipline used by many modern witch-cults, such as that headed by the remarkable doyen of modern witches, Alex Sanders. Here is the Zohar, the principal book of the Kabbalah, on the Jewish Goddess: "[On the Sabbath] all is found in one body, complete, for the Matronit clings to the King and they become one body, and this is why blessings are found on that day." We have seen how the Christians persecuted sexual things, and persecuted women, endlessly. Such practices as sex for love which is religious were, and are, anathema.

Among the Jews, then, the Sabbath is a day of the week that has become the habitation of a female divinity. The biblical name *Shabbat* means the seventh day of the week, and it appears (according to Patai and Esther Harding) to have a definite connection with the Akkadian *shabbattu* or *shapattu*, which is the name for the feast of the full moon. Our own hypothesis would be that this celebrated sex for tribal or family values—the values of ovulation. If the Goddess was menstruating, then the woman down below was safely fertile. This might have been a later development, or an exoteric one.

It was a particularly Jewish invention to give this name and honor to the day of the week. Originally, however, the feast of the full moon called the *shabattu* was the feast *which celebrated the menstruation of the great Goddess.*

Esther Harding points very directly to this origin in her *Woman's Mysteries* when she says: "Ishtar, the moon goddess of Babylon, was thought to be menstruating at the full moon, when the sabattu, or evil day, of Ishtar was observed. The word *sabattu* comes from Sa-bat and means Heart-rest; it is the day of rest which the moon takes when full, for at that time it is neither increasing nor decreasing. On this day, which is the direct forerunner of the Sabbath, it was considered unlucky to do any work or eat cooked food or to go on a journey. These are the things that are prohibited to the menstruating woman. On the day of the moon's menstruation everyone, whether man or woman, was subject to similar restrictions, for the taboo of the menstruating woman was on all. The Sabbath was at first observed only once a month, later it was kept at each quarter on the moon's phases." (Which is to say, weekly.)

Esther Harding confirms also that this kind of menstrual celebration of the great Moon-goddess is still observed in the East: "In India, the Mother Goddess is thought to menstruate regularly; during these times the statues of the Goddess are secluded and bloodstained clothes are displayed as evidence that she has had her sickness. These cloths are very highly prized as 'medicine' for most illnesses." The ancient Greeks observed the festival of the menstruation of

Athena, whose "laundry" had to be washed at first monthly, then, as the meaning of the ceremony was lost, yearly: so much lost that modern scholars describe this ceremony and cannot see the womanly menstruation that it celebrates, or the meaning of the word "laundry."

Cohn says that the word "Sabbath" was "of course taken from the Jewish religion, which was traditionally regarded as the quintessence of anti-Christianity, indeed as a form of Devil-worship." But we have seen exactly what this word applied to devil-worship, that is, spiritual sexuality, means. As we have seen, according to Raphael Patai, the word "Sabbath" is *the name of the Goddess who is the consort of the Jewish God*. Just as in Tantric Hinduism, with its emphasis on sexual experience and visionary states, Shiva, the God, has his consort the Shakti (who, when she is menstruating, is called *Dakini*, the red goddess), so Jehovah had his lover, Sabbath or Shekinah. "The Sabbath" of the Jews has, according to Patai, become an empty observance whose true meaning has been neglected. "To this day, in every Jewish temple or synagogue she is welcomed in the Friday evening prayers with the words 'Come, O bride!' although the old greeting has long been emptied of all mystical meaning and is regarded as a mere poetic expression of uncertain significance."

But the significance is clear. Friday night, the eve of the Sabbath, is the time when man comes together with his wife, and the Shekinah of God fills the house. The Sabbath itself, Saturday, is kept holy, and no masculine business ventures or work is undertaken, for this is the time that must exist in the Goddess's holy afterglow of loving intercourse between man and woman. It is in this afterglow after sex that the things of God are revealed; the Tantrics called it Maithuna. So what more natural than that a term that applied to a rite of Tantric vividness and excellence, and which was the Goddess's name, should be applied also to rites which involved that "carnal" knowledge of women which was the word that Hebrew uses for all knowledge: for it was believed, rightly, that there is no true knowledge without feeling. In the Kabbalah, this is known as the sephira *Daath*. That it was applied in persecution to the rites of a woman's deity, which were hated and feared either because these rites existed among women, or because it was feared that they might grow to exist, is one of the tragedies of Europe.

That such rites were in certain communities highly developed among the Jews is certain. Scholem tells us of the Jewish apple weddings: "This is the meal of the field of holy apples . . . I sing in hymns / to enter the gates, / of the field of apples / of holy ones . : . Her husband embraces her / in her foundation, / gives her fulfillment, / squeezes out his strength . . ." for his Bride, the Sabbath, the day on which the light of the upper world bursts into the profane world of the other six days of the week.

This apple tree, the one that was partaken of at the Fall, the ancient moon-tree, *Yesod*, foundation of the woman, was the tree that Adam and Eve ate to become human. It is the tree of apples of the Song of Solomon, when the Lover consummates his strength with his Shulamite, the black sister.[6]

This black sister was once Lilith, the demon-goddess of menstruation and masturbation, intercourse with whom produced demonic mental forms. She attacked the child in the cradle, as the neglected menstruation-side of the mother may. But she, one of the two sisters, Eve for ovulation, Lilith for menstruation, Nephthys the midwife and nurse, Isis the child-bearer (goddess of Apuleius and the Thessalian witches that sent him on his quest) has not always been kept down by male misunderstanding.

We have heard her Song of Songs at the beginning of this book, we can trace her journeys to become the black Queen of Sheba with her animal foot, beloved of Solomon, his wisdom, or Shakti, that danced before the Lord God for the delight of creation; through the cults of the Black Virgin and the woman's Sabbath-rites of the witches, even to the present day, when her power and love is merely waiting to be accepted, if we do not leave it too late for the world. "Black" means "unknown." Robert Graves says of her: "The black Goddess is so far hardly more than a word of hope whispered . . . She promises a new pacific bond between men and women, corresponding to a final reality of love, in which the patriarchal marriage bond will fade away . . . she will lead man back to that sure instinct of love which he long ago forfeited by intellectual pride."

Ian Serraillier has a lively little tale told in active verse which is called "Suppose You Met a Witch." It is in Helen Hoke's *Spooks, Spooks, Spooks.* The witch in question is called Grimblegrum, a name such as one might adopt as a friendly family name privately for Mother in one of her monthly moods. The tale is meant, we should say, for eleven- to twelve-year-olds. Roland and Miranda are tied up together in Grimblegrum's sack, like boy and girl in the same body. Roland is a mild and dreamy boy, musical as a lark: he sings in the dark of the jolting sack. Miranda has a nimble wit, her brain busy as a hive of bees "at honey time." When they reach the witch's house, the children are tipped out on the glacier-minted floor. Roland chips it with his great boots, but Miranda is able to spring forward and snatch the magic wand from the witch's pocket.

Thereupon Miranda can call the tune. First, by waving the wand, she transforms the "house of cake" into a "cloud-reflecting lake" with herself and Roland two swans floating thereon, and the evil witch drowned far below in the water. This contemplative solution does not last long, for the witch pops up out of the water (traditionally, in "swimming the witches" they are detected because the water will not accept them and they do not sink), breaking up the calm reflective surface of the lake. Grimblegrum cannot however swim, and a crow rescues her by plucking her out of the water and flying her home, where, the children realize, she will dry off and put on her seven-league boots, with which she will be able to catch them up anywhere. So the children, still swans, fly away through the air, dreading the gobbling sound of the witch which comes after them through the air. They are nearly lost—they have one chance, and that is to make the magic transformation that will keep them safe. Miranda knows the answer:

> "I'll change myself to a rose of crimson hue,
> set in a prickly hedge," Miranda said,
> "and, Roland, as for you,
> you'll be a piper, and the magic wand
> your flute."

They change not a second too soon—just as the witch's boat touches ground beside them. The rose amazes and attracts the old woman:

> "O glorious goriest rose!
> I have sought you from afar,
> how I wonder what you are!"

croaks the witch, and:

> she gaped at that glorious and goriest of roses
> With the greediest of eyes and the nosiest of noses.

And asks the piper, disguised Roland (whose name means "famous country"; Miranda's name means "admirable"), whether she might pluck the rose for herself to wear. "Certainly," replies the piper but while the witch is off guard reaching for the rose, he plays his pipe so that she is compelled to dance round and round until she is torn and entangled by the thorns of the rose. When she is quite safe Roland:

> wiped
> the sweat from his brow. Then gently with his pipe
> he touched the rose. Out leapt Miranda
> to the ground.

And away home they run. The old witch caught in the hedge gets burned by a passing cowman who puts a match to it.

We don't want to be lubricious about this, but it does strike a chord, particularly with that "goriest" rose and that nice little magic pipe, with the feelings of a sexual initiation at puberty, while at the same time being a charming story. The witch is like an old witch of whom the young one is jealous, until she has acquired the magic power, the sexuality, to overcome her. The jealousy is harmlessly earthed, the contest is accomplished in the story, everyone laughs, and a relationship with one's real mother is preserved.

Our point is that such stories are excellent in that they subliminally accustom people to certain likely events they will encounter, and they present them in symbolic form, like the events of an initiatory rite, which does not preclude laughter, wit, and enjoyment. They optimistically suggest that the way out of a situation may be by having unconventional but perfectly appropriate thoughts. It has been noticed by Auden that, with the Bible, Grimm's Fairy Tales are one of the indispensable guides to life. Perhaps they indicate the form which the "Bible of the Goddess" can one day take.

Seven

The Mirror of Dracula

When vampires and others of the living dead look into a mirror, however, they have no reflection. This test is, in fact, one of the ways of spotting a vampire. Do they, perhaps, have no reflection *because they are that reflection?*

Stan Gooch, *Total Man*

Horror films are one of the great money-spinners for the film industry. In Britain, home of Christopher Lee, currently the most famous "Dracula," Hammer Films have contributed much to the export drive. *Frankenstein and the Monster from Hell*; *Demons of the Mind*; *The Satanic Rites of Dracula*; *Blood from the Mummy's Tomb*; *Vampire Circus*; *Twins of Evil*; *Countess Dracula*; *Creatures the World Forgot*; *Lust for a Vampire*; *The Vampire Lovers*; *Taste the Blood of Dracula*; *Dracula Has Risen from the Grave*; *The Vengeance of She*; *Frankenstein Created Woman*; *The Reptile*; *Dracula, Prince of Darkness*; *Hysteria*; *The Secret of Blood Island*; *Kiss of the Vampire*; *The Pirates of Blood River*; *The Two Faces of Dr. Jekyll*; *The Brides of Dracula*: these are only a few of the titles. The wording of them repays study in view of what we have said in this book.

Why do so many people pay good money to see films that the critical pundits almost without exception say are lurid nonsense? Why are millions of people attracted to the Dracula myth? Or to any of the other myths which are told in full gore-geous color by these films: not just the fable of the blood-sucking resurrector, the Count; or of the nobleman Frankenstein who sews dead people together again by science and makes them walk; but by the scores of other fairy tales told in celluloid whose chief aspects are terror and the shedding of blood? Horror films do indeed seem like Grimm's Fairy Tales for our time.

We believe that people go to these films because the stories are imaging for them inner facts that are not provided for them in any other way. The *frisson* that these films offer is not so far from a feeling of festival terror that explodes into harmless laughter or extravagance. When one sees the guts out, the true face of the monster, or the theater critic's smoking, hopping heart jetting crimson gouts that spatter, one is watching something that, normally, is concealed, now extravagantly revealed. It may be, however, that the revelation is a further concealment. One has enjoyed a conjuring-trick, and certain emotions are satisfied much as the Romans killed gladiators in order to direct attention from their crumbling frontiers.

One usually finds that the "horror" is worse in the anticipation than in the revelation. It also has an air of unreality—or distance. Most of these films are set in the past, in costume. What is inside the old dark house, behind the bland mask of the master waxworks maker? Is it not something that we really need to know, and which frightened people try to keep from us, because it is too frightful, they say, except as kitsch?

W. H. Auden tells us that detective stories are like this. In an essay in *The Dyer's Hand* called "The Guilty Vicarage," he says that the detective story addict's fantasy is of being restored to a state of "innocence," that is to say, presexual love. "The driving force behind this daydream is the feeling of guilt, the cause of which is unknown to the dreamer." Electing a murderer, and then dispatching him to the processes of the law, is one way of relieving this guilt, and restoring innocence: that murderess shed the blood, and we did not, therefore we are stainless. Thus Auden implies that detective stories have a ritual function, a magical one, like an unofficial church. They make suggestions about anxiety which the official church line does not: except in so far as Christians purport to solve that great mystery, "The Jesus Murder," also a horror story. It is reasonable to suppose that horror films, which have probably been seen by more people than have read the Bible, might have a similar function at least to detective stories. Freud said in his essay that the "Uncanny" is "that class of the terrifying which leads back to something long known to us, once very familiar."

One of the biggest money-makers of all time in the horror-film industry has been *The Exorcist.* In London alone at the height of its popularity it was playing in three West End cinemas, and yet seats were hard to come by. It has gone all over the world: millions of people have seen it. But it was continually pilloried by film critics and denounced both from the pulpit and by religious correspondents in newspapers. Cases were reported of members of the audience apparently being scared into traumatic neurosis by the film. A Dr. Bozzuto was quoted by *Psychology Today* (U.K.) for November 1975 as saying that it was not the violence of *The Exorcist* which produced these neuroses but because "it portrayed uncontrollable forces within the person, which could be unleashed by outside forces over which one had no control."

The story is of the demonic possession in modern times of a young girl, Regan. She is the daughter of a minor film-star, Chris MacNeil, who is divorced from the child's father. There is much tension in the household, which also comprises a married couple who are the housekeepers, and a young woman secretary, Sharon. The mother, Chris, is constantly quarreling by long distance telephone with the absent father. She is making a film about student revolution.

There is a subplot running parallel to this. A famous

exorcist, Father Merrin, is excavating the ruins of Nineveh. He has a revelation of a winged demon Pazuzu among the excavated statuary. It is an old enemy, and he seems to resign himself to a coming showdown, though the last exorcism he performed aged him terribly. Walking back from the ruins through the city streets, he is nearly run down by an old woman in a black coach, who careens unexplained thus into and out of the picture. There is also a young Jesuit priest, Father Karras, who later becomes Father Merrin's assistant in the last exorcism either of them will attempt.

Meanwhile, in the basement at home, twelve-year-old Regan has begun to make drawings and paintings of winged lions, and little clay sculptures resembling the Nineveh demon, Pazuzu. Sounds of rats scamper in the attic, but the traps laid by the butler, Karl, are not sprung. The mother, Chris, is disturbed at night by the scampering. She goes into the attic with a candle: it flares up mysteriously and then goes out. Down below Regan complains that she can't get to sleep because her bed is shaking so much.

Regan has been playing with her ouija board, and from it gets communications with a Captain Howdy, a gruff spirit who doubts whether her Mom is *really* pretty. The Captain expresses these criticisms in Chris's presence, as by ventriloquism. Film-star Chris throws a party. Her Director, Burke Dennings, is there, and, a great social catch, a real astronaut attends. Little Regan walks in, in her nightie, pisses copiously on the carpet, and predicts the astronaut's death: "You're going to die up there," she says to him. General consternation.

These excitements, and Regan's continued restlessness, prompt Chris to take her to a doctor, who prescribes tranquilizers, and submits Regan to frightening medical tests. In the first-draft film script, published in paperback with a transcript of the film, Captain Howdy tells Regan something she had already suspected: that her father went away because he didn't love his daughter much. Also, the doctor says that

Regan's bed-shaking is a "hyperkinetic behavior disorder." Asked to explain this jargon, the doctor says in the draft script and the novel that it is "A disorder of the nerves. You often see it in early adolescence," and that she is "overreacting" to depression brought about by the divorce.

Despite the humiliating and terrifying medical tests, and large doses of tranquilizers, Regan goes from bad to worse. Her bedroom furniture mysteriously moves about, attacking her mother with itself; and the bed still shakes. Now there is a new development. Regan's throat swells up and in a growling voice she shouts at the attending doctor: "Keep away! The sow is mine! Fuck me! Fuck me! Fuck me!" Regan is possessed.

Now despite all the doctors can do, a separate personality has developed in Regan of a powerful lecherous kind, uttering all kinds of sexual obscenities, and completely uncontrollable. The little girl's personality appears and disappears under this demonic manifestation, and her body becomes a battleground. Regan vomits green stuff copiously, and wounds open and close on her flesh. Somehow the neighborhood feels these events. The local Catholic Church is found desecrated, with a statue of the Virgin painted up like a whore, and an enormous phallus fixed to her lap. The film director, Burke Dennings, is found smashed on the stone paving below the house. He may have fallen down the street-stairs, but he was last heard of in Regan's bedroom. It becomes evident that Regan's demon, summoning preternatural strength, actually threw the poor drunk from her high window, managing to wrench his head round completely back to front. A schmaltzy police-inspector grows suspicious. A lay psychiatrist is called in, attempts to hypnotize the possessed girl, but gets his balls squeezed in the demonic fist of Regan's alter ego, instead.

At last the priestly psychiatrist, Karras, appeals to the Bishop for an exorcism, and the old expert, Father Merrin, is brought in, the doctors having failed. The priestly rites cannot control the demon either, and it levitates, vomits, shouts, curses, and confronts the priests with personalities known only to themselves, such as Karras's old mother, who has just died senile, raving with edema of the brain. The air turns icy, the Exorcist, Merrin, continues with his ceremonies, addressing the demon emphatically as "ancient serpent," but is vomited at for his pains. Eventually the old Exorcist, who has been taking nitroglycerine tablets for a bad heart, dies from the strain, and Karras finds his body at the bedside. Appalled at his mentor's death, Karras, who is a spare-time boxer, loses all sense of psychiatry, and slaps his patient Regan all over the bed. He calls upon the demon, "Take me! Come into me!" The demon obeys him, and for a moment we see Father Karras's face distorted with this personality as he advances on the little girl now freed of her possession and looking pale and terrified. We are probably meant to take the suggestion that at this point the priest is about to rape her. However, with a sudden realization of what he is about to do, Father Karras chucks himself out of the window and the demon is gone with him.

In the last scenes the convalescent Regan has completely forgotten all about these exciting events.

It was strong stuff to watch, and though we did our best not to surrender, the second time we saw the film, we were still deeply stirred. But it was not with terror, though the film seemed to say it should have been. Nor with pity, or disgust. It was exhilaration! We felt somehow that in this battle over the body of the little girl, we were on the side of the demon. So did the rest of the audience, on both occasions. They cheered the demon on in its exploits, as though it were a martial arts film! They were on the side of the little girl's new powers in her battle with the established authorities of medicine and church. We're not sure that the film meant this, though it was doubtless glad of all reactions. It might have been employing the well-known strategy of the Sunday tabloids of taking the opportunity of going thoroughly with exciting detail into events that it overtly deplored. What might have been supposed to appall us, delighted the audience's instincts—not with the shocked relish of covert sadism either, but with a kind of partisanship.

This double reaction made us look closely at *The Exorcist*. We wouldn't have felt this way if the tale had been quite straightforward. What was it really about, that it excited people so and in no wholesome manner? It was set in modern times, so there was no distancing, as in costume drama. Visually it was of a far higher standard than the average horror film, so everybody ought to have been quite frightened. Some were, by reports, but we didn't see them. People must have been enjoying something in the film which was not really about hell and demons, or to be avoided at all costs, like the films of the Nazi concentration camps. In the newspapers the consensus seemed to be that it was an evil film about evil. One eminent critic warned his readers about dwelling on such matters as demonic possession, but he appeared to see a different film from the one we and our fellow cinema-goers in Falmouth and London saw. We thought we should try to think what the film was actually about instead of assuming, as most of the press coverage did, that because the public packed the cinema, it was doing so in order to defile itself.

A friend of ours, who is a Greek Cypriot, took his mother on her first visit to Britain to see *The Exorcist*. He hoped to shock her, but she was completely unmoved. She said that she couldn't understand what all the fuss was about, since little girls growing up in Cyprus always behaved like that! This was the obvious first point. Regan was going through her puberty, under strain, in a divorced household, with an absent father with whom her mother continued to quarrel, by telephone. Mother and daughter were superficially on good terms, though an invisible playmate of Regan's, Captain Howdy, betrayed a certain suspicion of Chris's outward behavior and "prettiness." There was a lot of joshing-about between mother and daughter, like good chaps. This love felt shallow; the house was full of jumpy energy well before the possession started.

What then came upon Regan? The demon was uncontrollably sexual, shouting "Fuck me! Fuck me!" There was a great fuss among the critics about Regan masturbating with a crucifix. We quote from the transcript: "Chris has raced into the room but stops short when she sees Regan sitting on the violently shaking bed, legs apart, masturbating herself with a bloodied crucifix, clearly much against her will. Her features and expression shift to match the voices that speak through her mouth . . . The Regan/Demon pulls Chris's head down, rubs her face sensually against her blood-smeared pelvis, then lifts Chris's head and smashes her a blow across the chest." What then is this blood that the daughter smears on her hypocritical mother's cheeks? Has she masturbated so violently that she had injured herself? Is it the blood of her hymen? Or is it the blood of her first period?

Kinsey has shown that if a person does not masturbate at any other time, it is at the period that she will masturbate. The clitoris particularly is energized at that time. If menstrual blood came upon the girl Regan with its "moment of truth," its sexual power, its energy of "overreacting" to the mother's cover-up job and the divorce, and Regan's own jealousy of her mother's flirtation with the film director, then this is the natural way to regard the blood in this scene. It is the natural way to look at the "possession," too: Regan's "hyperkinetic disorder of adolescence" that so baffled the male doctors and priests. Real life knows this: the newspapers recently reported a case in which a young retarded girl was sterilized before her puberty because apparently there were fears that the parents could not handle their daughter when her menstrual periods came.

But what about the occult phenomena, and the possession itself? A standard book, *Possession*, by T. K. Oesterreich, says, "there develops in the psyche a sort of secondary system of personality which directs the person's life against his will. The subject loses control over a considerable number of his states, and it is this part of his personality which plays the obsessive role of a demon," and he says that though we often think of certain natural states as strange and contradictory, "There are naturally other states and functions which we repudiate but which nevertheless make good their claim as belonging to us." Our sexual being, particularly if we are not prepared for its advent, is one of these states that come upon us. It may be without warning: the menstrual taboo is so strong, and the subject so little discussed, that a mother may not tell her daughter to expect blood, and new feelings. Maternal rivalry or fondness may refuse to acknowledge the imminence of first blood. School will rumor what is to be expected, but the shock can still be great at this sensitive time. The girl may think that she has damaged herself, particularly if she masturbates. The Rev. Chad Varah started his phone-in service for people in despair after attending the inquest on a little girl who had killed herself because she thought her first period was VD.

Jung's first clinical writing—his medical dissertation—was on this subject.[1] He called the "possession" by the term "somnambulistic symptoms." He studied several cases similar to Regan's, in which he noted that a new character was forming in the person so possessed, and sometimes remained as the person's own permanent selves, to their advantage. He noted that "somnambulistic symptoms are particularly common in puberty," and he believed that future character was formed particularly at this time. Perhaps, he conceived, the "phenomena of double consciousness are simply new character formations" trying to break through and "in consequence of special difficulties" such as unfavorable circumstances "they get bound up with peculiar disturbances of consciousness." He says that difficulties oppose the formation of a future character and that "the somnambulisms sometimes have an eminently teleological significance," by which he means that they express the intentions, purposes, beliefs, and perceptions of that newly formed character. He says that "sometimes they give the individual the means of victory," and he mentions Joan of Arc, whose "voices" led the French to victory over the English in the fifteenth century. He says that the so-called occult phenomena can be dramatized split-offs from the dream ego, as can the communications that can undoubtedly be obtained from "table-turning." The ouija board can be the "preliminary expression of the motor components of an idea" belonging to this further personality. He speaks of the "exuberant fantasy which is so very characteristic of the puberty period. It is the woman's premonition of sexual feeling . . ." Stone's classic psychological study showed that the only measurable characteristic that differentiated girls who had had their first periods from those who had not, was an increased ability for reverie or daydreaming. In difficult circumstances or other particular conditions reveries may easily achieve dramatic form, as everybody knows. Helene Deutsch[2] quotes a case remarkably like Regan's. A fourteen-year-old suffered a psychotic attack on the second day of her first menstruation. She was brought into the clinic in Vienna, her face covered in rouge, her hair wild, dancing and laughing. She repeatedly lifted her skirt and used obscene language. She kept on saying *Politik*, and analytical treatment showed that this word was for her fused of two other words: *Polizei* and *dick* (in German, "police" and "fat"). Helene Deutsch says that "police" had to do with "prostitution," which in the girl's native country was under supervision by the police, and was to her a feared and prohibited idea. Probably a tempting one too. "Fat" meant "getting fat" in pregnancy. "It is difficult to imagine a more graphic representation of the typical anxieties besetting a girl in puberty than this composite word . . . Once again the first menstruation played the part of *agent provocateur*; it obviously overburdened the girl's whole psychological structure and her limit of tolerance was overstepped."

We have spoken of the festival of the *Hysteria* and its

serious psychological function in ancient times; this wild-haired, dancing, rouge-covered, twentieth-century maenad has discovered for herself what was once considered an appropriate celebration of the arrival of her new, sexual personality. There are no festivals for her, only doctors. Laing[3] tells the story of a girl of fourteen who is sent to hospital for treatment as a schizophrenic because she preferred to stare at a wall instead of watching television, lost weight through not eating as the rest of the family did, and washed in cold water and not hot like everybody else in the household. Laing points out that this girl behaved as people do when they embark on a course of meditation. She was by nature descending inward, as a practitioner of yoga does, ". . . a way of resting, calming, emptying, tranquilizing the mind. It seems to me," says Laing, "one of the natural functions, like sleeping, dreaming, waking, being interested in things . . . She had come across a normal natural resource, cultured out of her subculture. There may have been a competent meditation teacher (someone who had spent years and *years* staring at a wall, or nothing in particular) in town . . . However, instead of this being viewed as a possible avenue of temporary escape (the best action in some situations is to escape—this is not escap-ism) and a refuge . . . this is regarded as the prime symptom of a schizophrenic illness."

Yogic calming and stilling of the mind, detachment, is one way of dealing with exceptional conditions and attaining trance-state; the opposite of yogic meditation, zazen, samadhi, is the aroused and hyperactive state of shamanism, the rapture in which a situation is danced out or dramatized in trance for all to see, and, if necessary, to act upon. If these two kinds of reaction are deprived of their meaning or function, then they are regarded as madness: of the schizoid, or detached kind, or the participatory, frenzied, hysterical kind, respectively, in the person whose need of expression or depth of perception is so great as to force them into uncontrollable behavior. Our point is that if these energies find a receptacle, this behavior finds a social context, then it is seen to be full of meaning. The irony is that if we call these conditions madness, then we can benefit indirectly, through the doctors, like Freud and Jung, who would not have seen so far into human nature without the testimony of their mad people. We hasten to say that there are conditions that are considered unprofitable mere madness, even in cultures that recognize shamanism.

Once again, we must recall what shamanism is. A shaman is a tribal doctor or medium who can in states of trance speak with other sub- or super-personalities, or go on inner adventures that, recounted or dramatized, have social or individual relevance to the watchers. The ability to go into trance and to obtain information expressed by a dissociated personality is a skill that is highly developed in many cultures, but not our own. Fairy tales, for instance, may be the remnants of visions communicated by shamanistic religion, and the biblical "prophets" were certainly shamans. Accounts of the creative process, whether scientific or artistic, often speak in terms which recall magical practice: whether light dissociation, visionary experience, or solutions imparted in dreams.

How does a person become a shaman? Among the Mohave Indians, says George Devereaux, it is at the time of her first menstruation that a shamaness's abilities will begin to manifest themselves, if she is a woman; and Carmen Blacker, Briffault, and Eliade all imply that the original shamans were first of all women. What "abilities"? According to Jung, those of "Heightened Unconscious Performance" and of the "receptivity of the unconscious far exceeding that of the conscious mind." We "know" far more than we believe we know, and shamanism is a technique for recovering what convention decrees we should not appear to know. Among the Mohaves, "A girl's dreams are of special consequence at the time of her first menses. She is instructed to remember all the details, and to recount them to an older person, so that her future life can be predicted."

Regan was certainly trying to communicate deep feelings through her drawings of the winged energy of the lion—perhaps she was feeling the "winged pains" of the period coming—and the sculptured bird-demons, before the full shamanistic dramatization of the "possession" burst out. Miriam Van Waters surveying many peoples' customs tells us that at first period girls are wedded to supernatural beings, that the "women who are to be shamans assume their religious and medical functions at puberty," that it is then that they acquire the conversation of "special deities, or guardian spirits," and that she has such extreme power at this time that if she dreams certain disasters, the tribe puts her to death by fire. The Mohave girls are told that whatever they do at this time has significance for their futures, just as Jung said was the case for his European patients.

Evidently, then, our film-Regan was gifted, as a shamaness. No wonder Medicine and Church fought for the soul of this adolescent "wise woman." Whisnant and Zegans report that "the deritualization of menarche in American culture, which acknowledges little public importance of this event . . . may have deleterious effects upon female identity development . . ." and that the interviews in their study "highlighted the prevalent cultural view that menstruation is 'like a sickness,' something that's best ignored." Chris could hardly ignore her daughter's menstruation after the latter had smeared her cheeks with it. *The Exorcist* seems to be an allegory, then, of the return of these ignored and deritualized powers.

Thus, the first reaction of the doctors when Regan became disturbed was to give her a tranquilizer. It has been shown that tranquilizers after continual use may actually increase violence, by tamping it down, possibly because they decrease dreaming, and decrease sexual libido. Regan's disturbance, however, broke through the bell jar of the drugs, so then she was subjected to the painful inquisition of medical tests, arteriograms, and so forth, and to psychiatric inquisition. The camera emphasized the quasi-human and indeed demonic appearance of the diagnostic machines, bending down like great polished insects to inspect the terrified little girl's body. She had been bitten by the "ancient snake" of menstruation: Crawley's *Mystic Rose* shows that this image of being bitten by a snake that lives in the moon is a most frequent explanation of the blood of the period in many cultures; Eliade and Briffault agree. However deep the X-rays probed they could not find any such snake inside Regan. Cinematic X-rays would have shown in the moving pictures the serpentine undulations by which the body's organs keep their tone, but this would not have been thought significant or indicative.

To shamanize, Regan developed an alternative personality: the demon. The demon was a truth-teller. He could not conceal his sexuality; he demanded possession of the "sow" and to be fucked. He revealed to Father Karras the priest's guilt about his mother's death by speaking in her voice at the shamanistic bedside; and in the voice too of a beggar the priest had ignored in his hurry on the subway. Why was he called Captain Howdy at first? Later on, he was asked his name, and he gave it in backward-talk, which Karras recorded and played back at the local University's language-laboratory. The name then was *nowonmai*: "I am no one." Similarly Jung quotes a case in which a subpersonality converses in backward-writing and when asked who it is, answers "nobody." Nor is it "anybody" yet, since it is so rejected. But why "Howdy"? A friendly greeting; a family euphemism: "A visit from the Captain"; does the unconscious mind draw on unexpected knowledge to say *hodie*, the Latin for "today": today's the day, i.e., for the period; or is it using dream-language for "how to die" since Regan's former little girl personality must learn how to die in order to grow up? Perhaps her jealous mother would prefer her to remain a little girl. "Slut! you are too young!" That could be a jealous response to a daughter's period, with a slap to the face, if the demon hadn't got in first. For *The Exorcist* is a tragedy in that Medicine and the Church win against the woman. Regan remembers nothing of her experience: she is unchanged— and probably, when the film ends, still chemically tranquilized! A tranquilizing injection was the first medical resource, and the film-doctors were surprised that even with large doses of drugs, the manifestations continued unabated.

Why "sow"? Regan got deep enough for traditional images, the voices of ancestors, to break through. "Sowishness" is a German slang term for the period. But like snake, it is an ancient and once-holy image. Erich Neumann in *Origins* says, "The image of Isis sitting with wide-open legs on a pig carries the line, via Crete and Asia Minor, to Greece." In Crete, King Minos was suckled by a sow. The female genitals in Greek and Latin are called "pig." Most Goddess names, as is natural, derive from words or images for "vulva" or "womb." The cowrie shell was called "pig," and explicitly represents the vulva. The pig itself is a highly fertile animal, which, when sacrificed, can be employed for clothing and food and all manner of benefits, since every part of the animal is of use to us. In bad times, it eats its farrow, which thus return to the place they came from, and produce more fertility. The pig was the attribute of Demeter known as Baubo, whose "obscene dance" cheered the mourning Goddess and made her laugh, appearing even "in the supreme mystery of Eleusis."

The name of the demon is "Pazuzu." He was a compound of human, lion, and eagle, and is to be found as a bronze amulet in the Louvre. He is said to guard the Tree of Life, or bring disaster. "Ziza" is one of the names of Isis and the Ancient Egyptian liturgy speaks of the spirit of the dismembered Osiris coming and going in the house, and this signified, according to Massey, the departing and return of the blood of the menstrual period. To say that Isis "rides the sow" is sacred or visionary language for saying that she rides her fertile instincts, which include her so-called "swinishness" of menstruation. In secular form, we have the contemporary image of "riding the rag," which means menstruation. This at least is the train of association.

What does happen in the film, however, is that an apparition of Pazuzu, with enormous phallus, exactly like that of the "desecrated" Virgin Mary, and spread wings, appears at the shamanizing bedside, in the smoke of the icy air. It is as though Regan has separated herself from her sub-personality, literally her "possession," and imaged it to herself, like Jung's early dream, as the phallic womb, with outspread "wings" for flying (anatomically, the *ligamenta lata*) and the stimulated phallicism of the clitoris she has been masturbating. It is like the images of sexuality the witches make, the broomstick, and the goat-head womb-man, like a "desecration" of a virgin. But Regan has been made by the panic reactions of family, doctors, and exorcists to split it off from herself. She is ready to bestow the role of "Devil"—on another person—since she must not as a good little girl have such energies. She must bestow her sexual projection, her animus, on whoever may be there to respond to it. And, tragedy indeed—who is there to take and return to this woman her sexuality, what figure of instruction and authority? Why, a celibate priest! Who when he feels the sexual demon and the energies of life which his discipline seeks to destroy enter him has no recourse but to commit suicide! He does not know what to do with this thing between his legs, his "devil"! And the maturing girl is left with no partner, for she has risked all in this magical declaration. In this film-world of priests and authoritarian doctors there is no place for a developed woman. It is curious that the word "devil" can be derived from "bridge," just like the Pope's title of "pontifex maximus." We take the liberty of supposing that the "bridge" referred to is not only that between this world and the next, but that between person and person in sexual love, the bridge between the legs.

Some of the images are unforgettable, not because of their violence or disgust, but because of their place in the film. There is the vomiting, which, like convulsions and hyperactivity, can be the accompaniment of PMT, as can great energy. In the film, Regan's vomiting is contrasted with images of the celebration of a Mass. It is as though the priests have taken over the woman's role by dressing in black frocks, and preparing a religious meal at a table, caressingly, among whispers. Regan's response is to vomit copiously, as if to comment *unfit (or inappropriate) to eat*. Perhaps such a vibration arrives from the depths for the reason that the little white disks of the Host derive from the *selenoi* or moon-cakes of women's rites, mentioned by Raphael Patai, and the Mass is a blood-mystery. Here Regan's shamanistic comment is to masturbate with the image of the bleeding Christ as if to say: "Well! did a woman not bleed in sacrifice before Christ was ever thought of?" Certain Gnostic heresies were of that opinion.

In another scene Regan levitates from her bed, as if pinned to an invisible Cross, her eyes rolled up to show the whites like two full moons. The priests try to chant her down from her epiphany with the words: "The Power of Jesus Christ compels you! The power of Jesus Christ compels you!" But it doesn't so compel. This great dream-picture sinks back to the bed in its own good time, watched uncomprehending by the silly violent men sweating in their long frocks, badged with vomit.

As we have said, wounds break out and heal on Regan's flesh, as if to show on the skin her long beginning sequence of wise wounds that she will endure or enjoy in her adult menstruations. Her throat swells to accommodate and resonate the voice of her power, as Theo Lang says it swells due to hyperthyroid activity at the first period, but which Dodds says is the characteristic carriage of the head in Dionysiac ecstasy, and which you can see in vase-figures of the Maenads in the British Museum. Dodds comments that the swollen throat and tossing head "at all times and everywhere" is characteristic of this kind of religious hysteria, in the Greeks associated with the tearing of animals in blood-sacrifice. He quotes a description of possessive hysteria in which "the head was tossed from side to side or thrown far back above a swollen and bulging throat." In medicine, the subjective experience of a swelling throat in hysteria is known as *globus hystericus*. Its psychological meaning could be "unspoken words."

Then again, Regan twists around the head of the mother's drunken favorite, Burke Dennings; and in a high passage of the exorcism rite twists her own head through 360 degrees, right around, but without harm. Is this body-language for the passing of a threshold, of which the double-headed god *Janus bifrons* used to be held, as guardian, sacred: an emblem of the need to be aware of where one has come from, where one is going? Is it the Devil's two faces, one upper, one nether, with two languages, one outer, one inner? Is it a return to babyhood, and the energies of the infant who cannot turn her head to watch her mother pass behind? Does it have to do with being born again, a "birthing" as a woman, the head rotating through the birth-passage, in the smell and feel of birth-blood? Whatever the meaning, it was a startling image in the film, that at one time was a religious image. One may see it on ancient wells or baptisteries, as for instance, the tricephalon on the Mawnan Smith Well near Falmouth, Cornwall. Janus, the gatekeeper, gives his name to our month "January" that stands as the gate to the new year. His name was originally "Dianus," and he was brother-husband to Diana, just as Osiris was to Isis: twin and lover-in-the-womb. This Devil has seemed more beautiful to other ages and other peoples than he/she does to ours, though Arthur Koestler uses the idea of "Janus-faced holons" to construct a new, holistic biology.

Once again, this is conjecture. It was when Sharon, the young Secretary (who with Regan in happier days on a walk together met a mysterious and handsome "man on a gray horse"), lifts the little girl's pajama jacket off her emaciated body in the icy bedroom and shows the ignorant priest-psychiatrist words forming in raised weals on the skin of her belly. The shaman's womb writes on her skin for the priest to see her last appeal: HELP ME.

After that, it is technical to note that weal-formation has been shown to increase with premenstrual edema! One can see, however, the excessive edema also in Regan's bloated face. There is a further curiosity worth mentioning: that very un-American first name, Regan (nickname: "Rags"). It is not in the Oxford Dictionary of Christian Names—but most people will have met it all the same. It is the name of one of King Lear's villainous daughters in Shakespeare's play who with her sister Goneril, when her father gives her the opportunity, takes over completely the old King's rule. It is as though the matriarchs in this play attempt to return to power. However, male Kingship is restored, and Regan's dying words are that she would answer the accusations against her, except that she is suffering and would have to answer "from a full-flowing stomach" (V, iii, 75).

These films themselves are like a shamanistic overspill from minds full of terror and a sneaking suspicion that the world could be better than it is, were our conscious minds not such cowards. To our readers so far, the proposition that there is something kept secret and feared by all men, but which nevertheless insists on returning time and again, will be a familiar one. Let's restate the proposition. All one has to do is to accept that in all places blood is shed monthly. Then that the monthly period often roughly corresponds to the synodic moon-phases: that in a given woman the period may come at about the same phase of the moon each month, or that there is an event that seems to come at moon-intervals, or that is commonly associated with the tides and the moon, a monthly duality apparently reflected in the sky. That before the blood is shed, people's spirits may be low, and that they may be subject to strange fancies and dreams, depressions, or sudden demanding bursts of energy. That their personalities may seem to alter, and that they may suffer so much premenstrual tension that they become monsters of behavior compared to their normal selves. That husbands and families react strongly to these changes, and may become ill as a consequence. That old troubles of childhood may reemerge. That sexual feelings may change at this time, both in men and women. That when the blood is finally shed, there may be feelings of great relief and pleasure, especially if the flow is copious. That because the secret is kept, this blood seems to arrive mysteriously, and one may encounter it unexpectedly, in the toilet or in a waste-bin, and this can be frightening. That the smell of the blood can be sexually exciting, and yet inhibiting too, and what one takes in with one's first breath is the smell of blood. That the woman's sexuality may take on a different quality, due to the sensitivity of the womb and the unlikeliness of conception. That this sexuality may seem to our customs more of the "male" than the "female." That the time of menstruation is often an inward-turning time, when old memories walk, and monsters and angels of the inward mind are met.

Accept these facts, which are common experience to every woman and to every man who lives with a woman, whether it is a man-child with his mother or a husband with his wife—and further accept that because these are womanly matters, and matters of great moment and unacknowledged power, they are not talked about or commonly described in a society where the chief powers and consciousness are kept by the men. Regarding as it does the fully developed woman as a daunting competitor, this society attempts to suppress the powers of women as if they had never been. Further grant that the imaginations of people always and in every time and place attempt to express the secret thing in their instinct for wholeness, and if this secret thing is kept down, it will cause intolerable anxiety and monstrous images of itself to walk abroad: because it seeks expression in some form, to further its development, and this is also a human instinct—grant these easy concessions and many of the stories which we call "horror films" and flock to in our millions will reveal a deeper and more urgent meaning than their melodramatic surface would otherwise declare.

With these considerations in mind, let's look at a popular horror film with a remarkably promising title: *The Blood Beast Terror* (Tigon, 1967).

It is England in the 1840s. Two men have died after attacks by some mysterious assailant that drains the blood from their bodies, but still leaves a good deal of it coating their outsides. "Mind your clothes!" warns the Inspector. "The corpse is swimming in blood."

The sole witness of these attacks has heard a flapping and seen a something fluttering away into the night. He has gone around the twist about it, and can do nothing but shout "The Moth! The Moth!" from his picturesque nineteenth-century asylum cot.

Instead of paying attention to this man—who has seen so much that there is no other message his mind can form—the Inspector ignores the fact that a respected zoologist who lives nearby is an expert on moths, especially big foreign ones. The zoologist is called Professor Mallinger, played by the excellent Robert Flemyng in a collar like a plastic drainpipe. This strange surname is quite remarkably close to "malingerer," which is what unsympathetic people say about a woman brought to bed with a bad period.

The professor has a daughter, and he holds soirées for University students. In one of these the students perform a home-written melodrama, like a play within a play, in which a mad doctor revives corpses with electricity. Fresh corpses are preferred, which the hired grave-robbers create themselves to save time. There is an electric machine with a large display dial showing the electrical potential. A broad red band on the dial is prominently labeled "Danger."

The climax of the students' melodrama is when the play-doctor's daughter (acted by Miss Mallinger), victim of a railway-crash, is brought in ripped up and streaming with simulated blood. Galvanism is successful, but the machine pours too much energy into the daughter, the needle goes into the red danger-mark, and the dead girl rises up again to strangle her player-father, who is re-begetting her with his electrical machine. She immediatcly falls dead again, so that the stage is littered with corpses, as in Hamlet. But, like the play within a play in Hamlet, the students' theatricals give Robert Flemyng a hint for his own experiments. He pricks up his ears at the mention of galvanism: perhaps this new discovery will help him too.

Meanwhile, the daughter, having changed out of her blood-stained rags into a clean dress, goes for a walk with a new young man recently arrived from Africa with moths for Mallinger. The full moon swings through black clouds, and the moth-woman strikes again, the moon-moth. We realize that the Professor's daughter *is* "The Blood Beast Terror."

So does the Inspector, played with fine intellectual features by Peter Cushing. Too late! He rushes to the deserted mansion to find only piles of human bones. The Doctor and his monthly mothy daughter have fled. Are these the skeletons of the people that the daughter has eaten during her metamorphoses? Or are they the shells of her monthly selves? Perhaps when she changes from girl to moth, which has its skeleton on the outside, she has to shed those inner bones. She would certainly have to turn herself inside-out.

Now we are getting the suggestion of some terrifying miscegenation. Perhaps the Professor learned to fertilize moth eggs with his own semen. Or perhaps as a boy the excitement and fear of his mother's periods taught him to masturbate, and the fluttering flowery feeling was like the pumping of a moth's wings, but a moth that needed blood.

Ernest Jones in *On the Nightmare* says that semen becomes equivalent to blood in bad dreams. If the boy masturbates, he feels better; in due course his mother emerges from her menstrual seclusion, looking like her own daughter, years younger! Then, by this dream-logic, it remains the boy's responsibility to masturbate, and with his semen renew his own mother. In effect, thereby, she becomes his daughter. But what of his own renewal? We shall see.

The nefarious Professor and his questionable offspring have moved to another remote and even more opulent mansion in Sussex. By a remarkable coincidence, Inspector Cushing and his pubescent daughter have gone down there too, for an inn-holiday. These men are determined to do without women—except for daughters. The moth-girl—the moon is full again—drinks the handsome young gardener's blood. But the Professor too has designs on the Inspector's young daughter, who appears to be about twelve. He kidnaps her, in order to draw blood from her. Her first blood will be used to nourish a great winged personage now hanging suspended head-down in the cellars in a cobwebby cocoon. Blood must infuse this cobweb, in order that the devil-moth may have life.

This animus-moth in profile closely resembles Flemyng himself. He appears to be making a counterpart of himself acceptable as his daughter's mate. He applies crackling electrical energy to the pupa, but at the last moment becomes frightened at the close approach of this mystery. Instead of completing the experiment, he throws the lighted oil lamp at his own transforming pupa. The oil catches, and it burns, and instead of consummation there is consuming fire. It is a sad moment. Psyche made a similar error when she looked to see whether her lover was a serpent, and found him Cupid. Hot oil dropped from her lamp on his shoulder, he awoke, and, on his wings, fled.

Dr. Mallinger's act causes his frustrated daughter to metamorphose in fury before our eyes, red dress and all. The moth which she is, darts forward and satisfies itself on the Professor's blood. The Inspector's daughter is still tied to the blood-transfusion table, but is cut free and hurried out of the burning building without losing more than a token amount of blood. The Inspector sets light to a bonfire in the night-garden to which the great moth is drawn. Flirting with the fire, it singes its wings, and plummets to earth, dead.

This film must have arisen from appalling anxiety about the menstrual changes in a woman's temperament, and from a great fear of the blood. The Professor attempts to control this anxiety by using the blood and his sperm for "scientific" or "magical" purposes. Love-juices become scientific re-agents. He attempts to become a Moth-er on his own account, just as the film Frankenstein tries to create "scientifically," out of dead bodies and galvanizing sexual lightning, without recourse to women at all. How amusing his name is: "Barren" Frankenstein! This was the ancient doctrine, as given by Aristotle, that babies were made from menstrual blood and man's sperm: for where else does the monthly blood go during pregnancy? It was the old dream of the alchemists and magicians to create "homunculi" in test tubes out of menstrual blood and their own seed, without an inconvenient commitment to anyone in the slightest resembling Mother. Sometimes it works, as in Goethe's *Faust*, where the gifted and prophetic homunculus or mannikin in his gliding vial advises, like an Eleusinian initiate, that he who comes to the Mothers need never fear again; and mounts Proteus' dolphin to reach beyond a human state through the sea's multitudinous forms. His womb-vase shutters menstrually against Galatea's throne, and the seas are spread with erotic light, and one commentator says that thereby the sea is consecrated for the rebirth of humanity. In Somerset Maugham's fictional version of Aleister Crowley's life, however, self-elected forces of righteousness persecute *The Magician*, and break up his abominable vases for him. Some last-minute fear usually frustrates these attempts. Marlow's Faustus gets torn to pieces by demons, as by PMT.

What this mystery images, however, is the rediscovering of the power and virtue of the menstrual blood, and with its help, the remaking of oneself. If the blood is mixed with semen, as in intercourse at the period, then a homunculus will in a sense be created: a new self. We are re-created by acts of good sex, we re-create ourselves and each other. An aspect of this re-creation in a woman who believed her period was a bad thing would be to find that her senses and her erotic sensibility had a different but valid vocabulary at this time. Spiritually, a beneficent animus would be created. Perhaps this is what is behind the Osiris myth of dismemberment and return, and many other such myths. The stories would be guides and images to this magical restoration: dreams or visions recalled perhaps after intercourse. Certainly this is what the Tantrists say will happen with intercourse at the "forbidden" time.

Something of this feeling is in the lover of women, Goethe: the homosexual Maugham, however, finds horror in the idea. C. D. Daly postulates that a variety of male homosexuality may derive from fear of the mother's power and changes at the period, when the infant would take on and retain so-called feminine passivity. At the end of Faust, the hero is rescued from damnation by a heavenly rain of blood-red rose-petals that burn the sneering, fleeing Mephistopheles (who has been admiring the heavenly choirboys) like fire, but which allow the transformed soul of Faust to ascend. In Apuleius—which contains the story of Cupid and Psyche we have just mentioned—the hero is trapped in the form of a Golden Ass until he sees a vision of Isis, Goddess of the transformations, rising from the tide. Isis commands the Ass to eat from a garland of red roses carried by a priest in the procession coming from the celebration of Her mysteries. He does so, and rises, "goodlier than before."

For the Professor in our film there is no relief except to be sucked dry and burnt. The blood keeps on coming, as it must, and corpses swimming in it turn up in police-vans constantly. The CIA term for assassination is "ultimate demotion." So these young men are sucked of their blood and their youth by the mysterious moon-moth. They have been subjected to terminal castration, ultimate detumescence, and lie around, limp and bloodless, at the full moon, covered with the blood the woman doesn't need. The man who sees the origin of the plague, subject to nineteenth-century psychiatry, is not understood. Like the man who sees his mother naked, he is a lunatic, and can say nothing but "Moth(er) . . . Moth(er) . . . ," the single syllable rising from his swollen throat. Until he meets the doctor who can understand his message, who has stamped his foot on the earth and descended, like Faust, to the Mothers, he will not recover. Hysteria was once called "The Mother." Groddeck believed he derived his insight as a doctor from having bathed with his mother as a child when she was menstruating. He saw "the black, the white, and the red," the pubic hair, the white skin, the red menstruation, and had no fear; just as the societies named by Stephens who seem to have lost their aggressions have no menstrual taboo either.

The woman in the story turns into a strange, fluttering creature of blood that can fly and dart out of the darkness, like the womb with its bloody mouth, that comes in a swish of skirts, with a mothy fluttering in the vagina of sexual sensitivity at the "moment of the moon," the menstrual period. There is also the uncanny moth in Freud, which was to his patient like a woman's legs opening and closing. This is over-challenging to the male temperament, as the man prefers to have such things under his control, especially as he has the memories of his infancy to contend with, when his mother, suffering under the ignorance and guilt imposed on her by the Fathers, must have presented a similar challenge.

Was the old Professor Mallinger of the Moon with his mask of controlled terror—this acted countenance of Flemyng's was presumably meant to be read as an expression of scientific probity—the Inspector's daughter's inward initiator, who drew blood from her in a cellar of terror when the time had come for her to menstruate, like another, inward "husband" who caused her to bleed by the bite of his sharp needle? Was this a bad dream of the menarche of the daughter of a family, shared and transmitted among its members, and remembered and reimaged like shamanism or nightmares years later by men making horror films about their most inward fears? This would reduce the anxiety, showing these images to themselves and having them accepted by others paying to see them. Such films call up these unregarded forces in the film audience: forces just contained (in the allegory) by the police-action of the Inspector, who, using his intellect, selects and destroys his scapegoat. So we all feel better—until the Moon-Moth of Blood strikes again, in the same old place, the very next month!

This menstrual information is passed time and again across the mirror of the cinema-screen: Perseus' mirror in which the Gorgon can be viewed with safety—and dismissed. Dismissed because the art is usually bad, and clichéd, because its sources are disregarded by the conscious mind. Some of the great filmmakers have transcended the profitable commercial formula: Roman Polanski in his *Dance of the Vampires* gave us a comic homosexual circus, and a vision of tainted generations of vampire people that was so crammed and comical and well-constructed that it left no gaps full of unspoken secrets. He went on to make *Rosemary's Baby* in which the Devil impregnated an American housewife with the Anti-Christ. It is one of the few films in which the heroine is explicitly aware of her periods: Mia Farrow playing Rosemary rings the calendar to make her husband aware of the best time for having a baby. However, he has meanwhile joined a ring of Satanists, and a scaly devil with cat eyes comes to her at that time instead. The result is a devil's baby, regarded as a world-savior. Polanski made *Repulsion* in which

a solitary girl's mind disintegrates in blood and dismemberment. Then there was Vadim's *Blood and Roses, Et Mourir de
Plaisir* (1960) also a vampire film, in which the director's
wife's white dress spontaneously drenched itself with blood.

But it seems for the main part that these forces are
transmitted unconsciously, though great and ancient images
may be their vehicle. *The Gorgon* is an example (Hammer,
1964). In this film the delicious Barbara Shelley was every
month transformed into the appearance of a much older
woman, with a crown of snakes, who turned whoever looked
directly at her into stone statues. The unsuspecting victim
would feel something uneasy in the air, in the atmosphere of
his garden, say—he would go to the little fountain of water
and stare into the smooth pond, and in it he would at first
only see the full moon. Then—a shadow of something else
would pass. Turning to see what this shadow was, he would
catch a glimpse, and fall, turning to stone as he fell, a difficult
corpse to bury without comment in the normal way.

This epidemic of Gorgonizing in the remote village of
Vandorf comes to the attention of a famous Professor, played
by Christopher Lee, on the right side of the law for once, and
not sinister. He immediately discerns the nature of the
plague. Barbara Shelley—resembling a much older woman in
curlers (the snake-wig)—appears in the haunted palace on
the hill, seated on a red-cushioned throne, as in Jung's
childhood dream. The hero, guiding his sword-arm on a
mirror, strikes the monster's head off, but only the bleeding
corpse of the lovely girl remains. However, the plague is at an
end.

Freud in 1922 wrote a short paper on the "Medusa's
Head." In it he said that the stiffening to stone attributed to
a direct sight of the Gorgon's face is an erection of the penis,
sexually excited by the female genitals, but cold as stone
because it is frightened at their appearance, which Freud says
resembles most of all a castrated penis. Freud does not say so,
but the effect on the psyche must be enhanced if that

apparent wound is also bleeding, and if one's first sight is of one's mother's vulva.

C.D. Daly in numerous papers goes much further. He says that the castration fears are particularly aroused by the menstruating vagina, which bleeds like a wound or like a toothed mouth—*vagina dentata*—which had bitten off a penis, and most particularly, he says, because it recalls one's experience with one's mother when she was menstruating: a mixture of sexual excitement and extreme terror. He says that Freud is wrong in believing that the Father is the source of the castration fear: it is rather that the Mother's menstruation is the kernel of the Oedipus complex, and it is her great power at this time which has to be controlled by all the devices of patriarchal civilization, including the menstrual and incest taboos.

The Gorgon's head was a very important emblem for the Greeks and Romans. Apparently the word "Gorgon" derives literally from the phrase "the moon as it is terrible to behold." "Medusa" means "mistress." Neumann says that "the power of the Great Mother is too overwhelming for any consciousness to tackle direct," and Slater comments that this describes the mythmaking process, and that the Gorgon's head, frightening yet fascinating, represents the mother's genitals. Since the winged horse Pegasus, symbol of poetic inspiration, springs from the blood shed from the Gorgon's decapitation, this can signify the hero freed from the mysterious secret fascination, just as the Golden Ass resumes humanity by grace of the Goddess's roses. Perseus used the prize of the Gorgon's head to turn his enemies to stone, and it eventually took its place as the center-boss or omphalos of wise Athena's shield, which we have suggested is a symbol of the inner vagina or cervix of the womb. There it was known as the Gorgoneion, which became a protective amulet "not always with a hideous face, but sometimes beautiful in death." There is a large Gorgoneion shown at the museum at Bath, which is like a radiant bearded sun, full of life and strength. We have mentioned the sun's eclipses by the moon: smoked glass will reveal the solar prominences writhing like snaky locks. This Gorgoneion is part of the Bath ruins of the Roman temple of Minerva: the Roman goddess who corresponded to the Greek Athena. In Athens, the goddess Athena was the center of a menstrual cult of the women, in which her "laundry was washed," meaning her menstrual towels. Bayley tells of the ancient story of the moon-princess who gives you joy, or whose glance freezes like ice. Campbell says that the Gorgon represents Mother Nature herself, and the more she is excluded, the more terrifying her Gorgoneion will become.

One point of oddity, which is no more than a coincidence, is that the Gorgon, who is called here Megaera, is played by Barbara Shelley. The poet Shelley wrote a very menstruous poem about the Gorgon's head:

> Yet it is less the horror than the grace,
> Which turns the gazer's spirit into stone . . .
> A woman's countenance, with serpent-locks,
> Gazing in death on Heaven from those wet rocks.

What is more interesting is that the film's name for the Gorgon, Megaera, is not a Gorgon's name at all. It is the name of one of the Furies, born, according to Hesiod, from the blood of castrated Uranus, and avengers in particular of matricide and other crimes against kinship. However, in the same way as Perseus transforms the power of the Gorgon to his own purposes, so in Aeschylus' *Eumenides* the Furies are transformed into civic deities by the intervention of Athena. Similarly, in our film, Barbara Shelley's head is struck off under the direction of the wise old Professor, Christopher Lee, who wishes to protect his best student against being turned into stone by the woman's mysterious monthly "possession." In the same way, Keats's old philosopher Appolonius teaches his student Lycius hatred of the loving snakewoman, Lamia. Lycius, destroyed by the conflict, if not the Lamia's "death-breath," dies at his wedding-feast.

Why the snakes? A. P. H. Scott[4] points out that during an eclipse of the sun (during which the menstruation of women was thought by Pliny to be particularly dangerous), the moon's shadow rushing toward you across the land ripples with the refractions of the earth's atmosphere like snakes. The solar corona can also be observed wriggling like a crown of snakes round the moon's shadow, if you use smoked glass. However, we have also seen that it is a common cultural image of the menstruation that a woman is bitten by a snake-god who comes from the moon. The moon sloughs herself and renews, just as the snake sheds its skin, and so does the sexually undulant wall of the womb renew its wall after one wave-peak of the menstrual cycle: the woman renews her sexual self after shedding blood as the snake sheds its skin. The wavy waters of the tidal sea are comparable to swimming snakes, and a good vaginal orgasm can feel to one's penis like a sea undulant with such snakes: a sea which is, of course, tidal with the monthly period. In addition, if the menstruation arouses memories and fantasies connected with the experience of birth, remembered with great vehemence in magnified images, then the birth-cord twists like snakes, and the cervix of the womb during the preparation for the first stage of labor, dandles and undulates over the presented head of the baby about to be born. A baby lives in continual undulant motion surrounding its skin, until it is born into an unfamiliar stillness and light. There will be a crowning with the cervix of the womb which contracts with undulant movements, as does the pelvic floor, in snaky segments, and one will be crowned also with the vagina's lips. These images are expressed by certain African tribes who make their candidates for adolescent rebirth by circumcision wear high collars of horsehair, making the candidate look exactly like a baby just after the crowning. Fear of the snaky genitals may result in what Freud calls upward displacement away from the actual site of the fear, thus giving the head a crown of venomous serpents in order to direct the attention away from the genitalia. All in all, the Gorgon is a formidable guardian of the deeply feminine experience, who makes men "marble with too much conceiving." Partridge says that the word "Wife" came from "Wave."

A *Haunted House of Horror* (1969) is what the family house becomes if it is haunted by a restless and irritable woman, her wise "wound" unlistened to, changing to herself and others in her cycle, carrying change in her wake like a great menstruous ship. Should we not attend to these public dreams, the horror films, with the kind of attention we give private ones? Much of their content is sadistic, admittedly, and it begs the question to say that this reflects the age which we live in, which is sadistic and aggressive. Yet Stephens seems to show that aggression is linked with an avoidance of menstruation, and C. D. Daly tells us that all sadism is rooted in the menstrual trauma. In fact, if the age is not aggressive and sadistic on its own, it is at least partly these things because it is overmasculinized. If, as Daly suggests, sadism, the desire to shed blood or cause pain for pleasure's sake, is rooted in menstrual trauma and taboo, it is because the feminine role and quality is misunderstood and neglected.

In dreams, the woman is sometimes represented by the house which she loves and furnishes, and in which she carries out her transformations, for example, of cooking or decorating. The house is the body of the woman. In this film—or dream—*Haunted House of Horror*—murders with mutilation are committed again and again in a certain house by some unknown person. Yet the band of young people must repeatedly come back to this house in search of their thrills and adventure, fascinated and terrified, simultaneously mocking it and tempting it to commit yet another of its bloody murders. A new murder is their half-innocent adventure-quest.

At the climax of tension the criminal is revealed: it is the young man who as a child was locked into the cellar of this house, and his only comfort was the cold light of the moon. The result of this childhood experience is that when this moonlight shines, he must shed blood. Which he does, just before the police arrive in their cars, in a last revolting murder when he stabs another boy through the groin, replacing the penis of the young man with a bleeding castrated wound. His victim bleeds also at the mouth as he falls. The killer hacks at the limbs, cutting him "down to size," like any dying god scattered after his pride to be buried in the land to restore his fertility.

The film ends with the killer-youth running through the night-gardens of the haunted house, his shirt like a loosening skin or blood-drenched caul, the full moon shining above, and turning into a silver crescent down below, the long and bloody knife in his hand.

Shrink this bloody knife down and give it its complement, the other, waxing crescent, and put the sharp knives like white canine teeth into the gory mouth of Dracula, Prince of Darkness, and we have the great overriding image of the animus of menstruation of the horror films: the most popular of all the modern myths of the cinema.

With what a *frisson* Dracula stealthily raises the lid of his coffin, lips twitching off the crescent teeth, and rises to go hunting into the night for young ladies to bite so that their blood flows in a swooning satisfaction! With what courage the wise Dr. Van Helsing confronts the hissing monster, toting a Cross of Christ which pulsates luminously and brands the recusant vampire with its mark. With what panache the most famous of all vampires, Christopher Lee, glides with his white half-moon profile up and down darkened night-stairs, wrapped in his cloak of night with its blood-scarlet lining! How he snarls, his mouth set with moon-teeth and running with gore. How he expires in orgiastic convulsions as the sharpened stake penetrates him bloodily, and sticks in his heart like a vast erect phallus displaced from below, or like the bleeding spear of the legend restored to its Grail. How handsomely he crumbles to dusty reds and purples in the direct sunbeams, as dreams do, his countenance collapsing on itself like lion-face with a mane of dust, the eyes glaring, the ashes remaining to be gathered up by his disciples, mixed with undamaged teeth, for their instant alchemy of his resurrection into the next film by admixture of fresh blood. With what provisionality Van Helsing stands in his intellectual triumph as the wind sweeps the ashes away, or the swift river of life carries the vampire off under the ice, until the next time, when the moon is full again, and Dracula and his three wives creep out to terrorize young women again!

Dracula's saga was begun for our time by the red-bearded barrister Bram Stoker, who became the great actor Henry Irving's manager. Stoker was married to the beautiful Florence Balcombe, who was much admired by Oscar Wilde, and who was also, according to authorities, frigid as a statue. It is likely that a woman with an unsatisfactory sex life will have very bad menstrual disturbances. Was it some image of these that gave Stoker's subliminal mind the hint that formulated a myth of formidable power, out of the ferocity of a frustrated bleeding woman, crackling with energy and unacknowledged sexuality? It is certainly possible. The image satisfies at one and the same time man's fear of the unknown side of woman, her dark monthly place (Dracula films always show beautiful pictures of the moon); and also woman's own natural fascination with the side of herself forbidden to her by men. This side she feels, if it could get its chance, would be more than a match for the men. Dracula is shown in the films as almost a hero, defeated time and again by the masculine Christian and scientific virtues, turned ugly and menacing, but still an aristocrat coming from a long line of potent ancestors: the Devil, the secret initiator into blood, the other husband. How amusing, though, the insistent title "Count," when we think of the etymology of "mensuration" in the measure of the month. With regard to the rank, George Devereaux notes how in

Italy menstruating women were regarded as going up one: a peasant became a lady, a noblewoman the Virgin, and presumably the Virgin a goddess.

The first Hammer *Dracula* (1958) brought something new into the vampire story. In the earlier films, Bela Lugosi starred as the Count, and once, Lon Chaney Jr. The first innovation was the self-possessed sexuality of Christopher Lee's performances. He has the kind of saturnine masculine grace that does not exclude the feminine. It therefore fits him especially for roles that satanically challenge clear-cut accepted values, and it accommodates him especially to certain feminine eroticisms for these reasons. Bela Lugosi was indeed magnificent, and on stage his intensity was absolutely compelling, but his face was fixed into a mask of anger and spite, when he was not actually looking aristocratic, which meant expressionless. Christopher Lee's usual expression, on the other hand, really conveys the feeling that this man knows something that we don't: it is serene, like a religious master. When he is being bestial, it is exciting as well as frightening; not like a tantrum at all, but like animal electricity.

And there was what he did for his ladies too. Before they were bitten, they were chlorotic weak creatures with vapors, dressed in stiff constricting corseted garments, who spoke in faint and genteel voices expressing deep frustration. After their blood had been shed for the vampire, though (and it is always from the *neck*; as we say neck or cervix of the womb), and they had suffered their first death into their new lives as vampires—why, what creatures they became! The corsets were replaced by practical white unhampering shrouds, very free and easy, sometimes a little blood-stained to show the red on the white, with the black hair and the bright glances tossing above very low-cut shrouds displaying a great deal of rosy bosom. Their eyes shone, their gait was swift and vigorous, they spoke energy with every glance, and their smiles, full of bright teeth with handsome canines, like neat panthers, were flashing and free, like Keats's "La Belle Dame Sans Merci." At last there seemed some point in becoming a vampire! Dracula opened the permissive sixties with his chorus of happily bleeding women, with broad hints about sexual menstruation. The old Moon-Professor had come through, and had undergone a rejuvenation!

Those the lady vampires bit became infected with these joys also, though they began, before they gave themselves up to their rebirths, by feeling a bit tired, and retiring to bed, allowing their hair to fall over their neck-scars. All that withstood this renaissance of energies was the thin-featured Professor Van Helsing, often played by the intellectual countenance of Peter Cushing, who stood for the restrained and sexless virtues of the drawing-room and the laboratory.

A feature of the films is the climax when Van Helsing appears waving a Christian Cross, at which the vampires recoil, disconcerted and hissing venomously. If the adage that the gods of the former religion are the devils of the next, is true, it is easy to understand why the modern representatives of the pagan menstruating goddesses will be made to recoil from the Christian symbol in a society that is still nominally Christian. In effect, the blood of Jesus has taken away the power from the blood of the menstruating women, especially since Christianity is concerned principally with the values of ovulation, and women, not as representatives of the deity, but as breeding-stock to bring more sons of God into the world. Dracula is like an image of Jesus' elder brother, who is said to have been the fallen Lucifer; he is certainly at the opposite pole of the menstrual cycle, since he ushers people into a new life after death, rather than ushering new people into the world from the life before birth. We know that Christianity prefers to ignore the sexual energies, and particularly their most expert bearers, the women, and exalt instead masculine detachment. It is notable that the head on crucifixes is in 90 percent of cases turned to the right, which is like an image of the child emerging from the mother's legs. Doctors always prepare to deliver babies from the right-hand side of the bed.

Dracula's freer concerns with individual illumination and children born of the spirit at the time of blood is seen as the shadow of the Cross, which the light of the Cross dissipates. This too is the crossroads for the menstruating woman: that her sexuality if satisfied at her period will give her her own self-energy, but on the other hand she will inevitably proceed on her cycle and change to her instincts at ovulation, a fortnight later, that will if she has intercourse very likely dedicate her to nine and a half months of pregnancy and an unknown time of dedication to the child that is born as a result. It is no wonder that Dracula screams if he wishes to taste freedom once again before he is reborn as a helpless human child. It is this cross at which his female disciples quail.

Hammer's great contribution lies in showing Dracula as evil chiefly in the eyes of his opponents. If we use our own eyes, we can see with what vigor he lives through his periodic deaths, and with what pleasure, in comparison with the vapid diversions they are offered by established values, his women associates live. Indeed in later films we see him, like the other side of Christ that he is, with power over all animals, with the power of self-resurrection at will. He is magic, and he is the magic of the women expressed in masculine disguise, but he has been outlawed, and therefore declared evil, like the God of the Witches, of which he is a further manifestation. Can one doubt it as one sees him weep his tears of blood? The garlic that repels him was to Avicenna a "provocative of the menses," and a hastener of his change.

We have mentioned sadism, and there is a considerable literature of the vampiric sadist who treasures blood in actual and not film-life. A paper on this subject by Bergh speaks of the "symbolism" of the blood as a most important factor varying from case to case, but does not suggest in what this symbolism consists—except that in the patients cited the blood from which they obtained such pleasure was "an unobtainable object" or a "forbidden fruit" which "as his therapy progressed, proved to be his 'unobtainable' and 'forbidden' oedipal wishes toward his mother." Should one not say rather, to the "mother-world"; that is, a world in which women are provided with their full rights and knowledge? As we have said, C. D. Daly would immediately point to the events of the menstrual cycle as the source of this vampiric patient's sadism; he quotes instances in which sadists under analysis recall a desire to lick the bleeding genitals of their mothers; and Layard in the course of a study of an important Celtic tale from the Mabinogion says that "The hag's blood is a female symbol of deepest wisdom and a knowledge of opposites." It is the flight from this blood-wisdom of the female that is reconstituted into sadistic fantasies in the male psyche both in actuality and in films.[5]

Recently, Christopher Lee has played a heretical clergyman dedicated to bringing into the world by means of cruel birth-magic an avatar of "Ashtaroth," a demon (*To the Devil a Daughter*, Hammer-Terra, 1976). It is indicative that this "Ashtaroth" is persistently referred to as "him," whereas, of course, Ashtaroth was the great Goddess of the Middle East. Lee, however, takes up again his "other husband" role: there is a rite shown in which he has intercourse with the mother of his child, which he later sacrifices, simultaneously with his golden image as "Ashtaroth" having intercourse with a young nun of his heretical order. Thus he is both literal father and divine lover in the one ceremony.

Later in the film, the young nun is to be made a super-woman, or avatar of Ashtaroth, by being baptized with the blood of the baby film-fathered by Lee. We are shown a scene in which this baby is born bloodily—apparently by scratching its way through its mother's belly. The legs of the woman in labor are fastened together with special white ribbons which Lee kisses first. In its manifest meaning, this is in our opinion one of the most revolting scenes ever filmed; but its latent meaning is that the mother of the child wishes to sacrifice herself for her belief that her death will give the child a special magical potency. She is a willing sacrifice; as is another woman in the film who transfuses her blood into bottles by repeatedly squeezing a rubber bulb until her hand weakens and she dies. The blood here is used in making a magical circle. Layard discusses this role of "willing sacrifice" by blood-shed in the figure of the Hare as Moon-animal, both in mythology, and in a case history in which a young woman becomes a "superwoman" compared to her former self, through dream analysis of her *mother*. The crux is an acceptance of the "willing sacrifice" of the moon-animal by the mother.

In the film's climax, the young nun is rescued by a writer of black magic tales before the blood-baptism occurs, though we are allowed to conclude that since a drop of blood has fallen on her forehead, she *may* after all have become the avatar. The novelist breaks Lee's head with a stone, which makes it bleed, and kills him. This might indicate that the desired change should take place *within* the black magic practitioner, and that he should not involve innocent victims, or attempt to create menstrual allegories by killing his children. He should baptize himself with blood—but it wouldn't be the same thing, of course, since he doesn't have periods. However, the embittered and passionate skull is split with a little yoni-wound, like a third eye.

However, according to Mr. Cecil Williamson's remarkable museum, "The Witches House," in Boscastle, Cornwall, women were said to abort their dream- or demon-conceived babies, and to hang them on a special tree for purposes of oracular prophecy. This type of rite has always been rumored of Gnostic practices; and makes its appearance in modern times among individual women as the fantasy of the "jelly-baby." There is of course no reason why this should not have taken place as a self-determined act by women wishing to gain power and mastery over their feelings and life-energies, though we nowadays find it difficult to stomach in this form, particularly as a religious practice. Such imagery is, however, as Jung shows, in transmuted form, behind the symbolism of the Mass. We might also conclude that such rites may be "psychodramas" enacted in the outer world at a time when the interior mastery of the images has been endangered. Above, we have suggested that fertility rites of blood-sacrifice may have been instituted as the women lost some hold on the meaning of their monthly changes, or wished to convey its feeling to the male people, or had them taken over by those same male people wishing such feelings for their own, and the magical blood too. This is what appears to have happened in *To the Devil a Daughter*. Much play is made of the inverted Christian Cross: it is most unusual to see an upside-down metal cross as a neck-ornament, especially on a nun! However, just as the Christian Cross is *arms open*, so is the magical inverted cross *legs open*; and this corresponds to the ancient image of the Sheela-na-Gig, from whose open legs and spread vulva all the world's goods flow. In our film the takeover quality by the male principle is illustrated by this Sheela-na-Gig posture being duplicated by the male image of "Ashtaroth," with Lee's features, legs spread apart so as to make this inverted cross. The posture is exactly seen in the New Guinea *dilikai* figures and we have mentioned the image of Isis riding a sow, image of fertility and the giver of the world's domestic goods. So not only does the male practitioner take the Goddess's name, he takes her ritual posture also!

Even more recently, United Artists have made a film of *Carrie*, in which a girl's terrifying poltergeist and telekinetic abilities are linked with her late menarche. Her powers are unleashed to destroy a town when at a high-school ball she is drenched by a practical joker with a bucket of pig's-blood!

We have in front of us at this moment a fine still from *Famous Monsters of Filmland* for December 1975 illustrating the film *The Incredible Professor Zovac*. It shows what must be the archetypal gesture of all horror films, from Dracula onward. The monster carries off, cradled in his arms, the defenseless heroine, in order to wreak his unknown will on her. Who does not remember how Dracula in his cloak stoops like a wave of blood-lined darkness to lift and carry off the unconscious form of his lady victim, without so much as puffing, but gliding effortlessly with her in his arms, his moon-face intently in profile? In our *Famous Monsters* still, the monster is a black man with a great iron-toothed collar around his neck: he has bolting eyes, and teeth like crescent moons: the tusks which, as Layard explains, in Malekula represent the waxing and waning moon, and therefore a cult concerning the underworld. Jung says that the lunar crescent symbolizes duality; and Neumann remarks that "the terrible gullet of death or the devouring womb that he must pass through consists of two crescent moons that are everywhere connected with the great dark Goddess of the night."

The victim here is a white lady, traveling with her throat stretched and her bosom thrust out and her eyes closed, leaning back in those dark arms, unconscious of, or resigned to, her fate. Time and again this is the badge of these films and their poster; and most of them are concerned with frustrating the loving monster of his prey, hunting him with dogs, burning him in bonfires, catching him in collapsing laboratories and castles, shooting him down in swamps, or burying him in sulphur. But of course he always returns.

We began this chapter with an epigraph from Stan Gooch's excellent *Total Man*. He shows that one can look at brain structure as a dialectic between old brain and new, as it might be a dialogue between the ancient powers of a Dracula and the modern science of a Van Helsing, deeply suspicious of the old ways. Or it might be seen as a dialectic between body-consciousness and cerebral consciousness, between the provisional conscious mind and the body-rooted images of the unconscious mind, with their wisdom rooted in genetic processes and the formative energies that make us human beings. It is the one energy with the two faces, like Janus.

Gooch sees this reflected historically in the displacement of the shamanistic and possibly matriarchal Neanderthal people by the clever and heartless patriarchal Cro-Magnon warriors. There may or may not have been an original matriarchy. What is certain is that each person starts his or her life under a mother's rule, expressed by body-language, since it is too early for spoken language, and that the mother's body-language reflects the changes of her menstrual cycle. It has been shown that the apparently random gestures of a young baby's limbs are such a language expressing responses to his mother and his environment generally. It is certain too that the neurological structure of every person's body reflects a division between the intellectual powers of the new brain or neocortical structures, and the older, limbic brain.

It is of course this limbic region that we suppress with our tranquilizers, whether we administer them to counteract premenstrual tension or for any other reason. And it is this region of older powers that is visited each month by Every-woman in the so-called "regressions" of her period. Old and sometimes frightening images arise from these places, with their bodily wisdom, their wounds and their healing which "happen of themselves." All the people of folk tale and fairy story live there, the little people, the talking animals, the magicians and merlins, and it is their stories that are retold in magnified images of terror by the cinemas of the new brain. But these powers are friendly ones. Gooch shows how the main brain-trunks communicating between old and new brain cross over, as the light reflecting in a mirror crosses over in making its image. Why is it that Dracula has no reflection? Because he *is the reflection: you are on the other side of the mirror.*

Epilogue

We have yet to see the "Bible of the Goddess" written for modern times. We have suggested that it should come from mental processes that are more akin to the creativity of the artists than to the reductionisms of science. We believe that the polarization between science and art is unnecessary and is likely to prove deadly. All the testimony shows that the creative process of discovery is the same process in both science and art. Perhaps our next evolutionary step as a species might be to develop a "science of the imagination" that does not neglect the inner life. If we do not, then it is likely that we shall perish.

It is acknowledged that the process which leads to discovery in science and to the creation of new works of art involves a creative surrender and a rhythm. No artist, no scientist, no poet can make works by a deliberate act of will: one has to accumulate insights and data with one's conscious mind, and then one knows one has to forget the "I," the "ego," to forget one's preconceived ideas, and to allow the more "unreasonable" and ancient aspects of the mind to find the pattern to one's material. There is a descent, and a return, with the knowledge and prize of inner riches.

We believe that the pattern of this descent and return was learned by the women from their menstrual cycle, and imparted to their male partners, who have taken it for their own, and forgotten their teachers. We think that the physical experience made possible the mental one. This subject deserves another book, but let us indicate how it may be by offering a short scenario of a creative process. Let us suppose that a woman artist is setting out to paint a picture of God, and let us comment aside on the creative process as she undergoes it from a much-respected masculine source, *The Hidden Order of Art* by Anton Ehrenzweig. We shall see that the latter speaks of fragmentation and reintrojection (that is, descent and return) in an abstract and purely mental sense, while what the woman (or any other artist) actually undergoes is far different. In our little sketch we suppose that the woman is actually menstruating, but has not yet—not until she actually finishes the picture—seen the analogy between her creative struggle and her feminine experience. In the following Ehrenzweig speaks in the italics.

"Any work of art functions like another person, having independent life of its own. An excessive wish to control it prevents the development of a passive watchfulness towards the work in progress that is needed for scanning half consciously its still scattered and fragmented structure . . ."

Our woman artist is painting a picture of God, and no doubt He will emerge on the canvas in just such a manner of growth; but what a wise attitude also to take to bodily processes: watchfulness without painful fear or straining. Maybe it won't hurt this time, though in painting a picture there is always a moment of apprehension before the creative changes begin, a breathless time, like a taboo hour. (How "scattered and fragmented" is the literature of femininity, so far.)

"We have seen," continues Anton Ehrenzweig, in this *The Hidden Order of Art, "how 'accidents' that crop up during the work could well be the expression of parts of the artist's personality that have become split off and dissociated from the rest of the self . . ."*

"Damn it!" says our woman artist painting God, as she

knocks over a jar of brushes, "I must be going to have a period!"

"Fragmentation, to a certain extent, is an unavoidable first stage in shaping the work and mirrors the artist's own unavoidably fragmented personality . . ." says Anton.

"My clothes don't fit today; I snapped at my boyfriend; I don't fit in a man's world at these times," says our woman artist, as her first brushstrokes, to an outside observer appearing almost arbitrary, begin to sketch out the structure of her painting of God.

And *The Hidden Order of Art* continues, *"The artist must be capable of tolerating this fragmented state without undue persecutory anxiety, and bring his powers of unconscious scanning to bear in order to integrate the total structure through the countless unconscious cross-ties that bind every element of a work to every other element . . ."*

And as our woman artist adds to her canvas brushstrokes of blood red that she does not yet understand are an essential part of the picture, yet which she knows must be there if it is to be a true picture, Ehrenzweig concludes: *"This final integrated structure is then taken back (reintrojected) into the artist's ego and contributes to the better integration of the previously split-off parts of the self . . ."*

And as Ehrenzweig finished his confident discourse on male creativity, our woman artist suddenly realizes that her picture is finished. She steps back in order to see as a whole what she has been painting. She needed to paint a picture of God, and she has done so. Now she sees it and cries out with astonishment and joy: "Why—She is menstruating, just as I do!"

Afterword— The Menstrual Mandala

The Wise Wound since 1978

Mandala: A pattern which is effective in connecting one part of experience with another, and the contemplation of which leads to insight. A mandala has a center, a boundary or circumference, and cardinal points. It often depicts a rhythm, which one can see at a glance in a single image. The simplest form is that of the wheeled cross, and this is the most ancient symbol known. The moon cycle, with cardinal points at full and new, first and last quarter, forms just such a mandala. The menstrual cycle can take a similar shape, with menstruation and ovulation, and the start of preovulation and premenstruation, as its cardinal points.

I Myths and Secrets

The essential message of *The Wise Wound* was that menstruation is a great and neglected resource. It is also an evolutionary force. In modern times it has been not only neglected, it has operated as a persecution, in which women are treated as inferior, because they bleed monthly, and, apparently, uselessly. Thus neglected, menstruation has turned into a sickness. Its language has been pain and sorrow. Once, it was honored by sayings such as "Woman partakes of immortal being, because she bleeds and still lives."

To masculinist science and religion, women are essentially breeders of children. They have only an ovulatory function. Their other half, the menstrual half, is neglected. In this side of their being they are the conveyors of imaginative and creative energies, and initiators into creative modes of sexuality. This was and is our message.

The Wise Wound was the first book ever published to show the range of that neglected area. When it first came out, in 1978, there was nothing else like it at all, and a lot of people were taken by surprise. It is wonderful how its message has spread, and how so many women have responded to truths in it which are self-evident once they are pointed out. Many lives have been changed by accepting, even experimentally, its suggestions and propositions. "Only look; trust the bleeding."

Of course our book is not at all the sole factor in this revolution. Such ideas are in the air when the time is ripe for change. Many felt as we felt, and have developed their parallel statements. One consequence is that menstruation can be discussed nowadays much more freely and openly among women, and men with women. Of course it means too that the word "menstruation" can be used in sit-coms, and menstrual jokes cracked in Monty Python films. But also it means that the valiant Greenham Common women can say "Warfare is disguised menstruation" and be understood. Nor is it a small thing when a Channel 4 TV series[1] can include at peak-viewing time a discussion of menstruation as one of the ways of redeeming time from its objective, industrial aspect, and restoring to people the certainty and value of subjective, personal time in the inward-looking that menstruation can bring Everywoman every month.

In the space available to us in this Afterword we'd like to hint at some of the more striking developments that have come to our attention in this subject since *The Wise Wound* was first published. That the pattern of the woman's cycle is the instigator of all cultural patterns and of social evolution was suggested by us (Chapter IV, pp. 149–53) in 1978, and subsequent anthropological work both independently done and stimulated by our suggestions does seem to show that this is true. The way that folklore and religion holds at its heart the mystery of woman's redeeming blood is supported now by much distinguished work, part of which we will later summarize. But such is the nature of the woman's contribution that this is not a matter of merely intellectual patterns, interesting and potent though these may be. It is personal and it is here and now. The fertility cycle operates in every household where there is a woman; beneficently if accepted, in sorrow and frustration where it is rejected.

Truly there is wisdom in the Hindu description of a woman as a "house-goddess" or the Anglo-Saxon term for a wife as "linen-goddess": weaver of the clothes, the table-linen, the bed-linen, the grave-linen, and of fate. We shall show how this "weaving" of influences is literally true when we come to discuss menstrual synchrony. Men are deeply involved, their very dreams and body-cycles are responsive to the women's: men are involved in Nature mediated to them by the power of the cycle, again beneficently if they allow it, and in sterile and sorrowful trouble if they do not. Some of the advances we will detail have been made by men, as it were, repenting their male tyranny, and becoming, as we pleaded originally, "earnest students of the women."

Let's begin by citing a study by woman, that has become widely available, and which honors the "Wise Blood" throughout. This is Barbara G. Walker's *The Woman's Encyclopedia of Myths and Secrets*.[1]

Myths and Secrets is an extraordinary handbook for feminist debate. Its assemblage of facts and conjectures travels all the way from Alpha to Zurvan, and from ancient history to modern times. It builds on established scholarship, which it often stands on its head, for the underlying theme is that all formulations of religion and philosophy are built upon the woman's capability not only of giving physical life but with it of evolving and enhancing mental life also. Woman is the true educator, because she has direct experience of undivided existence. Men, by comparison, are lost, wayward, distracted, and falsifying creatures, and this accounts for the unconvincing nature of male-founded religions. Woman imparts spiritual knowledge, which is also physical knowledge, or carnal knowledge, by bearing the child and forming the home into the eternal patterns—the home and the hearth being the origin of all temples and churches—by sexual initiation, and by a privileged access to cosmic rhythms, "because of their natural menstrual body calendar." This theme runs through Barbara Walker's book.

History's horror arises in the misunderstanding and neglect of what women offer—in the holocaust of the witches, in which millions of "wise women" learned in these mysteries were sacrificed to a male god; and in the degradation of erotic knowledge. Barbara Walker's article on "Prostitution," for example, tells us (p. 821) how in Hebrew the word *hor* means a hole, cave, or pit, and that these were synonyms both for the prostitute and the Goddess she served. The *yoni* of this Goddess was represented by a hole, cave, pit, or pool of water in the sanctum of the temple. Thus also, the Latin word was *puteus*, a well or pit, source of the Spanish *puta*, "whore" . . . "To dive into such water was a symbol of sexual intercourse. Communing in this way with a holy whore, man could realize the spiritual enlightenment called *horasis*. This word appears in the New Testament (Acts 2:17) misleadingly translated 'visions.'" It is clear how pejorative later times have made these words and acts.

The book, though called an "encyclopedia," is intensely readable; and its great length (1,124 pages) ensures bounty, not boredom; its illuminating information is a treasure-house, not a miser's cave; it is abundant. The theme of "wise blood" and sexual enlightenment resulting in *caritas*, beauty, and kindness, or Hindu *karuna* (the combination of mother-love, tenderness, comfort, mystical enlightenment, and sex) runs through the book. The article on "Menstrual Blood" is a chief focus of its correspondence with and corroboration of *Wise Wound* matters. She points out as we do that in other languages, the majority of words for menstruation honor it, being synonymous for the sacred, for spirit, supernatural, deity, and it was known as a "blessing" before it was ever thought of as a curse (*The Wise Wound*, p. 49).

Indeed the "wise blood" was equated with the very springs of creation. She comments on the biblical test "But there went up a mist from the earth, and watered the whole face of the ground" (Gen. 2:6). The original meaning was not, apparently, "mist," but what appears in other Middle-Eastern scriptures as "the Nether Upsurge": a fountain of life-giving uterine blood, of "female fluid from the deeps, bursting forth to meet a male fluid from the deeps, bursting forth to meet a male fluid from the clouds" (p. 724).

Moreover, according to Walker, the Bible's story of Adam was taken from an earlier myth in which a Goddess created man from moon-blood and clay (*adamah*: "bloody clay"). The same derivation applies to the Koran, since in pre-Islamic Arabia "Allah was the Goddess of Creation, Al-Lat" (p. 635).

Menstrual blood was not only the prime material of creation, but the source of creative inspiration, even to the gods. It was, in Greece, the "supernatural red wine" given by Hera to the gods. In Hinduism, Kali-Maya invited the gods "'to bathe in the bloody flow of her womb and to drink of it; and the gods, in holy communion, drank of the fountain of life—(hic est sanguis meus)—and bathed in it, and rose blessed to the heavens.'" In much the same way the Norse God Thor owed his enlightenment and eternal life to bathing in a river of menstrual blood, and Odin was similarly powerful by stealing the "wise blood" from the Mother Goddess's triple caldron, and drinking it. Indra's theft of knowledge from the Primal Matriarchs via their menstrual blood is another parallel: the mystic drink *soma*, corresponding to ambrosia, the food of the Greek gods, was "wise blood." Again, Egyptian pharaohs ingested an ambrosia called *sa* which was called "The blood of Isis." The Persian god-food *amrita* apparently had the same moon-source. Celtic kings were divinized by drinking "red mead" of the Fairy Queen Mab "whose name was formerly Medhbh or 'mead.' Thus she gave a drink of herself . . ." It is not surprising therefore that the medieval churchmen believed that the communion wine of the witches was menstrual blood. In the legend of Thomas Rhymer the wizard, the Fairy Queen told him that she had a "bottle of claret wine . . . here in my lap" and invited him to lay his head there. Evidently the witch is initiating her "wise man." Walker points out that "claret" meant literally "enlightenment" and that there was a saying "the man in the moon drinks claret" (pp. 635–7).

The references range ever more widely and convincingly. Naturally she cites Tantrism (as we do in our Chapter V), whose rites depend on menstrual blood, and suggests a Tantric influence on the courtly-love movement and in medieval romance, as she does also in the article "Romance" (pp. 859*ff*). There is also the Taoist way of "immortality," by a man's absorbing the red yin juice from a woman's Mysterious Gateway. Here again, the woman is the initiator. There are further references (pp. 635–641) to the Maori, who would color anything sacred red, calling the color menstrual blood; to the red Easter eggs of Greece and Southern Russia and the rebirth of Greek mystics from the menstrual river Styx; to the love feasts of the Early Christians, in which the menstrual blood and semen of the worshippers was consumed as the holiest of sacraments. She gives many more instances of the universal reverence accorded to menstrual blood, and its polar opposite, the taboo, which makes of the holy thing something incredibly polluting. The bearer of it is therefore the bearer of both sacred and malign powers. As we have also pointed out, this taboo has been a very efficient instrument for controlling and denigrating women's real power, for "one does not bother to tie up a puppy with a steel cable" (*The Wise Wound*, p. 61).

The picture adds up, just as we said in *The Wise Wound*, to the idea of the menstruation and its "wise blood" as a precious and powerful thing, essential to the welfare of gods and humans alike.

II   Here and Now

What does this mean to Everywoman, now, in practical terms? One thing is that woman is seen as a bearer not only of children, but of some infinitely powerful initiatory magic. In *The Wise Wound* we said that this magic was an evolutionary force that arose because by virtue of the menstrual cycle in the human being (as opposed to the estrus cycle of animals), sex and pair bonding evolved not only for reproduction of the species, but for personal initiation and development (*The Wise Wound*, pp. 149–159).

We pointed out the importance of the sexual "high" at the period on pp. 88–96 and in Chapter V. Most sex books have ignored this surge of feeling and masculinist science has tended to say that it cannot occur, despite the protestations of women that it does. The reason given is that it would be "nonadaptive" as you can't increase the species by sex at this time, or only very rarely. Thus science ignores inner events, calling them by the curse-word "subjective," pretending that life-altering events do not occur in sexual partnership. Honorable exceptions to such books are Sheila Kitzinger's,[3] of which more later, and the few that draw on the Eastern tradition, such as Nik Douglas and Penny Slinger's *Sexual Secrets*.[4]

The point we wish to make in immediately practical terms is that the evidence is overwhelming that menstrual blood was once rightly honored, as it should be still. This brings pride into the bleeding instead of shame. With proper pride comes the need for self-determination and self-mastery. If woman is the initiator, why should she take a back seat? Immediately all those experiences which are valued by women and put down by men take up a new position. Loving sex takes a new place, as does the value of intuitions, visions, dreams, and feminine magic of all kinds.

What books like Barbara Walker's make outstandingly clear is that the images of folklore and legend are not idle tales, but a map of self-discovery for the woman. They are the universal and shared dream-images, and a knowledge of them is an atlas for inner exploration. How can they be "merely subjective" if women of all ages have shared them, and they still arise spontaneously today in women who take their dreaming and their menstrual cycle seriously, seriously enough to make a menstrual mandala? (See below.)

This is not contradicted at all by those important developments since 1978 which show that a disposition to menstrual distress is accentuated by certain contemporary nutritional deficiencies, and that it can be alleviated by adding Evening Primrose Oil, Vitamin B_6 and other food supplements to the diet.[5] This looks like a surefire "objective" treatment, but what the books on it neglect to mention is that with the improvement of the menstrual trouble there also comes increased dreaming in parallel with heightened creative energy. This must be used too; it is what the PMT concealed. Society apparently has amplified the menstrual taboo by creating a diet that is OK for men but which harms the woman's menstrual cycle. Where sleep and relaxation were once impossible, now they return, but the dreams and fantasies which accompany them are all the more remarkable and insistent. They will be found to contain collective woman's imagery, such as Barbara Walker describes, running in parallel and inner conversation with the enhanced waking life.

With the easing of PMT the "other side of things" is apt to become more haunting, with feelings of how wonderful the dreams and fantasies are, and "how I wish I could *use* them; or at least understand them."

It's the same thing as happened to Penelope Shuttle in 1971 when she began dreaming so intensely (*The Wise Wound*, pp. 4–6). The pattern of her spontaneous dreaming was that of an ancient mystery of women, the descent of Persephone to the Underworld mourned by her mother Demeter, and Persephone's return with previously unregarded treasures from that dark land. In practical terms the treasures included a relief of her physical menstrual troubles, and an increase in creativity at the menstrual time (also an improvement of eyesight). The realization that her own inner menstrual processes had brought up an ancient initiatory pattern was equally important, as it resulted in a new attitude in her to the period and its processes, and eventually led to *The Wise Wound*. The period now had meaning, and this included a feeling of solidarity with women in those ancient times.

It is the time and the place to affirm now that Penelope Shuttle's experience *is the norm and not the exception*. This has been made overwhelmingly plain not only during our research for *The Wise Wound* but in scores of workshops and discussions with women and with other workers in the field—it is also the lesson of history, as will further emerge. Even though these truths are becoming increasingly self-evident, one can still visit a psychotherapist with remarkable and disturbing dreams that appear to require an answer in women's terms, and get a readout which takes no account of the menstrual cycle and its transformations. Our advice is to ask any therapist one might happen to be consulting whether they have any experience and knowledge of menstrual dreaming, and whether they know *The Wise Wound* or any other book on those themes, and take it from there. As we showed (*The Wise Wound*, pp. 50–57), menstruation is a subject from which psychotherapy has turned its face, and no advantage can come of that.

III *Dreamers of the Real*

We have often been asked whether we can give any practical guidance on the patterns of menstrual dreaming. This needs another book. More than dreaming is involved. The menstrual mandala is like a hologram—each part of the pattern can reproduce the whole, seen in the right light. In the space we have at present, it is impossible to do more than hint at the basic shapes. It must be remembered that this work is going on, now, and the authority is not ourselves or any other writer on this theme, but rather the deepest experience of individual women and men. Books can tune you into the experience that you knew you were having but couldn't quite see; it is a good idea to use suitable books in this way—rich books, such as Barbara Walker's, from which you can pick and choose things that relate to your own experiences.

It is not only the dreaming life but the waking life also which are involved. The cycle is a pattern of feelings and perceptions which is individual to each person, but a pattern which, in this age, because of the neglect of women's matters, seems often *patchy* and unconscious. We recommend therefore *knowing your pattern* even more than interpreting it, which can come later. We call this pattern the *menstrual mandala*. As will be seen, it can take various forms.

There's no mystery about making this mandala. It is simply a way of seeing the whole rhythm at a glance. The way we do it is to keep a journal both of waking events and dreams, and mark in Penelope Shuttle's cycle-day, together with the dates of the calendar month. The onset of menstrual bleeding counts as day one. In addition to the written record, one page per month in the notebooks we use is given over to the days arranged in a circle, like a menstrual clock, with day one at the top, the calendar days marked in, the phases of the moon, the dates of ovulation, and any notable dreams, feelings or waking events. Simply by drawing a circle like this, quite a rough diagram, one can see the shape and length of a month's cycle, and compare it to other months. Symmetry shouldn't be sought for, though it may emerge. For the details one can use it like an index to the journal. Making such a chart is not only deeply interesting, with the regularities and repeated happenings in it, but it actually seems to regularize the cycle. One's cycle responds to sincere interest, just as dreams do.

Another way of doing it is to make a flat monthly chart, on the pattern designed, for example, by Bristol Women's Health Group. As they say, "If you want to find out more about your own cycle it is best to learn from a woman who has charted her own cycle for a number of years," or you can write to them for advice.[6] The sample chart they have printed is very informative, showing clearly the rhythms in ovaries and womb, and how the changes are reflected in temperature, cervix changes, mucus changes, mid-cycle spotting, ovulation pain, etc. Judith Higginbottom (see below) uses a very beautiful chart of the year's moons.

Then again, you can superimpose several months to make a spiral mandala, twisting and turning through the lunar year. You can see the repeated events, dreaming, sexuality, length of period, degrees of feeling, and the rest, clustering like markings on a seashell along the path of the helix. There must be many ways as yet not invented of declaring this interior geometry. An artist could make of her months a conch big enough to enter, and contemplate from within; a scientist could find unguessed-at rhythms and patterns of coinciding events in the markings of the helix. The shape is that of the spiderweb, beloved by the Greenham Common women, with the spiral lying superimposed upon the radiating cardinal points.

It's a simple matter to add to any kind of chart a record of feelings if they are especially notable at a particular part of the cycle, on particular days. As we've suggested, these so-called "subjective" events are fully as important as the "objective" ones. The two are complementary. As one grows increasingly interested, the record can grow in pattern and detail almost without trying. One will begin to find one's way about what may have been chaos. One can navigate. One can anticipate when one feels most like doing certain things, or when one feels like nothing, or terrible, as the case may be. One knows when quiet times, or the reverse, are needed, to make best use of one's life-energies.

Simply as a result of this habit of attention to what is going on, it will not only seem natural to record one's dreams with each cycle day, but the dreams will start coming. As we said (*The Wise Wound*, pp. 97–100) fluent dreaming can actually replace PMT. You may say "oh, I don't dream" but the fact is that once one begins to look inward in this way, the dreams do come.

It is fascinating to see how they change as the cycle changes. To give an example of just one person's "month" of dreams, on Day 1 she dreams she sees the new moon, she tells her husband to take his glasses off so he can see it too. On Day 19, the last day of her ovulation (and when the ovum if it were fertilized would be preparing to implant) she dreams of picking up a beautiful fat baby from his cot, he smiles, he is her son, he is too young to speak but he says "Mummy, Mummy": even the ovum will seem to speak through dreams.

On Day 22 there is the beginning of a premenstrual discomfort with a dream of teeth being filled, and a resistance to a "big complicated injection of opium or some other drug" which the dreamer sees as the approach of menstruation itself with its vivid and almost psychedelic happenings. On Day 23 there is a dream of a recently dead friend as a Joan of Arc figure (among women Joan is a frequent image signify- ing important feminist qualities) and a rich brown river flowing near by. On Day 3 of the period there is a dream of a man who collects the dreamer and takes her beyond a barrier prohibited to ordinary visitors. This is seen as the animus accompanying the dreamer through her change of state in the menstrual time, which may involve affirming certain "masculine" qualities.

This may seem "pat," but the fact is that such dreaming patterned to the cycle *is the rule rather than the exception.* The only difference between this dreamer and any other is that she is practiced, and by practice she has got to know the fluctuations of her cycle. Again, on the night preceding Day 1 of her period (which came in the afternoon of this day, after making love) she dreams of sitting at her desk, with a small nuclear bomb in her hands. She splits it in two and takes out the center, the timing mechanism. She bites this and crunches it, eats it like a nut. Then she throws the now harmless halves away in the garden. Thus she finds the kernel or kore of the menstrual time-bomb, and it is food; and food for love too as there is a flood of sexual feeling.

During another cycle she has a beautiful ovulation dream of a concert, and of children, and a professional man who is a singer (and about whom are articles in the Sunday paper), who says little, but who has a strong calm presence. There is a city, the buildings are beautiful, golden, calm, there are restaurants. These are ovulation, nurturing values, the singer is a strong masculine figure, calm and certain, well-founded in his profession, who has qualities appropriate to a husband and father, civic and domestic harmony prevails, he is an animus of the ovulation. This was on Day 16.

On Day 17, there was a dream of a pregnancy. There is one big contraction, cramping. The dreamer goes down a country lane, to hospital. The doctor talks to her, reminds her that he delivered her of a child before. The dreamer says confidently, "This time it will be different, easy." As she was not in outer reality pregnant, the dream shows how passing the mid-cycle need to conceive has been made easier by study of the meaning of her cycle and its changes. Ovulation is for many women a most difficult time, which includes the physical distress and the depression sometimes known as *mittelschmerz* which is associated with a combined fear and desire for pregnancy. One may feel as ovulation passes that a life has been lost. This feeling can contribute to premenstrual depression. Thus, on another occasion our dreamer was on Day 28 "late for rehearsal. The orchestra plays Elgar, *Gerontius*. The music finishes as I walk up the corridor, with a pint of milk in my hand from which I am drinking. I apologize to the conductor for missing rehearsal. He smiles and says, 'Next week we do *From the House of the Dead*.'" Conception at ovulation has been missed, and the dreamer is herself drinking the milk that a child conceived at that ovulation would have needed. Instead the milk is returned to the dreamer's body, to become menstrual blood flowing from the House of the Dead, which is how ovulation sees the unoccupied menstruating womb.

However, this premenstrual dream was followed by the wonderfully positive menstrual dream about the nuclear bomb already recounted which, with its rise of willingly accepted libido, had its creatively sexual consequence in the outer world.

IV   Coloring the Menstrual Mandala

Only by finding the pattern of the great rhythm or tune that goes through one's body, sensing it inwardly, can one release these mental-physical energies called "ovulation," "menstruation," "anima," "animus," and the rest, so that they permit each other, interpenetrate, braid with, inform, and line with each other. Then, say, a depression becomes a decision, one is prepared for "highs" and can use them to the full; or withdraw into the "lows" and discover their content. Every woman experiences changes of personality, as a recent TV commercial acutely showed, with the wife and mother being alternately clown, schoolmaster, cordon bleu chef, and frogman-at-bathtime. The advertisement is for some beverage that soothes one sufficiently so that the ranges of role do not shock, distress, or irritate.

There is an inherent wisdom in the idea, for as everybody knows, while one is in one role, one cannot imagine coping with another task that may be looming in prospect. How much more so this is with the tuning between nature and women. One can dance to this tune like a puppet, the strings pulled jerkily; or with the artistry of the prima ballerina, who knows that the framework of the symphony she is dancing to is meant to reveal, not conceal, the whole range of her nature. This conscious passing between role and role, or between capabilities, is the meaning in the dreams of being ushered by a dream personage (who is also oneself) "beyond a barrier prohibited to ordinary visitors"—the "ordinary" here referring, alas, to the kind of woman that society wishes to remain in her ordained gender-role, unconscious of her capabilities.

Filling in one's journal with dreams, feelings, disappointments, and triumphs is, then, coloring the menstrual mandala, the round; and it is remarkable to see how themes return at various times of the month, how they grow and change. To be conscious of this is to begin to be mistress of it. Many women find that they distinguish different times of different emotional tones and interests. Taking merely as example a thirty-one-day cycle, the records of which are at hand, one woman finds Days 6–9 rather calm and detached, like gentle convalescence from the period. Day 9 is for her the beginning of the run-up to ovulation, so she expects a change. Her husband comments on a marvelous warm smell, like fresh-baked bread, in her bedroom on the morning of that day. It is still for them a sexual low, but during the next few days she is conscious of increasing sexuality. This comes to a series of enjoyable peaks during Days 12 to about 19, with a corresponding transition into a fresh range of feelings. This is followed for both partners with a withdrawal of outer energies, and intense dream activity seems to replace it during the premenstrual week, from about Day 22 on. This is the time when PMT may manifest, though if this usually quite violent dream activity is recorded and enjoyed, the distress is usually much lessened, even though it may contain disgusting, mutilating, or otherwise horrifying images. It is the "horror film" time! (See Chapter VII.) Strange as it may seem, these dreams can be enjoyed in the way a good horror film can be enjoyed in certain moods. In our example, the woman dreamer does just this, while the man partner does not have this degree of self-possession in his dreaming. He is inclined to have nightmares during her premenstrual time; and if he's going to get a cold, this is the time he catches it (see *The Wise Wound*, pp. 46–50, 80–81).

Then at Day 31 or thereabouts, at the peak of energy or tension, there is a sudden change, often heralded in the dreams, and the "red visitor" is there. There is a complete change in the atmosphere of the house. The man partner frequently finds a creative resolution in his work at this moment, the woman also, but not as cataclysmically as he does. Sexual energy of a different coloring begins again between them, and lasts until the bleeding finishes.

This partnership has learned an important lesson which we believe must always be followed when the woman has a strong rhythm; that her rhythm and not his real or imagined desire should call the tune, if they want creative and satisfying sexual relations.

Thus for people in a sexually active relationship, the pattern of sexuality though it may be changing and flexible needs to be known. To attempt sex with a woman when she is in a sexually low phase of her cycle is a disastrous thing to do. Both may think, or the woman may be persuaded by her partner, that it's OK to try, but it is really introducing an alien strain into the music.

This fact is likely to annoy the male partner initially. Men, if they follow the conventions of our society, like to feel they are in control. But the male rhythm of desire, strong as it may be to him, seldom matches in depth the rhythms of the woman, though his love can entrain them. Thus a woman may often not menstruate when her lover is away, and her period starts on the day of his return. This is not a romantic fiction, but a fact we have observed on numerous occasions.

When the partners do match together in a natural rhythm, then the control and sensitivity needed to become deeply orgasmic seems to emerge of itself. At menstruation, sex can sometimes be so satisfactorily ransacking that it seems that one has had the entire period in a few minutes, so both partners must be sure that they know the woman's blood to be a glory and not a "mess." The partners, knowing the best times to make love, will find not only that they learn by nature the basic Tantric disciplines for prolonged inter-course, but that their peaks and valleys of libido correspond. People are inclined to invent desire or deny it for sex-political reasons. We are speaking here of something deeper and far more natural.

All this can be a natural result of filling in the mandala. Sheila Kitzinger, in her *Woman's Experience of Sex*, has a fine diagram of the pattern of "Libido and the Menstrual Cycle" on page 61, and wise words to go with it (p. 80): "For some women lovemaking without orgasm is unsatisfying and they feel they have missed out on something precious. For others the journey holds more richness and delight than the getting there. For others again, the love they feel for another human being contains a deeper satisfaction even than orgasm. Each woman has a right to define her own sexual identity and the nature of her sexual fulfillment." We'd add to this that the "right to define" should be based on actual knowledge, knowledge that woman can find within herself, based on the menstrual mandala's music.

V ·Do Men Menstruate?

Whether a man has an inherent rhythm of his own is still in dispute, as it was when we wrote *The Wise Wound*. There has been quite a deal of research on this, but the results do seem to be variable: various rhythms have been proposed, from a forty-eight-hour rise of libido to a three-monthly hormonal flux, but there is much disagreement.

The reason for this seems to be that the man's own inherent rhythms, if they exist, are often overlaid by the menstrual rhythm he picks up by reflection from his female partner (and, it would appear, in childhood from his mother). The mechanism may be pheromonal, as with menstrual synchrony between women (details of this later), but the fact remains that if you look for a *menstrual* rhythm in a man who lives with a woman, you will find it. We have observed this very frequently in the dream-rhythms—the male partner is quite likely to have, say, ovulation dreams of his own or another's pregnancy, and violent and bloody premenstrual dreams full of fighting animals. He may have initiatory menstrual dreams of passing through dark waters, of having a lake of blood where an eye was plucked out, or a menstrual dream of incontinence (uncontrolled flow is one of the fears a woman may have about her period—that it might arrive unexpectedly, staining her clothing) or of a black man (a reflection of the menstrual animus in the woman) and a woman lover with a golden skin. We cite these examples from numerous records, and again, a reflection of menstrual events in the household in men's dreams *is the rule rather than the exception*.

We mentioned that a man may very well experience premenstrual distress, followed by a creative resolution. For example, one man during his wife's premenstrual week dreamed of a tube train, and a fire that had started in another compartment. Uniformed officials rush around, the dreamer is to be burned, he is terrified, nothing can prevent it. Then by an act of will the dreamer accepts his fate—and the emergency dies away. The following day in waking life, a piece of work reveals its solution. Here, the menstrual increase of libido in his partner was registered in the dream and the dreamer sees in his depths that he must not fight this, but adjust his attitude. With women, the dream of being burned as a witch is quite a frequent premenstrual dream, or, rather, nightmare. Acceptance of the fire-energy then leads to initiation into magical powers in the dream, and in waking life, the rise of energy operates creatively. If men as well as women begin to study the menstrual mandala in partnership these interactions reveal themselves, often very quickly.

Childhood and husbandly ailments are frequently the means the woman's rhythm uses to express itself, if it is kept unconscious. We propose the other way, in which the rhythm is not only acknowledged, but imaginatively investigated. It will be found that the children's dreams naturally and spontaneously declare the mother's rhythms. They do so in imagery which is often more vivid and unmistakable than it is in grown-ups.

Daughters may begin to menstruate at an earlyish age nowadays, and much sympathy must be given to the violent and pure expression in dream and fantasy-life of the new experiences. A frequent nexus in the family which is not yet much talked about in the psychological literature is when an elder daughter is at the peak of her fertility just as the mother is entering the run-up for menopause, with all the doubts that in our culture attend that. The influence of the mother's worry and even jealousy of her daughter at this stage can be profound, and is a very common source of mental and physical trouble in the daughter. Once the menstrual influence is seen, however, as in so much else, the pattern becomes clear, and useful work on the situation can be done.

It does seem likely that people who study the cycle by means of the menstrual mandala or other means have an easier menopause, and after the menopause both dreams and waking events do appear to keep something of the cyclical pattern. This area is even more underresearched than menstruation itself has been. Animus encounters appear to be basic to self-integration in menopause. For one woman brought up in a strict religious sect in her childhood, this was a confrontation and negotiations with a devil-figure. There is a useful and interesting book by Ann Mankowitz which gives some suggestive case histories.[7]

When there is menstrual synchrony among the women in the house, the men in it have two choices: they can become students of the matter, or form a masculine solidarity in opposition, which more often happens. The women in the household may themselves become students of the great rhythms they produce. We have suggested in *The Wise Wound* (Chapter V) that this has been the way of certain cultures in the past, and this is supported now by impressive new anthropological work which we shall touch on in a moment.

One researcher, Margaret Henderson, using oral and prostatic (rectal) temperatures, did appear to find a "testiculation" rhythm in men that corresponds with the ovulation temperature rise in women.[8] Her work opens fascinating perspectives. It is known that women can "cycle" together. She shows that men have a temperature cycle that can synchronize with women's, and that the men's temperatures can also cycle together, as with two gay males, living together in the same house. She says, "I have developed a great respect for the message these subtle temperature changes are giving me. So like researchers studying liquid crystals I am slowly learning this temperature language."

The male prostatic temperature changes are "remarkably similar to the temperature changes occurring at the same time in women—even to the characteristic threshold of 36.6°C . . . Other parts of the male temperature cycles also bear a striking resemblance to those of the female. There is a variable temperature peak during the first few days—followed by a phase of middle-range temperatures before the 'ovulation-type' pattern . . . In the last phase of the cycle is the major difference; where the women's temperature levels remain high and correlate with her progesterone, the male's temperatures tend to fall off more quickly, unless the preceding peak was small."

Her subsequent work seems to show, as we argue from the

dream evidence, that the male cycle is profoundly influenced by the female's. One man's wife was pregnant, and then lactating; his "testiculation" cycle continued, but was less sharply defined than before pregnancy, but he showed differences in amplitude between the pregnant and lactating phases. His temperature remained up, with no cycle, at the time of the birth, and started again when his wife returned from hospital. Another male who started out with a cycle synchronous with his wife's, found that when she went on a combined oral contraceptive, that he started a shorter cycle. After three months on the Pill his natural temperature cycle had been completely abolished and he had become very restless and went off for a holiday. On his return his wife went off the Pill and they settled down happily again. Another male who was severely depressed and whose wife was taking an oral contraceptive, was found to be "cycling" but out of phase with his wife.

In another case, the wife's periods were becoming very widely spaced due to the approach of menopause. The man did not show the typical male cyclic pattern except when his wife "cycled." When she did not, he showed increased day–night temperature changes. He also started to seek younger female companions who had a cycle, as though he could not bear to be without a female-induced rhythm. On the other hand, a male with a young female partner who was not ovulating continued to cycle in a normal male "testiculating" pattern. When she started to cycle again, it was as though she picked up *his* rhythm, as she started to cycle in synchrony with him. As Margaret Henderson says at the end of her paper, "no man or woman is an island—each individual when he or she is born becomes an integrated part of a larger pulsating social body."

VI   *Love without Reproduction*

Sexuality is not the only way, of course, that the rise of libido in the menstrual pattern can be expressed. The above examples of male–female synchrony suggest that the matter touches every aspect of our lives. However, one of the natural doorways to enhanced living is the sexual experience, and it is everybody's birthright. It is to be remembered that Western society is against fully achieved sexuality except as a means to the propagation of the species. This is why menstrual studies have been neglected for so long. It also seems to be why there are constant obstacles in the way of finding the fully satisfactory contraceptive method. As Sheila Kitzinger says (op. cit., p. 194), "When all is said, there is obviously no perfect method of birth control at the moment—certainly no single one that is right for everybody. It is more a matter of finding out what is available and then working out your personal equation." In this the male partner must also take responsibility, but "only when women take action can there be some development towards fully shared responsibility for contraception" (p. 196). Knowledge by both partners of the menstrual mandala is a contribution to this responsibility. (Even on the Pill, with its "imposed" cycle, the dreaming-feeling pattern of menstrual-ovulation events can continue, though, it seems, naturally enough, in a more muted form than in the natural cycle. For some, the Pill's mandala can be more easily manageable, like an introduction to the full cycle.)

There are obviously forms of sexuality in which there is no risk of conception, among gay partners clearly, and with refined techniques of oral sex. Also, "For others again, the love they feel for another human being contains a deeper satisfaction even than orgasm . . ." and there is a sense in which the discharge of the orgasm is an explosion of energies which can under certain circumstances be released more slowly and calmly. Most couples know at some time or other in their lives, that a naked embrace leading to sleep and dreaming, a "skin-sleep," can be fully as satisfying as an orgasm achieved by vaginal penetration. With this type of intercourse at the fertile times, there is of course no risk of conception. The menstrual mandala would be the guide to such possible times. The genitals touch (beware of partial ejaculation) and the rise of excitement that this normally produces is not assisted by deliberate action, but allowed to modulate and glide into full-body feelings that drift in and out of dreaming, sometimes in full tactile consciousness— touch moves into dream, and dream into touch. There are very subtle feelings of flow sometimes within and sometimes between the bodies. Usually for these kinds of experience a couple must have the kind of accord and interest in each other that the mutual investigations into the menstrual mandala can produce. The position sometimes called the "scissors" is very suitable (the woman lies on her back, and the man lying on his side clips the further thigh between his legs; her other leg goes over his hip).[9] There is an old book by Rudolph Von Urban[10] that gives detailed instructions, but it is marred by a horror of masturbation and a fear of the clitoris and of sexual fantasy. The "scissors" is also a splendid position for customary forms of intercourse, precisely because the partners can sleep without breaking their embrace.

Mutual masturbation properly done is another way of achieving sexual satisfaction without a risk of conception, and can lead into a wonderful "skin-sleep." Massage[11] and aromatherapy techniques are well worth exploring and experimenting with; since the menstrual synchronies we have emphasized as being such an important part of the whole business of relation are very probably mediated in part by chemical pheromone mechanisms, it would seem natural to use the properties that inhere in plant pheromones, or essential oils. There is much modern information on this,[12] and it is also traditionally Tantric. Aromatherapy is a physical treatment which has strongly psychological dimensions, close to waking dreams. Smells take one deeply inward. Thus Clary

Sage oil with Ylang-Ylang put into a hot bath will treat PMT, but an important part of the treatment is the relaxation and daydreaming in the bath.

Kitzinger writes very appositely on "natural" methods of contraception, and these may well result from work on the menstrual mandala. She says (p. 192): "If you are to be successful in using any of the 'natural' methods you need to know your body and your menstrual rhythms really well. It is not enough to rely on a calendar. But women who have got in touch with their bodies in this way, who know exactly how they feel prior to and during ovulation and understand the changing physical sensations of the cycle, are enthusiastic about it . . ."

It's clear that the "physical sensations" are not "merely physical." The experienced worker with her menstrual mandala knows how well she can "see" into the body. The fact that she can do this challenges one of the basic assumptions of masculinist science: that mind and matter are wholly distinct, that subjective and objective are an absolute dichotomy. In working the menstrual mandala one obtains by subjective means results that are also objectively true. In this way you have an inner authority from the body which is effective in both worlds, while the way of masculinist science is to set up outer authorities to which one must defer.

Thus people feel lost and alienated in the modern world, which is so much outwardness and so little inwardness. People feel that they have been emptied by the modern world. Particularly have women been emptied by the various strategies we have described (*The Wise Wound*, pp. 36–71) for denying or muting those inner rhythms that give privileged access to themselves, to other people and, it may be, to cosmic rhythms such as the moon's.

Working with the menstrual mandala is a way of restoring what has been lost. The dream-experience of the cycle is the same as the cycle-experience of the dream. Knowing the conditions of her sexuality, her temperature range, the condition and sensation of mucus, the position and degree of opening of her cervix, is simply another aspect of our dreamer dreaming, say, that her menstruation is a nuclear ("kore") bomb that she can turn into a nutrient that is not breast-milk for a child.

Thus the psyche-soma split, the Cartesian dualism, is healed at a stroke. Men do not have this advantage by nature. They cannot without the help of women achieve a true and lasting inner authority. Men seem to carry their bodies around with them like a machine they don't quite know what to do with. Women know naturally how precious life-in-the-body is. Our bodies are ourselves. We are not ghosts living inside robots. Such care cannot make atomic bombs. This is another meaning of that bomb dream. Make food of love, not war.

VII   Simple Relaxation a Key to the Mandala

Orgasm is not only the "huge, tingling shudder," the "delicious faint," the "clutch of butterflies let loose inside," or "like having a good strong bowel motion," "long satisfying yawns," "coming in colors," ". . . like having a baby; you build up to a climax (labor pains) then you push the baby's head out," described by some of the women in Kitzinger's book, it is also the "good feeling all over" and the "unfocused elation and heightening of the senses" which Judith Higginbottom (see below) says can also be a characteristic of the menstrual state itself.

This "afterglow" is much commoner than many people think, and one of the states of body-mind most to be valued. It is the creative state, an awareness which combines in one condition the characteristics of waking and vivid relaxed dreaming. Once again, in this common experience, the split between conscious and unconscious minds is healed. It is the magic state of profound alert relaxation. It is easy to prepare for this experience and to make it more frequent by adopting some process of regular relaxation. Once one is accustomed to entering this state, the benefits are extraordinary.

So far as the menstrual mandala is concerned, relaxation makes the transition between the various stations of the cycle much more easy. It increases dream recall. It helps alleviate menstrual distress. It improves sex, and heightens one's enjoyment of life generally. A regular daily practice of relaxation helps one's creativity—one can enter relaxation with a problem, and find when one emerges that one can see a solution, which may come suddenly and unexpectedly, or gradually, so one can see its full workings. One may have a puzzling dream, and find that during relaxation that one redreams the dream, and can relate to it better.

We've found that the best idea is to start a relaxation method during the first quarter of the cycle, when the bleeding has stopped, say about the sixth or seventh day. By the time that premenstrual feelings come around again, one is practiced, and daydreaming or reverie on chosen images can take over from the tension. We have devised a simple relaxation method that we have used ourselves and taught to scores of women and men, both for creative purposes and for easing menstrual distress. This method is given in an appendix to this Afterword. You can make a recording of the instructions on a cassette and play them to yourself. You can rerecord as you adjust the working to your own preferences, since each person eventually develops their own variation. It is a kind of womb-breathing or womb-soothing (with the implication that "sooth" also means "truth"). There are many methods of inducing relaxation response or meditation, and of those on the market, we can also recommend Peter Russell's *Relaxation Made Easy* with Rosalind Shanks.[13]

The menstrual mandala is any device one uses to make the cycle's events and their shape plain. As we said above, Penelope Shuttle uses a diary and a diagram like a round calendar. She marks in the moon's phases, as she is interested in the way her cycle hovers much of the time between thirty and thirty-three days, and the way in which it alters so that her period never seems to come on the quarter-moons, but usually near the full or new moon. She likes to keep her bedroom curtain drawn back as the room faces the South, so the moon shines in. She is a poet and a novelist as well as a mother, and finds, as any working woman will, that the roles conflict. It seems to her that during the school holidays, when she has less time for intense creative work, her cycle tends to move around so that her periods come near the new moon. When she is engaged most of the day on creative work, it seems that her cycle has altered so that her menstruation comes on the full moon. She believes that it is possible that there can be two kinds of cycle for a woman. One of these we call the Mother Cycle, where ovulation is at the "traditional" time of the full moon, and menstruation on the new moon. As the Menakers' work we quoted in *The Wise Wound* (pp. 168–71) shows, this may very well be the pattern for conception and birth, with the majority of births occurring on the full moon.

If this is the traditional correlation of the cycle with the moon's phases, it is possibly because woman's traditional role has been that of a Mother. However, Penelope Shuttle also believes that there is another pattern corresponding with the moon's phases, and that is when the full moon, as it were, produces not the egg, but the blood tide. That is, on the Mother Cycle, the culmination of the rhythm is the ovulation, and this would be, on this theory, at the full moon, which is the usual time for fertility rites. But women are not only Mothers, and so seemingly partake of another rhythm as well.

The ancient image is that the ovum, containing all the potentialities of the creation of a physical person, if not fertilized, releases these energies for the use of the individual woman and her partner, in menstruation. On the other cycle, the culmination of cycle events would be the menstruation and the vivid experiences which attend it, rather than the ovulation, and, on this theory, the blood culmination would occur in the full light of the moon. It is as though on one cycle, the Mother's, dedicating herself to the continuation of the species, the full moon summoned the egg from the ovary; and on the other, which one could call the "Medial"[14] or "Wise Women" cycle, it summoned the blood from the womb.

The Mother and the Wisewoman, Witch, or Midwife meet in the delivery room. If the Menakers are right (and they have published an additional paper to the one we quoted[15]) this is likely to be a full moon event. The Midwife (if she is not a menopausa) would be menstruating. This would deepen the blood-mysteries of birth, and might even stimulate labor. At birth there would be a triple-blood: of the Mother, of the Placenta, and of the Midwife. The vibrant and pheromone-laden atmosphere of the birth-room would imprint on every-body there the importance of the womanly blood-mysteries. The mystery would be compounded by another type and example of all blood-sacrifice, which is not just the Mother, nor even the Menstruating Wisewoman but the sacrificed Placenta slaughtered at birth. The placenta is made of our own body, and is like a twin brother or sister in the womb. It feeds us, it responds to our moods or desires in that archaic place, it mediates between us and the body of the mother, we see or otherwise sense the great tree or bridge of our umbilicus drawing on the beneficence of that Other who is present and sustaining during the long bodily pilgrimage in which we recapitulate all the stages of evolution until we are ready to be born. Then, at birth, that Brother or Sister is killed to give us life. It feeds us like the Grail, it dies for us like Jesus on the Cross.

This scenario raises many more questions and opportunities for psychological and anthropological research than we have space to pursue here. There is a lot of evidence for sentience in the womb, and a prima-facie case (as for instance in Laing and Peerbolte[16]) for an adult memory of womb events. It is only when women's studies have made progress against current established prejudice that we shall have certain knowledge of what actually happens at these deep times, and how we can improve the conditions of life by studying the events before and during birth and connect them up in one mandala with childhood and adult life.

VIII   Does the Moon Menstruate?

In *The Failure of the Sexual Revolution* (Mentor, 1974), George Frankl described how while our society remains class-conscious it can never be truly free, sexually or otherwise. He attributes class hierarchies to the Oedipus Complex, that is, to the phallic conflict between males for the favors of the women themselves, favors defined by the men as acceptable to themselves. Thus the true nature of women is altered and repressed. The basis of the class war on this argument is the sexual class war. Frankl points out that for women in the patriarchal system "God does not speak to her, only to man . . . she ceases to believe in the spontaneity and the demands of her sexual urges . . . for that would make her a being in her own right . . . female cultural symbols will emerge . . . Women would again develop their divinities, their principles and ideas in a recognizable manner as distinct cultural entities, and it is high time that this should happen if we are to be saved from the aggressive mania of the male Gods."

In the sexual class war a female solidarity must develop which transcends class barriers; a catalyst in this can be the menstrual mandala, since the subjective-objective knowledge that comes by this means is not dependent on a particular education, income, or social standing. In the development of female solidarity, practical investigative work is needed which is uninfluenced by preconceptions.

One outstanding piece of work was done during 1978–80

by Judith Higginbottom, the feminist filmmaker based in Devon. She called the project "Water into Wine." She wrote to some fifty women, asking if they would be prepared to record the correlations between their menstrual cycles and the cycle of the moon, and also give an account of their feelings and dreams associated with the cycle. In the event twenty-seven women actively cooperated in the work. This, with Judith Higginbottom, made the appropriate moon-number, like a Moon-College, of twenty-eight. She says: "When this work started, I had very clear ideas about gathering information about possible relationships between the menstrual and lunar cycles, about links between lunar/menstrual cycles and dreaming, creativity, tension, depression, and various details of physical, bodily changes that occur at different stages of the menstrual and lunar cycles. As the months progressed, I found that in addition it was also a study of the effects of using lunar and menstrual cycles as a measure of time; to some extent the structuring of our time according to these cycles . . . I have read of societies without artificial light in which all the women ovulate at the full moon and menstruate together at the old/new moon. I felt that there must be a strong sense of sisterhood between women in such societies. There is no such sense of sisterhood in our society, where women experience menstruation as a curse, alone and in secret . . ."

The work was carried out during a period of thirteen lunar months, from 29 December 1978 to 16 January 1980. Very beautiful moon-calendars—a form of menstrual mandala—were developed to chart the cycles. These duplicated sheets showed the phases of the moon for each day, and one can see in it in one glance the pulsing of light through the lunar year of thirteen months. Several important sets of results from this group of women emerged. The first was that due to this act of attention the women grew interested in the menstrual changes, and menstrual distress actually diminished in some of the women who were accustomed to regard their cycle as a regular torment. Another result was Higgin-bottom's defining of a "menstrual state." She says: "Many women find that just before menstruation their mental state or consciousness undergoes a marked change. This may be experienced negatively as PMT or depression, or in other ways. I discovered as I began to experience menstruation positively, rather than as an illness or curse, that before menstruation I was experiencing a very positively altered state of consciousness. This state is quite unmistakable . . . It is a very powerful state . . ."

Among its characteristics she distinguishes (1) increased creativity. Most ideas and decisions about work are made at this time; confused ideas and concepts become clear; (2) All the senses are intensified. "Sometimes the world may seem like an overwhelming rush of colors, sounds, and other sensations"; (3) Emotions are also heightened; (4) Thought processes become instinctive, seem to be experienced physically. "The split between the self and the physical environment disappears"; (5) Increased sexual awareness; (6) May be experienced as a visionary or ecstatic state of reverie and meditation, almost trancelike. She says: "I discovered that this state has been experienced by many other women, and that in other societies it has been used positively, like menstrual dreaming. It has been used as a source of prophecy and inspiration. Women shamans and witch doctors have used this menstrual state as a source of their power." In the original documents of the project the compiled letters, often very beautiful, show that "Most of the women noticed the 'menstrual state' at least slightly at some time during the 13 months."

In addition, a particular set of dream imagery and events was associated with the menstrual state. This was timeless shared imagery, apparently collective to the women, as we suggested above in discussing Barbara Walker. The sea and water featured, with sea and water creatures; red objects and clothing were often seen; powerful male animals, or seeing oneself as male; sexual dreams, and dreams with Goddess figures, strong, powerful, and helpful women; and visionary dreams which revealed solutions to problems. "I dreamed I was standing on the beach . . . It was very dark and moonless (because the moon was at the end of its cycle). It was so dark that I couldn't see anything but I could hear the sea . . . I walked towards the sea. When I reached it I walked into it . . . until the water reached my thighs. Suddenly hundreds and hundreds of small silver fishes were leaping out of the water all around me. I was confused about why I could see them when it was so dark. I said 'For whom but me will the fish of the laughing ocean be making welcome?' I woke and my period was starting." Again: "I dreamed I was standing on the sand dunes . . . a flood tide was racing between the dunes . . . a man with blond hair was there to teach me about synthesizers. I explained to him that I wanted to express my menstrual cycles as music, and he showed me how to do this . . ."

Further, "the majority of the women taking part have their periods around either the full or the new moon, and very few have their periods at the lunar quarters." As we suggested above, this bears out the idea of two kinds of cycle. Higginbottom herself had watched her own cycle over a two-year space of time, and had noted that it averaged thirty-four days, and this is four to five days longer than the lunar cycle. However, her period almost always came at the new or full moon (as Penelope Shuttle's also did). This means that her cycle was lengthening or shortening to stay in phase with the lunar cycle. She says, "I have only noticed this effect since I have lived in the country, away from artificial lighting."

Because Judith Higginbottom described her work in the television program we mentioned at the beginning of this Afterword ("About Time"), many thousands more women must now be aware of some of the possibilities inherent in their cycle, possibilities freely available but almost entirely neglected by society.

Nobody should be surprised to find that men—who, after all, are also a part of the process—feel gladness and a sense of liberation with the emergence of truths which have been overlaid by the patriarchal paradigms. Men as people have also labored under them, due as they are to the rejection of female knowledge. Men are very much concerned in the work of reparation. There is nothing for it but for them to become students of the women if they are to be people. This must not be seen as another attempt at male takeover, nor should it be allowed to become so. How can it be, when the source of knowledge and vitality is that same spring, fountain, or pool in the inner temple of "wise blood" which Barbara Walker shows is so universal in wisdom-stories, and which belongs to the women alone?

Among the men who have achieved honorable studentship in what has been hitherto an extraordinarily masculine preserve—social anthropology—is Chris Knight, whose published anthropological papers are truly remarkable, and who is preparing a book for a wider audience called *The Greatest Myth on Earth* (in preparation for RKP). His wealth of solid anthropological and scientific data shows that it is very likely indeed that the dual rhythms of menstruation and ovulation run behind all culture and all human society, and that human society originated with knowledge of the menstrual cycle, as we also suggested in Chapter IV of *The Wise Wound*.

Until *The Greatest Myth on Earth* actually comes out, there are three important papers by Chris Knight that we'd like to consider briefly. The first is "Levi-Strauss and the Dragon."[17] Here (as in the other two papers) he brings evidence that at some time in the past women lived in the kind of kinship proximity that enabled them to synchronize their menstrual periods. This menstrual synchrony, according to Chris Knight, beat out a great cultural pulse, the two peaks of which were the surges of energy produced by ovulation on the one hand, and menstruation on the other. This is the beat which underlies the establishment of human society. Women ensured that this happened by ritual means. As we said in *The Wise Wound* (p. 164), the assurance that the moon actually synchronizes the period is less important than the assurance that by using ritual moon-imagery women can cause synchrony.

At the two culminations, one relating to birth and a bond with the husband, and the other, menstruation, relating to a return to womb and interfeminine values, the two different sets of cultural structures arose. Ovulation related to getting a husband, tribal values, the bearing of children, overt social symbolism, public speech and customs. Menstruation related to feminine values, sibling values, magic children, prophetic speech, and shamanism. Both sets of values have been altered and perverted, indeed inverted, by the men, who were not able to participate in the feminine blood rituals, except by surrogate means; the positive side of the menstrual energy was in particular concealed and it was the men who seemed to have the "wise blood" which they produced by means of contrived and artificial rites.

In particular, the female solidarity which enabled women to undergo these two basic experiences of birth and menstruation with the knowledgeable support and participation of their sisters, was by and large forbidden by the men. In Australian Aboriginal society, for example, the men made propaganda that, if women associated for these purposes, the tribes would be visited by various disasters, principally floods brought about by a never-ending rainy season, by the power of the great Rainbow Serpent.

Chris Knight shows that the Rainbow Serpent in these myths, far from being the visitation of the angry male phallic god, is in its origin a myth which declared that very solidarity of the women which was altered and repressed. He very movingly reinterprets the important myth of the Wawilak Sisters in the Aboriginal rock-paintings in the light of the menstrual experience: the Rainbow Serpent being the name of their dance and celebration and emblem of their joy, the great snake of the rainbow that took them up to heaven. To replace this, the men substituted ceremonies of their own that were cruel parodies of the women's bloodshed. Incidentally, this myth bears out the observation of the two cycles mentioned above—one sister menstruates as the other gives birth (*The Wise Wound*, pp. 63–4).

In his "Menstruation as Medicine"[18] Knight shows how under certain conditions the usual menstrual taboos are reversed, and menstrual blood becomes a healing medicine instead of a maleficent polluting substance; indeed it is the latter because of its inherent great power as a medicine. He draws on a remarkable paper by Tom Buckley[19] on the survival of ancient positive rites of menstruation and their resumption as a source of inspiration among contemporary Yurok women: "According to the old menstrual laws, a woman should isolate herself during the flow 'because this is the time when she is at the height of her powers.' Such time should not be wasted in mundane and social distractions, nor in concerns with the opposite sex. Rather, all of one's energies should be applied in concentrated meditation on the nature of one's life, 'to find out the purpose of your life.' It is a time for the 'accumulation' of spiritual energy . . ."

Possibly his most striking paper is "Menstruation and the Myth of Matriarchy"[20] in which he points the way to a truly feminine culture; not, as is usually thought, "culture" belonging to men, and women being a part of "nature"; but a fully human alternative culture based on undeniable and ineluctable feminine events fully understood and employed by the women.

He discusses the lunar logic of fairy tales and magical myths, and how woman's power "grows with the moon and comes and goes with it" and how "Through their bodies and, in particular, through their reproductive organs, women are felt to have a peculiar and privileged access to 'medicine' of a kind which is dangerously independent of male cultural control . . . it is probably just such all-pervasive and untrammeled 'witchcraft' which the myths of matriarchy depict as 'catastrophic' for men." This was the basis of witch persecution. It is also the basis of the power of fairy tales. In looking for the one tale with respect to which all fairy tales will appear as variants, one authority was drawn to those in which a dragon kidnaps a princess, and the hero succeeds "in traveling to another world by some magical means in order to ravish the dragon and rescue his bride . . . such things as flying steeds, birds, flying boats, or flying carpets—magical means of travel obtained from a witch—transport the hero between home and the world beyond, this to-and-fro movement forming a counterpart to the alternating sexual availability and non-availability of the bride . . ."

The myths and tales are lunar, with an essential logic of "metamorphosis, of 'death' and 'rebirth.' Unlike the sun, which (except during eclipses) is always its own self, the moon is periodically its own opposite—each month it is devoured by a dark shadow, which may be conceptualized as a 'wolf,' a 'jaguar,' and huge 'frog' or some other monster . . . In numerous cultures, a woman—like the moon—is regarded as turned into her own opposite during (menstrual) seclusion . . ."

He discusses tales like The Sleeping Beauty, Jack-and-the-Beanstalk, Cinderella, and Little Red Riding Hood. If there is a central theme to the "wide variety of fairy tales" it is metamorphosis and rebirth to a "higher plane" and seeing the "animal side of herself" for the woman.

He quotes many tribal myths concerning the yielding up of power by the woman to the man, for instance, *How Woman Lost Her Flute*, which recalls Serraillier's contemporary tale we quote (*The Wise Wound*, pp. 259–261), and *How Woman Lost the Moon*. "A woman took the moon from the water and hid it in her house under some firewood, intending to cook and eat it later. But while she was out, her husband, aided by his brothers, broke into the house and stole it."

In certain cultures women are seen through menstruation

and childbirth to "come into direct contact with the mysterious weather-changing and 'skin-changing' forces which men seek to control . . . ," in another the "rains themselves are 'the menstrual flow of Woman Shaman'—the prototype shaman from which all shamans derive their powers" and without the great secrecy of men's rites the fiction of their mastery of these powers could not be maintained, for "Were women able to peruse at close quarters the 'menstruation' and 'childbirth' of men, their amusement could cause the entire enterprise to collapse in hilarity."

In short "women may appear to men as a threat because they do seem so 'naturally' capable of tuning in, with their own body-rhythms, to the life-renewing forces of the cosmos. When men try to 'menstruate,' it is in order to make their own bodies collectively resonate with such rhythms." (Thus bloody war becomes a masculine source of inspiration, as the Greenham Common women know.) Under the "rule of men," when "men tune in to the cosmic rhythms it is not in sympathy or harmony with women's menstrual rhythms, but in competition with them and at women's expense. Menstruation as a tuning-in system is taken away from women in a 'political inversion' which then makes a women's own menstruation the opposite of what it is supposed to be . . ." as in the contemporary taboos we have discussed in *The Wise Wound*.

There is much more discussed in this paper than we have space to detail. There is a useful up-to-date summary of findings on menstrual synchrony, and other articles in the book in which Knight's appears are concerned with this matter. Referring to Yurok women who have revived ancestral menstrual customs, he says that the cultural context, its permission, ensures that their internal rhythms, in Buckley's words, have "profound . . . implications . . . in dictating the temporal structuring of activities for entire households," and this means for the entire culture. (There is a clear similarity with the "moon-colleges" we discussed in Chapter V of *The Wise Wound*.) Knight says: "To the extent that women, as an entire gender-group, 'rule' it is neither nature nor political violence which dictates life's 'temporal structuring.' It is a rhythm internal to womankind, rooted in solidarity, sustained by the whole of culture and inseparable from the periodicity of the moon." Her capacities for menstruation and childbirth and for forming the bonds associated with motherhood and sisterhood become, in this eventuality—"the sources of her centrality to culture and her privileged access to its regulative mechanisms and power." He concludes by saying: "The potentiality for feminist liberation—for the experience of being physiologically feminine in a context which *engenders* collectivity and *confers* full social power—is a potentiality which has always been latent *within culture itself*."

We have tried to make a mandala of this short Afterword by traveling round from mythology to ordinary life again and back to mythology, hopefully showing by this serpentine move that these apparent opposites nourish and inform each other, just as the two opposites of ovulation and menstruation and their qualities and capacities combine in the menstrual mandala, in the shape we call feminine individuality.

There is so much more we could have written, extending each of our chapters in *The Wise Wound*. Horror films continue to provide a depraved folklore of the fear of feminine power; even more depraved now than then, they make our chapter above look almost innocent. Among the good films there is *Company of Wolves* from a short story of Angela Carter's in her *The Bloody Chamber*,[21] a retelling of the Red Riding Hood fairy tale. *The Incubus* and *The Entity* are fables of how a woman gains power by incubating her menstrual dreams. A distinguished film, Cassavetes's *Lovestreams*, afflicts the philanderer hero with his sister heroine's menstrual furor, when she fills the house with animals. At a moment of crucial insight, he hallucinates her dog, her animal representative, as a wise, bearded animus. The film reads out, with Cassavetes's conscious knowledge or not, like a man's dream of his wife's premenstruation. These fables and mythology are the shadow side of the religious dimension, for the divinities of one religion become the devils of the next.

We would have liked to discuss the ordination of women as Christian priests, and how, if women were able to take an active part in the formation of a liturgy, rhythms and meanings now concealed might emerge in a developing Christian myth. Indeed, religions in which women have primacy and full ordination have always existed, as Barbara Walker's book shows in full measure, and as we pointed out in the Witchcraft chapter of *The Wise Wound*. It is wonderful to know from Janet and Stewart Farrar's *The Witches' Way*[22] that *The Wise Wound* has been playing a serious part in the considerations of this developing religion of Wise Women who train Wise Men.

A whole book could be written on the beauties and healing intricacies of dreaming and its relation to the menstrual cycle. Several more *Wise Wounds* could be written; and we hope they will be, but not just by ourselves, but as part of the great flood of truly revolutionary knowledge that will come with the liberation of this hitherto "dark" side of women.

Appendix Relaxation
Practice Outline

1. Lie comfortably, but not as for ordinary sleep. This is a special sleep, between sleeping and waking. Normally we plunge straight into sleep, and wake up suddenly too, so we know little of the events that occur during the transition. This transition between sleeping and waking, between conscious processes and unconscious wisdom, is the creative state. One can lie on the floor, the neck slightly propped, the body covered with a blanket. The skin becomes very relaxed, silky and warm, so one must conserve heat.

2. Select a spot or crack on the ceiling, a little above one's eyes' normal level of sight. Stare at this spot, without blinking. Let it be the only visible thing in the world, and let your attention flow between you and the spot. But *at the same time* remind your body what it feels like to go to sleep, the limbs heavy and warm, the sinking and floating feeling, and how the eyes, when one is sleepy, insist on closing. Allow your open eyes to feel this wish for sleepy closing, but do not allow them to close yet.

3. Continue to remind your body of how it feels to sleep peacefully and let the sleepy feeling increase in your eyes until they cannot remain open, and drop of their own accord. As they close, feel the small pleasant shock of transition

between the waking world of light and the warm sleepy darkness in your own head and body.

4. Now, with the eyes always closed, attend to your big toe on the left foot. Don't move it, just know it is there. Feel its existence, the space it occupies, its warmth. Now do the same for your right big toe. Allow this gently focused awareness to spread to your other toes, and then to the soles of your feet, the heels, and slowly to the whole foot. You can now feel the touch of the whole skin of your foot. Be aware of the warmth of it too, and the heaviness.

5. Allow the feeling of warmth, heaviness, and touch to spread inward, so that you seem to feel the bones, relaxing, melting to the touch. Let the warmth and relaxation spread up to the ankles, the shins, the calves of the legs, slowly, warmly and gently, to the knees and to the thighs with their weight, and the buttocks that feel the warm weight of the floor pressing upward, of the whole earth. Let the flood of warmth and relaxation and awareness spread over your belly and over the small of your back. Let the bones of your pelvis melt, and let the warmth and the relaxation travel up your back and over your shoulder blades like warm soft dark hands caressing. Let it travel over your chest, where the breath is coming and going of its own accord, without you having to do anything to help it. Let the relaxation travel to your neck, and soften your jawline, and to the back of your neck, and soften it there. Let it travel down your left arm, warming it in sections, melting the bones, and travel out of your fingers, which are so relaxed they seem to stretch far out into the distance. And from the right shoulder down the right arm and out of the fingers. Let it travel over your face, which simply rests without expression on its bone, serene as the face of a buddha. Allow the space between the eyebrows to widen, and the brow to become broader, and be soothed by soft warm hands, and the relaxation to travel over the scalp like warm oil spreading under the hair. If there are thoughts or pictures flashing now, let them come, and then let them

go, and allow the relaxation to spread over the back of the head down the nape of the neck and down the spine, as though there were a tap at the base of the spine, and it was open, and all tension was draining away to the center of the earth.

6. Now attend only to the breathing. Watch it come and go slowly of its own accord, as it will. Breath is the link between conscious and unconscious, the door; for we can consciously direct our breath or, as now, allow it to come and go as it will. Breath responds to the whole universe inside you, and outside you.

7. Only pay more attention to the outbreath, which is the relaxing breath. Feel your relaxation deepen a little more each time you breathe out. Now imagine that you are breathing out an inch or two below your navel. Let the breath come out at this place, which seems open. You may feel a warmth there as you do this, or a tingling. Allow any thoughts or dream pictures to come, look at them, let them go, and return to your breath, your breath that is coming and going of its own accord, an inch or so below your navel, and relaxing you further with each outbreath. Stay in this very pleasant place as long as you have determined.

8. When you are ready, imagine you are a diver, ready to return by your own buoyancy from a great depth to the light above. Count backward from twenty as you come up from those depths, pausing occasionally to remember them, and think that your eyes will open as you reach the number one.

9. Open your eyes, and move very gently, carefully at first. Think about what has happened. Take notes very gently, for things alter as you move.

10. Many people get remarkable experiences involving imagery, waking dreams, sudden vivid insights, and the sheer unexpected pleasure of deep relaxation the first time they try this method. Generally speaking, it is best to promise oneself to do it every day for about twenty minutes or more for a fortnight. That gives it a chance. We have shared this

technique with some hundreds of people, and everybody who has given it this chance reports considerable benefits: in dream-recall, creativity, improved health, and alleviation of menstrual distress. Everybody alters the sequence and the details to suit themselves as they become practiced. Often one can start with an intention, such as a puzzling dream and a request for illumination, forget the intention while initiating the relaxation, and recall it again while doing the "womb-breathing" (men included). Often then the redreaming or solution is seen as in a magic mirror of the outbreath in the lower abdomen. We have known painters do this, and watch their painting develop a further stage, in the relaxation. Everybody develops it as they differently wish. You can make a tape-recording to listen to while relaxing, and rerecord as you find the instructions that suit you best.

11. Remember at the beginning, if you are doing relaxation by yourself (or recall it to anybody you are guiding into relaxation), that it is very easy to wake up from this relaxation if there is any emergency. It is also best, however, to take the phone off the hook. If somebody you are guiding wishes to remain "down there" and resists returning, you can ask them why. They usually say "It's so nice . . ." and one should let them stay there. It will sometimes develop into a brief nap. In any case, the relaxation is very refreshing. One should gently accustom oneself to taking simple notes, as part of the menstrual mandala.

Notes

CHAPTER I: THE SCIENCE OF BLEEDING

1 Haupt (1902) p. 29.
2 Suarès (1972) pp. 140–142. The Hebrew appears to evoke the goblet roundness of the changing moon. The actual appearance of the womb's cervix in the vagina may be involved. See Chapter V, pp. 178ff.
3 Suarès (1972) loc. cit.
4 Allegro (1970) pp. 72–73; Dames (1976) pp. 110f assimilates womanly knowledge, "cunning" and "cunt"; Bakan (1965) pp. 278f shows that the god-name "Daath" or "Knowledge" means "carnal knowledge."
5 Sollberger (1965) pp. 97–98. Wilson and Rennie (1976) pp. 46–56. Southam and Gonzaga (1965) quoted by Sherman (1971). For sensory and EEG changes see our note 48 to Chapter II. Tightrope walking: Johnson (1932).
6 This astonishing fact will be returned to in Chapter II, pp. 53ff.
7 Benedek (1952) appears to be an honorable exception. It is indeed a pioneering work, but it must be noted from its Chapter II, pp. 12f, that all the women contributing presented severely maladjusted symptoms. We criticize further in our Chapter II, pp. 87f.
8 Masters and Johnson (1966) p. vi plead for "physiologic fact rather than phallic fallacy" in teaching sex education and diminishing pornography. Their own was the first systematic factual study.

9 Few good love-books appeared before the 1960s, and even then they were marred by controversy or obsession, e.g., against homosexuality, or for/against "clitoral" or "vaginal" orgasms. Comfort (1972), though he believes that homosexuality is a "major sex problem" (p. 235), is otherwise to be recommended for imagination, precision, and tolerance. (Dr. Comfort is also a noted poet.) The love-book in English which is a sound guide to both technique and inner experience has yet to appear.

10 The consensus is examined further in our Chapter II, p. 41ff and notes. Eysenck (1973) and Sherman (1971) summarize the main work, which is characterized by uncertainty as to whether physical or psychological causes are chiefly responsible for menstrual distress, and by strong indications that the two aspects cooperate by "feedback."

11 Menstrual stage has been identified by dreams (Benedek and Rubenstein: 1942), by verbal productions (Benedek, 1963) and by personality questionnaires (Moos *et al.*, 1969; Ivey and Bardwick, 1968); but for many women "You hear no sounds of the hammer, but the building and destruction is ceaseless" (Bloom and Van Dongen, 1972 p. 212).

12 Von Franz (1974) p. 115.

13 Standard attitudes are: "the womb weeps bloody tears for its loss"; the "uterus weeps in memory of the ovum departed 14 days previously"; "the monthly abortion of the decidua of the unfertilized ovum"; "a woman menstruates because she does not conceive"; "Nature's physiological flaw"; "Nor do we know why, in the reproductive economy, women and monkeys are the sole members of God's creation to be afflicted with this inconvenience"; all quoted by Bloom and Van Dongen (1972) p. 212.

14 Llewellyn-Jones (1971) says that periods do not usually return for six months, if the mother is breast-feeding, but that 10% menstruate by ten weeks after childbirth, 20% by twenty weeks, and 60% by thirty weeks. He says: "Even if the menstrual periods start, breast-feeding can be continued as the quality of the milk is not altered during menstruation." We say that the *emotional* quality of the feeding *is* altered, depending on whether the mother has good periods or not. This fact seems to have been neglected by authorities, with the exception of Sylvia Close

(1972), who says that the feeding baby may suddenly go on strike, even though the breasts are full, from two months on: "The reason for this strange behavior seems to be associated with the mother's menstrual cycle—either the onset of menstruation or her premenstrual tension to which the baby reacts. It is thought that at this time the familiar smell of either the breast-milk or the mother is slightly different" (pp. 54–55). She recommends a relaxing, scented bath.

15 ". . . mammalian, including human, tissue starts as female in fetal life, regardless of the chromosomal sex . . . a clitoris is not a little penis; rather, anatomically, a penis is an androgenized clitoris. . . ." Robert J. Stoller in Strouse (1974) p. 345. Also Money and Ehrhardt (1973) pp. 7f.

16 Wilson and Rennie (1976) p. 25. Zuckerman (1949) thought that the uterus might not be a purely passively reacting organ, but perhaps had "an underlying rhythm of its own" (p. 1034). Cauthery and Cole (1971) suggest that prostaglandin may pass into the blood from the endometrium (p. 127).

17 If the authorities agree on nothing else, they agree that emotional life affects the menstrual cycle, and vice versa (Eysenck (1973), Sherman (1971)).

18 Bloom and Van Dongen (1972) p. 209. The flagrantly omitted feedback sequence is from vagina-womb in sexual experience, to conscious and subconscious, to hypothalamus, to pituitary, to ovary, to womb again. But clocks do not, so far as we know, have important inner experiences.

19 Gooch (1972) pp. 281–282: "The autonomic system is governed and shaped by the subjective reality of the internal environment—a reality differing from that of the objective, external universe."

20 It was once thought that menstruation and animal "heat" were equivalent (Ellis (1936) vol. I, part I, pp. 98ff) but there was controversy as to whether the ovulation occurred in association with menstruation (as it does with animal "heat") or at some other time of the cycle. See also Chapter II, note 48 below.

21 Weideger (1975) p. 31. Broadhurst in Eysenck (1973) accords general agreement to Arey (1939): average 29.3 days. Weideger objects to the "magic number" of 28. We agree that it is and

should not be incumbent, but offer an explanation of the number's recurrence in Chapter IV.

22 Wilson and Rennie (1976) p. 36.

23 McClintock (1971); Dewan (1969); see our Chapter V.

24 Bloom and Van Dongen (1972) p. 213.

25 Bardwick *et al.* (1970) p. 21.

26 Fourfold structure is only useful if it accords with people's experience, though it does correspond with the physiological events described, and certain others, as for instance the fourfold cell patterns observed microscopically (Gold (1975) pp. 135f). We merely suggest this pattern as a guide. J. Redgrove in Colquhoun (1971) p. 211 says ". . . the cycle has two main points, ovulation and menstruation. For convenience it is often divided into four phases, pre-ovulatory, ovulatory, premenstrual and menstrual." Significantly enough, one handbook of psychiatry gives four phases but leaves menstruation itself out! (Tredgold and Wolff (1975) p. 216: estrogenic, ovulation, progesterone and premenstrual phases). Nothing could be more indicative of the attitude of medical psychiatry to menstruation. The estrogenic phase is selected as the time for coitus, while "As progesterone production diminishes the woman becomes less loving and mature." We show in Chapter II how this attitude insultingly begs the question. Ellen Zimmermann and Mary Brown Parlee (1973) divided into four phases for their empirical study of behavioral changes: menstrual, follicular, luteal and premenstrual. Some authors (e.g., *Encyclopaedia Britannica* 1974) divide threefold, leaving menstruation as a phase out altogether; many others distinguish five phases: follicular, ovulation, postovulatory, luteal, and menstruation, for physiological or statistical reasons. It depends what you are measuring. Some of the confusion has been due to the fact that only quite recently have people begun to think of the *ovarian* cycle as distinct from the *womb* (or menstrual) cycle. Then the two linked cycles of three events each would come together like a Star of David: two linked triangles with six points altogether; and then the logical division would be sixfold. In measuring *experience*, however, many women tend to think of a cycle of about four weeks, during which there will be varying kinds of emphases. Wilson

and Rennie (1976) p. 11 show how directly opposite the two cycles are: "When referring to the menstrual cycle, day one is considered as the day on which menstrual bleeding commences . . . In the ovulation cycle the day of the LH peak is day zero and the next day is day one." The two day ones will usually be separated by a fortnight or more.

CHAPTER II: THE MENSTRUAL EPIDEMIC

1 The foreword to Dalton (1969) calls PMS "the commonest disease in the world"; Coppen and Kessel (1963) show that ". . . the incidence is great enough to raise doubts about the propriety of considering dysmenorrhea as abnormal" (Eysenck (1973) p. 174); "the frequency of dysmenorrhea found by various authors ranges between 3 and 90 per cent of all women in child-bearing age" (Svennerud (1959) pp. 7–8); "Depending on the definition of the premenstrual syndrome, estimates of its incidence have ranged from 25 per cent to nearly 100 per cent" (Sherman (1971) p. 134); "The premenstrual syndrome has been described as the commonest endocrine disorder, and Rees (1958) states that the figures for incidence range from 25 to 100 per cent, depending on definition . . ." (Dalton (1964) p. 39); "It is estimated that from 25 to 100 per cent of women suffer from some form of premenstrual or menstrual emotional disturbance . . . Eichner makes the discerning point that the few women who do not admit to premenstrual tension are basically unaware of it, but one needs only to talk to their husbands, or co-workers, to confirm its existence" (O'Conner *et al.* (1973) quoted by Weideger (1976) p. 47). Moos (1969) lists fifty symptoms attributed to PMS. The literature on the negative effects of the menstrual cycle is very extensive. It is summarized by the above authors, and by Parlee (1973), who also criticizes its assumptions. She points to lack of experimental controls, and, most cogently, that nobody has ever looked for favorable effects of the menstrual cycle. The incidence of dysmenorrhea is said to be low in Russia, where the status of women is high (Eysenck (1973) p. 174).

2 See our note 10 to Chapter I. Sherman (1971) pp. 128ff surveys

the literature, and throughout her summary shows how multifarious the uncertainty is. Authority after authority disclaims sure knowledge of the causation or cure of spasmodic or congestive dysmenorrhea or the premenstrual syndrome. Dalton (1964) is confident of a hormonal etiology, but concludes that it is "not yet possible to prove" (p. 35). The following quotation from Koeske (1975) is noteworthy: "One recent investigator (Wineman 1971) has found that sympathetic arousal characterizes the premenstrual phase of the cycle. Following Schachter and Singer (1962), emotionality should result from the interaction of this arousal with emotional labels provided by the situation. The simultaneous operation of a cognition linking negative moods and the premenstruum could result in the discounting of situational factors and an emphasis on biology (a type of internal attribution) in explaining negative but not positive moods. This attributional pattern, then, could reflect not the actual incidence of positive and negative moods as premenstruation, but the extent to which women's negative but not positive moods are seen as explained by biology. Exaggeration of the likelihood or recall of negative moods with a reversal for positive moods might also result. Acceptance of this attribution pattern might then adversely affect women's self-esteem. Valins and Nisbett (1971) have argued that a vicious circle of self-condemnation and anxiety may result when negative behavior patterns are internally attributed and situational factors discounted . . . Women . . . attributed more personal causation for emotionally expressive behavior. These tendencies, if widespread, could predispose women to suffer guilt, anxiety, and depression as a function of their belief in the biological explanation of premenstrual tension and might make action to alter upsetting situations more unlikely. As part of a complex attributional chain . . . this belief may represent one of the more significant aspects of socialization on female personality . . ." (pp. 477–478). We have characterized this "chain" and "vicious circle" independently in our treatment of "howlback."

3 Melody (1961) p. 440. He refers to premenstrual distress as "a biosocial disorder" and says it is the "commonest condition for which American women consult doctors" (p. 439).

4 Santamarina (1969); Melody (1961); figure for tranquilizers given in "Too Calm for Comfort," *Daily Express*, 14 March 1975; the white paper *Better Services for the Mentally Ill* (HMSO 1975) says that one in seven women consult their family doctor for psychiatric stress; *BMJ* leader, 21 October 1967.

5 *BMJ* leader, 21 October 1967, pp. 125–126. Jean and John Lennane (1973) argue that if you accept a psychogenic origin for such disturbances, then this leads to an approach to their management which is irrational and ineffective. We have tried to show that to restrict one's views of femininity to the physiological is both insulting and irrational. Please see further notes and documentation to this chapter for the extent of the controversy, particularly note 6 below. The possibilities of a developed psychological medicine have hardly been explored as such. For what these promise, see our pages *passim* and, for instance, Kent (1969), who says (pp. 7–10, p. 51): "It is the function of psychotherapy to release the parts of the personality which have been repressed by frightening images . . . If we are to revive and broaden a function, such as the menstrual cycle . . . The energies that bring about destruction can be diverted to build up new growth patterns . . . We may compare the human organism with a house divided into many compartments, all connected by communicating passages. During sickness certain compartments may develop unhealthy conditions . . . In psychotherapy the house is felt as a living unit through which streams or waves of forces and power are flowing . . ." These may show themselves as images, a person falls into a daydream and "has flashes of ideas which he does not like . . ." or nightmares. It is easy to interpret the crises as "negative therapeutic reactions" as Freud did. Thus rejected, they may easily become worse. The analyst's task is to see them as what they are: "the release of powerful energies hitherto unknown." As Reich (1958 p. 420) remarks: "But if one penetrates the distortion, a wide vista opens up on a vast realm of human experience, rich in truth and beauty. It is the realm from which all the great deeds of genius emerge."

6 Broadhurst in Eysenck (1973) p. 174 is an invaluable summary. There is a "lack of uniform views," and a tendency for psychi-

atrists to recognize "a strong psychosomatic component, while many of the gynecologists considered psychogenic aspects relatively unimportant." The distinction may, therefore, be imposed by medical specialization, and not by the menstrual troubles themselves. One activity that unites body and mind, gland and psyche, is sexual activity, which is noted by Masters and Johnson (1966) p. 126 as a technique that has been learned for the release both of "excessive uterine irritability and the symptoms of pelvic vasocongestion when present at menstrual onset," in other words for the relief of both congestive and spasmodic symptoms. We cannot find that this idea has been much followed up. Sexual activity is hormone and psychological treatment in one! One can take a similar view of hypnotherapy, particularly effective in dysmenorrhea. Sherman's review (1971) says there is dysmenorrhea, psychic amenorrhea, and the PMS, and all except dysmenorrhea are partly psychogenic. She shows how the fashion changes from psychological interpretation, as for instance that women hate menstruation "as a symbol of their femininity" (Weiss and English (1957)) to her own two-pronged conclusion (p. 141) that "it is now clear that primary dysmenorrhea is physically, not psychologically, caused. It is equally clear that psychic factors can affect menstruation. This is particularly plain in the case of amenorrhea. There is definite evidence of cyclic mental and physical changes. There is some evidence for a psychogenic etiology of cyclic symptoms, and it seems probable that there are cases of disturbed menstrual functioning caused by faulty attitudes. However the prevalence of the premenstrual symptoms make it clear that this cannot be solely a neurotic phenomenon." The "prevalence" might just as well mean that many women are in a neurosis-producing situation! and as for the rest, you *can* have it both ways. There is really no human need for this rigid body-mind separation, and what the menstrual problem is clearly trying to tell the scientists is that the two aspects belong together, and are particularly close in women. Separation of mind from body may well be a predominantly masculine characteristic. Fisher (1973) reviews the literature and says ". . . it is clear that one cannot with confidence assert that dysmenorrhea is or is not caused by neuroticism or some species of personality maladjustment" (p. 125). Pistilli (1975) says "the exact nature of the premenstrual syndrome remains unknown" (p. 16). Weideger (1975) p. 57 criticizes in detail the theory that water retention is the cause of premenstrual syndrome. Shainess (1962) p. 357 says: "While physiologically, the endocrine and water-balance changes probably account for a feeling of tension, weight gain (in part), breast engorgement and nipple tenderness, and, to some degree, headache, all other symptoms comprise an ancillary group that is psychogenic in origin." She finds dysmenorrhea to have a physiological basis in some patients and a large psychogenic component in others. Amenorrhea was largely psychogenic. She finds a correlation between a good mother-daughter relationship and a favorable introduction to the experience of menstruation. Louise Brush's empirical study (1938) accords with this. So does Weideger (1975). Shainess extends her idea of menstruation as a "nodal area of high potential for enhancement or impairment of the self" (1961) to the idea of a "new feminine psychology" concerning itself with the "'nodal points' in every girl's development." These are "the menarche, the development of breasts—organs not visibly present at birth, but growing as harbingers of puberty (and a significant development totally overlooked by Freud, to the best of my knowledge), defloration, pregnancy, delivery; the larger rhythms of pregnancy weaving through the smaller rhythms of menstruation, and finally the menopause . . . The psychology surrounding them is *the only psychology* which can justifiably be called 'feminine psychology'" (Shainess (1972) pp. 295–296). She omits lactation from her list, however. Herzberg and Coppen (1970) studying psychological changes in women taking the Pill suggest that the psychological and somatic components of PMS "may be produced by different mechanisms" (p. 163). Karen Horney's important but neglected 1931 paper is of the opinion that libido—sexual energy—is increased as a result of menstruation, and in her opinion is involved in the normally experienced premenstrual depressions, which are nearer the experience of most women than actual depressions within the menstruation. Ms. Horney says that the premenstrual depressions have nothing to do with a neurotic interpretation of the bleeding. What they do have to do with in some women is that the sexual power and desire has—from whatever circumstance—to be repressed. The anger they feel at the renunciation is converted into depression. With other women the inhibition is more inward: the cause is rather the intense wish for a child, which is awakened by the approaching period and repressed with equal intensity, thus causing depression. The relief that such women experience when the period actually begins is due to the fantasy of pregnancy ceasing. In menstruation, sacrifice sometimes stands in the foreground. Chadwick (1932) p. 11 refers to "the monthly neurosis of women . . . which Freud describes as the sudden intensification of libido, which leads to an outbreak of recognizable neurosis." Karen Paige (1972) thought that religious practices would affect menstrual distress. Among 298 women, the Jewish women, with severe bans on intercourse during menstruation, suffered the most difficulties. The Catholic women, whose belief it would be that suffering was God's law for women, also had frequent menstrual distress, particularly insofar as they lived out their religiously ordained female role, with no purpose in life outside the home and rearing of children. The conclusion seems to be that menstrual problems tend to come if the menstrual taboo is accepted.

7 Dalton (1969) p. 48.

8 Crabbe (1975) p. 4.

9 Excellent criticisms of Freud's writings on femininity by Juliet Mitchell, Elizabeth Janeway, Margaret Mead, and Robert J. Stoller will be found in Strouse (1974). More radical objections are given in Chesler (1972). Neither book has much to say on menstruation itself, beyond what we have mentioned: that the bleeding reinforces castration-fear, where that exists. Many of our quoted writers on menstruation, e.g., Shainess (1961), Houseman (1955), remark on the sparsity of Freud's treatment of the subject, if not on its partiality. Chadwick (1932) points out how silent psychoanalytic literature has been on the subject. To us, Skultans (1970) p. 646 concisely puts her finger on the problem with her references to the 1931 essay on female sexuality, in which "the subject is significant by its complete

absence" and to the note on p. 36 of *Civilisation and Its Discontents* (Freud, 1930), concerning the iron repression of an original sexual attraction: "The taboo on menstruation is derived from this 'organic repression' as a defense against a phase of development which has been surmounted. All other motives are probably of a secondary nature. (Cf. C. D. Daly, 1927.) *This process is repeated on another level when the gods of a superseded period of civilization turn into demons*" (our italics). The indexes of the Standard Edition of Freud give the sparse references, which are mostly asides.

10 e.g., Dalton (1969) "changeable personalities of at least half the female population" p. 59; "it wasn't the true me" p. 62; "a totally different person" p. 111.

11 Dalton (1969). On p. 115 she points out how the child's reactions of insecurity may increase the mother's stress and therefore PMT and therefore the child's reactions by a "howlback" circle. The reference to baby-battering is in a letter to the *BMJ* (Dalton 1975). Dalton (1969) Chapter 23 says "no evidence of male cycles," but Ellis (1935) I (1) pp. 112f examines evidence and says men have sexual cycles.

12 Parlee (1973) p. 456.

13 Chesler (1972) pp. 70–71.

14 Margaret Drabble in a BBC broadcast talk "Words" on 14 September 1975. According to her letter in the *Guardian*, 21 October 1975, a BBC executive objected to her discussing menstruation on the program.

15 Skultans (1970) p. 643.

16 We are indebted to Theodora Abel and Natalie Jaffe (1950), Louise Brush (1939), Virginia Larsen (1963) and to various personal communications for this selection of names.

17 Daly (1943) pp. 151–152; on p. 161 he says that the omission of menstruation from psychology is due to "hysterical amnesia." See also our index and bibliography under "Daly."

18 Rank (1929) p. 51. Roazen (1976) pp. 395–396, 403–404, 411.

19 Groddeck (1950) particularly Letter XII.

20 Klein (1975) pp. 224–227. Klein (1975b) pp. 318–319: she reviews Chadwick's *Woman's Periodicity* with an understanding of "how the common and neurotic attitudes of man and woman to

menstruation are transmitted to children and, in turn, how they again show the same kind of disturbances when they are grown up . . . and how they transmit the same problems again to the new generation: in this way neurosis is transmitted from generation to generation."

21 A. Freud (1965) p. 195. "The first external laws with which she confronts the infant are concerned with the *timing* and *rationing* of his satisfaction . . ." In this passage particularly (ibid. pp. 142–143) there is a great sense of the rationality of the mother's decisions. We wish to say how apposite and wise we find much of Klein's and A. Freud's writing, and we are here only calling attention to what we believe is an important omission. "The more completely we succeed in bringing both the resistance and the defense against affects into consciousness and so rendering them inoperative, the more rapidly shall we advance to an understanding of the id" (A. Freud (1968) p. 41). This is our aim also.

22 Cf. "Amenhorrhea". Eysenck (1973) pp. 172–173. The facts quoted extend the notion of the cycle profoundly sensitive to external experience. So does Chapter 4 of Dalton (1969) "Emotions and the Menstrual Clock." They need to be considered in conjunction with Chesler's (1972) and Szasz's (1971) arguments that psychiatric practice selects scapegoats; and Fisher's (1973) observation that "raises the possibility that the menstrual experience is somehow specifically helpful to women with serious psychiatric symptomatology" (p. 122). We have offered the notion of a helpful "moment of truth" that festers psychologically if ignored. Chillingly, in the Nazi concentration camps ". . . the menstrual process ceased suddenly on a mass scale, and with it the libido also became passive" (Weinstock (1947) p. 235). Martius (1946) found that amenorrhea, excessive fatigue, backaches, intractable constipation, underdevelopment of the womb, and discoloration of the vaginal entrance were found in 50–60% of women in labor battalions, 85% of women imprisoned for major crimes, and 100% of Jewish internees in concentration camps. He mentions hormone treatment, but says that cure can only come by settlement of populations. Gyöngyössy and Szalóczy (1971) write of "the ovulation-

inhibiting effect of modern living" and call it a "*civilization disease.*" Mall (1958) indicated how insulin, chloropromazin and reserpine treatments in mental hospital treatment masked natural rhythms, including the menstrual ones. A. E. Rakoff in Michael (1968) shows how vulnerable the human menstrual cycle is to outside disturbances. "Endocrine mechanism in psychogenic amenorrhoea" (Teja 1976) shows how important it is to differentiate puberty psychosis from schizophrenic illness.

23 26m quoted in the *Daily Express*, 14 March 1975, in an article that worries on the extent to which people are prescribed pills that are accused by critics of "leading to aggression and . . . often accentuate the patient's original problems." According to the anonymous author in an article in *Undercurrents* No. 19, Dec. 1976–Jan. 1977, pp. 34–35, "The advertisements for tranquillizers and anti-depressives . . . depict women fifteen times as often as men . . ." ". . . women do take twice as many tranquillizers and anti-depressants as men. . . ." A table given shows that in 1971 in the U.K. 8.9% of men, and 19.1% of women took "anti-anxiety sedative medicines," and in the U.S.A. the figures were 8.0% and 20% respectively!

24 Dalton (1969) p. 129. Rosemarie Patty and Marcia Ferrell (1971) have also studied "The Motive to Avoid Success and the Menstrual Cycle."

25 Devereaux (1950) p. 253.

26 Campbell (1965) pp. 60, 64, 72, 52.

27 Briffault (1927) vol. 2, pp. 421f. This great feminist book should be read as a corrective to Frazer, particularly his chapters in this vol. XIX "The Witch and the Priestess"; XX "The Lord of the Women"; and XXI "The Resurrection and the Life." Briffault's information has not been challenged, though he was criticized by Estermark for his biological theories and by Lowie for his view that matriarchy was always and everywhere the primal condition. He is a source for the scholarly Neumann (1955), Levy (1948), Thomson (1965) and others, but not Kerényi. Briffault should be read in the three-volume reprint, especially vol. 2. Harding (1955) draws upon his information.

28 Van Waters (1913) p. 400. Also pp. 396, 399–403. Van Waters (1914) pp. 89–93, 105. Devereaux op. cit. concurs that menar-

che is the time a women becomes a shamaness or witch. Ford (1945) p. 9 notes of the Lepcha of India that after menstruation begins, a divinity "peculiar to women makes love to them in their dreams *each month*" (our italics). Examples summarized from several sources by John H. Field in Webb (1975) pp. 30–37. Bettelheim's (1955) material also accords with this view, as does Briffault (vol. 2, pp. 543ff).

29 Stephens (1961, 1962); his views are corroborated by the empirical psychological data that are available according to Kline (1972).

30 Slater (1968) p. 461; Benedict quoted p. 413.

31 Weideger (1975) pp. 117f. She had a good chapter on "Taboo" pp. 85–113. Ford (1945) remarks of 64 societies from the Yale Cross-Cultural Survey, none "was specifically reported by the ethnographer to permit intercourse during menstruation."

32 Laing (1960) pp. 39f. Recent discussion on Laing's ideas suggested that schizophrenia in its nonbiochemical aspect was generated by a damaged "sense of consistency" (e.g. *Listener*, 28 Oct. 1976, letters p. 553). A menstrual period in an unhappy woman will produce such an inconsistency in a child's environment, and we suggest that the woman's disturbance is produced by society's inconsistency toward her femininity.

33 Crawley (1927) suggests this in his theory of "Inoculation" by which one sex adopts properties of the other in order to withstand the dangerous charge of union (I, pp. 285ff). De Martino (1972) suggests a theory of magic by a controlled dissolution of the "presence": a magician or shaman learns to do this, and the anguish of an untrained person in the face of natural forces is "his will to retain his identity when confronted with the threat of losing it." If the "presence" is lost, the person becomes infinitely sensitive to his environment or to suggestion, for instance, "if his attention is caught by branches moving in the wind, he will imitate this movement." The state is sometimes called "olonism" or "echopraxia" (pp. 81f).

34 A close sexual association involves not only physical realization of the other partner's nature, but also playful or experimental changes of role and ability. This mingling of individual natures has its counterpart in the mingling of genetic material in the

offspring. With extreme "ovulatory" polarization, this genetic mingling will be the chief aim; a person will be reborn in his/her child, and this will be the only purpose of a sexual connection. Ferenczi compares in "Thalassa" the desire to merge with another, and the pang of parting, with the primal cell-fusion of the gametes, and the first subdivisions of the ovum.

35 Coined by Richard Dawkins, "Memes and the evolution of culture," *New Scientist*, vol. 72, 28 Oct. 1976, p. 208.

36 Bettleheim (1955) e.g. p. 177, p. 231, pp. 207ff and pp. 61–63 "The Men-Women" and pp. 227ff "The Secret of Men." Judith Brown's level-headed survey (1963) confirms the role of such ceremonies in sex-role acceptance, and, where women contribute to subsistence activities, the giving of "special assurance of competence." Ford and Beach (1951) speak of and describe examples of the "instruction" given, as does Van Waters. The Apache girl's puberty ceremonies were notable: she has the power to bless and help others, is identified with the culture heroine. This contrasts with most other Apache rites, born of crisis and fear (Opler (1972)) p. 1144, who criticizes some of Judith Brown's assumptions. Hogbin's "The Island of Menstruating Men" (1970) is a very rich ethnographical work that does not proceed to psychodynamic theories. However, it is clear from it that penile mutilation arises from a sexual anxiety not shared by the women, that the male bleeding is regarded as cleansing in the spiritual sense by the men, and that the women in Wogeo "enjoy a higher status than is customary in New Guinea," thus corroborating some of the notions we put forward in this and subsequent chapters.

37 Chesler (1972) p. 56.

38 Daly (1935).

39 Groddeck (1950b) pp. 24–25.

40 Frazer (1922) pp. 933–934.

41 Buxton (1973) Part V, Chapter 21, particularly pp. 391f; Turner (1967) esp. Chapter III "Colour Classification in Ndembu Ritual."

42 De Beauvoir (pp. 335–342) has a powerful evocation of the disgust that can be aroused in a woman of powerful intellect by the inconsistency of her menstrual cycle.

43 Fully discussed in Dalton (1964); summarized succinctly in Janowsky (1966) and in Dalton (1969). In the last, a particularly cogent statement on p. 139 says that 50% of the women investigated were in their paramenstruum in studies of: newly convicted prisoners; disorderly prisoners; schoolgirls punished at school; women requesting doctor's home visit; accident admissions; sufferers from acute mental disturbance; employees reporting sick; acute surgical and medical admissions; viral and bacterial infections; mothers of sick children. Parlee (1973) surveys the field and concludes that while there are undoubtedly widespread effects, the statistical and control procedures leave much to be desired; moreover, researchers look for illness and not benefits, and so find them. Sherman (1971) in her survey gives support to the actuality of adverse monthly changes, and says that it is "possible that more careful attention to adverse monthly changes might prevent the development of more serious mental disturbances . . ." and ". . . much more attention to research and to education in these matters is indicated." The kidnapping of Dr. Herrema was reported in the press during 1975: the *Daily Mail* on 1 November mentioned that sanitary towels had been passed in. Groddeck (1950) says that most rapes are committed during menstruation, and Kroger and Freed echo this. We have not been able to find a more recent study on rape which even mentions menstruation. Burial granted to menstruating suicides: Wetzel and McClure (1972), who review the menstrual suicide data.

44 Wright (1967) pp. 16–18. Newton (1975) and in Zubin and Money (1973).

45 See Snaith and Coxon (1969).

46 Danielle Rapoport's study reported in *New Scientist,* 25 Nov. 1976, p. 449. Leboyer's book (1975) is impressive and moving.

47 Masters and Johnson (1966) pp. 124–126. The menstrual fluid would ejaculate with such force as to clear the vaginal barrel without touching the speculum blades. Masters and Johnson (1975) confirms the use of masturbation for relieving menstrual cramps.

48 Havelock Ellis's humane discussions (1935), though they might seem anecdotal and overlimited by modern standards, are

warmly recommended, particularly I (1) pp. 98ff in "The Phenomena of Sexual Periodicity"; II (3) pp. 67f "Sexual Education," and II (2) pp. 213ff "The Menstrual Curve of Sexual Impulse." The last gives fascinating case studies, including dreams, from which Ellis concludes that there is a double crest in the "menstrual wave of sexual desire," one during or around menstruation, and the second at midcycle. He says that there is "the indication of a tendency of the menstrual cycle to split into two" and that establishing this curve would seem to be a "notable advance." Ellis also emphasizes the importance of erotic dreams, and their relationship to the enhancement of the senses in "hysteria" (I (1) pp. 201ff). He took the view of his time that menstruation, because of its sexuality, was analogous to the "heat" in animals. This is a half-truth (though sufficient to lead to a neglect of his opinions), since ovulation does not normally occur then, but at midcycle. This was not agreed until roughly 1920. On the theory of "adaptation," sexual libido would have to be highest at the time when the species would benefit by offspring, at midcycle. Thus the fact of a sexual peak at menstruation was neglected in scientific circles. McCance *et al.* (1937) show in their review this partiality for ovulation in action: "It is satisfactory that the greatest degree of desire should precede ovulation, but if, as Zuckerman (1936) maintains, the human sperm can rarely live in the female generative tract for more than two days, it is difficult to see why seven days should elapse between the period of maximum desire in the female and her time of ovulation." Indeed it is, unless the sexuality has some other function than that of reproduction. They too, however, record a dual crest, one during or shortly after menstruation, and, in married women, another at the expected ovulation time. Their sample of single women did not show the ovulation-crest. R. D. Hart (1060) reviewed the literature, which on balance agreed with her finding that in 59% of her married woman subjects, maximal libido was associated with menstruation, and less with midcycle ovulation. An early survey by Georgene Seward (1937) found that most authorities "find that in the majority of women increased sexual desire is reported either just before, after, or before and after the hemorrhage. This bimodal curve is difficult to explain in terms of homology with the estrus in lower mammals" (p. 184). Ford and Beach (1952 pp. 221ff concurs. Sherfey (1972) believes with Kinsey that 90% of women are more sexually active during the luteal phase, in the presence of progesterone, and that this time of premenstrual congestion is exactly comparable to "heat" in animals (p. 98). Clearly more study is needed, which ought to include (as Money and Ehrhardt (1972) p. 223 criticizing Udry and Morris (1968) said) some notice of the quality as well as the quantity of experience. Diamond *et al.* (1972) found visual sensitivity increased at midcycle, and believed that this made coitus more likely at midcycle. It may merely mean that the sexual sensitivities introverse, changing quality. They quote studies that show auditory and olfactory response also declining. Introversion may also be indicated by de Baenne's finding that the EEG can slow at the beginning of menstruation, and then present an "abnormal" picture (1942). Roubicek *et al.* (1968) also find this slowing at menstruation. Wineman (1971) showed changes of balance in the autonomic nervous system through the cycle. Shader *et al.* (1968) find libido changes more pronounced in highly anxious women, and in women raised in "upper class families." Which came first, though, the anxiety or the libido? Barbara Sommer (1973) questions these findings in parallel with Parlee's doubts—and says of the measurements: "When social or psychological expectations of menstrual debilitation are altered, the effect disappears" (p. 532). Zimmermann and Parlee (1973) show further doubt of the accepted laboratory measurements. This sensitivity of laboratory and questionnaire results is commented upon in our note 2 above. Swanson and Foulkes (1968) also refute Benedek, and find sexiest dreams during menses. Kleitman (1939) found increased dreaming also.

49 Fluhmann (1936) p. 121.
50 Kinsey (1965) p. 610.
51 Money and Ehrhardt (1972) p. 223.
52 Jung (1973) p. 404. Jung (1957) pp. 3ff gives a fascinating account in his medical dissertation of what the onset of periodical sexual feeling in puberty meant in terms of dreams and "occult phenomena" including enhanced sensory perception

and even "the psychology of the supra-normal, that of genius" (p. 4). It is unfortunate that he did not interpret the phenomena in terms of the menstrual cycle, or see the cycle's significance to the life of a woman—instead it appears as rather an irrelevance. Jung (1963) pp. 129–30 pooh-poohs a "lunar vampire" fantasy.

53 Masters and Johnson (1966) pp. 124–126.
54 Fisher (1973) pp. 199–201.
55 Weideger (1975) pp. 123–127.
56 Bardwick *et al.* (1970) p. 8; p. 37.
57 Benedek (1952) p. 158.
58 Campbell (1965) pp. 160–164.

CHAPTER III: AMIMUS, ANIMAL, ANIMA

1 Judith Kestenberg in Chapter 3 "Menarche" of Lorand and Schneer (1961).
2 Introduction to *The Portable Jung*.
3 These half-submerged references to menstruation in Jung's formulations, from which they may take their power, is the subject of a further book in preparation by Peter Redgrove, *A Feminist Jung*. A fascinating and consistent account is in "The Psychological Aspects of the Kore" (Jung 1959), though the only overt reference to menstrual blood implies archaic observance. He speaks of the *nekyia*, a descent into the Underworld for the "treasure hard to attain" connected with "offerings of menstrual blood to the moon"; "drinkings of blood and bathings in blood"; a maiden-goddess in white carrying a black monkey; he quotes an "Indian" woman saying "A woman's life is close to the *blood*"; and dreams of snakes, blood, and sacrifices: "in order to enter the temple precincts one has to be transformed into an animal"; a black-clothed countess with red hair surrounded by spirits; and many other interesting features that, read out as we suggest, with menstruation in mind, make immediate sense apparently beyond Jung's intention. On p. 363 the mandala, lotus, and "golden flower" are the "rose-wreath" womb. Other references include: opposites listed, Jung (1963b) p. 3; the goal of the work discussed, pp. 487ff, 533ff; p. 141 "the slaying of the dragon . . . first, dangerous, poisonous stage of the

anima . . ."; *succus lunariae* (juice of the moon-plant) and moon-bitch, pp. 152–153; "finally, the mixture must not lack the thing that really keeps body and soul together: human blood, which was regarded as the seat of the soul. It was a synonym for the red tincture, a preliminary stage of the lapis; moreover, it was an old-established magic charm, a 'ligament' for binding the soul either to God or the devil, and hence a powerful medicine for uniting the *unio mentalis* with the body. The admixture of human blood seems to me unusual if one assumes that the recipe was meant literally" (p. 485).

Jung also expresses surprise at the literal presence of blood in "conjunctio Solis et Lunae" on p. 440. White woman and red slave are discussed on p. 93 of Jung (1967), Mercurius and the Philosophical Tree in separate essays, with a section on "the mysterious rose-colored blood" and the Tree on p. 292: we suggest that Mercurius is the Western version of the "spirits of the menstruation" that Van Waters and other say come upon the girl at menarche; and that the figure of the Tree should be assimilated to the fruiting ovaries of the woman.

Jung (1976) in his Tavistock lectures remarks: "The inferior function is always associated with an archaic personality in ourselves . . . There we have an open wound, or at least an open door through which anything might enter" (p. 21).

The menstruum of the whore is mentioned in Jung (1954) p. 284, with the "foul deposit" (also in Jung (1968) p. 289n). The whole essay "Psychology of the Transference" pp. 164ff takes new and relevant life when read with the cycle of renewal of the menstrual process in mind. As he says (p. 250), the work or *opus* becomes "an analogy of the natural process by means of which instinctive energy is transformed, at least in part, into symbolical activity." The "maternal fount" and "my red wine" are on p. 282. The transforming tincture is "spiritual blood" on p. 197, and "out of the monstrous animal forms there gradually emerges a *res simplex*," meaning an inward unity. That this is seen by Jung as a "spiritual child" is condensed for us in Jolande Jacobi (1962) p. 118: "Thus there is a natural complementarity between the sexes, not only on the physical level where it gives birth to the 'bodily child,' but also in the mysterious stream of images which flows through the depths of their souls and joins them together to engender the 'spiritual child' . . . once a woman has become aware of this, once she knows how to 'handle' her unconscious and let herself by guided by her inner voice, then it will be up to her . . ." Esther Harding (1955) echoes this (p. 239). It is an inner conjunction: "Mysterium Coniunctionis," the title of Jung's last major work (1963b) on alchemy, which is also packed full of material requiring reinterpretation in the feminist sense. Of particular interest is the section on "Luna" and "The Dog" pp. 129ff, that speaks of the tree of sun and moon, which is a red and white coral, or a sponge planted in the lunar sea that has blood and sentience. "If thou wouldst handle the plant, take a sickle to cut it with, but have good care that the blood floweth not out, for it is the poison of the Philosophers." "Therefore pull down the house . . ." is on p. 150. Red Adam, who renews himself in a bath and has two faces, is discussed on pp. 383ff. The Golden, and the Severed Head, as *prima materia* is on p. 434, with a reference to the Song of Songs, which, with its "black and comely" Shulamite is seen elsewhere as an alchemical drama, having to do with Solomon and the Queen of Sheba who "gave her body and blood to the disciples" and "the transformation of the feminine element from a serpent into a queen" (pp. 376ff).

4 Fisher (1973b) pp. 72–77, p. 85, pp. 181–182. Di Nardo (1974) has recently shown that there is a tendency toward less menstrual distress in women with more positive body-attitudes. Dancers have always been rumored to suffer little from dysmenorrhea.

5 C. G. Jung often equates Grail, *Krater*, center, uterus, philosophical stone, life-giving vessel, e.g., Jung (1968) p. 179n where it is approached by a spiral, which is like a changing cycle, through a "virgin forest," drawn in a letter "from an unknown woman. She writes that she has pains in her uterus." In the forest there are swarms of monkeys. Jung's interpretation begins: "The anima reports that there are painful processes going on in the life-creating center. . . ." He neglects here, as elsewhere, that a characteristic of any uterus, spiritual or physical, is that it menstruates, for which a goblet of blood is the natural image, the Grail. In Jung (1971) he equates alchemical *vas* with uterus

in commenting upon "The Song of Songs" (pp. 233ff). The spiral is a symbol both of the moon's phases and of the vulva, Eliade (1958) p. 156.

6 Kent (1969) demonstrates, with case histories, that "The changes in biological function are accompanied by changes in the capacity for image formation." In one male patient "The emerging capacity for image formation and the release of new energies on the biological level stimulated orderly and sequential events . . ." (p. 115). He says (p. 138) that "Image formation is a spontaneous activity of the unconscious. Such activity can be so severely curtailed by repression that it leads to externalization phenomena such as hallucinations." Layard (personal communications) would thus analyze the hallucination in the same manner as with a dream-image. Kent continues: "The more the unconscious is relieved of restrictive pressure, the more spontaneous activity of the unconscious is released on the bodily and imaginative levels." This is Jung's "active imagination" and his "transcendent function" of creativity, though he rarely reported remission of physical symptoms; it is also the spontaneous imagery of hypnosis and meditation. It is also fantasy or fancy: a great disservice is done in contrasting "fancy" with "imagination" as Coleridge does, if this distinction leads to a neglect of the growth-areas which "fancy" represents, the free play of the mind in a state of reverie in which, as Koestler shows, new connections and discoveries are made, not in the arts alone, but in the sciences also. Kent, as physician, suggests good biological reasons why we "regress" and why it is "necessary to regress in order to overcome immaturity" (p. 255). It is because the organism plays to develop, and to understand and release its natural energies, however inconvenient these may be to society organized on its present lines. In terms of the practice of reforming oneself by consulting animal images, as in yoga or totem-dancing, or the witch-flight (our Chapter VI, p. 227), this impulse may occur spontaneously in the form of hallucinations or compulsions. Kent comments on the case thus (p. 116): "The forces which appeared in the first place as embryo developmental forces revealed their evolutionary origin in archaic images such as a neckless and limbless fish with a straight spine, or as a

powerful ape with a pointed snout and long fangs. The archaic vestiges were experienced as potential for remolding and enriching the organism. Under the regime of repression the animal forces acted as restrictive potentialities tearing the organized part of the organism to shreds. The patient experienced very keenly the unintegrated potentials of animal origin and the way in which he frantically built up a false personality to counteract the disruptive activity within." We are suggesting that just as menstruation opens up rifts in the false stereotyped personalities that women may have to adopt, so it is an opportunity to contact these potentials—which may at first show themselves in an unevolved state. Thus, a hallucination of red ants on a doorway at menstruation integrated swiftly to a warm-blooded playful red ape, and as his play was enjoyed, he then acquired the power of speech. Then the conversation with "animus"—the form in which these repressed energies frequently appear in women's dreams or fantasies—can begin.

7 On the question of the meaning of the words "devil" and "demon": Partridge gives one origin of the latter word as "daemon," meaning guardian spirit. The word probably filtered through monkish Latin, which gave it the evil connotation. "Devil" or "diabolus" apparently goes back to a translation of the Hebrew "Satan" meaning "traducer." It also means to throw (*ballein*) across (*dia*). The word "traduce" in the OED can mean not only to "put over" meaning to deceive, but also "to lead over." Slater (1968) pp. 96–97 quotes Ferenczi discussing the genital act and the penis as "bridge" between external reality and the internal reality of the womb. This is as the snake "symbolized the bond between the hero and Mother Earth," and he compares them to the wool fillets with which the *omphalos* at Delphi was decorated: "the fillets worn by suppliants and seers represented a similar tie—a kind of ancient 'hot line.'" We give reason later for interpreting the cone-shaped *omphalos* or hub at "Delphi" or womb, as the visible cervix of the womb, which was thus honored as the bridge between life and death, phallus or umbilicus. The seep of blood like a red-dyed fillet would be visible at menstruation. We have seen how often the snake is figured as is the counselor or "other husband" to women at their

first period, and the Devil is often referred to, for instance in exorcism services, as "Ancient Serpent." Therefore as we said before, the Devil is sexuality, particularly menstrual sexuality. In Jung, the devil, Mephistopheles for instance, is the Shadow: life-giving if he is "assimilated." For Freud, according to Bakan (1965) p. 211, "The pact with the devil is therefore really a pact with the Super-Ego not to help human beings in getting these things but to stop preventing them in doing so." This recalls T. S. Eliot's definition of inspiration as less something that is added to one, but rather something which is taken away that acted as a barrier to inspiration. It is interesting that in modern times the "visit of a male relative" is a frequent euphemism for the period. Markale (1975) says that the Devil "being etymologically the one who 'throws himself across,' prevents things happening according to the current norm" (p. 171).

8 Eliade (1960) gives fascinating summaries of these "approaches to the sacred" for both men and women in his Chapter 8; animal language is discussed pp. 60f.

9 Jung (1976) p. 21. His important 1913 vision (Jung 1963, pp. 172f) ends with an "intolerable outpouring of blood—an altogether abnormal phenomenon, so it seemed to me . . . I abandoned all further attempt to understand" and he attributed it to the approach of war.

CHAPTER IV: DOES THE MOON MENSTRUATE?

1 Brown (1976) is an excellent discriminating introduction to this new science: astro-archaeology.

2 O'Neil (1976) is an admirable summary of "Time and the Calendars." He confirms Briffault's opinion that the calendar originated in moon-phases (p. 47); he says of our calendar: "What a strange hodge-podge in which nothing quite fits anything else! The weeks don't quite fit the months of the year; to make the months fit the year real Moon periods are abandoned; the years are never exact solar tropical periods . . ." (p. 13).

3 Berry (1973).

4 This alternative tradition of the Garden is traced by Armstrong (1969).

5 Campbell (1965) p. 103n.

6 Bakan's (1965) absorbing chapter on "Sexuality in Jewish Mysticism and Freudian Theory" is recommended p. 271. Also Waite discusses in his chapter "The Mystery of Sex." Patai (1967) is also recommended very strongly, e.g., "Sabbath and Sex" pp. 246f.

7 Samples of this work will be found in Lee and Mayes (1973); Fisher *et al.* "Cycle of Penile Erection Synchronous with Dreaming (REM) Sleep" pp. 235ff (no research appears to exist on feminine excitation and REM sleep); and Snyder "Toward an Evolutionary Theory of Dreaming" pp. 378ff.

8 Campbell (1965) pp. 162–163.

9 The Mooseheart records are suggestive (Reymert and Jost 1947). In 5,562 menstrual cycles of girls from 10 to 18½, the mean length was 29.8 days; there was a seasonal variation in the cycles, the shorter ones in the winter and the longer in the summer. More girls reached menarche in the summer and winter than in the autumn or spring. So there is definitely environmental sensitivity with, one presumes, a subjective component also.

10 Gay Gaer Luce (1972) is recommended as an introduction to the subject, and has an excellent bibliography. Sollberger (1965) is more technical.

11 Gauquelin's work was recently examined by independent committees, who admitted its soundness, but who were not able to provide explanations for the undoubted effects (*New Scientist*, p. 428, 26 Feb. 1976).

12 Feedback is implicit in the procedures described in standard texts, e.g., Hartland (1971) and Ambrose and Newbold (1968), but was put forward explicitly as a theory of hypnosis by Nick Humphrey in *New Scientist*, 2 Sept. 1976: "Hypnosis explained, or how to escalate suggestibility" (pp. 185 186).

13 Quoted by Bayley (1912) I p. 188 in a chapter called "The Fair Shulamite" in which he traces through folklore images of neglected and restored femininity.

14 Briffault (1927) III pp. 183–184.

15 Benjamin Walker, in *Man, Myth and Magic*, no. 67, p. 1876.

CHAPTER V: DID THE ANCIENTS HAVE WISDOM?

1 Allegro (1970); Massey (1883); Kerényi (1975). The last is our chief source for information on the Hera cults.

2 Mentioned in Howey (1972) p. 133; advanced also by Lyle Borst in his *Megalithic Software* reported in *The Times*, 31 Jan. 1976.

3 Thomson (1965) pp. 220ff, 231ff.

4 Cf. Layard (1972).

5 Morton Smith (1963). There is no need to insist that there was genital intercourse. An initiation could have taken place after suitable preparation in a state of extreme suggestibility by the laying on of hands. The seeing of visions and the alteration of body-image is a staple of modern medical hypnotherapy, and there are modern cults who claim profitable visionary adventures from simple relaxation and massage techniques. One set of methods, which is even known by its initiates as the "Christos" experience, is described in Glaskin (1974), though his account would be improved by some cultural cross-reference and critical discussion such as is provided by Tart (1972, 1975). Our point is that the exquisite sensory sensitivity, particularly of the skin, and the mental openness that commonly goes with the flow, and could have been the origin of menstrual seclusion customs, could also have been the occasion for the kind of physically mediated reveries that it is easy to develop on the personal level. Cecil Williamson: personal communications.

6 To the best of our belief, this fact has not been noticed before in modern times. The "omphalos" is discussed in notable books, such as Jane Harrison (1962) and Butterworth (1970) with numerous illustrations, and the discussion takes on new vitality and value if it is understood by self-examination or consulting a gynecology textbook that the sacred object is carried in every case by Everywoman herself in her own secret place. The cults of the dead are also cults of the unborn, and of informative ghosts whose communications are associated with womb-structures. Leroi-Gourhan (1968) illustrates many Stone Age markings, including the mysterious "cup marks" hitherto difficult of interpretation, that may have this significance. Marshack's (1972) arguments for Stone Age moon-menstruation-fertility calendars gain great force, though he

thinks in terms of vulva- and not cervix-images. Dames (1976) interprets Silbury Hill as a birth-image, a constructed goddess-belly, or an eye, which by reflections from water-surfaces built around the hill he says must have produced a pageant of moon-birth and suckling at fertility-festivals. He does not note the conical hill's resemblance to the cervix, like any "sacred mountain" with its flattened peak and its status as axis where two worlds touch: literally true of the womb's entrance. Butterworth p. 26 notes how the word "omphalos" is a stumbling-block: "the word should properly describe depression, not the opposite thereof"!

7 Wiener's (1966) intricately documented theories on external chemical messengers are fascinating and important; Davis (1971) provides a readable introduction. Klock (1961) quoted by Bermant and Davidson (1974) and Michael *et al.* (1974) offer evidence of pheromone communication in the human menstrual cycle as do Udry, Morris, and Waller (1973).

8 Garrison (1964) has a chapter on "The Fragrance of Being": his is an inoffensive guide to simple sex-rituals, and does not mention menstrual rhythms. Grant (1973) notes the female Tantric initiates were known as "'the sweet-smelling ladies' (*suvasinis*)."

9 The sources for our conjectures about Eleusis include Kerényi's excellent short essay in Jung and Kerényi (1963): the horned child born; the process "to be pursued, robbed, raped, to *fail to understand*, to rage and grieve, but then to get everything back and be born again"; "Men, too, entered into the figure of Demeter and became one with the goddess"; the inner act of surrender to a death; also Kerényi (1976); Otto in Campbell (1955); Mylonas (1961); Thomson (1965).

10 Campbell (1968) takes a parallel view in that he implies that the Grail's meaning that few have questioned is the language of dreams. In von Eschenbach, Parzival asked the correct question on his second visit to the Grail castle.

11 Quoted Markale (1975) p. 179. He may underplay menstruation, but provides useful corroborative information in that he does equate sexual paradise with the menstrual flow (p. 74); mentions that prophecy is connected with "a woman's disease" (p. 143) and that the Gnostic Phibionites in their specially

menstrual rites "By rejecting procreation as the purpose of sexuality, they allowed women to enjoy their bodies fully once more" (p. 171). He quotes de Gourmont's *Lilith*, which he says "is denouncing the taboo imposed on the type of love that consists of the total possession of two people without any biological purpose. But since, within this kind of love, woman would regain all her alarming powers . . ." she and her consort are depicted as two demons, Satan and Lilith (p. 159). On p. 151 he regards man as "nondivinity" opposed to woman's "divinity," and traces the forcing-underground of Lilith (pp. 154ff) and notes the conflict of the daughters of Lilith with the daughters of Eve. This last is in his chapter "The Rebellion of the Flower-Daughter": it is to be noted that menstruation was called "the flowers" presumably because it is not the offspring, the fruit.

CHAPTER VI: NINE MILLION MENSTRUAL MURDERS

1 Weiberbünde and Männerbünde summarized in Eliade (1960) pp. 204ff.

2 La Fontaine (1972) pp. 135ff.

3 *Redbook*, vol. 132, April 1969, pp. 94ff.

4 *Time*, 22 Oct. 1956.

5 Margaret Mead, *Redbook*, vol. 138, pp. 49ff. Mary Chadwick (1931, 1932, 1933) pointed out the psychoanalytic likeness between witch-beliefs and menstruation. She quotes modern patients who converse with the Devil. She, as a Freudian, thought witchcraft, and the menstrual experience, regressive. Sherman (1971) p. 126 also comments on this. Schmiedeberg (1933) says the connection corresponds with the ideas of primitive people.

6 Scholem (1965) is very clear about the importance of Sabbath; it is when "the light of the upper world bursts into the profane world" and it was important for Torah scholars to "perform marital intercourse precisely on Friday night" for the reason that the earthly union was symbolic of the heavenly marriage between God and his Bride, Sabbath or *Shekinah* (pp. 139ff). The advent of the Shekinah was transformed into the "holy apple orchard" and there were hymns sung: "Go, my beloved, to

meet the Bride,/Let us receive the face of the Sabbath . . ."
Scholem is here describing Jewish Kabbalist sects; Patai (1967)
implies that the notion is an orthodoxy, but vestigial, and has a
whole chapter on this aspect of *The Hebrew Goddess* called "The
Sabbath–Virgin, Bride, Queen, and Goddess." He relates Jewish
observances to the early history of this Goddess—the Canaanite
Ashera and Astarte—showing quite clearly that this Mediterranean love- and moon-Goddess was shared by many peoples. It
seems very likely to us that this name Sabbath was retained apart
from Jewry to denote a festival of the moon-goddess, since that
had been its usage for thousands of years; but was also used by
the Christian persecutors to associate the supposed witches with
things Jewish, thus redoubling the hatred. As Cohn remarks
(p. 101): "The term 'sabbat,' like the term 'synagogue,' was of
course taken from the Jewish religion, which was traditionally
regarded as the quintessence of anti-Christianity, indeed as a
form of Devil-worship." It is interesting that in the Middle Ages
one of the reasons for hating Jews was that it was supposed that
the Jewish men, as well as the women, menstruated. We are
supposing that witchcraft had become by exile the menstrual
side of a Goddess cult: forced into this polarization by the
supremacy of the male nonmenstruating Christian God. The
reported cannibalism of witches could be a propagandist exaggeration derived from the view that menstruation was the blood
and body of an unconceived child. It was in this way that the
feminine energies found their formulation: whether in the
fantasies of individual women delirious under torture, or in
organized cults. Any cults need not have been *very* organized: as
we know, witch-beliefs are similar all over the world because the
archetypes are so strong. They would arise again in any group
of women interested in the resources of their minds, particularly
in an age that gave nothing to women's minds. Scholem says that
the Shekinah at times "tastes the other, bitter side, and then her
face is dark" and that this is moon-symbolism: she is also called
"The Tree of Death" (p. 107) and has "alternating phases." This
new moon darkness is also the ideal time for "'meditation on the
Messianic secret,'" because the disappearance of the moon
signifies the horror of exile (p. 153). The Shekinah is "'the

beautiful virgin who has no eyes'" since she has lost them from weeping in exile. Add to this the saying that the Messiah will come when the moon shines as bright as the sun, and one might conclude—as Kluger (1974) almost does—that the Jewish Messiah will embody the restored spirit of the exiled menstrous *moon-woman*. Daly suggests this about the Hindu Kali, and that she is black, like the Shulamite and the Queen of Sheba, because we will not look at her. It is we who have lost our eyes, then, not she. Briffault (1927) confirms that the Sabbath was originally lunar, and therefore menstrual, and of the women.

CHAPTER VII: THE MIRROR OF DRACULA

1 Jung (1957) pp. 3ff.
2 Deutsch (1973) vol. 1, pp. 184f. Altschule and Brem (1963) report on "Periodic Psychosis at Puberty." Teja (1976) comments on the danger of confusing such a psychosis with schizophrenic illness: puberty psychosis must be differentiated for "therapeutic, prognostic, and theoretical reasons." Whisnant and Zegans (1975) report on the harm "deritualization of menarche in American culture" may do. Van Waters as long ago as 1914 complained that "in modern life 'we neglect the puberty of the mind'" (p. 105). The *Daily Mail* for 24 June 1976 gave a report of a retarded girl of 11 who was hysterectomized for fear that it would not be possible to cope with her at her menstrual periods. Schmiedeberg (1931) points out that menstruation is sometimes considered to be a punishment for masturbation—an unfortunate cathexis if the period brings the desire to masturbate simultaneously with the blood, as if one had wounded oneself. The only guard is education.
3 Laing (1976) pp. 91ff.
4 "Aeschylus, Astronomy and Sex" by A. P. H. Scott, privately circulated by the New York Institute of Technology, 1974. He gives the etymology of "Gorgon" as "the Moon as it is terrible to behold"; Campbell's etymology for "Medusa" is "Mistress."
5 Bergh and Kelly (1964) quote a range of actual cases of "Vampirism." In one case, intensive psychotherapy revealed that "the blood symbolized to the patient 'an unobtainable object,' or

'forbidden fruit,' which, as his therapy progressed, proved to be his 'unobtainable' and 'forbidden' oedipal wishes towards his mother." They do not refer to Daly (1935), which would have illuminated this case: the mother's menstruation is clearly the source of the vampiric compulsions. Lévi-Strauss (1973) discusses the links between vampire-bats and menstrual blood.

AFTERWORD—THE MENSTRUAL MANDALA

1 "About Time" 12 June 1985. A book based on the series was published: Christopher Rawlence (ed.) *About Time* (Jonathan Cape, 1985).
2 Harper & Row, 1983.
3 Sheila Kitzinger, *Woman's Experience of Sex* (Penguin, 1985).
4 Hutchinson, 1979.
5 Books that discuss this include:
Dr. Ann Nazzaro and Dr. Donald Lombard with Dr. David Horrobin, *The PMT Solution* (Adamantine Press, 1985).
Caroline Shreeve, *The Premenstrual Syndrome* (Thorsons, 1983).
6 Bristol Women's Health Group, c/o 5 Dover Place, Clifton, Bristol BS8 1AL.
7 *Change of Life: A Psychological Study of Dreams and the Menopause* (Inner City Books, 1984).
8 Margaret E. Henderson, "Conditions related to the menstrual cycle in women and evidence for a male hormonal cycle." Paper given to the Women's Health Conference, University of Queensland, 25–29 August 1975.
9 This appears to be the position illustrated but unnamed on pp. 134–135 of Alex Comfort's *The Joy of Sex* (Simon & Schuster).
10 Rudolf von Urban, *Sex Perfection* (Rider, 1952).
11 For example: Gordon Inkeles and Murray Todris, *The Art of Sensual Massage* (Unwin, 1977).
12 For example: Maggie Tisserand, *Aromatherapy for Women* (Thorsons, 1985).
13 Supplied by Human Potential Division, Encyclopaedia Britannica International Ltd., Mappin House, 156–162 Oxford Street, London W1N 0HJ.
14 "Medial Feminine": "one who mediates the unknown." Used by

Nor Hall for the Sibyl as the Old Wise Woman. Her chapter on the Sibyl of Menstruation is another important contribution. Nor Hall, *The Moon and the Virgin* (The Women's Press, 1980, pp. 161–188).

15 "Lunar Periodicity with reference to live births," *American Journal of Obstetrics and Gynaecology*, vol. 98, no. 7, pp. 1002–1004.

16 R. D. Laing, *The Voice of Experience* (Allen Lane, 1982). M. Lietaert Peerbolte, *Psychic Energy* (Servire Publishers, Wassenaar, 1975).

17 Chris Knight, "Levi-Strauss and the dragon," *Man*, vol. 18, no. 1, March 1983.

18 Chris Knight, "Menstruation as Medicine," *Soc. Sci. Med.* vol. 21, no. 6, pp. 671–683, 1985.

19 Thomas Buckley, "Menstruation and the power of Yurok women: methods in cultural reconstruction," *American Ethnologist*, vol. 9, no. 1, Feb. 1982, pp. 47–60.

20 Chris Knight, "Menstruation and the myth of matriarchy," in *Blood Magic—New Anthropological Approaches to Menstruation*, eds. T. Buckley and Alma Gottlieb. Forthcoming CUP (US).

21 Penguin, 1981.

22 Robert Hale, 1984, Chapter XV.

Works Cited

The dates given refer to the editions we have consulted.

ABEL, Theodora M., *and* JOFFE, Natalie F. 1950. Cultural backgrounds of female puberty. *American Journal of Psychotherapy*, vol. 4, 1950, pp. 90–113.

ALLEGRO, John M. 1970. The Sacred Mushroom and the Cross. London, Hodder and Stoughton, 1970.

ALTMAN, M. *et al.* 1941. A psychosomatic study of the sex cycle in women. *Psychosomatic Medicine*, vol. 3, no. 3, July 1941, pp. 199–225.

ALTSCHULE, Mark D., and BREM, Jacob. 1963. Periodic psychosis of puberty. *American Journal of Psychiatry*, vol. 119, 1963, pp. 1176–1178.

AMBROSE, Gordon, *and* NEWBOLD, George. 1968. A Handbook of Medical Hypnosis. London, Ballière, Tindall and Cassell, 1968.

AREY, L. B. 1939. The degree of normal menstrual irregularity. *American Journal of Obstetrics and Gynecology*, vol. 37, 1939, pp. 12–29.

ARMSTRONG, John. 1969. The Paradise Myth. London, Oxford University Press, 1969.

AUDEN, W. H. 1963. The Dyer's Hand and other essays. London, Faber and Faber, 1963.

BAKAN, David. 1965. Sigmund Freud and the Jewish Mystical Tradition. New York, Schocken Books, 1965.

BARDWICK, Judith M., DOUVAN, Elizabeth, HORNER, Matina S., GUTMANN, David. 1970. Feminine Personality and Conflict. Belmont, California, Brooks-Cole Publishing Company, 1970.

DE BARENNE, Dorothea D., *and* GIBBS, Frederic A. 1942. Variations in the electroencephalogram during the menstrual cycle. *American Journal of Obstetrics and Gynecology*, vol. 4, 1942, pp. 687–690.

BAYLEY, Harold. 1912. The Lost Language of Symbolism. London, Ernest Benn. Seventh impression 1974.

DE BEAUVOIR, Simone. 1953. The Second Sex. Harmondsworth, Penguin Books, 1972.

BENEDEK, Therese. 1952. Studies in Psychosomatic Medicine: Psychosexual Functions in Women. New York, The Ronald Press Co., 1952.

BENEDEK, Therese. 1963. An investigation of the sexual cycle in women: methodologic considerations. *Archives of General Psychiatry*, no. 8, 1963, pp. 311–322.

BENEDEK, Therese, *and* RUBENSTEIN, Boris B. 1939. The correlations between ovarian activity and psychodynamic processes: I. The ovulative phase. *Psychosomatic Medicine*, vol. 1, no. 2, April 1939, pp. 245–270; II. The menstrual phase, ibid., vol. 1, no. 4, Oct. 1939, pp. 461–485.

BENEDEK, Therese, *and* RUBENSTEIN, Boris B. 1942. The sexual cycle in women. *Psychosomatic Medical Monographs*, vol. 3, nos. 1 and 2, 1942, Washington DC, National Research Council.

BENEDICT, Ruth. 1934. Patterns of Culture. Boston, Houghton Mifflin, 1959.

BERGH, Richard L. Vanden, *and* KELLY, John F. 1964. Vampirism: a review with new observations. *Archives of General Psychiatry*, vol. 11, pt. 5, 1964, pp. 543–547.

BERMANT, Gordon, *and* DAVIDSON, Julian M. 1974. Biological Bases of Sexual Behaviour. London and New York, Harper and Row, 1974.

BERRY, Constance, *and* MCGUIRE, Frederick L. 1972. Menstrual distress and acceptance of sexual role. *American Journal of Obstetrics and Gynecology,* vol. 114, no. 1, Sept. 1972, pp. 83–87.

BERRY, Patricia (ed.). 1973. Fathers and Mothers: Five Papers on the Archetypal Background of Family Psychology. Zurich, Spring Publications, 1973.

BETTELHEIM, Bruno. 1955. Symbolic Wounds: Puberty Rites and the Envious Male. London, Thames and Hudson, 1955.

BETTELHEIM, Bruno. 1976. The Uses of Enchantment: The Meaning and Importance of Fairy Tales. London, Thames and Hudson, 1976.

THE HOLY BIBLE. 1611. London, The British and Foreign Bible Society, 1969.

THE HOLY BIBLE. 1952. Westminster Study Bible: The Holy Bible: Revised Standard Version. New York and Glasgow, Collins, 1952.

BILLIARD, Michael, GUILLEMINAULT, Christian, *and* DEMENT, William. 1975. A menstruation-linked periodic hypersomnia. *Neurology,* vol. 25, May 1975, pp. 436–443.

BLACK, Matthew, *and* ROWLEY, H. H. 1962. Peake's Commentary on the Bible. London, Nelson, 1962.

BLACKER, Carmen. 1975. The Catalpa Bow: A Study of Shamanistic Practices in Japan. London, George Allen and Unwin, 1975.

BLATTY, William Peter. 1974. On The Exorcist: from Novel to Film. London and New York, Bantam Books, 1974.

BLATTY, William Peter. 1971. The Exorcist. London, Blond and Briggs, 1971.

BLOOM, MAX L., *and* VAN DONGEN, Leon. 1972. Clinical Gynaecology: Integration of Structure and Function. London, Heinemann, 1972.

BMJ. 1967. Leading article: Dysmenorrhoea. *British Medical Journal,* 21 Oct. 1967, pp. 125–126.

BRIFFAULT, Robert. 1927. The Mothers. London, George

Allen and Unwin; New York, Macmillan; London and New York, Johnson Reprint Corporation, 1969. 3 vols.

BROWN, Barbara B. 1975. New Mind, New Body; Bio-Feedback; New Directions for the Mind. London, Hodder and Stoughton, 1975.

BROWN, Frank A. 1972. The "clocks" timing biological rhythms. *American Scientist*, Nov.–Dec. 1972, pp. 756–766.

BROWN, Judith. 1963. A cross-cultural study of female initiation rites. *American Anthropologist*, vol. 65, 1963, pp. 837–853.

BROWN, Peter Lancaster. 1976. Megaliths, Myths and Men: An Introduction to Astro-Archaeology. Poole, Blandford Press, 1976.

BRUSH, A. Louise. 1938. Attitudes, emotional and physical symptoms commonly associated with menstruation in 100 women. *The American Journal of Orthopsychiatry*, vol. 8, 1938, pp. 286–301.

BURLAND, Cottie, *and* FORMAN, Werner. 1975. Feathered Serpent and Smoking Mirror. London, Orbis Publishing, 1975.

BURR, H. S., *and* MUSSELMAN, L. K. 1936. Bio-electric phenomena associated with menstruation. *Yale Journal of Biology and Medicine*, vol. 9, 1936, pp. 155–158.

BUTTERWORTH, E. A. S. 1970. The Tree at the Navel of the Earth. Berlin, Walter de Gruyter, 1970.

BUXTON, Jean. 1973. Religion and Healing in Mandari. Oxford, at the Clarendon Press, 1973.

CAMPBELL, Joseph. 1965. The Masks of God: Occidental Mythology. London, Secker and Warburg, 1965.

CAMPBELL, Joseph. 1968. The Masks of God: Creative Mythology. London, Secker and Warburg, 1968.

CAMPBELL, Joseph (ed.). 1955. The Mysteries: papers from the Eranos Yearbooks. New York, Pantheon Books, 1955.

CAMPBELL, Joseph. (ed.). 1971. The Portable Jung. New York, The Viking Press, 1971.

CASTALDO, V., *and* HOLZMAN, P. S. 1967. The effects of

hearing one's own voice on sleep mentation. *Journal of Nervous and Mental Disease*, vol. 144, 1967, pp. 2–13.

CAUTHERY, Philip, *and* COLE, Martin. 1971. The Fundamentals of Sex. London, W. H. Allen, 1971.

CHADWICK, Mary. 1931. Menstruationsangst. *Zsch. f. psychoanal. Päd.*, vol. 5, 1931, pp. 184–189.

CHADWICK, Mary. 1932. The Psychological Effects of Menstruation. New York and Washington, Nervous and Mental Disease Publishing Company, 1932.

CHADWICK, Mary. 1933. Woman's Periodicity. London, Douglas, 1933.

CHESLER, Phyllis. 1972. Women and Madness. New York, Avon Books, 1972.

CLARKE, W. K. Lowther. 1952. Concise Bible Commentary. London, SPCK, 1952.

CLOSE, Sylvia. 1972. The Know-how of Breast-feeding. Bristol, John Wright, 1972.

COHN, Norman. 1975. Europe's Inner Demons. London, Chatto-Heinemann for Sussex University Press, 1975.

COLQUHOUN, W. P. (ed.). 1971. Biological Rhythms and Human Performance. London and New York, Academic Press, 1971.

COMFORT, Alex (ed.). 1972. The Joy of Sex. New York, Simon and Schuster, 1972.

COPPEN, A., *and* KESSEL, N. 1963. Menstruation and personality. *British Journal of Psychiatry*, vol. 109, 1963, pp. 711–721.

CRABBE, Julie Lebach. 1975. Menstruation as Stigma. University of Colorado, Ph.D. 1975. Ann Arbor, Michigan, Xerox University Microfilms, 1975.

CRAWLEY, Ernest. 1927. The Mystic Rose. London, Spring Books, 1965.

DALTON, Katharina. 1964. The Premenstrual Syndrome. London, William Heinemann, 1964.

DALTON, Katharina. 1969. The Menstrual Cycle. Harmondsworth, Penguin Books, 1969.

DALTON, Katharina. 1975. Paramenstrual baby battering. *British Medical Journal*, 3 May 1975, p. 279.

DALY, C. D. 1927. Hindu-Mythologie und Kastrationskomplex. *Imago*, vol. 13, 1927, pp. 145–198.

DALY, C. D. 1928. Der Menstruationskomplex. *Imago*, vol. 14, 1928, pp. 11–75.

DALY, C. D. 1935. The menstruation complex in literature. *Psychoanalytic Quarterly*, vol. 4, 1935, pp. 307–340.

DALY, C. D. 1935. Der kern des oedipuskomplexes. *Int. Z. Psychoanal.*, vol. 21, 1935, pp. 165–188.

DALY, C. D. 1943. The role of menstruation in human phylogenesis and ontogenesis. *International Journal of Psychoanalysis*, vol. 24, 1943, pp. 151–170.

DAMES, Michael. 1976. The Silbury Treasure: The Great Goddess Rediscovered. London, Thames and Hudson, 1976.

DAVIS, Flora. 1971. Inside Intuition: What We Know about Non-Verbal Communication. New York and London, McGraw-Hill, 1971.

DELANEY, Janice, LUPTON, Mary Jane, *and* TOTH, Emily. 1976. The Curse: A Cultural History of Menstruation. New York, E. P. Dutton, 1976.

DEUTSCH, Helene. 1973. The Psychology of Women: A Psychoanalytic Interpretation. Vol. 1: Girlhood. New York and London, Bantam Books, 1973.

DEVEREUX, George. 1950. The psychology of feminine genital bleeding. An analysis of Mohave Indian puberty and menstrual rites. *International Journal of Psychoanalysis*, vol. 31, 1950, pp. 237–257.

DEVEREUX, George. 1953. Why Oedipus killed Laius. *International Journal of Psychoanalysis*, vol. 34, 1953, pp. 132–141.

DEWAN, E. M. 1967. On the possibility of a perfect rhythm method of birth control by periodic light stimulation. *American Journal of Obstetrics and Gynaecology*, vol. 99, issue 7, December 1967, pp. 1016–1019.

DEWAN, E. M. 1969. Rhythms. *Science and Technology*, vol. 20, 1969, pp. 20–28.

DIAMOND, Milton, DIAMOND, A. Leonard, *and* MAST, Marian. 1972. Visual sensitivity and sexual arousal levels during the menstrual cycle. *The Journal of Nervous and Mental Disease,* vol. 155, no. 3, 1972, pp. 170–176.

DIX, Carol. 1976. The Pill: the inside story. *Guardian,* 18 Nov. 1976.

DODDS, E. R. 1973. The Greeks and the Irrational. Berkeley, Los Angeles, London, University of California Press, 1983.

EAYRS, J. T., *and* GLASS, A. 1962. The ovary and behavior. In ZUCKERMAN, S. (ed.). The Ovary, vol. 2. New York and London, Academic Press, 1962.

EHRENZWEIG, Anton. 1967. The Hidden Order of Art. London, Weidenfield and Nicolson, 1967.

ELIADE, Mircea. 1958. Patterns in Comparative Religion. London and New York, Sheed and Ward, 1958.

ELIADE, Mircea. 1960. Myths, Dreams and Mysteries. London, Collins, 1968.

ELLIS, Havelock. 1935. Studies in the Psychology of Sex. New York, Random House, 1942. 2 vols.

ERICKSON, Milton H. 1960. Psychogenic alteration of menstrual functioning: three instances. *The American Journal of Clinical Hypnosis,* vol. 2, no. 4, April 1960, pp. 227–231.

EYSENCK, H. J. (ed.). 1973. Handbook of Abnormal Psychology. 2nd edition. London and New York, Pitman, 1973.

FAERGEMAN, Poul M. 1955. Fantasies of menstruation in men. *Psychoanalytic Quarterly,* vol. 24, 1955, pp. 1–19.

FERENCZI, Sandor. 1938. Thalassa. New York, Psychoanalytic Quarterly, 1938.

FISHER, Seymour. 1973. The Female Orgasm: Psychology, Physiology, Fantasy. New York, Basic Books, 1973.

FISHER, Seymour. 1973b. Body Consciousness. London, Fontana-Collins, 1976.

FLUHMANN, C. Frederic. 1956. The Management of Menstrual Disorders. Philadelphia and London, W. B. Saunders, 1956.

LA FONTAINE, J. S. (ed.). 1972. The Interpretation of Ritual: Essays in Honour of A. I. Richards. Tavistock Publications, 1974.

FORD, Clellan Stearns. 1945. A comparative study of human reproduction. Yale University Publications in Anthropology no. 32. New Haven, Yale University Press; London, Humphrey Milford, Oxford University Press, 1945.

FORD, C. S., *and* BEACH, F. A. 1952. Patterns of Sexual Behaviour. London, Eyre and Spottiswoode, 1952.

FRAZER, James George. 1922. The Golden Bough. Abridged edition, London, Macmillan, 1963.

FRENKEL, Richard E. 1971. Remembering dreams through auto-suggestion relationship of menstruation and ovulation to the auto-suggestion dream recall cycle. *Behavioural Neuropsychiatry*, vol. 3, nos. 3–4, 1971, pp. 2–11.

FREUD, Anna. 1965. Normality and Pathology in Childhood. Harmondsworth, Penguin Books, 1973.

FREUD, Anna. 1968. The Ego and the Mechanisms of Defence. London, The Hogarth Press, 1976.

FREUD, S. 1930. Civilisation and Its Discontents. London, The Hogarth Press, 1975.

FREUD, S. 1931. Female sexuality. Medusa's head. *Collected Papers*, vol. 5. London, The Hogarth Press, 1950.

FREUD, S., *and* BREUER, J. 1955. Studies on Hysteria. New York, Avon Books, 1966.

GARFIELD, Patricia L. 1974. Creative Dreaming. New York, Simon and Schuster, 1974.

GARRISON, Omar. 1964. Tantra: The Yoga of Sex. New York, Avon, 1973.

GAUQUELIN, Michel. 1969. The Cosmic Clocks: From Astrology to a Modern Science. London, Peter Owen, 1969.

GINDES, Bernard C. 1953. New Concepts of Hypnosis. London, George Allen and Unwin, 1953.

GLASKIN, G. M. 1974. Windows of the Mind: The Christos Experience. London, Wildwood House, 1974.

GOLD, Jay J. (ed.). 1975. Gynaecologic Endocrinology. New York and London, Harper and Row, 1975.

GOOCH, Stan. 1972. Total Man: Notes Towards an Evolutionary Theory of Personality. London, Allen Lane, The Penguin Press, 1972.

GORE, Charles, GOUDGE, Henry Leighton, *and* GUILLAUME, Alfred. 1928. A New Commentary on Holy Scripture. London, SPCK, 1928.

GRANT, Kenneth. 1973. Aleister Crowley and the Hidden God. London, Frederick Muller, 1973.

GRAVES, Robert. 1952. The White Goddess. London, Faber and Faber, 1952.

GRAVES, Robert. 1965. Mammon and the Black Goddess. London, Cassell, 1965.

GRINNELL, Robert. 1973. Alchemy in a Modern Woman: A Study in the Contrasexual Archetype. Zurich, Spring Publications, 1973.

GRODDECK, Georg. 1950. The Book of the It. London, Vision Press, 1950.

GRODDECK, Georg. 1950. Exploring the Unconscious. London, Vision Press, 1950.

GUTMANN, David. 1970. Feminine Personality and Conflict. Belmont, California, Brooks-Cole Publishing Company, 1970.

GYÖNGYÖSSY, A., *and* SZALÓCZY, P. 1971. The ovulation-inhibiting effect of modern living. *Psychosomatic Medicine in Obstetrics and Gynaecology*, 3rd Int. Congr., London, 1971, pp. 589–592. Karger, Basel, 1972.

HANNAH, Barbara. 1962. The Problem of Contact with Animus. Guild Lecture No. 70. London, The Guild of Pastoral Psychology, February 1962.

HARDING, M. Esther. 1955. Woman's Mysteries. New York, Pantheon, 1955.

HARRISON, Jane Ellen. 1962. Epilegomena to the Study of Greek Religion and Themis. New York, University Books, 1962.

HART, R. D. 1960. Monthly rhythm of libido in married women. *British Medical Journal*, vol. 1, 1960, pp. 1023–1024.

HARTLAND, John, 1971. Medical and Dental Hypnosis and its Clinical Applications. London, Ballière Tindall, 1971.

HARTMANN, Ernest. 1967. The Biology of Dreaming. Springfield, MA, Charles C. Thomas, 1967.

HARTMANN, Ernest. 1966. Dreaming sleep (the D-state) and the menstrual cycle. *The Journal of Nervous and Mental Disease*, vol. 143, no. 5, 1966, pp. 406–416.

HAUPT, Paul. 1902. The Book of Canticles. Reprinted from *The American Journal of Semitic Languages and Literatures*, vol. XVIII, pp. 193–245; vol. XIX, pp. 1–32. Chicago, The University of Chicago Press, 1902.

HEALTH BOOK COLLECTIVE, The Boston Women's. 1971. Our Bodies, Ourselves. New York, Simon and Schuster, 1971.

HERTZ, Dan G., *and* JENSEN, Mogens R. 1975. Menstrual dreams and psychodynamics: emotional conflict and manifest dream content in menstruating women. *Br. J. Med. Psychol.*, vol. 48, 1975, pp. 175–183.

HERZBERG, Brenda, *and* COPPEN, Alex. 1970. Changes in psychological symptoms in women taking oral contraceptives. *Brit. J. Psychiatry,* vol. 116, 1970, pp. 161–164.

HMSO. 1975. Better Services for the Mentally Ill. London, HMSO, October 1975.

HOGBIN, Ian. 1970. The Island of Menstruating Men: Religion in Wogeo, New Guinea. Chandler, Scranton, 1970.

HOKE, Helen (ed.). 1974. Spooks, Spooks, Spooks. London, Chatto and Windus, 1974.

HORNEY, Karen. 1931. Die premenstruelle Verstimmungen. *Zsch. f. psychoanal. Päd.*, 5, pp. 161–167, 1931.

HOUSMAN, Harold Stephen. 1955. A psychological study of menstruation. University of Michigan Ph.D., 1955. University Microfilms Inc., Ann Arbor, Michigan, 1955.

HOWELLS, John G. 1971. Modern Perspectives in Psychiatry. Edinburgh, Oliver and Boyd, 1971.

HOWEY, M. O. 1972. The Cults of the Dog. Rochford, C. W. Daniel, 1972.

HOWKINS, John, *and* BOURNE, Gordon, 1971. Shaw's Textbook of Gynaecology. Edinburgh and London, Churchill Livingstone, 1971.

IVEY, M. E., *and* BARDWICK, Judith M. 1968. Patterns of affective fluctuations in the menstrual cycle. *Psychosomatic Medicine*, 30, 1968, pp. 336–345.

JACOBI, Jolande. 1962. The Psychology of C. G. Jung. London, Routledge and Kegan Paul, 1962.

JANOWSKY, David S., GORNEY, Roderick, *and* KELLEY, Bret. 1966. The curse—vicissitudes and variations of the female fertility cycle. Part I. Psychiatric aspects. *Psychosomatics*, vol. 7, July–August 1966, pp. 242–247.

JANOWSKY, David S., GORNEY, Roderick, *and* KELLEY, Bret. 1966. The curse—vicissitudes and variations of the female fertility cycle. Part II. Psychiatric aspects. *Psychosomatics*, vol. 7, Sept.–Oct. 1966. pp. 283–287.

JENNINGS, Hargrave. 1887. The Rosicrucians: their rites and mysteries. London, George Routledge, 1887.

JOHNSON, G. B. 1932. The effects of periodicity on learning to walk a tight-wire. *J. Comp. Psychol.*, vol. 13, 1932, pp. 133–141.

JUNG, C. G. 1954. The Practice of Psychotherapy. Vol. 16 in Collected Works. London, Routledge and Kegan Paul, 1954.

JUNG, C. G. 1956. Symbols of Transformation. Vol. 5 in Collected Works. London, Routledge and Kegan Paul, 1956.

JUNG, C. G. 1957. Psychiatric Studies. Vol. 1 in Collected Works. London, Routledge and Kegan Paul, 1957.

JUNG, C. G. 1959. The Archetypes and the Collective Unconscious. Vol. 9, Part I in Collected Works. London, Routledge and Kegan Paul, 1959.

JUNG, C. G. 1963. Memories, Dreams, Reflections. London, Collins and Routledge and Kegan Paul, 1963.

JUNG, C. G. 1963b. Mysterium Coniunctionis. Vol. 14 in Collected Works. London, Routledge and Kegan Paul, 1963.

JUNG, C. G. 1967. Alchemical Studies. Vol. 13 in Collected Works. London, Routledge and Kegan Paul, 1967.

JUNG, C. G. 1968. Psychology and Alchemy. Vol. 12 in Collected Works, 2nd edition. London, Routledge and Kegan Paul, 1968.

JUNG, C. G. 1971. Psychological Types. Vol. 6 in Collected Works. London, Routledge and Kegan Paul, 1971.

JUNG, C. G. 1973. Experimental Researches. Vol. 2 in Collected Works. London, Routledge and Kegan Paul, 1973.

JUNG, C. G. 1976. Analytical Psychology: Its Theory and Practice. The Tavistock Lectures. London and Henley, Routledge and Kegan Paul, 1976.

JUNG, C. G., *and* KERÉNYI, C. 1963. Essays on a Science of Mythology. New York, Harper and Row, 1963.

JUNG, Emma. 1957. Animus and Anima. Zurich, Spring Publications, 1974.

JUNG, Emma, *and* VON FRANZ, Marie-Louise. 1960. The Grail Legend. London, Hodder and Stoughton, 1971.

KENT, Caron. 1969. The Puzzled Body: A New Approach to the Unconscious. London, Vision Press, 1969.

KERÉNYI, C. 1967. Eleusis: Archetypal Image of Mother and Daughter. London, Routledge and Kegan Paul, 1967.

KERÉNYI, C. 1975. Zeus and Hera. London, Routledge and Kegan Paul, 1975.

KING, Francis. 1971. Sexuality, Magic and Perversion. London, Neville Spearman, 1971.

KING, Stephen. 1975. Carrie. London, New English Library, 1975.

KINSEY, Alfred C., *et al.* 1965. Sexual Behavior in the Human Female. New York, Pocket Books, 1965.

KITZINGER, Sheila. 1972. The Experience of Childbirth. Harmondsworth, Penguin Books, 1972.

KLEIN, Melanie. 1975. The Psychoanalysis of Children. London, The Hogarth Press, 1975.

KLEIN, Melanie. 1975b. Envy and Gratitude and Other Works. London, The Hogarth Press, 1975.

KLEITMAN, N. 1939. Sleep and Wakefulness as Alternating Phases in the Cycle of Existence. Chicago University Press, 1939.

KLINE, Paul. 1972. Fact and Fantasy in Freudian Theory. London, Methuen, 1972.

KLUGER, Rivkah Schärf. 1974. Psyche and Bible: Three Old Testament Themes. Zurich, Spring Publications, 1974.

KOESKE, Randi K., *and* KOESKE, Gary F. 1975. An attributional approach to moods and the menstrual cycle. *Journal of Personality and Social Psychology*, vol. 31, no. 3, 1975, pp. 473–478.

KROGER, William S., *and* FREED, S. Charles. 1956. Psychosomatic Gynaecology: Including Problems of Obstetrical Care. Glencoe, Illinois, The Free Press, 1956.

LAING, R. D. 1960. The Divided Self. Harmondsworth, Penguin Books, 1965.

LAING, R. D. 1976. The Facts of Life. London, Allen Lane, 1976.

LAKE, Frank. 1966. Clinical Theology. London, Darton, Longman and Todd, 1966.

LANDAUER, K. 1931. Das menstruationserlebnis der Knaben. *Zsch. f. psychoanal. Päd.*, vol. 5, 1931, pp. 175–184.

LANG, Theo. 1971. The Difference Between a Man and a Woman. London, Sphere Books, 1973.

LARSEN, Virginia L. 1963. Psychological study of colloquial menstrual expressions *Northwest Medicine*, vol. 62, 1963, pp. 874–877.

LAYARD, John. 1944. The Lady of the Hare: being a study in the healing power of dreams. London, Faber and Faber, 1944.

LAYARD, John. 1972. The Virgin Archetype: Two Papers. New York, Spring Publications, 1972.

LAYARD, John. 1975. A Celtic Quest: Sexuality and Soul in Individuation. Zurich, Spring Publications, 1975.

LEBOYER, Frederick. 1975. Birth without Violence. London and Australia, Wildwood House and Rigby, 1975.

LEE, S. M. G., *and* MAYES, A. R. (eds.) 1973. Dreams and Dreaming. Harmondsworth, Penguin Books, 1973.

LENNANE, K. Jean, *and* LENNANE, R. John. 1973. Alleged psychogenic disorders in women: a possible manifestation of sexual prejudice. *New England Journal of Medicine*, vol. 288(6), Feb. 1973, pp. 288–292.

LEROI-GOURHAN, André. 1967. The Art of Prehistoric Man in Western Europe. London, Thames and Hudson, 1967.

LÉVI-STRAUSS, Claude. 1972. Structural Anthropology. Harmondsworth, Penguin Books, 1972.

LÉVI-STRAUSS, Claude. 1973. From Honey to Ashes. London, Jonathan Cape, 1973.

LEVY, Gertrude Rachel. 1948. The Gate of Horn. London, Faber and Faber, 1963.

LLEWELLYN-JONES, Derek. 1971. Everywoman: A Gynaecological Guide for Life. London, Faber and Faber, 1971.

LOESER, A. A. 1943. Effect of emotional shock on hormone release and endometrial development. *Lancet,* vol. II, 1943, pp. 418–519.

LORAND, Sandor, *and* SCHNEER, Henry. 1961. Adolescents: Psychoanalytic Approach to Problems and Therapy. New York, Paul B. Hoeber, 1961.

LUCE, Gay Gaer. 1972. Body Time. London, Temple Smith, 1971.

MCCANCE, R. A., LUFF, M. C., *and* WIDDOWSON, E. E. 1937. Physical and emotional periodicity in women. *Journal of Hygiene*, vol. 37, 1937, pp. 571–605.

MACLEAN, Una. 1971. Magical Medicine: A Nigerian Case-study. Harmondsworth, Penguin Books, 1971.

MCCLINTOCK, Martha K. 1971. Menstrual synchrony and suppression. *Nature*, vol. 229, 22 Jan. 1971, pp. 244–245.

MAIR, Lucy. 1969. Witchcraft. London, Weidenfeld and Nicolson, 1969.

MALL, G. 1958. Zur diagnostik und therapie periodisch rezidivier psychosen. *Conf. neurol.*, vol. 18, 1968, pp. 171–179.

MARKALE, Jean. 1975. Women of the Celts. London, Gordon Cremonesi, 1975.

MARSHACK, Alexander. 1972. The Roots of Civilization. London, Weidenfeld and Nicolson, 1972.

MARTIN, Ian C. A. 1975. Blood, sweat and tears: some psychiatric aspects of menstrual disorder. *Nursing Times*, 13 Nov. 1975, pp. 1830–1832.

DE MARTINO, Ernest. 1972. Magic Primitive and Modern. London, Tom Stacey, 1972.

MARTIUS, H. 1946. Fluchtamenorrhöe. *Dtsch. med. Wschr.*, vol. 71, 1946, p. 81.

MASSEY, Gerald. 1883. The Natural Genesis. 2 vols. New York, Samuel Weiser, 1974.

MASTERS, William H., *and* JOHNSON, Virginia E. 1966. Human Sexual Response. Boston, Little, Brown and Co., 1966.

MASTERS, William H., *and* JOHNSON, Virginia E. 1975. The Pleasure Bond. New York, Little, Brown and Co., 1975.

MAUGHAM, W. Somerset. 1956. The Magician. London, Heinemann, 1956.

MEAD, Margaret. 1950. Male and Female. Harmondsworth, Penguin Books, 1962.

MELODY, G. F. 1961. Behavioural implications of premenstrual tension. *Obstetrics and Gynecology*, vol. 17, 1961, pp. 439–441.

MENAKER, Walter, *and* MENAKER, Abraham. 1959. Lunar periodicity in human reproduction: a likely unit of biological time. *American Journal of Obstetrics and Gynaecology*, vol. 77, April 1959, pp. 905–914.

MICHAEL, R. P. (ed.). 1968. Endocrinology and Human Behaviour. London, Oxford University Press, 1968.

MICHAEL, Richard P., BONSALL, R. W., *and* WARNER, Patricia. 1974. Human vaginal secretions: volatile fatty acid content. *Science*, vol. 186, 24 Dec. 1974, pp. 1217–1219.

MOFFATT, James. 1958. The Moffatt Translation of The Bible. London, Hodder and Stoughton, 1958.

MONEY, John, *and* EHRHARDT, Anke A. 1972. Man and

Woman, Boy and Girl. Baltimore and London, the Johns Hopkins University Press, 1972.

MOOS, R. H., KOPELL, B. S., MELGES, F., YALOM, I., LUNDE, D. T., CLAYTON, R. B., *and* HAMBURG, D. 1969. Fluctuations in symptoms and mood during the menstrual cycle. *Journal of Psychosomatic Research*, vol. 13, 1969, pp. 37–44.

MOOS, R. H. 1969. Typology of menstrual cycle symptoms. *American Journal of Obstetrics and Gynaecology*, vol. 103, 1969, pp. 390–402.

MORGAN, Elaine. 1972. The Descent of Women. London, Souvenir Press, 1972.

MURRAY, Margaret Alice. 1921. The Witch-Cult in Western Europe. Oxford at the Clarendon Press, 1962.

MYLONAS, George E. 1961. Eleusis and the Eleusinian Mysteries. Princeton, Princeton University Press; London, Routledge and Kegan Paul, 1961.

DI NARDO, Patricia Gambitta. 1974. Psychological Correlates of the Menstrual Cycle. Saint Louis University Ph.D., 1974. Ann Arbor, Michigan, University Microfilms, 1974.

NEUMANN, Erich. 1954. The Origins and History of Consciousness. London, Routledge and Kegan Paul, 1954.

NEUMANN, Erich. 1955. The Great Mother: An Analysis of the Archetype. London, Routledge and Kegan Paul, 1955.

NEWTON, Niles. 1975. Trebly sensuous woman. *Psychology Today* (U.K.), vol. 1, no. 1, April 1975, pp. 34–38.

O'CONNOR, J. F., SHELLEY, E. M., *and* STERN, Lenore O. 1973. Behavioural rhythms related to the menstrual cycle. *International Institute for the Study of Human Reproduction*, New York, 1973, p. 7.

OED. 1971. The Compact Edition of the Oxford English Dictionary: Complete Text Reproduced Micrographically. Oxford University Press, 1971.

OESTERREICH, T. K. 1966. Possession: Demoniacal and Other. Secaucus, New Jersey, Lyle Stuart Inc., 1966.

O'NEIL, W. M. 1976. Time and the Calendars. Manchester University Press, 1976.

OPLER, Morris E. 1972. Cause and effect in Apachean agriculture, division of labor, residence patterns and girls' puberty rites. *American Anthropologist,* vol. 74, 1972, pp. 1133–1146.

PAIGE, Karen. 1969. The effects of oral contraceptives on affective fluctuations associated with the menstrual cycle. University of Michigan Ph.D., 1969. Ann Arbor, Michigan, University Microfilms, 1970.

PAIGE, Karen. 1973. Women learn to sing the menstrual blues. *Psychology Today* (U.S.), vol. 7(4), Sept. 1973, pp. 41–46.

PARLEE, Mary Brown. 1973. The premenstrual syndrome. *Psychological Bulletin*, vol. 80, no. 6, 1973, pp. 454–465.

PARLEE, Mary Brown. 1974. Stereotypic beliefs about menstruation: a methodological note on the Moos menstrual distress questionnaire and some new data. *Psychosomatic Medicine*, vol. 36, no. 3, May–June 1974, pp. 229–240.

PARTRIDGE, Eric. 1966. Origins: a short etymological dictionary of modern English. London, Routledge and Kegan Paul, 1966.

PATAI, Raphael. 1967. The Hebrew Goddess. New York, Ktav Publishing House, 1967.

PATTY, Rosemarie Anderson, *and* FERRELL, Marcia M. 1974. A preliminary note on the motive to avoid success and the menstrual cycle. *The Journal of Psychology*, vol. 86, 1974, pp. 173–177.

PISTILLI, J. 1975. Stereotyped perceptions of women as a function of menstrual cycle phase and physical attractiveness. Kent State University Ph.D., 1975. Ann Arbor, Michigan, University Microfilms International, 1975.

PORACH, Lee Bowman. 1970. The relationship of masculine and feminine identification to dream scores, and to menstrual cycle reactions. University of Virginia Ed.D., 1970. Ann Arbor, Michigan, University Microfilms, 1970.

RANK, Otto. 1929. The Trauma of Birth. New York and London, Harper and Row, 1973.

RAWSON, Philip. 1973. Tantra. London, Thames and Hudson, 1973.

RAWSON, Philip. 1973b. The Art of Tantra. London, Thames and Hudson, 1973.

REICH, Steven Kenneth. 1972. The Effects of Group Systematic Desensitization on the Symptoms of Primary Dysmenorrhea. The University of New Mexico, Ph.D., 1972. Ann Arbor, Michigan, Xerox University Microfilms, 1973.

REICH, Wilhelm. 1958. Character Analysis. London, Vision Press, 1958.

REISS, M. 1958. Psychoendocrinology. London, Grune and Stratton, 1958.

REYMERT, Martin L., *and* JOST, Hudson. 1947. Further data concerning the normal variability of the menstrual cycle during adolescence and factors associated with age of menarche. *Child Development*, vol. 18, 1947, pp. 169–179.

REYNOLDS, Evelyn. 1969. Variations of mood and recall in the menstrual cycle. *Journal of Psychosomatic Research*, vol. 13, 1969, pp. 163–166.

ROAZEN, Paul. 1976. Freud and His Followers. London, Allen Lane, 1976.

ROSENBLUM, Art, *and* JACKSON, Leah. 1974. The Natural Birth Control Book. Boston, Tao Publications, 1974.

ROUBICEK, J., TACHEZY, R., *and* MATOUSEK, M. 1968. Electrical activity of the brain during the menstrual cycle. *Ceskoslovenska Psychiatrie*, vol. 64(2), 1968, pp. 90–94.

SANTAMARINA, B. A. G. 1969. Dysmenorrhea. *Clinical Obstetrics and Gynaecology*, vol. 12, 1969, pp. 708–723.

SARKAR, Sarasi Lal. 1943. A study of the psychology of sexual abstinence from the dreams of an ascetic. *International Journal of Psychoanalysis*, vol. 24, 1943, pp. 170–175.

SAVRAMIS, Demosthenes. 1974. The Satanizing of Woman: Religion Versus Sexuality. New York, Doubleday, 1974.

SCHMIEDEBERG, M. 1931. Psychoanalytisches zur Menstruation. *Zsch. f. psychoanal. Päd.*, vol. 5, 1931, pp. 190–202.

SCHOLEM, Gershom G. 1965. On the Kabbalah and Its Symbolism. London, Routledge and Kegan Paul, 1965.

SCHWENK, Theodor. 1965. Sensitive Chaos: The Creation of Flowing Forms in Water and Air. London, Rudolph Steiner Press, 1965.

SEWARD, Georgene H. 1934. The female sex rhythm. *The Psychological Bulletin*, vol. 31, no. 3, March 1934, pp. 153–192.

SEWELL, Elizabeth. 1960. The Orphic Voice: Poetry and Natural History. London, Routledge and Kegan Paul, 1960.

SHADER, Richard I., DI MASCIO, Alberto, *and* HARMATZ, Jerold. 1968. Characterological anxiety levels and premenstrual libido changes. *Psychosomatics*, vol. 9, July–August 1968, pp. 197–198.

SHAINESS, Natalie. 1961. A re-evaluation of some aspects of femininity through a study of menstruation. *Comprehensive Psychiatry*, vol. 2, 1961, pp. 20–26.

SHAINESS, Natalie. 1962. Psychiatric evaluation of premenstrual tension. *New York Journal of Medicine*, vol. 62, 1962, pp. 3573–3579.

SHAINESS, Natalie. 1972. Towards a new feminine psychology. *Notre Dame Journal of Education*, vol. 2, no. 4, 1972, pp. 293–296.

SHELDRAKE, Peter, *and* CORMACK, Margaret. 1974. Dream recall and the menstrual cycle. *Journal of Psychosomatic Research*, vol. 18, 1974, pp. 347–350.

SHERFEY, Mary Jane. 1972. The Nature and Evolution of Female Sexuality. New York, Vintage Books, 1973.

SHERMAN, Julia A. 1971. On the Psychology of Women: A Survey of Empirical Studies. Springfield, Charles C. Thomas, 1971.

SILBERMANN, Isidor. 1950. A contribution to the psychology of menstruation. *International Journal of Psychoanalysis*, vol. 31, 1950, pp. 258–267.

SKULTANS, Vieda. 1970. The symbolic significance of menstruation and the menopause. *Man*, vol. n.s. 5, 1970, pp. 639–651.

SLATER, Philip E. 1968. The Glory of Hera: Greek Mythology and the Greek Family. Boston, Beacon Press, 1971.

SMITH, Morton. 1974. The Secret Gospel. London, Victor Gollancz, 1974.

SNAITH, Linton, *and* COXON, Alan. 1969. Dick-Read' Childbirth Without Fear. London and Sydney, Pan Books 1969.

SOLLBERGER, A. 1965. Biological Rhythm Research. London and New York, Elsevier, 1965.

SOMMER, Barbara. 1973. The effect of menstruation on cognitive and perceptual-motor behavior: a review. *Psychosomatic Medicine*, vol. 35(6), Nov. 1973, pp. 515–534.

STEPHENS, W. N. 1961. A cross-cultural study of menstrual taboos. *Genet. Psychol. Monogr.*, vol. 64, 1961, pp. 385–416.

STEPHENS, W. N. 1962. The Oedipus Complex: Cross Cultural Evidence. New York, Free Press of Glencoe, 1962.

STONE, C. P. *and* BARKER, R. G. 1939. The attitudes and interests of premenarcheal and postmenarcheal girls. *Journal of Genetic Psychology*, vol. 54, 1939, pp. 27–71.

STROUSE, Jean (ed.). 1974. Women and Analysis. New York, Grossman, 1974.

SUARÈS, Carlo. 1972. The Song of Songs. Berkeley and London, Shambala, 1972.

SVENNERUD, Sven. 1959. Dysmenorrhoea and absenteeism. *Acta Obstetricia et Gynecologica Scandinavica*, 38, Supp. 2, 1959

SWANSON, Ethel M., *and* FOULKES, D. Dream content and the menstrual cycle. *Journal of Nervous and Mental Disease*, vol 145, 1968, pp. 358–363.

SZASZ, Thomas S. 1971. The Manufacture of Madness: A Comparative Study of the Inquisition and the Mental Health Movement. London, Routledge and Kegan Paul, 1971.

TART, Charles T. 1972. Altered States of Consciousness. New York, Anchor Books, 1972.

TART, Charles T. 1975. Transpersonal Psychologies. London, Routledge and Kegan Paul, 1975.

TEJA, Jagdish S. 1976. Periodic psychosis of puberty: a

longitudinal case study. *The Journal of Nervous and Mental Disease,* vol. 162, no. 1, 1976, pp. 52–57.

THOMSON, George. 1965. The Prehistoric Aegean. New York, The Citadel Press, 1965.

TIKTIN, Morris. 1966. Menstrual Tensions and Marital Satisfaction. University of Oregon, Ph.D., 1966. Ann Arbor, Michigan, University Microfilms Inc., 1966.

TREDGOLD, Roger, *and* WOLFF, Heinz (eds.). 1975. UCH Handbook of Psychiatry for Students and General Practitioners. London, Duckworth, 1975.

TREVOR-ROPER, H. R. 1967. Religion, the Reformation and Social Change: and other essays. London, Macmillan, 1967.

TURNER, Victor. 1967. The Forest of Symbols: Aspects of Ndembu Ritual. London and Ithaca, Cornell University Press, 1967.

UDRY, J. R., *and* MORRIS, N. M. 1968. Distribution of coitus in the menstrual cycle. *Nature,* vol. 220, 1968, pp. 593–596.

UDRY, J. R., MORRIS, Naomi, *and* WALLER, Lynn. 1973. Effect of contraceptive pills on sexual activity in the luteal phase of the human menstrual cycle. *Archives of Sexual Behaviour,* vol. 2, no. 3, 1973, pp. 205–213.

ULANOV, Ann Belford. 1971. The Feminine in Jungian Psychology and in Christian Theology. Evanston, Northwestern University Press, 1971.

VAN DE CASTLE, Robert. 1971. The Psychology of Dreaming. New York, General Learning Corporation, 1971.

VAN WATERS, Miriam. 1913. The adolescent girl among primitive peoples. *Journal of Religious Psychology,* vol. 6(4), 1913, pp. 375–421.

VAN WATERS, Miriam. 1914. The adolescent girl among primitive peoples. *Journal of Religious Psychology,* vol. 7, part 1, 1914, pp. 32–40, 75–120.

VON FRANZ, Marie-Louise. 1970. An Introduction to the Interpretation of Fairy Tales. New York, Spring Publications, 1970.

VON FRANZ, Marie-Louise. 1972. Problems of the Feminine in Fairy-Tales. New York, Spring Publications, 1972.

VON FRANZ, Marie-Louise. 1974. Number and Time. London, Rider, 1974.

WAITE, A. E. Undated. The Holy Kabbalah. New York, University Books, undated.

WEBB, Peter. 1975. The Erotic Arts. London, Secker and Warburg, 1975.

WEIDEGER, Paula. 1975. Menstruation and Menopause. New York, Alfred A. Knopf, 1975.

WEINSTOCK, Eugene. 1947. Beyond the Last Path. New York, Boni and Gaer, 1947.

WEISS, Edward, *and* ENGLISH, O. Spurgeon. 1957. *Psychosomatic Medicine*, 3rd edition. Philadelphia, Saunders, 1957.

WETZEL, Richard D., *and* MCCLURE, James N. 1972. Suicide and the menstrual cycle: a review. *Comprehensive Psychiatry*, vol. 13, no. 4, July–August 1972, pp. 369–374.

WHISNANT, Lynn, *and* ZEGANS, Leonard S. 1975. Menarche in American culture: deritualization may be harmful. *Roche Report; Frontiers of Psychiatry*, 15 Jan. 1975, p. 3.

WIENER, Harry. 1966, 1967 and 1968. External chemical messengers. I. Emission and reception in man. *New York State Journal of Medicine*, vol. 66, no. 24, 15 Dec. 1966, pp. 3153–3170. II. Natural history of schizophrenia. ibid., vol. 67, no. 9, 1 May 1967, pp. 1144–1165. III. Mind and body in schizophrenia. ibid., vol. 67, no. 10, 15 May 1967, pp. 1287–1310. IV. Pineal gland. ibid., 1 April 1968, pp. 912–938.

WILSON, E. W., *and* RENNIE, P. I. C. 1976. The Menstrual Cycle. London, Lloyd-Luke, 1976.

WINEMAN, E. W., 1971. Autonomic balance changes during the human menstrual cycle. *Psychophysiology*, vol. 8, no. 1, 1971, pp. 1–6.

WINGET, Carolyn, *and* KAPP, Frederic T. 1972. The relationship of the manifest content of dreams to duration of childbirth in primiparae. *Psychosomatic Medicine*, vol. 34, no. 4, July–August 1972, pp. 313–320.

WRIGHT, Erna. 1967. The New Childbirth. London, Tandem Books, 1967.

YOUNG, J. Z. 1971. An Introduction to the Study of Man. Oxford at the Clarendon Press, 1971.

ZIMMERMANN, Ellen, *and* PARLEE, Mary Brown. 1973. Behavioral changes associated with the menstrual cycle: an experimental investigation. *Journal of Applied Social Psychology*, vol. 3, no. 4, 1973, pp. 335–344.

ZUBIN, J., *and* MONEY, J. (eds.). 1973. Contemporary Sexual Behaviour: Critical issues in the 1970s. Baltimore and London, The Johns Hopkins University Press, 1973.

ZUCKERMAN, S. 1949. The menstrual cycle. *The Lancet*, vol. 1, 18 June 1949, pp. 1031–1035.

Index

407

words, meanings of, *see* etymology

Wortman, Richard, pineal research, 179

Wright, Erna; painless childbirth, 82, 184; relief of M pains, 85

Yeats, W. B., 255

Yoga, 16, 164, 201, 272, 372; animal postures, 130; Tant-

ric, 166–167, 215, 222, 233, 257, 377

Young, J. Z., on pair formation, 152

Zimmermann, Ellen, 354

Zubin, J., and Money, J., evolution of sex activity in primates, 153

Zuckerman, S., sex activity of primates, 153, 353, 367

About the Authors

Penelope Shuttle is a noted feminist poet and novelist. Her most recent collection of verse is *The Lion from Rio* (O.U.P. 1986), and her work is represented in various anthologies including *The Penguin Book of Contemporary British Poetry*. She has also published five highly praised novels, including *Rainsplitter in the Zodiac Garden* (Boyars 1977) and *The Mirror of the Giant* (Boyars 1980), both of which have been translated into French (Hachette). She is currently working on a new novel and a volume of short stories.

Peter Redgrove read science at Cambridge, has worked as a research scientist and scientific journalist, and is regarded as one of the country's leading poets. He has published nine books of verse with RKP, the most recent of which was *The Man Named East* (1985), seven novels, also with RKP, and is well-known as a playwright, having won the Italia Prize in 1982. He trained as a lay analyst with Dr. John Layard during 1968–69. He is currently writing a further nonfiction study called *The Black Goddess and the Unseen Real*.

Penelope Shuttle and Peter Redgrove live together in Cornwall with their daughter, Zoe.